THE MAKING OF
THE TRIPS AGREEMENT

PERSONAL INSIGHTS
FROM THE
URUGUAY ROUND NEGOTIATIONS

Edited by Jayashree Watal and Antony Taubman

WORLD TRADE
ORGANIZATION

World Trade Organization
Rue de Lausanne 154
CH-1211 Geneva 21
Switzerland

Tel: +41 (0)22 739 51 11
Fax: +41 (0)22 731 42 06

www.wto.org
publications@wto.org

WTO Online Bookshop
http://onlinebookshop.wto.org

ISBN 978-92-870-4025-1
French version 978-92-870-4026-8
Spanish version 978-92-870-4027-5

Designed by Messaggio
Printed by WTO Secretariat

Cover photo "Peace" (1925), by Genevan artist Luc Jaggi (1887-1976), which adorns the left side of the main entrance of the Centre William Rappard, home of the WTO. (c) WTO/Pierre-Yves Dhinaut. This image recalls the reference in the Preamble of the WTO TRIPS Agreement to the shared emphasis among WTO members on "the importance of reducing tensions by reaching strengthened commitments to resolve disputes on trade-related intellectual property issues through multilateral procedures".

All photos copyright WTO unless otherwise indicated.

CONTENTS

NOTES ON CONTRIBUTORS

Editors

Jayashree Watal

Jayashree Watal is Counsellor in the Intellectual Property Division of the WTO. She represented India in the Uruguay Round TRIPS negotiations from 1989 to 1990. She has published widely on the law and economics of IPRs and also teaches these subjects at the postgraduate level in several universities.

Antony Taubman

Anthony Taubman is Director of the Intellectual Property Division of the WTO. He was previously Director of the Global Issues Division at WIPO, and has worked as a patent attorney and diplomat. He has authored numerous works on TRIPS and the law and policy of international IP, and has held several academic research and postgraduate teaching posts.

Contributors

Lars Anell

Lars Anell is Chair of the Swedish Research Council. During the Uruguay Round, he was Chair of the TRIPS Negotiating Group from 1986 to 1992. Subsequent roles included Permanent Representative to the European Union in Brussels from 1992 to 1994 and Senior Vice President of AB Volvo from 1994 to 2001. He has undertaken different academic assignments and has authored several books.

Mogens Peter Carl

Mogens Peter Carl is the former Director-General of Environment and Director-General for External Trade at the European Commission. He was the chief TRIPS negotiator for Europe during the Uruguay Round. He has held the role of personal representative of the French Minister for Energy, Environment and Energy.

Thomas Cottier

Thomas Cottier is Emeritus Professor of European and International Economic Law at the University of Bern and the former Managing Director of the World Trade Institute. He served on the Swiss negotiating team of the Uruguay Round, first on dispute settlement and subsidies, and later led Swiss negotiations on TRIPS. He was Deputy Director General of the Swiss Federal Institute of Intellectual Property and has served on several GATT and WTO dispute panels. He has published widely in the field of WTO law.

Catherine Field

Catherine Field is the former Deputy General Counsel in the Office of the US Trade Representative. She is now semi-retired and consults for the Office of the US Trade Representative. During the Uruguay Round negotiations, she was an Associate General Counsel and legal advisor to the U.S. delegation on TRIPS. In 1993, she also participated in the negotiations on the Dispute Settlement Understanding and the Marrakesh Agreement Establishing the WTO.

David Fitzpatrick

David Fitzpatrick is a barrister, solicitor and occasional academic lawyer, and is now semi-retired. He was a police prosecutor and colonial civil servant in the Attorney General's Chambers of the Hong Kong Government from 1981 to 1993. From 1987 to 1992 he was seconded to the Trade and Industry Branch as legal adviser to Peter Cheung Po Tak during the TRIPS negotiations.

A.V. Ganesan

Arumugamangalam Venkatachalam Ganesan is the former Commerce Secretary of India and was the chief negotiator for India during the Uruguay Round for most of the period from 1989 and 1993, when he was closely associated with the TRIPS negotiations. From 2000 to 2008, he was a Member and Chairman of the Appellate Body of the WTO.

John Gero

John Gero is the former Canadian Ambassador to the WTO, WIPO and UNCTAD in Geneva from 2008 to 2012. As Counsellor at the Canadian Mission to the GATT from 1987 to 1991, he was the Canadian negotiator for TRIPS in the Uruguay Round. He has worked for over forty years in the fields of international development, trade promotion and trade policy.

Matthijs Geuze

Matthijs Geuze is Head of the International Appellations of Origin Registry in the Brands and Designs Sector of WIPO. As a member of the GATT/WTO Secretariat from 1989 to 2002 he assisted the Uruguay Round TRIPS Negotiating Group, and was subsequently Secretary of the Council for TRIPS.

Adrian Macey

Adrian Macey is Senior Associate at the Victoria University of Wellington Institute of Policy Studies. In 1987, he became Counsellor and Consul-General at the New Zealand Embassy in Geneva. In this capacity he took part in the Uruguay Round dispute settlement negotiations and the TRIPS negotiations. From 2006 to 2010 he was Climate Change Ambassador for New Zealand

Umi K.B.A. Majid

Dato' Umi Kalthum binti Abdul Majid is a Judge of the Court of Appeal in Malaysia. She negotiated the TRIPS Agreement as Senior Federal Counsel in charge of GATT matters in the Advisory and International Law Division of the Malaysian Attorney General's Chambers. Following this assignment, for the last 23 years she has held many high-level posts in Malaysia.

Adrian Otten

Adrian Otten is the former Director of the Intellectual Property Division of the WTO from 1993 to 2008. Between 1986 and 1993 he was Secretary of the Uruguay Round TRIPS Negotiating Group. Prior to joining the GATT Secretariat in 1975, he worked on international trade policy issues in Brussels and London.

Jörg Reinbothe

Jörg Reinbothe is Professor at the European Institute at the University of Saarbrucken, where he teaches IP law. He was a member of the EC delegation to the Uruguay Round TRIPS negotiations. He was subsequently Head of the Copyright Unit in the European Commission, where he represented the European Community at WIPO and various other international and European fora. He has published a number of books and articles on IP issues.

Jagdish Sagar

Jagdish Sagar is a copyright and entertainment lawyer in India. As a civil servant in the Indian Ministry of Human Resources Development, he participated in the TRIPS negotiations on copyright-related issues in 1990, and was closely involved in drafting major amendments to the Indian copyright law enacted in 1994.

Piragibe dos Santos Tarragô

Piragibe dos Santos Tarragô is Ambassador of Brazil in the Netherlands. He was the chief TRIPS negotiator for Brazil during the Uruguay Round from 1987 to 1993, and later in the non-agricultural market access negotiations in the Doha Round from 2003 to 2005. He has been a career diplomat since 1974.

Thu-Lang Tran Wasescha

Thu-Lang Tran Wasescha is an IP Consultant and part-time Counsellor at the Swiss Federal Institute of Intellectual Property. She is a former Counsellor in the Intellectual Property Division of the WTO. She was deputy head of the Swiss TRIPS negotiating team in the Uruguay Round, and in charge of the implementation of the TRIPS provisions in the Swiss domestic law. She served as Legal Officer and Principal Legal Officer in the Industrial Property Division of WIPO.

Antonio Gustavo Trombetta

Antonio Gustavo Trombetta is Ambassador of Argentina in Switzerland. He was the TRIPS negotiator for Argentina from 1989 to 1993, when he was based in the Permanent Mission of Argentina to International Organizations in Geneva. He subsequently held several posts in the Argentinian Government, including that of Special Advisor to the Secretariat for Industry and Trade, and to the Secretariat for Agricultural Policy; Under Secretary for Trade; and Chief of Cabinet of the Minister of Foreign Affairs.

Hannu Wager   Hannu Wager is Counsellor in the Intellectual
                               Property Division of the WTO, and serves as
                               Secretary to the Council for TRIPS. During the
                               Uruguay Round TRIPS negotiations, he
                               participated in the coordination and collaboration
                               between the Nordic countries (Finland, Iceland,
                               Norway and Sweden) and represented them in
                               the Geneva negotiations from 1991 to 1993. He
                               also represented Finland at WIPO and various
                               other international and European fora. He has
                               published extensively on IP issues.

FOREWORD

As we mark the 20th anniversary of the WTO, it seems appropriate that we should put a spotlight on the TRIPS Agreement which also turns 20 this year. When the TRIPS Agreement came into being in 1995, it introduced substantive and comprehensive disciplines on intellectual property rights (IPRs) into the multilateral trading system. It had a significant impact on national intellectual property (IP) regimes the world over, with the most significant changes experienced in the developing world. Indeed, in 1995, and earlier in the negotiations leading to the conclusion of TRIPS, the international IP system was largely seen as a trade interest of the developed economies. Today, the picture differs dramatically. Some middle-income countries are among the major users of the global IP system, and many other developing countries are increasingly engaged with it.

The adoption of the Doha Declaration on the TRIPS Agreement and Public Health in 2001, and its subsequent amendment, encouraged this shift in perceptions. Today the Agreement is no longer seen as a one-sided imposition of the strong IP laws of developed countries on the developing world. Rather, experience has shown how it serves as a benchmark for legitimate policy-making, balancing protection of IPRs with the interests of users and the general public.

This volume tells the story of how that balance was achieved. It helps us to understand how the text of the Agreement was constructed – from a brief negotiating mandate to a sophisticated and balanced agreement that has stood the test of time. Moreover, it illustrates that, contrary to the general belief that the negotiations were dominated by a stark North-South division, large parts of the TRIPS text were developed through the resolution of intra-North differences or through alliances that cut across North-South boundaries, including on copyright, patents, trade secrets, test data protection and geographical indications. The general need to reconcile different legal systems was also an intra-North challenge. The provisions on enforcement saw many compromises made by developed countries to ensure an overall goal of ensuring balance and fairness, as well as with a view to limiting impediments to legitimate trade.

The accounts in this volume from negotiators from Argentina, Brazil, Hong Kong, India and Malaysia show how developing countries made crucial contributions to the Agreement that today give testament to their substantive and farsighted engagement in the negotiations.

I recommend this book not just to TRIPS specialists but also to all those who are interested in learning about how a complex and sensitive subject came to be successfully negotiated in the Uruguay Round.

I would like to congratulate Jayashree Watal, Antony Taubman and their colleagues in the IP Division for their dedicated efforts in collecting these important accounts, first in the organization of a Symposium which sparked discussion of the TRIPS negotiations, and later in their hard work in bringing this present volume to fruition. I also want to thank the negotiators and former Secretariat staff for taking the time to engage in dialogue at the Symposium and then preparing this unique and irreplaceable set of perspectives on the negotiations.

Roberto Azevêdo
WTO Director-General

PREFACE

Jayashree Watal

This book was conceived in mid-2014 when members of the Intellectual Property Division (IPD) of the WTO began to reflect on what facets of the Agreement on Trade-related Aspects of Intellectual Property Rights (TRIPS) could be highlighted for WTO members and the public at large in 2015, a year marking the 20th anniversary both of the WTO and of the entry into force of the TRIPS Agreement. The IPD, under the leadership of its Director, Antony Taubman, planned a capacity-building Symposium on the TRIPS Agreement and a book on TRIPS negotiations, informally dubbed the "TRIPS@20" project. This project was in large part delegated to me, which I carried out with the able assistance of Karyn Russell and my other colleagues in the IPD. The Symposium was financed by WTO's Institute for Training and Technical Cooperation (ITTC) as part of the Secretariat's programme of technical assistance and capacity building for WTO members in the TRIPS area. It was held back-to-back with the TRIPS Council in February 2015 in order to facilitate the wider participation by both Geneva and capital-based TRIPS Council and other WTO delegates. A central objective of the Symposium was to bring together key TRIPS negotiators and GATT Secretariat staff who crafted the original text. The broader purpose for us in the IPD was to "bring TRIPS home", namely to take ownership of the Agreement and try to shape a fact-based discussion on it in 2015. We organized two other sessions to evaluate the legal and economic aspects of TRIPS and to look at emerging issues in the TRIPS area and possible responses to them.

It took many months of hard-core detective and diplomatic work on my part to track down the whereabouts of key TRIPS negotiators, whom I had known during the negotiations in the Uruguay Round but with whom I had lost touch over the years. I was delighted to have a good reason to seek them out again in order to get them to commit to participating in the capacity-building Symposium and the book project. One of the first persons I contacted was Ambassador Lars Anell, who was Chair of the TRIPS Negotiating Group in the Uruguay Round, and who is currently Chair of the Swedish Research Council. He delivered a thought-provoking and substantive keynote address drawing from his vast experience in the Swedish Government, private sector and research organizations and sprinkled it liberally with his unique sense of humour. We thought it best to reproduce his speech verbatim and this is appended to the book.

The other indispensable figure from whom we wanted a firm commitment was the true guiding spirit behind the TRIPS negotiations, Adrian Otten, who worked in the GATT Secretariat, was Secretary of the TRIPS Negotiating Group and continued working on the subject as the Director of the IPD until 2008. Fortunately for us, Adrian lent his enthusiastic support to the project and devoted an inordinate amount of his time to guiding me closely in planning and executing both the Symposium and the book, right up to the final stages.

Thanks to the Internet, help from Geneva-based delegates and a lot of luck, I was able to track down most of the key TRIPS negotiators from both developed and developing country members of the WTO. We could not have held the Symposium or written this book without a voice from the United States, which was the major driver behind the inclusion of intellectual property in the Uruguay Round. I was lucky to have caught Catherine Field between jobs in the United States Trade Representative. Despite being one among many members of the US negotiating team, she worked hard to make this project a success. The European Communities (EC) played a crucial role in bringing about a balanced TRIPS Agreement, and so I was particularly happy when Mogens Peter Carl, leader of the European TRIPS negotiating team throughout the Uruguay Round, supported us enthusiastically. Fortunately, I was already in touch with A.V. Ganesan from India and we were indeed privileged that he undertook the travel necessary to participate in the Symposium and contributed to the book with his characteristic sincerity of purpose. John Gero, who played an important bridging role in the TRIPS negotiations, recently retired from his post as Permanent Representative of Canada to the WTO in Geneva and readily accepted to return for the Symposium and to reproduce his insightful contributions for this book.

I was happy to learn that two key negotiators from Latin America, Antonio Gustavo Trombetta from Argentina and Piragibe dos Santos Tarragô from Brazil, are Ambassadors of their countries in Europe. They were gracious enough to take time away from their duties to participate in the Symposium and contribute substantive chapters to the book, despite having moved on to many other subjects in the course of their diplomatic careers. Both freely shared their views in a frank, disarming manner and we learned about many new facets of the issues they faced during the TRIPS negotiations. I am particularly proud to have managed to track down the intrepid TRIPS negotiator from Malaysia, Umi K.B.A. Majid, whom I persuaded to temporarily leave her important position as a judge in the Court of Appeal of her country to join us on our trip down memory lane. Peter Cheung and David Fitzpatrick were both available and ably represented the Hong Kong perspective at the Symposium, and David Fitzpatrick contributed an important chapter to the book. A chance meeting with Adrian Macey in December 2014 at a climate change conference in Lima, Peru, brought him on-board to discuss the original dispute settlement proposal he initiated during the TRIPS negotiations, which he explains in his contribution.

As they were based in Switzerland, it was relatively easy, although no less important, to co-opt Swiss TRIPS negotiators Professor Thomas Cottier and Thu-Lang Tran Wasescha and my colleague and the Nordic countries' copyright negotiator Hannu Wager, as well as ex-GATT staffer Matthijs Geuze. Well after the project began, I managed to persuade two other negotiators who were unfortunately not at the Symposium, Jörg Reinbothe and Jagdish Sagar, respectively members of the EC and India TRIPS negotiating teams, to contribute chapters to this book. All the contributions have enriched the book and we are truly grateful for the authors' time and efforts.

I was truly saddened that one of the central figures in the negotiations, Sivakant Tiwari from Singapore, could not be with us to share his memories as he passed away in 2010. Also, while I was able to contact some other key TRIPS negotiators such as Michael Kirk and Bruce Wilson of the United States, Patrick Smith of Australia, Shozo Uemura of Japan, and Thosapone Dansuputra of Thailand, who all contributed immensely to the making of the TRIPS Agreement, they were unable to join us for the Symposium or in the book project.

The programme of the Symposium and some of the presentations made there are available at www.wto.org/tripsat20. Adrian Otten's presentation at the Symposium is a curtain raiser to his chapter in this book and has already been used by many who wanted to learn of the timeline and main issues in the TRIPS negotiations. Other panellists were Mogens Peter Carl, A.V. Ganesan, Catherine Field, John Gero, Antonio Gustavo Trombetta, Piragibe dos Santos Tarragô, Thomas Cottier, Thu-Lang Tran Wasescha, Umi K.B.A. Majid, Peter Cheung, David Fitzpatrick, Adrian Macey, Hannu Wager and me. We all spoke extemporaneously to describe various aspects of the TRIPS negotiations in response to questions asked by our able moderator, Adrian Otten, and we reacted spontaneously to what others said, creating a fascinating account of personal recollections and lessons learned from the historic TRIPS negotiations.

A clear message that came out of this session of the Symposium, albeit surprising for some, was that the making of the TRIPS Agreement, even on controversial issues such as patents or test data protection, was also characterised by an informal intra-North dynamic rather than only a North-South dynamic as is usually presumed. Another key factor for the success of TRIPS was the constructive environment engendered by mutual respect among negotiators and the trust inspired by the competence and skill of the Secretariat team and the Chair of the Negotiating Group. Several chapters in this book reiterate these messages, including those of Adrian Otten, John Gero and Thomas Cottier.

The feedback from those who participated in the Symposium was positive and we were encouraged to pursue the book project, seeking written contributions from those who were closely involved with the making of the TRIPS Agreement. Contributors to this volume who participated in the Symposium met the day after and discussed ideas about the structure and nature of the book, as well as the concrete outlines and chapters that had already been submitted. It was clear from the outset that most authors had long left the subject of TRIPS behind and preferred personal accounts of various aspects of the negotiations, with adequate freedom to pursue their own style and substance. The book does not claim to be an authoritative or complete history of the TRIPS negotiations but it is certainly the first time that the key negotiators have been able to corroborate each other's first-hand accounts of the negotiations written from different perspectives. This volume is undoubtedly a valuable contribution to our understanding of the TRIPS negotiations.

Before this book, the closest we could come to piecing together a near-complete story of TRIPS negotiations was from the informal records kept by the GATT Secretariat. The GATT documents speak for themselves in revealing the major changes that took place in developing the TRIPS text, showing that most of the text was negotiated by 1990, beginning in right earnest with the June 1990 composite text, moving to a very detailed November 1990 text that was sent to the Brussels ministerial meeting in just six months, and then to the almost final ironing out of compromises, mainly on the patent complex, reflected in the December 1991 Dunkel Draft. The final TRIPS negotiated text in December 1993 made only two changes to the 1991 text. While only two derestricted texts, namely those of July 1990 and December 1991, are appended to this book, all other texts are readily available for consultation on the WTO website (a link is given at www.wto.org/tripsat20).

This book is the result of the collective effort of many months of preparation, writing, editing and re-structuring, and I am very grateful to all the contributors for the time and effort each devoted to the Symposium and the book. Without the financial and logistical support provided by the ITTC, we would not have been able to hold the Symposium or the subsequent meeting to discuss the book project – for this we owe a debt of gratitude to Bridget Chilala and her able team. I am deeply obliged to Antony Taubman for his wisdom, guidance and enthusiastic support for the project and, most of all, for his thoughtful contributions to the two introductory chapters of this book. I would also like to thank Adrian Otten who unstintingly gave his time to guide us through the planning of the session in the Symposium and the book project. I gratefully acknowledge the help and support received from Karyn Russell of the IPD at all stages of the project and, last but not least, I am truly grateful to Anthony Martin and Jaci Eisenberg of our publications unit for their superhuman efforts to produce the book on a tight schedule.

LIST OF ABBREVIATIONS

ACTA	Anti-Counterfeiting Trade Agreement
ASEAN	Association of Southeast Asian Nations
CBD	Convention on Biological Diversity
EC	European Communities or European Commission (context-dependent)
EU	European Union
EFTA	European Free Trade Association
EPC	European Patent Convention
FRAND	Fair, reasonable and non-discriminatory
FTAs	Free trade agreements
GATS	General Agreement on Trade in Services
GATT	General Agreement on Tariffs and Trade
GDP	Gross domestic product
GSP	Generalized System of Preferences
GIs	Geographical indications
HIV/AIDS	Human immunodeficiency virus/acquired immune deficiency syndrome
IP	Intellectual property
IPIC Treaty	Treaty on Intellectual Property with Respect to Integrated Circuits (Washington Treaty)
IPRs	Intellectual property rights
MFN	Most-favoured nation
NGOs	Non-governmental organizations
OECD	Organisation for Economic Co-operation and Development
R&D	Research and development
TNC	Trade Negotiations Committee
TRIMS	Agreement on Trade-Related Investment Measures
TRIPS	Agreement on Trade-Related Aspects of Intellectual Property Rights

UNCTAD	United Nations Conference on Trade and Development
UNESCO	United Nations Educational, Scientific and Cultural Organization
UNICE	Union of Industrial and Employers' Confederations of Europe
UPOV	International Union for the Protection of New Varieties of Plants
US	United States
WCT	WIPO Copyright Treaty
WIPO	World Intellectual Property Organization
WPPT	WIPO Performances and Phonogram Treaty

DISCLAIMER AND EDITORIAL NOTE

Disclaimer

The opinions and conclusions contained in this book are the sole responsibility of the individual authors and do not reflect the views of any institutions to which the authors are or were affiliated. This includes contributions prepared by staff of the World Trade Organization (WTO) Secretariat. None of the chapters purports to reflect the opinions or views of WTO members or the Secretariat. Any citation of the chapters should ascribe authorship to the individuals who have written the chapters. This book should not be viewed as advancing any form of legal interpretation or any policy position, and no views or analysis in this publication should be attributed to the WTO, its Secretariat or its members.

Editorial note

Please note several editorial points followed by the editors of this book.

Every time the word "country" appears in relation to GATT or WTO membership, it must be read as including customs territories. Any state or customs territory having full autonomy in the conduct of its trade policies may join ("accede to") the WTO pending approval by WTO members.

GATT document MTN.GNG/NG11/W/71, Negotiating Group on Trade-Related Aspects of Intellectual Property Rights, including Trade in Counterfeit Goods – Communication from Argentina, Brazil, Chile, China, Colombia, Cuba, Egypt, India, Nigeria, Peru, Tanzania and Uruguay, 14 May 1990, lists 12 parties to the document; this is evident in its title. However, Pakistan and Zimbabwe later associated themselves with this group, bringing the total to 14 parties.

In the case of the European Union, the term "European Communities" (EC) is used for references prior to when the European Union gained legal personality on 1 December 2009. The authors of this book use the terms relevant to the period covered by their contribution.

The French term "*demandeurs*" used in the text may be understood to mean the WTO member or GATT contracting party requesting a particular outcome, according to the context.

Finally, the seasonal references in the contributions – autumn, winter, spring, summer – all refer to the Northern Hemisphere, since the TRIPS negotiations took place in Geneva, Switzerland.

Part I

Introduction, context and overview

Revisiting the TRIPS negotiations: Genesis and structure of this book

Antony Taubman and Jayashree Watal

The 1986 Punta del Este Declaration inaugurated a set of negotiations on "trade-related aspects of intellectual property rights" as part of the Uruguay Round mandate for multilateral trade negotiations. These negotiations led, ultimately, to the conclusion of the TRIPS Agreement, an integral element of the single undertaking constituting the legal framework for the newly established WTO which came into existence in 1995.

The TRIPS Agreement was the product of an unusually successful and effective multilateral negotiation process. The Agreement, and the negotiations that led to it, have since spawned a voluminous scholarly and academic literature. That literature still lacks a full inside perspective of the negotiations and thus can overlook some of their most distinctive and instructive characteristics. Few of the original negotiators - who mostly worked in other professional or official roles in their subsequent careers - have set down their reflections on the process, and their potential contribution to a richer and more informed account of the negotiation process has been scarcely tapped. Equally, with multilateral norm-setting on IP mostly at a standstill, and regional and bilateral avenues proving to be more active in this field, collective sense of how to make multilateral negotiations "work" is potentially ebbing away.

The widely felt need to develop a more informed and objective understanding of the TRIPS negotiations was the genesis of a symposium convened in February 2015 which drew together many of those who participated in the making of the text of the TRIPS Agreement. Stimulated by and building upon the spirited and instructive discussions at the Symposium, this volume gathers together unique insights into the negotiating process, and seeks to illuminate the process that led from an ambiguous and somewhat uncertain negotiating mandate to what became a transformative instrument in the field of trade, and the most wide-ranging and influential multilateral treaty to date in the field of IP.

This volume therefore aims to fill a gap in the literature on TRIPS by providing important insights into the TRIPS negotiations centred on the individual accounts of a wide spectrum of key participants in the negotiations, who were invited to look back on the experience from the vantage point of twenty years after the entry into force of the TRIPS Agreement. It is not an authoritative history of the negotiations that produced the Agreement, still less a guide to its legal interpretation. The authors were invited to provide their personal recollections of the process itself, and to reflect upon the actual practice of making of the TRIPS Agreement and the practical skills they applied in making negotiations work. The contributors therefore discuss what the negotiations achieved, how that outcome was achieved and what lessons this process and outcome could offer today's policymakers and negotiators. Additionally, as many of the negotiators remain active in policy spheres, they also reflect on the enduring relevance of the TRIPS Agreement and consider the possible avenues for multilateral work on IP issues today.

These individual accounts are expressly personal and informal in character, and are not presented as representing the past or current view of any participating government or of the GATT or WTO Secretariats. A conscious effort has been made to ensure a wide spectrum of views representative of the diverse array of active participants in the negotiations; but the views captured in this volume are not comprehensive: it proved practically impossible to capture insights from all those involved.

The aim of this project - this volume, and the Symposium that renewed dialogue between the original participants in the making of the TRIPS Agreement - is to provide today's negotiators, policymakers and analysts, whether in government service, in civil society, industry, or academia - with a fresh understanding of the TRIPS negotiating process. What interests drove negotiations forward? What can we understand about the practical management and conduct of negotiations in an area that is at once politically sensitive, technically demanding and multidisciplinary? How exactly were these negotiations structured and organized? How were understandings reached so as to produce a balanced and wide ranging final text?

Any such negotiation is a one-off, and perhaps the same convergence of institutional, commercial and wider geopolitical factors that produced the

TRIPS Agreement is unlikely to be closely replicated in the future. Nonetheless, there are valuable practical lessons to be learned from the negotiations, particularly key elements of negotiating know-how that may otherwise have been lost to view and would then have to be painstakingly relearned. These diverse individual accounts help us to understand the distinct roles of negotiators, Chair and Secretariat, as well as how negotiators sought to balance matters of principle and good policy against simple commercial or political trade-offs.

The TRIPS negotiations drew together countries at different levels of economic development and involved intensive engagement with a range of substantive fields of IP law and policy. The negotiations also followed a clear trajectory from discussion of the mandate and overall direction, to submission of concrete proposals, to the engagement with substantive issues, to close textual negotiations and final agreement on the text. While this volume is structured to cover this diverse set of perspectives in the following five parts, it is clear that many contributions span the subject of several parts, and allocating them to one or other part of the volume was inevitably somewhat arbitrary:

> Part I: Introduction, context and overview

> Part II: Anatomy of the negotiations

> Part III: Perspectives from the developed world

> Part IV: Perspectives from the developing world

> Part V: Negotiating substantive areas of TRIPS

Part I contains this general introduction to the book followed by a thematic overview of the contributions that describes the context of the TRIPS negotiations and summarizes the views of the contributors on key themes recurring throughout the book. It also discusses substantive issues addressed in the negotiations and negotiators' observations relevant for the contemporary scene.

Part II gives a series of accounts of and reflections on the overall negotiating process from GATT Secretariat staff and TRIPS negotiators. Several contributions in this part are written from the particular perspectives of the delegation on which that author served, but also draw broader lessons from the negotiating process.

This part begins with a key contribution by Adrian Otten, a central figure in the GATT and WTO Secretariats who has 25 years of unequalled experience with the development and implementation of the TRIPS Agreement both before and after the establishment of the WTO. His chapter describes the formal and informal negotiating processes and sets the scene for the later contributions to this volume. It can be used as a compass to guide the reader through the rest of this book: other contributors add layers to his foundation. His contribution provides an authentic timeline and background of the negotiations starting from the Tokyo Round, and systematically runs through the seven years it took to complete the Uruguay Round. He describes the growing perception at the time that the future of the multilateral trading system depended on some recognition of the importance of intellectual property protection. Mr Otten makes the vital observation - which is developed further in other chapters - that the conventional narrative of the TRIPS negotiations as being defined by North vs South negotiating camps overlooks the more complex and diverse structure of negotiations, with North-North differences at times proving to be more intractable.

Thomas Cottier, the lead Swiss negotiator and one of the most thoughtful trade law scholars on TRIPS, reflects on the nature of the Agreement that emerged from the negotiations, laying emphasis on its ground-breaking character as a trade agreement setting standards for domestic regulation, with deep roots in existing domestic law (especially in developed countries). He analyses the role of informal plurilateral processes and the active lobbying role of the private sector. His pen-sketches of the main actors involved in the process, both in the GATT Secretariat and in the delegations, further leaven this personal account. He also reflects on the practical modes of working that made the negotiations a success.

John Gero negotiated on TRIPS for Canada and has elsewhere been described as a bridge between negotiators from the developed and developing worlds. He analyses the human and institutional factors that contributed to the success of the negotiations, singling out, as many others do, the competence of, and the trust placed in, the Chair and the Secretariat. He attributes the outcome to the ability of hard-working negotiators to bring creativity to the negotiating method, but also to their willingness to engage with each other on the substance of the issues at stake, guided by domestic practices, and to the dynamics of shifting alliances that cut across the full economic and political spectrum of negotiators, beyond conventional North-South boundaries.

Mogens Peter Carl, the lead negotiator for the European Commission, assesses the reasons for the success of the negotiations and evaluates the results in today's context. He sets the negotiations within their full historical context, describing the pivotal period of the relaxation of East-West confrontation, the resultant political transformations, and a period of economic optimism as the chief factors behind the success of the Uruguay Round. He offers an insider's account of the distinctive manner in which the EC delegation prepared for and engaged in TRIPS negotiations, and its unique model of engagement with stakeholders and the member states of the European Communities (EC). Mr Carl maintains that the TRIPS negotiations cannot be reduced to classical trade "bartering" but were founded on a more reasoned public policy basis for moving forward, spearheaded particularly by the EC. More recent work on access to medicines illustrates for him how balance was already built into the text, particularly on compulsory licences and parallel imports. While TRIPS rules remain generally legitimate today, he makes a strong plea for a major review in the light of "signs of age" and emerging gaps, for instance, on copyright protection for software, patent trolls and the un-stemmed tide of trade in counterfeit goods.

Matthijs Geuze, a GATT Secretariat official during the negotiations, describes how certain elements of the TRIPS text came together, and gives insights into the personal dynamics that made the negotiations function effectively. He points to the care taken by the Secretariat in compiling the Composite Draft Text of June 1990 that formed the foundation of the textual negotiations on the Agreement, the "constructive ambiguity" that produced outcomes in some areas that remain sensitive today. On the relationship of the TRIPS Agreement with WIPO treaties, he notes the impulse that TRIPS gave to participation in other non-WTO IP treaties, as well as the complex question of the relationship between TRIPS obligations and those under the WIPO conventions it incorporates by reference. He shares his memories on the informal and collegial approach taken at times to work on matters that squarely divided delegations.

Part III sets out the perspectives of several developed country negotiators. While the negotiating dynamics cannot be accurately portrayed as a simple North vs South trade-off between two monolithic sets of interests, it is clear from the accounts in this part that developed country economies were the *demandeurs* who, on the whole, actively sought an agreement on trade-related aspects of IP rights as central to their goals for the Uruguay Round, even while they differed greatly on what this should mean in practice, and indeed failed to bridge some significant policy divides. Some of the contributions to this part could well have been placed in Part II, as they give valuable additional perspectives on the genesis and political context of the TRIPS negotiations, analyse the full negotiating process and draw useful lessons for future negotiations.

The United States was the principal *demandeur* in the area of TRIPS and was represented by a large and specialized negotiating team. Catherine Field, a key member of that team, gives a systematic account of the successive phases of the negotiations, highlighting the importance of IP as a major offensive objective for her delegation. The formulation of the mandate and progress in the negotiations was rooted in domestic trade policy considerations in the US and the use of the Generalized System of Preferences and Special 301 mechanisms to bring about improvement in IPR protection in foreign markets. She stresses that the US and others had sought to address IP enforcement standards in the GATT framework for over ten years before the pivotal mid-term decision on TRIPS in 1989 that set the foundation for substantive negotiations. Ms Field attributes the outcome to certain negotiating axioms and illustrates how they produced outcomes on patents (a "mixed bag" which only partly achieved US goals), trademarks, geographical indications, and general principles and exceptions, including the import of introducing a strong most-favoured nation principle to IP. Current issues such as patents and standards, patent trolls and IP and competition policy require careful solutions, but these can be achieved within the existing TRIPS framework.

From the viewpoint of a Swiss negotiator, Thu-Lang Tran Wasescha recreates the atmosphere of the negotiations and their multilateral context, starting with the failed revision of the Paris Convention on the Protection of Industrial Property, and goes on to describe the role of the Swiss negotiating team as well as the Swiss Government approval processes. She provides a unique account of how the Swiss negotiating position was developed in a complex and actively democratic federal system, and how her delegation sought to substantiate negotiating positions through careful explanation. Equally, "constructive ambiguity" was needed to forge a delicate and finely balanced agreement. She offers a detailed analysis on the dynamics and interests driving the negotiations on patents and GIs, explaining why Switzerland was particularly active in these areas.

Jörg Reinbothe reviews the challenges that confronted the European Commission in representing a diverse group of distinct member states at a time of evolution in EC IP law. Many contentious issues had to be resolved between EC member states, thus repeating the discussion that invariably took place in the context of TRIPS negotiations between developed and developing countries. The EC experience illustrated how a principle of subsidiarity could apply also in multilateral norm setting. He assesses the EC's achievements against its negotiating objectives and the effect of TRIPS in the making of IP law elsewhere. While the EC secured notable gains especially on copyright and on enforcement, Mr Reinbothe maintains that the TRIPS Agreement was a success for all negotiators in that it was true to widely-shared principles while adding value in several domains, and also formed the basis for norm-setting in other fora.

Part IV offers a range of perspectives from developing country negotiators, including accounts of those who, being less ambitious for an outcome on TRIPS, sought to safeguard domestic policy interests within the negotiated outcome, while obtaining other benefits from the multilateral trading system and blunting the impact of unilateral trade measures. Nonetheless, despite the common themes, developing country negotiators actively pursued several diverse trade interests, as is evident from their accounts. In this part, too, there are contributions that could have been placed in Part II or in Part V, as they review the overall process as well dealing with specific sections of the TRIPS text. They are nevertheless placed in this part as they predominantly describe the negotiating process and results from the perspective of a developing country delegation or of the developing world more generally.

A.V. Ganesan negotiated on TRIPS for India at several stages, from 1987 to 1989 and again from 1991 to mid-1993, and played a key role in negotiating what became known as the Dunkel Draft in December 1991. He traces the approach taken by developing countries in general and India in particular from the launch of the Uruguay Round onwards. Initially, India took the position that substantive norms of IPRs were not included in the mandate for negotiations. After agreeing to discuss these in April 1989, India then went on to defend its laws which notably excluded product patents for chemicals and pharmaceuticals. Mr Ganesan describes the reasons for India's positions with respect to product patents on pharmaceuticals and other sensitive issues through the various phases of negotiations. He acknowledges that India failed to get its demands met in the final stages before the Dunkel Draft and subsequently, yet reflects that TRIPS may be "a blessing in disguise for India" because India can assure foreign investors of its compliance with standard international IPR norms and thus better manage trade frictions.

Piragibe dos Santos Tarragô, who represented Brazil in the TRIPS negotiations from 1990 to 1993, reviews the major events in chronological order. He traces the evolving positions of Brazil in such sensitive areas as pharmaceutical and chemical patents and copyright protection of software as it took a tactical approach with an eye to gains in other areas of the Uruguay Round. He characterises this evolution as a move from "staunch opposition" to "somewhat hesitant acceptance" of the text. Developing countries were faced with relative unity among the *demandeurs*, saw the need to strengthen the multilateral system in the face of unilateral action and sought to secure export interests in other sectors. Mr Tarragô underscores the compelling need for the effective preservation of policy space for developing countries to promote development and the public interest. He reviews the significance of negotiations on patents - the conscious concessions made were offset by the maintenance of flexibilities and a role for compulsory licensing as a policy tool.

Antonio Gustavo Trombetta negotiated for Argentina, and sets his account of the negotiations within the global and national political and economic shifts centred on 1989, a critical and decisive year in the TRIPS negotiations. He contrasts his country's offensive interest in ensuring greater market access for its products in the agriculture negotiations with a set of defensive interests pivoting on a range of public policy concerns, particularly the impact of pharmaceutical patents on the cost of medicines. Mr Trombetta acknowledges the impact of unilateral action on IP protection as a spur to cover IP disputes within the multilateral dispute settlement system. He concludes on a realist note: the TRIPS Agreement was not a perfect agreement, and only part of a broader framework, but constituted unprecedented regulation in the area of IP.

Umi K.B.A. Majid, Malaysia's negotiator, offers a perspective of a "small, developing, Muslim majority country that is very reliant on foreign investment" and a net importer of IP. She describes how she engaged with the negotiating process to deal with issues that had sensitive implications in a domestic context and argues that smaller delegations had to rise to a particular challenge to ensure their presence was felt. She underscores the significance of bilateral factors in encouraging developing countries to engage with multilateral standards. Ms Majid illustrates how the sensitive issue of GI protection, particularly for products of the vine, was dealt with to take account of regulatory diversity. The distinct situation of Malaysia could be accommodated, including through a footnote allowing for administrative enforcement action. She gives compelling examples of the need for all participants in negotiations to voice their concerns and positions clearly and firmly.

David Fitzpatrick's particular expertise in negotiating for Hong Kong was a deep knowledge of due legal process in enforcement as a former prosecutor and litigator. His account focuses on two issues of concern to Hong Kong as an important trading economy with an established IP system: parallel importation and enforcement. He identifies some of the features that enabled Hong Kong to make a distinctive contribution to the substance of the negotiations, given its significance as a trading economy and its extensive experience with the suppression of counterfeit trade within an established legal system. Mr Fitzpatrick highlights the importance of the issue of parallel importation in a negotiation concerning "trade-related" aspects of IP. Recalling the controversial character of this question, which could not be resolved in the negotiations, he characterises the outcome as an "honourable draw". Looking to the implementation of the enforcement part of TRIPS, he cautions against bias towards domestic firms in the enforcement of IP.

Part V looks closely at the negotiations in three substantive areas of TRIPS, which had contrasting negotiating dynamics: the texts on patents, on copyright, and on the settlement of disputes. TRIPS largely gives effect to existing international copyright law in the form of the Berne Convention for the Protection of Literary and Artistic Works, but added several key updates in economically significant sectors. The TRIPS Agreement broke new multilateral ground on patents against a backdrop of long-standing North-South dissent. Dispute settlement was contentious and uncertain until late in the negotiations, as it proved difficult to establish the proper place of IP disputes within the overall dispute settlement mechanism.

Jayashree Watal negotiated on all aspects of TRIPS (save copyright) for India in 1990, when much of the TRIPS text was developed. She provides a comprehensive account of the key developments in the critical area of patents within the TRIPS Agreement. Her contribution complements the overview of India's negotiating positions provided by A.V. Ganesan. A key part of her account, crucial for understanding the structure and content of the TRIPS text, concerns the negotiation of the text on compulsory licensing, which drew together the notion of government use and compulsory licensing under the broader heading of "use without authorization of the right holder", and the resultant absence of restrictions on the available grounds for such authorization. She attributes the balanced outcome to support from key developed country negotiators on aspects of public policy, as well as an overall negotiating environment characterized by cooperation, coalition-building and compromise.

Hannu Wager, who represented the Nordic countries focusing on copyright issues, sets the TRIPS negotiations in the broader context of the development of international copyright law, in particular the differences between the civil law tradition of authors' rights and the more utilitarian Anglo-Saxon tradition followed by the US, the UK and Commonwealth countries in general. They included the treatment of moral rights and a set of issues concerning the initial ownership of copyright and transfer of rights. Mr Wager also discusses the different approaches to the protection of performers, phonogram producers and broadcasting organizations within these traditions, and how these differences were bridged in the negotiations. Finally, he describes how international IP law evolved since the 1970s with respect to two new areas of information technology, namely computer software and layout-designs of integrated circuits, and how this evolution influenced the way these issues were addressed during the TRIPS negotiations.

Jagdish Sagar was India's copyright negotiator and also oversaw the initial implementation of the TRIPS copyright provisions into Indian law. His contribution therefore describes the history of the already high level of copyright protection in India in the light of its economic interests in films, music and software, and gives an update on India's position on the WIPO Internet Treaties that followed TRIPS. His contribution is important in understanding why the US and India were largely on the same side when it came to copyright protection. Yet there were differences between these two delegations on copyright issues, for example on the "impairment test" in the TRIPS rental rights provisions for films.

Adrian Macey negotiated both on TRIPS and on dispute settlement for New Zealand, giving him a unique vantage point. His chapter describes the debate over whether or not there should be a stand-alone dispute settlement mechanism for TRIPS. Citing the Uruguay Round documents, he outlines the distinct concerns that were raised by the *demandeurs* and the developing countries on dispute settlement and potential trade sanctions in other sectors for violation of IPR standards, or "cross-retaliation". Mr Macey outlines the role of a New Zealand proposal drawn up with the support of Colombia and Uruguay to bridge across these concerns, noting that many of the ideas in this proposal found a place in the Dispute Settlement Understanding (DSU). He points to the irony that cross-retaliation has been authorized by the WTO several times for use by developing countries against their developed country trading partners, revealing the resultant dispute settlement system to be a "two-edged sword".

The central figure in the negotiations, Ambassador Lars Anell, who chaired the TRIPS negotiating group and whose indispensable role as a thoughtful, fair and effective leader is acknowledged with much respect throughout this volume, gave a keynote address at the February 2015 Symposium reviewing the negotiating experience but also looking forward to today's public policy challenges for the IP system (see appendix 1). Indeed Ambassador Anell's reflections serve as a powerful link between the remarkable, productive and enduring work of the TRIPS negotiators almost a generation ago, and today's complex policy environment within and beyond the field of IP.

It was striking, when the TRIPS negotiators came together many years later for the Symposium, to hear of their continued engagement with the policy domain: apart from reflections on the TRIPS negotiations, the conversation was imbued with knowledgeable concern about contemporary public policy issues and the need for the multilateral system to continue to play its proper, balanced role. For this is the essential message that we can glean from the narratives drawn together in this volume: the TRIPS negotiators ultimately transcended the bare logic of trade negotiations, the simple zero-sum exchange of concessions. The accounts here show that the work of the negotiators evolved into a true - if contested and pressured - dialogue about what constitutes a proper policy balance in the field of IP, and how to define an adequate level of regulatory convergence internationally while leaving essential policy space.

For many, such a negotiation could not be successful without mutual respect, intellectual curiosity and creativity, and a willingness to listen to one another and to learn from those who offer practical expertise. The TRIPS negotiations become a case study in how to address a very practical challenge today: how to conduct a set of multilateral negotiations in a politically sensitive and technically challenging area where trade interests and regulatory imperatives overlap and intersect.

As the negotiators themselves point out in this volume, today's world differs considerably from that in which the TRIPS Agreement was negotiated and concluded, and the multilateral system confronts new and ever more complex challenges. Therefore, the TRIPS negotiations are unlikely to provide a simple template to be applied to contemporary issues in the same manner. Yet the goodwill, intellectual curiosity, mutual respect and skill of the negotiators, the leadership and drive of a respected Chair, and the trust invested in a professional and neutral Secretariat are all ingredients that would surely support and facilitate future negotiations.

The growing recognition of the TRIPS Agreement as a touchstone of policy legitimacy and balance, and as a framework for appropriate levels of regulatory convergence and preservation of domestic policy space is, however, the essential legacy of the negotiators. The following chapter seeks to distil the core lessons for today's policymakers and negotiators from the diverse accounts provided by the negotiators as a further guide to the indispensable individual chapters that follow, giving unique and irreplaceable insights into the making of the TRIPS Agreement.

2

Thematic review: Negotiating "trade-related aspects" of intellectual property rights

Antony Taubman[1]

TRIPS: reframing international intellectual property law

The entry into force of the TRIPS Agreement, along with the inception of the WTO in 1995, was a turning point for multilateral governance and a catalyst for transformation of law, policy and international relations in IP and in a host of related policy fields. Through the linking concept of "trade-related aspects" of IP rights, the TRIPS negotiations reframed both the international governance of IP and the very conception of "trade" within multilateral trade law and policy. The period since the Agreement entered into force has undoubtedly been the most active, the most intensively debated and the most geographically and economically diverse phase of intellectual property law-making and policy-making processes ever experienced: national legislative texts on IP notified to the WTO TRIPS Council now amount to over 4,500 official document references.

Yet twenty years is a brief period in the history of international IP law. IP was the focus of some of the first multilateral conventions in any field, and of the first attempts at multilateral regulatory convergence: the Paris Convention for the Protection of Industrial Property of 1883 and the Berne Convention for the Protection of Literary and Artistic Works of 1886 were negotiated during an earlier phase of economic integration, when it was recognised that the absence of an agreed framework for IP protection adversely affected commercial relations involving industrial products, branded goods and creative works. The initial negotiations in the 1880s were followed by a series of amendments over successive decades, and by further multilateral conventions; these agreements - especially the Paris and Berne Conventions - have proved to be remarkably resilient throughout all the change and upheaval of the 20th century and today still constitute much of the legal backbone of international relations in IP.

The TRIPS Agreement was consciously built upon this established framework, yet its very purpose was to be a dramatic departure from it: hence, it both reaffirmed the multilateral law of IP and fundamentally restructured its base. The conclusion and entry into force of the Agreement precipitated concern that it would not only subvert the existing multilateral IP system but would equally taint the multilateral trading system, particularly through its incorporation into the WTO dispute settlement mechanism; critics were concerned about its potential impact on sound domestic policy-making and upon the stability and legitimacy of the trade law system. And the period since the Agreement was concluded has unquestionably been the most dynamic and challenging time ever for the IP system in general.

Hence it is remarkable that, in the turbulent times of rapid social, technological and economic change that followed its conclusion, the TRIPS Agreement largely sustained its relevance and legitimacy. Its essential built-in balances have not been revisited by WTO members - apart from one specific case[2] - and the reported experience with its implementation across a wide spectrum of the WTO's membership has been a record of balanced, diverse and suitably tailored domestic policy-making,[3] rather than bare legal compliance backed by the threat of trade disputes.[4] While few may have predicted it, this more positive outcome is arguably of a piece with the logic and content of the Agreement as a legal text, and with the decisions taken about its place within the legal and institutional framework; hence, to understand the role and impact of the Agreement today, it is essential to understand its origins and above all how the text was crafted.

In 1986, when trade ministers from the bulk of the world's trading nations launched the Uruguay Round, the most complex and ambitious set of multilateral trade negotiations to be undertaken at the time, the IP negotiating mandate responded to the concerns of some that the existing legal and institutional multilateral framework for IP no longer represented "a functioning multilateral rule of law".[5] The Punta del Este Declaration directed negotiators to address "trade-related aspects" of IP rights. The original mandate was somewhat indeterminate: indeed, as many contributors to this volume recall, the first phase of the TRIPS negotiations largely constituted a debate over what "trade-related aspects" should be included, and how that understanding should structure the negotiation outcome. The results of these negotiations - the TRIPS Agreement - far exceeded most expectations in its coverage and its reach behind the border into the domestic domain, and in how its implementation would be monitored and enforced.

The Agreement emerged as the most comprehensive and far reaching international treaty on IP to date, covering as it did a wide sweep of substantive subject matter, as well as the administration and enforcement of IP, and the settlement of disputes between trading partners over IP. It also set out, for the first time in international IP law, the underlying public policy rationale for IP protection, and it provided policy space sufficient for countries at different levels of development to take measures to balance the interests of the right holders with the public interest in access to and use of protected content. Having been negotiated and then administered in a trade forum, it inevitably forged enduring legal, policy and institutional links between IP and the multilateral trading system. Its effects - and, more so, its perceived effects - have been profound, not only on the domestic IP laws and systems of the WTO's members, but on the international legal architecture and multilateral institutions concerned with both IP and trade.

Today, it is three decades since trade ministers at Punta del Este framed multilateral negotiations on IP in terms of their "trade-related aspects" - more as a diplomatic formula to facilitate production of a mandate than as a substantive concept to guide and inform negotiations. The Agreement itself entered into force over twenty years ago, and its main provisions were largely settled by negotiators four years prior to that, in 1991. We have since gained twenty years' practical experience with its effect on national law and policy in many legal systems across the globe, with its practical role in the management of trade relations and disputes and its influence on bilateral and regional trade agreements. This passage of time potentially offers a clearer perspective from which to assess the dynamics and importance of the negotiations and to distil their essential lessons for the future - both in administering the existing agreement and in developing new ones.

From this perspective, the TRIPS text, while a pragmatic negotiating outcome and an artefact of the inevitable give-and-take and ambiguities of trade negotiations, has come into clearer focus as a sound and legitimate framework not merely for resolving disputes between trading partners, but also for sound and balanced domestic policy-making responsive to national needs and circumstances. This creation of a new benchmark for legitimacy in IP policy-making is the most abiding and consequential outcome of the TRIPS negotiations, and it is only by closer attention to the distinctive qualities of the negotiating process that we can understand how this was achieved. Indeed, closer familiarity with the negotiations enables us to discern that the goal of creating a platform for sound, balanced and practically-informed policy may have been a shared, if mostly tacit, negotiating objective for many. The abiding effects of the final negotiated outcome can also be traced from a closer consideration of the structure and organization of the negotiations and their internal dynamics, the external driving factors and an exploration of how earlier, inconclusive work within the GATT purely on counterfeit trade ultimately yielded a comprehensive behind the border treaty on domestic regulatory convergence and on standards for domestic law enforcement and legislation.

From "trade-related aspects" of IP ...

The catalytic, linking concept of "trade-related aspects" of IP can now be seen as an acceptance, in effect, by trade policymakers and by trade negotiators that IP was indeed trade-related - in the very practical sense that a comprehensive set of trade agreements could only be concluded if recognition of the value and significance of IP in the contemporary international economy was part of the deal. In turn, this realization stemmed from growing anxiety within industrialized economies about their longer-term competitiveness, and recognition that their capacity to create jobs depended in part on advances in innovation - gains that could be lost if innovation and creativity was not adequately protected. Already by the late 1970s these concerns had centred on counterfeit trade - at that time, the most immediate threat to the producers of intangible value embedded in international trade. Progress towards the 1986 Punta del Este mandate, and during subsequent phases of negotiations, can be mapped against an increasing realization and consequent political acceptance - in some cases, grudging - that positive IP standards had to be a part of multilateral trade law if the Uruguay Round was to conclude successfully. Less clear at that time, but increasingly apparent in the period since the TRIPS negotiations, has been the wider recognition of the objective economic and commercial significance of the knowledge component of trade in goods and services, and thus the trade policy significance of IP - for instance in contemporary analysis of global value chains.[6]

The structure and character of the international economy when ministers established the Punta del Este mandate had differed considerably even from the state of affairs apparent at the time the negotiations concluded in 1994: several contributors in this volume chart the effect of these broader economic and geopolitical shifts on even the internal dynamics of the TRIPS negotiations. Today, twenty years later, the transformations already evident at the time the TRIPS Agreement entered into force are even more profound and fundamental, and yet the Agreement – as a legal text and as a framework for economic relations – proved to be uncannily fit for purpose for the new economy. These developments include a vast increase of the geographical scope of the trading entities encompassed within the international trading system, and a progressive shift of the centre of gravity of economic activity (and, later, of innovative activity) away from the traditional concentration in the industrialized world, but they also include a transformation of the very nature of the trade conducted within that system.

At the centre of this transformation of global trade was the progressive recognition of the value added by the intangible knowledge component of globally-traded goods and services, and its significance for trade policy and negotiations. But dealing more directly with the knowledge embedded in international trade in goods and services also meant crossing traditional disciplinary boundaries and policy domains, and engaging other areas of expertise and administrative competence. In turn, this meant that trade law and institutions engaged the interest of a much wider range of public policymakers, officials and analysts than those in the traditional trade policy community: TRIPS negotiators relate how their domestic consultations on the negotiations necessitated the construction of new consultative mechanisms so as to draw together all needed policy perspectives and expertise.[7] This was a conceptual and bureaucratic challenge even for those developed economies that were already more conscious of the increasing critical importance of the knowledge component of trade in goods and services, and yet a far greater challenge for developing country negotiators. The accounts of two Swiss negotiators - Thomas Cottier and Thu-Lang Tran Wasescha (chapters 4 and 9, respectively) - combine to present an absorbing case study of a cross-sectoral and federal consultative process that produced a consolidated stance for a country with strong domestic IP interests. Equally, A.V. Ganesan, Piragibe dos Santos Tarragô and Antonio Gustavo Trombetta recount that a strong defensive interest of developing countries was to preserve policy space so as to ensure scope to consider and develop alternative approaches in sensitive areas, rather than being pressured to adopt through a trade negotiation the exact same approach on IP and regulatory issues that developed economies had established for themselves (chapters 11, 12 and 13, respectively). India's approach in the area of patents exemplifies how these defensive interests were carried through to close textual negotiations (as described by Jayashree Watal, chapter 16).

... to trade in IP

Yet, paradoxically, from today's perspective, the most remarkable and visible "trade-related aspect" of IP was not foreseen by the TRIPS negotiators, still less in the mandate for TRIPS: that is the very tradeability of IP in itself, the burgeoning of international transactions at the individual consumer level that are defined by purchasing access to content protected by IPRs. In 1986 the Internet was a limited tool for academics and researchers, unknown to most of humanity who were largely oblivious to its potential economic and social impact. And the very character of trade was perceived essentially to concern transactions in physical objects that passed across borders and could be counted and measured as such - things you could drop on your foot, as the familiar parlance put it. Yet the impact of globalized communications networks and increasingly accessible information technologies was also beginning to be felt. In 1993, seemingly the earliest year for which such statistics were kept, only 0.3 per cent of the world's population had access to the Internet; today, this figure is close to 44 per cent. The Internet is a major conduit of global commerce, creating a seemingly borderless online global market, enabling vast markets in intangible products and trade in knowledge and creative content as such, shorn of the physical carrier media that had long served as a proxy for this form of valuable trade.

It is only since the conclusion of the TRIPS Agreement that we have seen the emergence - and in some industry sectors, the more recent predominance - of new consumer markets in digital products such as music, software, books, journals and audiovisual works, suggesting the development of a form of trade in IP as such, and the emergence of IP as a tradeable good in itself.[8] The Agreement was not drafted expressly to promote or to enable trade in IP as such: nonetheless, this form of international trade has flourished within the convergent set of standards established by TRIPS. David Fitzpatrick recalls that, at the time of the TRIPS negotiations, the full impact had yet to be felt of the new technologies that are currently revolutionizing content distribution models in the copyright sector; the negotiators did not "indulge in futurology", and so did not address the thorny IP issues raised by the online environment (chapter 15). It was only in 1999 that Indonesia and Singapore, in a thoughtful contribution to the WTO's electronic commerce work program, observed that books, music and software had been traded as goods "because they had to be delivered in the form of a carrier [medium]", and that such products "without a carrier medium are intangible goods considered under the ambit of intellectual property rights" and thus speculated whether they could be "simply considered as trade in [IPRs]".[9]

TRIPS negotiations forged a transformation of international IP law ...

The significance of the transformation in international IP law wrought by the TRIPS Agreement is apparent in three fundamental ways. While these three features are now an accepted, integral part of international law and its administration, it is striking that none of them was preordained by the original negotiating mandate, nor could even be readily predicted from it. Accordingly, it is only through understanding the internal dynamics and external driving factors of the negotiations that one can fully trace the character of these three interrelated transformations:

- *Substantively*, through the effective recognition that trading partners have a legitimate interest in how, and how well, their firms' IP is protected in export markets, not merely as a political claim but as a matter of substantive trade law commitments. This is the essential legal logic of an agreement on standards of IP protection as an integral component of the Marrakech outcome and as an expression of the *demandeurs'* claim that adequate and effective protection of IP should be recognized as a prerequisite for trade. This pivotal transformation of international trade law was the import of the critical choice made in the course of the TRIPS negotiations, extensively discussed in this volume, and confirmed in the decisive year of 1989, to work towards agreement on minimum standards for "adequate" IP protection and not only the articulation of general policy principles, nor exclusively to focus on trade in counterfeit goods.

- *Administratively and institutionally*, with the incorporation of trade-related aspects of IP as an integral responsibility of a newly created international organisation, the WTO, establishing it definitively as one of the institutions involved in the international governance of IP alongside WIPO, and adding IP as covered subject matter to the scope of the trade policy review process.

- *In the practical management of trade relations*, following the decision to incorporate IP commitments within a uniform dispute settlement mechanism administered by the WTO, integrating IP into the same system that is applied to more conventional trade disputes, with the unexpected – but entirely logical - consequence of giving WTO members the opportunity of using the threat of cross-retaliation by withdrawing IP benefits to enforce respect for rules in more conventional market access areas covered by the multilateral trading system.

In essence, the result of the negotiations was that international IP law would become a branch of international trade law, structurally and substantively, in the form of the TRIPS Agreement, even though the legal and policy rationale for this move was far from settled (and is still debated today), and even though it retained its own character and identity as a distinct branch of international law, administered mostly by WIPO. This reconceptualization of IP law and of trade interests meant a country's interests in the IP system would be defined, asserted, defended and litigated in the domain of trade law: not only for WTO members, but for all others that sought to be integrated into the global economy. The conclusion of the TRIPS Agreement was in effect a formal multilateral recognition of a broader paradigm shift, with significant consequences not only for IP law and policy across the globe, but also for mainstream trade law and for the institutions - multilateral, bilateral and regional - which manage trade relations between nations - a paradigm shift that can be traced to past GATT work on counterfeit trade and changes in US trade law in 1984. In this sense, the Agreement continues to find an imprint in the numerous bilateral and regional trade agreements that now incorporate IP as a trade issue. And this three-way convergence - minimum standards for protecting IP, a new international trade organisation overseeing those standards and a rigorous dispute settlement mechanism to deal in a balanced and fair way with frustrated expectations - is now firmly entrenched in today's international system.

... but to yield a zero-sum deal or a balanced framework for policy-making?

Despite its complex character, this convergence between streams of international law is typically characterised in zero-sum terms - for instance, as trade trumping policy, or economic law trumping human rights law. Indeed, much of the analysis of the Agreement pivots on assumptions and perceptions of the objectives and character of the negotiating process - largely characterising it as an all-or-nothing trade-off between the industry interests of the North and the public policy interests of the South. Yet this conventional model lacks nuance and depth, and above all offers little insight into the actual dynamics of the negotiations and the specific ways in which important and diverse policy interests were secured; it runs the risk of reifying inflexibilities that are not present in the treaty text, and foregoing opportunities for positive-sum gains that serve public policy interests. The derestricted formal documents from the negotiations are an inherently limited source of information, and do not enable a full understanding of the largely informal process and dynamics, nor of the considerations and assessment of interests that yielded the negotiating outcome. Still less do they enable lessons to be learned that may be of broader application as the international community continues to strive for consensus on how to adapt and apply the IP system, and other forms of domestic regulation, to advance common interests in promoting social and economic development in a coherent way that still accommodates necessary policy space for distinct national needs and interests.

Yet the narrative accounts gathered together in this volume - particularly when they reflect on the second stage of the negotiations, once the mandate question had been largely resolved - give a general impression that the negotiators did not see their essential task in zero-sum terms, nor in terms of one set of interests trumping another. The picture that emerges is a kind of dialectic, supported by a willingness to engage with the issues and to negotiate the most acceptable course guided by domestic experiences and an openness to learn from respected experts. The balance and quality of the negotiated outcome help us to understand today why many of the more dire predictions about the impact of TRIPS have not come to fruition (see, for instance, Jayashree Watal, chapter 16, discussing post-TRIPS pharmaceutical prices in India). This helps explain why the Agreement has proven to be a more flexible document, more accommodating of diverse domestic policy needs and priorities, than both its critics and its proponents anticipated at the time. In turn, this explains why implementation of the Agreement has proven to be less contentious in character than was feared. The expected avalanche of dispute settlement claims aimed by developed against developing countries has not eventuated: indeed, the predominant pattern in TRIPS dispute settlement was one of contention between developed economies, partly reflecting the continuation of policy differences already apparent during the negotiations.

The outcome on dispute settlement meant that not only the provisions of TRIPS itself, but also the pre-existing Paris and Berne Conventions, would be interpreted and applied in a trade law context. Even so, despite some concerns, multilateral IP law did not fragment into a TRIPS version conflicting with a WIPO/UN version, due in part to pains taken to ensure coherence both during negotiation and in subsequent interpretation. And the concept of "trade-related aspects" of IP did not mean ignoring the wider public policy questions of social welfare and economic development. Rather, the Agreement has proven to be a nuanced and balanced instrument and an expression of sound policy thinking, and it can still today enable fair and balanced public policy and defend against the excessive influence of sectoral interests and specific actors in domestic policy-making. It is impossible, in reading this volume, not to conclude that this positive outcome can be attributed in large part to the skill, expertise and professional focus of the negotiators, and to their awareness of the need for coherence and sound public policy (see Mogens Peter Carl, chapter 6).

This policy awareness is indeed evident in the very logic and structure of the Agreement: one of the striking achievements of developing country negotiators, well documented in this volume, was to build public policy safeguards into the text. They also articulated, for the first time in a multilateral IP instrument, the policy rationale for the IP system. Article 7 of the Agreement stipulates that IP protection should "contribute to the promotion of technological innovation and to the transfer and dissemination of technology, to the mutual advantage of producers and users of technological knowledge and in a manner conducive to social and economic welfare, and to a balance of rights and obligations".

This conscious embedding of public policy guidance and the construction of policy space within the Agreement were not a mere face-saving exercise in soft law, but rather - as several of the accounts directly attest - were a part of deliberate defensive negotiating strategies maintained and executed by developing country negotiators, with a view to the longer term, even though this was at the cost of substantive concessions elsewhere in the text (see Piragibe Tarragô, chapter 12). The subsequent experience of TRIPS implementation in the intervening period provides support to the understanding of the negotiators. By one reading, to secure a balance between protection of IP and public interest, all features incorporating a balance in the Agreement must be given full weight and meaning (see A.V. Ganesan, chapter 11). In effect, there is considerable opportunity for TRIPS implementation to include attaining public policy goals through sound policy-making, not simply passing legislation to achieve passive, formal compliance with the letter of the law of TRIPS.

This more nuanced picture both of the negotiations and of the treaty text they produced should not imply, however, that all negotiators' interests were secured and negotiating objectives attained, nor that the outcome did not entail serious concessions; still less, that the Agreement as concluded was an ideal outcome from any point of view, but especially from the perspective of the developing countries that had initially opposed substantive standard-setting. Indeed, the accounts that emerge from the negotiators bear witness to the difficulties in accepting certain concessions on significant provisions of the text, with serious policy implications - both from an offensive and a defensive point of view. Perhaps the least known aspect of these negotiations, however, is the extent to which developed countries (generally perceived as the winners of the TRIPS negotiations) individually gave ground on significant points of law and policy.

The making of the TRIPS Agreement was imbued with a strong sense of the policy issues at stake. But it was a tough set of trade negotiations conducted under significant external pressures, and entailing necessary compromise and suboptimal deal-making. Antonio Trombetta's clear-sighted analysis of the negotiations makes it clear that the Agreement was not the ideal outcome for the set of interests he was defending (chapter 13); likewise Catherine Field records some areas where the Agreement falls short of the interests the US delegation was working to secure, and where the Agreement forced change in US domestic law (chapter 8). The hesitation to reopening the text at a late stage (see Adrian Otten, chapter 3) and the ultimate agreement to accommodate specific demands on two substantively unrelated issues - compulsory licensing of semiconductor patents and the grounds for taking a complaint on TRIPS under the WTO dispute settlement system (discussed in Catherine Field, chapter 8) - illustrates the pragmatic character of the negotiations, driven as they were by a complex of sectoral interests and the overarching goal of a credible and coherent agreement. Nonetheless, many of the negotiators developed, and showed at the February 2015 Symposium and in this volume, an informed, judicious, practitioner's grasp of the complex public policy dimensions of IP, an awareness that helped shape the treaty text in key parts.

Insights into negotiations for today's TRIPS debates

The keynote address at the February 2015 Symposium by the widely respected Negotiating Group Chair Ambassador Lars Anell gave a sweeping review of contemporary IP policy challenges, and reminded us that the TRIPS negotiators did not settle many of the policy issues they grappled with, as these issues remain current and contested today, in some cases still more than ever, with some policy differences evident in the negotiations finding expression in the resort to the WTO dispute settlement mechanism (appendix 1). Within the broader multilateral context, the Agreement has helped provoke and frame debate on a host of public policy questions, ranging from public health to climate change, and debate about the linkage of TRIPS with human rights and other spheres of public international law. Debate and analysis continue about its very character and legal effect as an international legal instrument - at a time when the IP component of trade and the public policy role of IP systems are both more important than ever - and its legal and policy implications are still uncertain. Active and important debate and analysis centred on the Agreement continues at several levels concerning:

- The place and legitimacy of an agreement on substantive IP standards within the framework of trade law, and in particular the negotiating dynamics that brought the Agreement to fruition, given the perception that it was only the consequence of a wider negotiating deal forming part of a set of trade-offs with other sectors. A related, continuing question concerns whether the outcome would work to the overall benefit of developing countries, which had initially resisted the expansive interpretation of the TRIPS mandate.

- Specific legal questions, many relating to the exact scope and character of the commitments entered into under the Agreement and the legitimate scope for domestic discretion and flexibility within TRIPS standards.

- Fundamental systemic questions within the realm of trade law, such as the legal basis of a dispute under TRIPS: whether complaints can only cover non-compliance with treaty obligations, or could extend to frustration of treaty objectives and the nullification and impairment of expected benefits. This was a matter that negotiators could not resolve at a late stage, and passed to the TRIPS Council for resolution.

- The consequences for international governance, not merely in substantive international IP law, but also concerning its interplay with law and policy in several other areas such as health, the environment, food security, climate change and several strands of human rights law.

The present volume is not intended to, and will not in practice, settle any of these four lines of important debate about TRIPS, which continue to this day. However, the insights from the making of TRIPS that this unique set of authors provide will certainly inform and illuminate these essential debates, and may help future negotiator and policymakers chart their way through this perennially difficult terrain. The following chapters by individual negotiators discuss the negotiating dynamics of the Agreement and probe the assumptions and sets of interests driving the negotiations, the nature of the negotiating process, specific choices made during the negotiations and the reasons behind them, the considerations that led to concessions in the area of TRIPS as against expected benefits in other sectors, and the political economy background in which newly recalibrated economic interests in international IP made their presence felt through a range of trade and political channels.

Analysing the TRIPS negotiations

The negotiating dynamics are anatomized most effectively by the key Secretariat figure in the negotiations and in the subsequent administration of the TRIPS Agreement: Adrian Otten, whose account serves as the keystone of this volume. He contrasts the peripheral reference to IP in pre-existing GATT law with the growing perception that the future of the multilateral trading system depended on some recognition of the importance of IP protection and accommodation of IP interests within the trade policy mix. He tells us in unambiguous terms that the driver behind the inclusion of TRIPS in the mandate for the Uruguay Round was the United States, following the Trade and Tariff Act of 1984. His narrative traces how the negotiations moved from the initial standoff over the mandate, through a process of initial understanding the factual background and diverse negotiating objectives, and were transformed by the pivotal, mid-term decision that enabled negotiation on substantive standards, finally leading to a close and intensive textual negotiation that involved diverse alliances and a resolution of significant North-North differences along with institutional and dispute settlement questions. His account therefore serves as the core of this book, with the other individual perspectives by negotiators and Secretariat staff illuminating and expanding upon his thematic framework (chapter 3).

Distilling these diverse narratives, this chapter draws out the main themes identified by the contributors, who have analysed the negotiations at several levels:

- The place of the negotiations within the Uruguay Round, including the trade-offs and linkages with other areas of negotiation

- The external political and other factors that drove the negotiations, and that influenced evolving negotiating positions

- The role of non-state actors

- Sources of legal standards and the multilateral institutional linkages – within the GATT and elsewhere, notably in WIPO

- The influence of the outcome on regulatory convergence

- The anatomy and dynamics of the negotiations, including the origins and the evolution of the negotiating mandate.

TRIPS negotiations within the Uruguay Round

The genesis and negotiation of TRIPS was a pragmatic initiative, resolved by creative negotiators in the overall context of the Uruguay Round, a negotiating platform that offered unprecedented opportunities for market access in areas of interest to developing countries. The major economies had reassessed their economic and trade interests, saw IP protection in foreign markets as critical to those interests and therefore insisted that their need for more effective IP protection be integral to any multilateral trade deal. Developing countries were not won over at the level of principle: many accepted the deal only as a trade-off for gains elsewhere, cautioning against legal harassment upon the conclusion of the treaty, but – as this book records – they had negotiated hard for the text to include provisions to preserve their policy interests in ways that have been since demonstrated as providing effective safeguards. The accounts of Piragibe Tarragô and Antonio Trombetta in particular bring out the importance of the trade-offs with market access for agricultural products and the key role that these played at various stages of the negotiations, but most crucially in April 1989 and December 1991 (chapters 12 and 13, respectively). The TRIPS negotiations were a realist diplomatic process: in essence, each party asserted and defended their interests, and sought to accommodate those of others, in the hope of achieving a balanced outcome that could be acceptable in a domestic context.

While the comprehensive nature of the Uruguay Round gave opportunities for trade-offs between sectors of negotiations, and this was a major impetus to the negotiations and conclusion of the TRIPS Agreement, TRIPS were not a monolithic set of interests that remained essentially the province of developed countries, to be traded off against market access elsewhere. This finished character of TRIPS - a seasoned and carefully curated articulation of a balanced framework for domestic IP policy-making, rather than a checklist reciting a set of unilateral demands - is surely what has enabled its consolidation as a widely-accepted basis today for legitimate balance in the protection, administration and enforcement of IP.

When discussing the dynamics of the negotiations, Mogens Peter Carl comments on the general assumption that the TRIPS Agreement is a consequence of a mercantilist trade-off between different trade sectors, suggesting that this analysis can be overstated. He observes that negotiators may make concessions while persuading themselves they are acting in their own interests. In his view the TRIPS negotiations did not have the character of a traditional bartering, but enabled consideration of what amounted to good policy (chapter 6).

This analysis provides support for the growing understanding today that the policy framework and principles articulated by TRIPS are not, for the most part, a bare set of diplomatic formulae, but rather represent something of a compromise agreed upon to codify a kind of best practice in policy terms. This applies not merely to the substantive standards, but still more so to the enforcement provisions, the negotiation of which is revealed as a process of articulating due process and appropriate balance. The exceptions that prove this general rule - those areas of text that bear the hallmarks of what authors describe in diplomatic parlance as "constructive ambiguity" (as Matthijs Geuze and Thu-Lang Tran Wasescha recall in chapters 7 and 9, respectively) - lie principally in areas where disagreement over policy is most pronounced and lingers today. In this vein, several authors discuss geographical indications, which remain a divisive issue today. Even the careful crafting of provisions relevant to local working requirements has not, apparently, put a decisive end to a legal and policy debate that continues today.

External political and economic drivers

All accounts point to 1989 as the pivotal year, internally and externally, for the negotiation of TRIPS. It was a critical and decisive time for the negotiation process, the point of inflexion when the focus turned to the concrete elaboration of substantive standards. It was also a remarkable year in global politics that led a recalibration of negotiating stances that put a substantive outcome within closer reach of the negotiators.

No negotiator operates in a vacuum, and several contributors to this volume emphasize the influence of dramatic changes in the international realm, particularly the fundamental political and economic realignments culminating in the fall of the Berlin Wall in November 1989. In 1986, when the Uruguay Round mandate was framed, many countries maintained centrally-planned economies and import substitution policies. While economic liberalisation was continuing apace, particularly in East Asia, there was arguably no fully international or global trading system. Several negotiators reflect on the impact of this transformation.

For Peter Carl, the relaxation of East-West confrontation and the resultant political transformations, producing a period of economic optimism and a unique "political and psychological context", was the chief factor behind the success of the Uruguay Round in general (chapter 6). Thomas Cottier also stresses the significance of the geopolitical changes of 1989, which for him had the effect of changing "the rules of the game" as countries turned to market economy precepts, noting the significance of appropriate levels of IPRs to attract much-needed foreign direct investment (chapter 4). From a developing country perspective, Antonio Trombetta also centres his account on the global political and economic shifts of 1989 - "of magnitudes unknown up until then" - and their implications for an economy such as Argentina, when it became clear that its positive economic interests lay in ensuring greater market access for agricultural products through trade negotiations in that area (chapter 13).

Well before the Uruguay Round came to an end in 1994, many countries had embarked on a fundamental structural transition to a market-based economy, leading over time to near universal engagement with a globalized marketplace. Adrian Otten therefore sees these changes as "a reflection of the *Zeitgeist* and a great stimulus to it", as TRIPS was going with the grain of economic policy thinking and reform underway at the time (chapter 3). It must be noted that the paradigm shifting 1989 mandate came in April, a good seven months before the fall of the Berlin Wall. A.V. Ganesan and Piragibe Tarragô also highlight the wider political context: the importance of new governments more disposed to market-friendly policies and to the economic role of the private sector and foreign investments (chapters 11 and 12, respectively).

Another important factor for many negotiators, particularly but not only from the developing world, was the compelling defensive interest in dealing with the consequences of the growing leverage of IP interests in domestic trade policy processes of developed economies, notably in the US. Indeed, these accounts taken together directly illuminate the existing understanding of how the multilateral turn represented by TRIPS was impelled in part by the actual and feared impact of unilateral action - essentially, pressure from the US Special 301 process, which expressly envisaged trade sanctions against countries that did not provide adequate and effective standards of IP protection and enforcement to US entities. For some negotiators, this was a spur to advancing negotiations to ensure that IP trade matters would fall within the multilateral trade dispute settlement system.

This unilateral trade policy process, which began effectively to be enforced in 1989, was also influential in shaping the character of TRIPS as a set of agreed multilateral standards that would define, in effect, what was adequate and effective for the purposes of reconciling mutual expectations of IP protection in the context of trade relations. Several authors, including A.V. Ganesan, Piragibe Tarragô, Antonio Trombetta and Umi K.B.A. Majid, dwell on the significance of this unilateral pressure and the resultant common desire to deal with trade tensions over the protection of IP through a multilateral dispute settlement system. This objective was by no means limited to developing countries and was also pursued by developed countries such as Australia, Canada and Japan (see chapters 11, 12, 13 and 14, respectively). As Catherine Field recalls, the US "was sending a strong message that maintaining access to its market was linked to having adequate IP protection". She highlights *inter alia* the determination of the US government to take trade action to address IP concerns as one reason for the acceptance of the more specific April 1989 mandate, and recalls that the United States successfully engaged with its trading partners as part of the Generalized System of Preferences process and under Special 301 to obtain IP improvements (chapter 8).

The role of non-state actors

Contributors to this volume recognize the impact of domestic players, including industry and other nongovernmental interests, in shaping their negotiating positions, but also in catalysing the TRIPS negotiating mandate in the first place. Thomas Cottier recognizes the influence of private lobbies at the outset of the negotiations, whose direct influence was particularly strong in the US delegation, but argues that these efforts do not alone explain the results achieved (chapter 4).

Industry interests especially were instrumental in getting IP - and the more concrete demand for substantive minimum standards - on the negotiating agenda, but did not determine the character of the outcome, which differed significantly from what key industry players had sought. Nevertheless, inputs from the private sector, in particular the common statement of views put forward in 1988 by the US Intellectual Property Committee, the Japanese Keidanren, and the Union of Industrial and Employers' Confederations of Europe, guided the *demandeurs* in formulating their own negotiating positions.[10]

Peter Carl notes that the European Commission, on the other hand, was much less exposed to external pressures from private parties, industry or non-governmental organizations (NGOs) (chapter 6). The contrast with the current multilateral environment on IP - which sees much more active and direct engagement with civil society and other policy voices - is remarked by several, including Thomas Cottier who in hindsight believes their involvement may have been beneficial in preparing an overall balanced result (chapter 4).

Industry interests from developing countries were also closely associated with the negotiations. Antonio Trombetta and Jayashree Watal both highlight how the Argentine and Indian generic drug industry groups and experts were closely following the negotiations and even liaising with their counterparts in other countries to safeguard their interests (chapters 13 and 16, respectively).

The focus on the role of non-state actors has limited explanatory value, however, and the essential analytical point that this volume bears out is that the negotiated outcome cannot be attributed simply to the private sector demands of TRIPS proponents or opponents. In particular the final text was very far from a passive imprint of the expectations of those interests that put "trade-related aspects" of IP on the multilateral trade agenda. Indeed, all negotiators describe a process of mutual learning, debate and negotiating give-and-take that yielded a balanced and nuanced document that articulated a number of concrete policy principles and recognized potential risks to legitimate trade from excessive IP enforcement and abusive licensing practices.

The sources of legal standards and links with multilateral institutions

The TRIPS Agreement was all the more momentous as a paradigm shift given that - of all the areas of law, policy and regulation that the newly formed WTO would cover - it was IP law that was the longest established and deepest rooted internationally. The TRIPS negotiators therefore made a critical decision not to address the drafting of standards *ab initio*. Negotiators elected to save time and enhance coherence by incorporating the substantive standards of the latest texts of the Paris Convention and the Berne Convention - the key WIPO conventions - directly into text, but also to draw on past WIPO work in some substantive areas still, at that time, unsettled in international law.

Several authors describe the complex implications for the TRIPS mandate and subsequent negotiations of faltering negotiations in WIPO - which had been seen as failing to respond effectively to the IP related interests of developed countries, and yet provided source material for the TRIPS text. The Treaty on Intellectual Property in Respect of Integrated Circuits - concluded at the mid-point of the TRIPS negotiations in 1989 and discussed by Hannu Wager (chapter 17) - provides a good illustration: this diplomatic outcome was perceived as weighted too heavily towards developing country interests and thus attracted virtually no ratifications (to date, only three parties have accepted or ratified the treaty), but the bulk of its substantive text was incorporated within the TRIPS text and thus it was given legal effect by an indirect route.

This incorporation of the WIPO treaties raised several technical legal questions, particularly of treaty interpretation (would provisions of Paris or Berne within the TRIPS Agreement differ from those same provisions in their original legal setting, and was there an hierarchy of provisions between the TRIPS Agreement and these earlier conventions?) which would only be resolved in subsequent dispute settlement. Further, while the existing WIPO instruments provided a surer foundation, they did not preclude differences in approach. As Adrian Otten and Hannu Wager note, even after the US had acceded to the Berne Convention, North-North differences continued to dominate the copyright negotiations with respect to moral rights and contractual arrangements (chapters 3 and 17, respectively).

Yet this critical decision by TRIPS negotiators ensured that trade-related standards on IP would be anchored within the existing corpus of multilateral IP law, and that in turn TRIPS would influence the WIPO legal system, for example on the so-called WIPO Internet Treaties in the area of copyright concluded in 1996. And the paradigm shift in international governance that the Agreement represented was immediately apparent in the form of concerns about its impact on WIPO as an institution, and in terms of the threat posed to the future coherence of international IP law.

The dynamics of WIPO work on IP standard-setting both before and during the TRIPS negotiations are well documented by contributors as a significant influence on the pace, content and outcome of the negotiations. Thu-Lang Tran Wasescha recalls that the TRIPS negotiations emerged from a period of failed attempts since the 1970s to update and reform the international IP framework in WIPO (chapter 9). Jayashree Watal tells us that during the Uruguay Round, WIPO undertook negotiations on patent law harmonization, a process that continued in parallel with the TRIPS negotiations. Indeed, despite the fact that this process did not succeed, TRIPS negotiators drew upon these materials as a substantive resource (chapter 16). The negotiators also drew extensively upon trade law principles and developments in the GATT. GATT work on a code on the suppression of counterfeit trade began in the 1970s, and GATT dispute settlement over the trade impact of discriminatory IP enforcement long preceded the finalization of the TRIPS text.

Catherine Field's contribution contains the most exhaustive analysis of the relationship between TRIPS and trade law. She stresses the significance of past GATT work on counterfeit trade and its link with domestic concerns about such trade in the US and other industrialised economies. She also explains how the TRIPS text on national and most-favoured nation (MFN) treatment is "an amalgam of both IP and trade principles, with the IP community unwilling to give up existing exceptions to national treatment and the trade community seeking to avoid 'free-riders'". She recalls that the MFN provision, which is drawn from trade law and does not exist in the WIPO conventions, was mainly proposed by the European Communities (EC), which had not benefited from the pipeline protection for pharmaceutical patents that had been provided for in the bilateral US-Korea agreement. She points out that the TRIPS MFN provisions are not subject to an exception such as Article XXIV of GATT that provides for regional or bilateral trade agreements or customs unions. The more "limited" and "specific" scope for MFN exceptions under TRIPS means that the benefits of so-called TRIPS-plus provisions in bilateral or plurilateral trade agreements should be automatically extended to all WTO members without discrimination. She analyses the role of MFN in the area of geographical indications (GIs), where the European Union (EU) and European Free Trade Association have agreed to protect particular GIs listed in bilateral trade agreements, while noting that to date members have chosen not to challenge such agreements in relation to the MFN principle. In considering exceptions more broadly, she contrasts the approach taken with that of the GATT: negotiators considered, but rejected, a general exception clause such as GATT Article XX. Instead, they settled on tailored exceptions specified for each IP right. She draws a link, however, with the IP enforcement exception under GATT XX(d), viewing the TRIPS enforcement provisions as an elaboration of the positive disciplines in this area.[11]

The one area that is treated identically in both the TRIPS Agreement and other areas of trade law is dispute settlement, since TRIPS largely adheres to the same system. The TRIPS Agreement differs in the formal terms applying to dispute settlement only in that non-violation and situation complaints do not currently apply to it. This exception is a subject of on-going negotiation in the TRIPS Council.

In describing more fully the status of IP in the pre-WTO GATT, Adrian Otten recalls the significance of dispute settlement on IP under the GATT, notably the seminal and timely ruling in Section 337 of the US Tariff Act in early 1989. This case demonstrated how the GATT dispute settlement system could handle complex IP issues and could prevent the abuse of IP rules as trade restrictive measures. He suggests that this experience helped boost confidence that "trade-related" IP disputes did have an appropriate place in the GATT/WTO dispute settlement system (chapter 3). On the politically sensitive negotiations on GATTability, Catherine Field notes that inclusion of TRIPS within the dispute settlement system was a top-level objective for the United States, in particular the aspect of trade retaliation (chapter 8).

Adrian Macey recounts how an exemplary middle player grouping of New Zealand, Colombia and Uruguay worked on a proposal on dispute settlement with the goal of enabling conceptual discussion and alleviating the divisiveness of this issue, highlighting the benefit of creative approaches to negotiations in sensitive or otherwise difficult areas. In analysing the debate over cross-retaliation (the possibility of withdrawal of concessions under another agreement in the event of non-compliance with TRIPS), he concludes that the symmetrical and balanced application of cross-retaliation has enabled developing countries to exercise leverage in disputes over more conventional market access obligations frustrated by developed country WTO members. He therefore describes the resultant dispute settlement system as a "two-edged sword", an unexpected development in that the principal exponents of cross-retaliation have in fact been developing countries, despite their opposition in the negotiations to this linkage, whereas the developed countries that advocated the prospect of cross-retaliation during the negotiations have seen it used to encourage their own compliance with dispute settlement rulings under other agreements (chapter 19).

In addition to pre-existing international IP and trade law, the TRIPS Agreement drew most of all from long-established domestic IP law - the practical desire being to limit changes to established domestic balances - but also to provide a positive source of concepts, principles and standards. Catherine Field relates that the US submissions laid down what it considered to be adequate and effective protection standards of IP, standards that were largely satisfied by US law and supported by business communities from the industrialized countries. The US negotiating team accepted proposals on what are now known as "flexibilities" that were in line with its own domestic laws, including use of patents by or on behalf of government upon payment of full compensation or compulsory licences to address anti-competitive behaviour. She perceptively notes that with regard to "must achieve" objectives of negotiators, a change to a country's domestic law or practice may be possible but a change to the core principle underlying the IP or other regime of the country may not be possible if the agreement has to be implemented as envisioned (chapter 8).

In this context it is worth noting that Jagdish Sagar, who negotiated on copyright for India, observes that the emerging standards from the TRIPS negotiations largely mirrored domestic processes and the strong national interest identified in software and the film industry; the approach on performers' rights more accurately reflected the cultural context of musicians in India, and overall in this area in view of specific domestic interests legislators elected to set standards beyond those of TRIPS in certain respects (chapter 18).

The EC negotiators recall that the process of formulating an EC-wide position on substantive issues, informed by the various domestic practices of its members, served as a precursor for the distillation of common standards for TRIPS. For the EC, it was a natural objective to seek to imprint its emerging common standards as multilateral standards in the TRIPS Agreement. Yet there was a two-way flow: Jörg Reinbothe describes how TRIPS provisions influenced the formulation of EU law itself, particularly in the field of enforcement. This experience in regional regulatory convergence also underscored specific IP-related principles of balance, reconciling IP with free trade and integrating with the existing multilateral IP system (chapter 10).

Developing country negotiators recall how, in some instances, their domestic enforcement standards already largely anticipated TRIPS provisions. David Fitzpatrick's description of the elaboration of the enforcement part of the Agreement, and Umi Majid's account of how she sought to preserve balance in the allocation of enforcement resources, both exemplify the benefit of experienced practitioners in crafting an informed, fair and effective set of provisions defining domestic enforcement of substantive standards. These two accounts help explain how these rules were shaped with a view to balance and procedural fairness, also taking account of actual enforcement experiences and their effects on trade. Notably, the TRIPS Agreement remained balanced between the two main legal systems, civil law and common law, particularly within its provisions on domestic enforcement (chapters 15 and 14, respectively).

Nevertheless, as Catherine Field's chapter records, sometimes even the TRIPS *demandeurs* found that they were negotiating altogether new or significantly revised standards in a range of areas covering both substantive law and its administration and enforcement, and in the case of industrialized countries, with only a brief period of 12 months for implementation (chapter 8). Hence, the norm-setting process takes on the character of a regulatory feedback loop rather than the imposition of a single regulatory template. This loop draws on and informs domestic standards for the IP system within a broad policy framework – a characteristic since borne out in the subsequent experience with TRIPS implementation among WTO members.

Other institutional linkages within the multilateral system are discussed as well. Adrian Otten recalls the role of the Organisation for Economic Co-operation and Development (OECD) in first placing IP on the multilateral trade agenda in the 1980s (chapter 3). Thomas Cottier characterizes the initial phase of negotiations as a North-South *dialogue de sourds* (dialogue of the deaf) defined by two opposing positions lacking in solid evidence and dominated respectively by doctrines developed in the OECD and the United Nations Conference on Trade and Development (UNCTAD). Developing country negotiators describe the role of UNCTAD in helping draft the initial submission of 14 developing countries in Spring 1990 that provided a solid basis for their substantial negotiating positions (chapter 4 and part IV, respectively).

A potential model for regulatory convergence

From the perspective of the quarter century that separates us from the conclusion of the bulk of its text, the TRIPS Agreement comes into focus as a model for a regulatory convergence treaty, expressing a balanced conception of good governance, specifying how its provisions are to be given effect and providing for sound public policy safeguards. Before the Uruguay Round, the essential functions and objectives of trade agreements were seen as to reduce obstacles to trade in goods and to limit discriminatory treatment: the basic purpose of trade law did not extend to setting mandatory positive standards for domestic regulation. The Uruguay Round came at a singular point of economic, political and technological change: the attendant recalibration of trade and policy interests precipitated a major transformation of trade law. Central to this paradigm shift was the acceptance that trade law commitments could legitimately reach behind the border and address areas of domestic regulation that had impact on trade.

Within this legal framework and trade policy context, the TRIPS Agreement comes into focus in retrospect as a precursor of a new kind of trade-related agreement – providing for convergence of standards by establishing broad policy principles and defining how they can be carried out domestically, while leaving latitude - policy space - for distinct needs and circumstances to be accommodated. Jörg Reinbothe recalls that the experience of standard-setting within the EC had enabled practical familiarity with the principle of subsidiarity, which in turn was highly pertinent for multilateral norm setting that left appropriate leeway for domestic systems (chapter 10).

Thomas Cottier emphasizes the groundbreaking character of the Agreement as a "regulatory convergence" multilateral trade Agreement setting positive standards for domestic regulation: it exceeded initial expectations to become a kind of base code for decades to come. Its standards had deep roots in existing domestic laws, particularly those of developed countries, and had the effect of extending some principles established at the domestic level to a wider range of economies. He singles out the provisions on fair and equitable procedures - based on established domestic traditions - as the first multilateral trade agreement on regulatory convergence, codifying principles that were entirely new to public international law, even if well-established in many national jurisdictions. The challenges to regulatory convergence are not necessarily North-South in character: he points out that difference on regulatory issues divided developed countries at the time of the negotiations and those differences were mirrored in the subsequent pattern of dispute settlement that took place principally between developed members. In any event, the outcome redefined and restructured international IP law. Furthermore, it altered the very character of international trade law by establishing harmonized positive standards with which domestic regulatory systems would have to comply, within a trade agreement that would reach well behind the border and stipulate how IP should be protected, going so far as to set forth the procedural principles for domestic courts and other authorities to follow (chapter 4).

The anatomy and dynamics of the negotiating process

It is critical to understand the full anatomy of the negotiating process - in terms of its chronology and distinct phases, the way in which interests were raised and accommodated, how and why compromises were reached and negotiating objectives were not fully achieved, and the practical tools employed to achieve the outcome. Diverse factors - positive interests defined by the shifting external trade, economic and industry environment; the defensive quest for a multilateral shield from unilateralism; and the failure to progress past work in GATT and in WIPO - all fed into the Punta del Este mandate for TRIPS negotiations. The conception of "trade-related aspects" in this mandate was shorthand for the IP dimension that multilateral trade negotiators would need to address. Yet it was an ambiguous formulation that hovered uncertainly across a range of divergent expectations.

From an ambiguous mandate...

Adrian Otten explains how the wording of the Punta del Este mandate on TRIPS necessitated an initial focus on clarifying and giving substance to that somewhat uncertain reference to "trade-related aspects". He notes that its only clear element was the reference to a code or agreement on trade in counterfeit goods along the lines of past GATT work. The mandate did open up further possibilities, although it seemed to "remain anchored in the world of the GATT and of trade in goods", and recognized concerns about the competences of other IGOs, especially WIPO (chapter 3).

Recalling that this mandate was open-ended, Peter Carl singles out the question of dispute settlement on TRIPS matters - a key outcome, now a major component of the multilateral trading system - that was not expressly covered in the initial mandate (chapter 6). Catherine Field locates the origins of the mandate's reference to "adequate and effective protection" of IPRs within the US Trade and Tariff Act of 1984, and its provision that denial of adequate and effective IP protection and enforcement amounted to an "unreasonable act, policy or practice" providing a basis for retaliatory action by the United States Trade Representative (chapter 8).

However, the reference to adequate and effective protection left open the question for many negotiators as to whether it required substantive standards to define such a level of protection. Thomas Cottier tells us of the 1987 Swiss proposal to build a TRIPS Agreement on the basis of existing GATT disciplines of nullification and impairment, developing normative principles and an indicative list of types of conduct considered detrimental to international trade.[12] This was rejected in favour of an approach covering minimum standards for IPRs (chapter 4).

... to negotiations on substantive standards...

Adrian Otten's account, reinforced by others, describes an initial wrangling over the import of this mandate, with even the EC taking until mid-1988 to accept that negotiations should cover substantive standards and internal enforcement of IPRs alongside the border measures contemplated in the counterfeit trade code, and many others only conceding that point as part of the April 1989 mid-term deal. He points to the practical impact this shift in focus had for many delegations who were faced with more complex domestic consultations, a challenge accentuated for the EC as it triggered a recasting of EC competences *vis-à-vis* its member states (chapter 3). Piragibe Tarragô suggests that this shift on the part of the EC was decisive in creating a sense that a treaty of substantive IP standards had become inevitable (chapter 12). In effect, it was the April 1989 decision that determined the full operational mandate of the negotiations. Indeed, a comparison of the separate elements of this decision with the table of contents of the TRIPS Agreement shows how closely the negotiators followed this structure, only leaving open the questions of GATTability and the institutional setting of the agreement once concluded.

The general view of the substantive TRIPS negotiations that emerges from this volume is of a more multipolar, balanced and nuanced negotiation process than is often depicted. However, the processes of information gathering and mutual learning - though valuable and well attested in many accounts - were not sufficient to carry forward negotiations, and without an external impulse the negotiations could have remained in the deadlock familiar from more recent attempts at multilateral norm-setting in IP. As Adrian Otten recounts, it was the sense of potential failure of the multilateral trading system apparent at the 1988 mid-term review, and awareness that refusal to negotiate on IP would not make those issues disappear, that ultimately led to political acceptance of the substantive approach. His analysis of the April 1989 decision on TRIPS stresses the value of clarity and precision in guidance given to negotiators. This reframing of the negotiation process explains the fundamental, even structural, trade-offs established at that time between the establishment of substantive standards on both availability and enforcement of IPRs on the one hand, and the reference to public policy goals and application of multilateral rule of law to IP disputes on the other. This enabled institutional questions – the so called GATTability of TRIPS and dispute settlement in particular – to be set aside for the final stages of the negotiations. Thus negotiations could proceed on text before it was even decided to establish a new multilateral organization, let alone the situation of TRIPS dispute settlement within it (chapter 3).

... to negotiations on text, informed by policy understanding

With a clearer mandate, greater understanding of negotiating positions and objectives, and a process of mutual learning underway, the path was clear for textual negotiations on content. The negotiators describe a progression from a procedural stand-off, wrangling over the negotiating mandate, towards an informed and thoughtful review of the principles of the IP system and a reasoned effort to capture the essence of good policy-making in different fields, while preserving significant latitude for domestic policy differences. What is presented is, without doubt, a pragmatic trade negotiation, but one that was increasingly informed by learning and debate about balanced policy settings, particularly in the view of the EC negotiators (see Peter Carl, chapter 6, and Jörg Reinbothe, chapter 10).

Factors enabling a successful outcome

The negotiators acknowledge the unique external factors - even the unprecedented, and likely unrepeatable, *Zeitgeist* - that not only put TRIPS on the negotiating table, but also drove forward the negotiations to an unexpectedly comprehensive and far-reaching conclusions. Yet the insiders' narratives about the very practice of negotiations - the internal dynamics, the practical negotiating know-how, the individual skills, expertise and personal qualities that were brought to bear - create a strong and convincing impression of a remarkable, memorable and instructive case study in effective multilateral process. Thomas Cottier identifies the processes of mutual learning, building of mutual trust, continuity of representation and the negotiating techniques used to build a common and comprehensive treaty text as "endogenous factors" for success. He recalls how trust and continuity engendered an environment in which problems could be discussed in a frank and open manner, enabling variant and conflicting interests to be aired while maintaining trust and mutual respect (chapter 4), a view echoed by others including John Gero and Jörg Reinbothe (chapters 5 and 10, respectively).

John Gero singles out the distinctive skills of the Chair and the importance of trust ultimately invested in the expertise and neutrality of the Secretariat. He observes that the challenges of framing IP standards within a trade law context inevitably lead to the formulation of new concepts and methodologies which recognised that trade negotiations now reached into areas traditionally reserved for domestic regulation. The question of non-violation disputes exemplified this challenge, as it was an established concept in traditional trade law, but uncharted territory when it came to IP. He also underscores the importance of engagement with the substance of the issues, maintaining that negotiators were closely and professionally engaged with the substance, and did not avoid tough issues. For him, a key factor in the result was the salutary effect of turning from more abstract, "theological" debates to an approach rooted in the actual practices of the negotiating countries, illustrating how this led to solutions in one of the most sensitive issues addressed: that of patenting life forms. This account reinforces the overall conclusion that a number of key TRIPS provisions have roots in the domestic practice of national jurisdictions, and thus were more grounded than a more abstract level of negotiation may have delivered (chapter 5).

David Fitzpatrick's account of the negotiations on enforcement measures exemplifies how seasoned practical understanding of domestic regulatory systems - in this case, IP enforcement - is vital for the creation of realistic and balanced international standards. Equally, understanding of the clear distinction between international-level standards and the choices taken to implement them domestically enabled negotiators to bridge between major legal traditions, particularly civil law and common law countries, and distinct legal conceptions of copyright (chapter 15).

Adrian Otten highlights the distinct and significant roles of each player in the negotiation process, particularly that of IP experts. The technical expertise and negotiating know-how of the central actors from both developed and developing countries "who were able to be constructive as well as hard headed in the pursuit of their national interests" are highlighted as key factors in the outcome (chapter 3).

Catherine Field recalls the need for trade negotiators and IP experts to learn from one another and respect distinct areas of expertise, and the acceptance of pragmatic compromises to yield a balanced outcome which nonetheless left some key issues unresolved. She attributes the outcome to four negotiating axioms: all participants should benefit; all should prioritize objectives and even accept difficult changes to their own regime (which applied to the US); there had to be a realistic assessment of what is achievable in the light of overall goals; and flexibility on the different ways progress can be achieved (chapter 8).

Thu-Lang Tran Wasescha stresses the value of substantiating negotiating positions through careful explanation, while recognizing that "constructive ambiguity" also remained necessary to forge a delicate and finely balanced agreement (chapter 9).

Several contributors tell us that the role of the Secretariat was essential: key factors that emerge from the narratives include its recognized technical expertise and neutrality, and its careful preparation of high quality supporting documents that were noted for being inclusive and accurate. Matthijs Geuze and Adrian Otten both attest to the scrupulous efforts taken by the Secretariat to ensure neutrality and quality in the supporting documentation (chapters 7 and 3, respectively).

Evolution from procedural deadlock to negotiations on substance

Several authors in this volume, beginning with Adrian Otten, tell us that the conventional narrative of the TRIPS negotiations being defined by North vs South negotiating camps overlooks the more complex and diverse structure of negotiations. North-North differences proved at times to be more intractable, and such divisions have persisted in dispute settlement and in other negotiations, such as contemporary bilateral and multilateral processes on GIs (chapter 3). In taking issue with "mythologies" of the negotiations, John Gero agrees that it is misleading to assume that the negotiations were essentially between North and South by illustrating the diversity of interests and shifting alliances that cut across the full economic and political spectrum of negotiators (chapter 5). Thu-Lang Tran Wasescha also charts the shifting alliances and diverse interests among developed economies, reinforcing the general impression that the negotiations evolved into a more nuanced and diverse set of interests, from an initial, already somewhat dated stand-off between "pro-IP" and "anti-IP" delegations (chapter 9).

This more nuanced, multipolar view of the negotiations is evidenced by several of the alliances recounted by the negotiators. They describe, for instance, how India, with a strong positive interest in the creative industries, was in some respects closer to the United States on copyright matters. A.V. Ganesan recalls that "the Indian film industry was as vociferous as Hollywood on the prevention of piracy of cinematographic works". However, in pointing to a number of intra-North differences in the areas of copyright, related rights, GIs and patents on life forms, he notes that these differences were of a different class and character than the North-South differences. Developing countries saw themselves as "hapless defenders" in these new areas, with no *quid pro quo* to gain from the Agreement, and indeed much to lose (chapter 11). Piragibe Tarragô and Antonio Trombetta echo these views and note the unity of the North on core demands as against the disunity of the South, and the latter lists the disadvantages suffered by developing country delegations, including the lack of technical expertise (chapters 12 and 13, respectively).

The negotiations on the patent complex within the TRIPS Agreement provide an instructive case study about the practice of multilateral norm setting in a regulatory field of major trade significance that has bearing on other crucial areas of public policy. Patents were a key area of ambition for some developed countries; others, such as Canada, played more of a mediating and bridging role on such issues, aligning more with developing countries on some questions rather than seeing their interests purely in terms of stronger standards (chapter 5). For Piragibe Tarragô and Antonio Trombetta, the conscious concessions made by developing countries in this area were offset by the maintenance of flexibilities, particularly compulsory licensing (chapters 12 and 13, respectively). Catherine Field acknowledges that the outcome on patents was a "mixed bag" which only partly achieved US goals, left some matters uncertain, and yet overall created a clear framework (chapter 8).

Umi Majid describes how she was able to defend Malaysia's interests in maintaining regulatory diversity and a balanced distribution of enforcement resources (chapter 14). Piragibe Tarragô observes that the enforcement standards set out in TRIPS were already largely effected in Brazil's law, and that Brazil sought to fend off expectations that IP enforcement should have preference over other fields of law. He was satisfied that this was achieved through the inclusion of a tailored caveat in Article 41.5.

The broad architecture of the Agreement itself manifests the idea of balance. Piragibe Tarragô recalls the determination of developing countries to incorporate references to the social, economic and technological rationale of the IP system in view of their concerns about the public policy consequences of stronger IP protection. These provisions were designed to ensure flexibilities as a safeguard against the impact of higher IP standards once it became clear that the "minimalist" preferences of developing countries could be sustained (chapter 12). This balance is also evident in the detailed text in more technical provisions which bear the hallmarks of effective negotiations by developing country delegations - a telling example being Jayashree Watal's account of India's role in the crafting of a provision on the sensitive question of compulsory licensing that left open the entitlement to specify grounds for the grant of such licences (chapter 16). While compulsory licensing is one of the most conspicuous and closely observed instances - in view of its pivotal policy significance - overall, the negotiators' accounts identify a number of key areas where the outcome reached contrasts very significantly with the initial objectives of *demandeurs*, and the expectations of the industries that helped put IP on the multilateral trade agenda.

Peter Carl argues that the goal of a comprehensive and balanced agreement is measured more in political and psychological terms than in concrete terms. The accounts in this volume arguably show that the idea of balance in the negotiations has progressively shifted from a political and psychological perception that a TRIPS Agreement was needed to balance market access elsewhere (very strong at the time of the 1989 mid-term deal) - an Agreement perceived essentially as negotiating coinage to buy a Uruguay Round deal - to today's widespread perception of the Agreement as embodying a legitimate conception of balanced policy in itself. Accordingly, the negotiators help us understand how the Agreement's text gives expression to an enduring conception of what amounts to "adequate" and "effective" protection of IP that is a reasonable precondition for trading relations. He also makes the perceptive point that what are construed as "concessions" in trade negotiations may actually be accepted, if tacitly, as representing worthwhile policy outcomes in any case (chapter 6). A.V. Ganesan, in the light of subsequent experience with its implementation, goes so far as to describe the Agreement today as almost "a blessing in disguise" for India, given that it provides assurance to foreign investors and technology suppliers, and enables India to avoid unnecessary trade frictions by referring any grievance over IP protection to the WTO dispute settlement mechanism (chapter 11). It is noteworthy, in this context, that India has brought a complaint against the EU, in part under the TRIPS Agreement, in order to defend its interests in the export of generic medicines.[13] In assessing the outcomes against the principal EC objectives, Jörg Reinbothe views the text as a success for all negotiators in that it remained true to broad principles that were widely shared (chapter 10).

Unquestionably, if TRIPS does have legitimacy and balance as a legal and policy instrument today, this is a consequence of the give-and-take of the negotiations and the efforts, well documented in this volume, of developing country negotiators to include effective policy safeguards which have since been shown to be effective in practice, for instance in the sensitive policy area of public health. Peter Carl maintains that the quality of the resultant TRIPS text is demonstrated by the fact that subsequent controversy over access to medicines could be largely resolved within the framework of the existing text, a view echoed by Catherine Field (chapters 6 and 8, respectively).

This understanding of the final agreement entails distinguishing the early diplomacy and divergence of interests that gave initial impetus to the negotiation mandate from the subsequent close textual negotiations. Jayashree Watal observes that the final package was much more balanced than some commentators assumed, drawing a clear distinction between the initial goals of *demandeurs*, and the actual outcome of a genuine multilateral negotiation, with concomitant checks and balances. She attributes this outcome to support from key developed country negotiators on aspects of public policy, as well as an overall negotiating environment characterized by cooperation, coalition-building and compromise (chapter 16). Similarly, Thu-Lang Tran Wasescha maintains that the TRIPS text was not the so-called monopolistic straight-jacket that some had feared, but has allowed for effective safeguards and flexibilities. She attributes this outcome to the spirit of collegiality and mutual respect in which even sharp differences could be aired without derailing the negotiations (chapter 9). Piragibe Tarragô and Antonio Trombetta acknowledge that the outcome entailed a fundamental shift in the stance of key developing countries. This was hesitantly accepted as it enabled a stronger multilateral trading system and opportunities for their major export sectors, yet they could defend their core IP interests through the preservation of policy space and flexibilities to promote development and public interest (chapters 12 and 13, respectively).

The importance of the multilateral approach is borne out in this context: Adrian Otten observes that the counterfactual to multilateralism in IP is bilateral negotiations, where the lack of collective weight of developing countries and the opportunity to exploit differences between major *demandeurs*, "could not be expected to yield as much flexibility or give it the same degree of legitimacy" (chapter 3). Indeed, while TRIPS has been used as a basis for further bilateral and plurilateral negotiations on IP, these have resulted in what some would see as TRIPS-plus provisions without the same balance that TRIPS contained.

Nonetheless, developed country negotiators – despite dramatic policy differences in some areas – showed greater coherence and resolve overall in pushing forward the TRIPS project, and several contributors comment on the considerable constraints faced by developing country negotiators, and the limited participation from the developing world, notably the African continent.

Negotiation as a practical craft

Substantively, the TRIPS Agreement is unique - both in defining core standards across the spectrum of IP, and in engineering a fundamental shift in multilateral governance by integrating those standards within the trade law system. Given the changed external circumstances, it is also a moot point whether it would be possible to negotiate, multilaterally, a similar treaty on TRIPS today. Yet the TRIPS negotiators' narratives of the making of the Agreement hold considerable practical interest for today's negotiators not least because of what might be termed the tradecraft of negotiations - the skill set and the practical tools that were developed and applied so as to make this a successful process, indeed one that outpaced negotiations in other sectors in the Uruguay Round.

Several negotiators underscore the logical progression of the negotiations. Thomas Cottier maintains that the organized and structured approach to the negotiations, proceeding from principles, general proposals, to a draft composite text and checklists of issues, was central to its success (chapter 4). Adrian Otten's account highlights the importance of the opening phase of negotiations which enabled both the collection of factual information and the opportunity to come to understand the different negotiators' concerns and objectives. This laid a surer foundation for subsequent substantive work. He views the ensuing detailed discussion of proposals and synoptic tables as an essential basis for subsequent negotiations: not least because trade negotiators, including those from developing countries, generally lacked IP expertise, but because discussions precipitated consultative networks in domestic capitals that could deal with the full range of issues under discussion (chapter 3). Clarity in the negotiating mandate, and the consequent shared understanding of the outline of the common objective, are described by many negotiators as catalysts for progress on substance, the 1989 decision clearly being pivotal, just as the imprecision in the initial mandate had earlier led to unresolved procedural debate. Yet even that initial period was productive, as it enabled the commencement of the information gathering and mutual understanding that Adrian Otten describes in particular. The Chair, Lars Anell, remarks that "[i]t had to be a slow start and a steep learning curve" (appendix 1).

The quality and inclusiveness of the supporting documentation is widely cited as a vital ingredient. Catherine Field confirms the practical value of a single, synoptic table that reflected all views as a practical foundation for substantive negotiations (chapter 8). Piragibe Tarragô acknowledges that the practical diplomatic tool of a composite negotiating text enabled negotiations to proceed despite greatly divergent levels of ambition in IP protection standard-setting (chapter 12). Thomas Cottier recounts how the Chair and the Secretariat compiled the delegation submissions carefully, initially indicating the source of each proposal and later deleting such authorship and provenance, thus enabling more rapid progress to be made, presumably because no one would be attached to their original text. Indeed such rapid progress was made using these tools that in the space of less than six months an almost complete draft of the Agreement was in place by December 1990 (chapter 4). Lars Anell recalls that, when "real negotiations were all but impossible", the "obvious solution" was for the Secretariat to prepare a composite text of different proposals as a basis for negotiations. Agreement could only be reached on the basis of a promise that "[l]iterally everything" that had been tabled was included, yielding the Chair's Draft of June 1990 that put the negotiations on a solid track. This process disclosed significant convergence already in some areas – "an abundant crop of low-hanging fruits" (appendix 1). This enabled negotiators to make progress despite continuing disagreements on structure and the GATTability question.

Adrian Otten narrates how work then ensued on this basis: the Chair held intensive informal consultations with delegations to produce a series of revised drafts, on his responsibility rather than as expressing a commitment from any delegation, and highlighting points of difference. This enabled work on non-substantive differences and on compromise language in more substantive areas. These texts gradually took on the look of draft agreements. The final stage, he recalls, entailed virtually continuous negotiations, directly between participants and under the auspices of the Chair, the latter through a so-called "10+10" group (10 developed and 10 developing countries, in practice open to any interested delegation), and "5+5" groups with variable membership, especially on the most difficult issues. Such smaller group meetings were followed by detailed reports by the Chair to meetings of all participants, provided also in writing, "to ensure transparency and give all participants an opportunity to react" (chapter 3).

All accounts attest to the individual qualities of the Chair, the Secretariat, and the negotiators, who were united by a common professional objective to produce a creditable outcome in the face of considerable pressure from the dynamics of the Uruguay Round. Continuity of representation and well-established domestic consultative networks helped ensure that the negotiators were able to engage fully and effectively. Many negotiators estimated that this particular kind of negotiation required the integration of knowledge from many different sources, and required learning from recognized experts. The negotiations were extremely complex as they were situated within a multilateral trade law framework, but also covered the then-distinct field of international IP, with its own established rules: an existing treaty structure and specific practices drawn from the development, administration and enforcement of domestic standards in multiple areas of IP. Respect for professional expertise and the willingness to learn from it extended beyond formal negotiating differences, and did not in themselves compromise competing negotiating positions – but it did mean that negotiating compromises, when they came, were more likely to be consonant with established ideas of good policy.

Summing up

The accounts of the negotiations show remarkable diversity in the interests pursued and in the negotiating objectives and priorities identified by each negotiator: a broad spectrum of interests had to be accommodated in the final text. Nonetheless, it is possible to discern several common themes that help to explain the abiding success of the negotiated outcome, and potentially provide guidance for future negotiators and policymakers. These elements of success, also widely discussed at the February 2015 Symposium, include the following:

- The progressive development of trust and mutual respect between negotiators. They took time to understand the interests and concerns behind negotiating positions. Additionally, continuity of representation fostered common understandings and a collective sense of purpose.

- The scrupulously distinct but equally important roles of the Chair, the Secretariat and the negotiators. The Chair led and guided the negotiations, while the Secretariat provided neutral, discreet and substantive support. The negotiators acknowledged their gaps in technical expertise and addressed their tasks with intellectual integrity, consulting judiciously with acknowledged experts so as to ensure the quality of the negotiated text.

- The clear, logical sequencing of the work. The factual background, broad principles and the overall direction of the negotiations were established before moving to an inclusive and intensive text-based process led to an outcome that has served effectively as a stable multilateral framework.

- The progressive shifts from procedural wrangling to an informed debate. Preliminary negotiations over mandate and diplomatic formulae moved towards a thoughtful and constructive deliberation on points of principle and policy. Elements of best policy practice were increasingly informed by a wide range of practical experience and lessons from domestic regulation in a cross-section of jurisdictions. This provided the negotiations with a stronger empirical base and a practical focus.

Overall, the external factors driving the negotiations emerge as nuanced, diverse and multifaceted. They are not accurately captured by a monochrome picture defined by developed country industry interests set squarely against developing country policy concerns. To be sure, this subtler and more polychromatic picture does not conflict absolutely with conventional characterisations of the negotiations as a trade-off between IP demands from the North and the quest for policy safeguards from the South. The accounts in this volume convincingly show how negotiators moved from diverse interests and disparate negotiating objectives towards the common goal of establishing a platform of adequate standards to serve as a foundation for a more stable and transparent multilateral order. In so doing, they sought a shared institutional and legal base, so as to ensure that the IP system and related areas of regulation would deliver on the economic and social policy objectives expected from IP law and policy.

TRIPS today and in the future

The TRIPS Agreement is a treaty of surprising resilience and adaptability that has been used as a basis for further multilateral and bilateral negotiations on IP in other spheres. The relative completeness of the text compared to other WTO agreements - in that its rules cover almost all areas of IP and provide for limited specific exceptions under the MFN principle - may be one factor behind its continuing relevance. Indeed, considering the text in today's trade policy environment, the original negotiators do not, in general, see any need for a major renegotiation or extension. Catherine Field points to the major changes technology has wrought in IP and the transformation of information itself into a tradable good, but she does not estimate that this warrants a rewriting of the rules (chapter 8). Even the need she acknowledges for a more coherent international approach to the application of IP competition and antitrust measures may not necessarily require a renegotiation, but rather solutions within the established framework. Nevertheless, Thomas Cottier sees a role for greater development of competition standards to set a regulatory ceiling complementing the minimum standards for IP protection (chapter 4).

In any event, in IP and other areas of regulatory convergence, treaty standards are largely not self-actuating; they require significant domestic capacity to be implemented both effectively and in a balanced way. Peter Carl points to the gulf between TRIPS provisions and their effective implementation: most WTO members have implemented the provisions in their national law, but problems remain with effective administration and enforcement, some abusive litigation practices and the erosion of consensus around the basic principle of IP protection (chapter 6). Even the issue that first led the GATT to work on IP matters, counterfeit trade, remains a major scourge today due in part to technological developments unforeseen in the TRIPS provisions on enforcement.

For some of the contributors, including Peter Carl, Catherine Field and Thomas Cottier, TRIPS rules remain legitimate today, but are showing some signs of age and emerging gaps, leading to different suggestions for reviews or further work within the TRIPS framework (chapters 6, 8 and 3, respectively). Peter Carl takes issue with the conventional view that multilateral negotiations are stalled due to unwillingness to accept the necessary compromises and concessions for classical economic reasons. Instead, he points to a less favourable external environment for negotiations, the political and psychological impact of globalisation, reactions to the ambitious outcome already achieved and the lobby against IP enforcement of both copyright and trademarks (chapter 6).

Can the TRIPS negotiations shed light on current difficulties in reaching multilateral agreement on IP standards? Adrian Otten concludes that the unique historical circumstances of the making of the TRIPS Agreement illustrate why it is now more difficult for the WTO to make headway. The very scale of the results on TRIPS, combined with the effectiveness of the WTO dispute settlement mechanism, has led to some governments being cautious about taking on any new obligations. The growing usage of the dispute settlement mechanism may "lead to a greater role for lawyers at the expense of deal-makers". The increasing political importance of NGOs has led to a wider range of actors and interests, but also raises "the political cost of making the compromises necessary in any international negotiation". Equally, global governance is at a time of renewed transition, with the effect that "a wider spectrum of countries must take the initiative if progress is to be made". The formal structures do provide for this work to be done, but it is ultimately a matter for attitudes to change "in both countries that formerly assumed leadership and those that now need to" (chapter 3).

The lessons for future IP negotiators and policymakers that can be drawn from these reflections are manifold, but the following broad themes emerge:

- Considerable work needs to be done to establish a clear and workable mandate. While the Punta del Este mandate put "trade-related aspects" of IP on the agenda, it was only with the creation of the clearer and more precise 1989 mid-term agreement that constructive work could begin in earnest, aided by detailed textual submissions from delegations.

- Negotiations are greatly assisted by understanding drawn from past domestic and multilateral experience, and the infusion of actual expertise, provided that there is an environment of intellectual curiosity, mutual learning and respect for divergent positions among the key negotiators.

- Negotiators benefit from a clear, comprehensive and neutral set of preparatory documents, and a trusted and expert Secretariat can contribute through the preparation of such materials. Creative solutions and bridging proposals from negotiators and the Chair of the process can help.

- Leadership is vital. Political leadership, understandings at the political level that give impetus to the negotiations and the leadership role of the negotiating Chair are key elements. Additionally, these leaders must be supported by active delegations who accept the need for compromise and, equally, the need for all negotiators to come away with a sense that they have achieved material gains.

- Negotiations on regulatory matters can be informed and actively assisted by considerations of good public policy and experience of good regulatory practice. Such considerations underpin the legitimacy of the concluded text and set the text in its intended operational context.

- Periods of hiatus in formal negotiations or of political uncertainty can be used to work on consolidation of the background understanding, the resolution of technical issues and bridging gaps.

The practical lessons of the TRIPS negotiations, and the insights the negotiators offer in this volume, should be of significant service to future generations of negotiators, and warrant the close attention of analysts, even if the exact circumstances that led to the TRIPS Agreement are unlikely to be repeated.

Looking back over the past two decades, it is clear that the fundamental notion of what constitutes "trade-related aspects" of IPRs has undergone a thorough transformation: something that was once the province of negotiators has now become a daily consumer experience for billions. Throughout this period of fundamental change, the TRIPS Agreement has proven to be flexible, managing sensitive policy issues such as public health. The comprehensive, relatively finished and flexible character of the Agreement suggests to some of its negotiators that it can retain its central role in international IP law and dispute settlement, and as a touchstone for legitimacy and balance in policy-making for years to come.

Endnotes

1   This chapter benefits from extensive conceptual and textual input from, and a close critical review by, Jayashree Watal; any errors or inaccuracies remain, however, the responsibility of the author.

2   A system of special compulsory licences expressly for the export of pharmaceuticals was introduced in order to provide an additional legal pathway for access to medicines, first through a waiver of TRIPS rules and later through a proposal to amend the Agreement. See https://www.wto.org/english/tratop_e/trips_e/factsheet_pharm02_e.htm#importing (last accessed 6 August 2015).

3   A record documented in the IP/Q/* series of documents prepared for the WTO TRIPS Council capturing its discussion on the distinct policy and legislative choices in the TRIPS area made by over 130 members. These documents can be consulted at http://docs.wto.org.

4   See Adrian Otten's and Adrian Macey's discussions of the pattern of dispute settlement (chapters 3 and 19, respectively).

5   See Adrian Otten, chapter 3.

6   See, for instance, Richard Baldwin, "Global supply chains: why they emerged, why they matter, and where they are going" in Deborah K. Elms and Patrick Low, eds., "Global value chains in a changing world" (WTO, 2013) (available at https://www.wto.org/english/res_e/booksp_e/aid4tradeglobalvalue13_e.pdf).

7   See, for example, Thomas Cottier, chapter 4.

8   See Catherine Field, chapter 8.

9   WTO document WT/GC/W/247, Preparations for the 1999 Ministerial Conference - Work Programme on Electronic Commerce - Communication from Indonesia and Singapore, 9 July 1999.

10 See in particular Catherine Field, chapter 8, and Thomas Cottier, chapter 4.

11 The concepts of national treatment and MFN as they apply in the GATT, the General Agreement on Trade in Services and TRIPS are outlined in a WTO Secretariat document prepared for the Working Group on Trade and Competition Policy, WT/WGTCP/W/114, Working Group on the Interaction between Trade and Competition Policy – The Fundamental WTO Principles of National Treatment, Most-Favoured-Nations Treatment and Transparency – Background Note by the Secretariat, 14 April 1999.

12 GATT document MTN.GNG/NG11/W/7/Add.2, Negotiating Group on Trade-Related Aspects of Intellectual Property Rights, including Trade in Counterfeit Goods - Submissions from participants on trade problems encountered in connection with Intellectual Property Rights – Switzerland, 5 August 1987.

13 WTO document WT/DS408/1, European Union and a Member State — Seizure of Generic Drugs in Transit – Request for Consultations by India, 19 May 2010. See one-page summary at: www.wto.org/english/tratop_e/dispu_e/cases_e/ds408_e.htm (last accessed 13 August 2015).

Part II

Anatomy of the negotiations

3

The TRIPS negotiations: An overview

Adrian Otten

As a former official within the Secretariat of the GATT/WTO with responsibility for TRIPS matters, my aim in this chapter is to set the scene for the contributions to this book of the negotiators themselves, by outlining the origins and various stages of the negotiations that led to the TRIPS Agreement. I will also make some general observations on the negotiations, in particular on how it proved possible to negotiate an agreement as substantial as the TRIPS Agreement and on why the WTO has been finding it difficult to achieve results comparable to those of the Uruguay Round of multilateral trade negotiations. I will, of course, do this from the perspective of a former Secretariat official; other chapters will add additional perspectives. I should add that I left the WTO Secretariat in 2008.

Background to the negotiations

Intellectual property in the GATT

Prior to the Uruguay Round, there was relatively little on IP in the GATT, at least explicitly. Despite this, there were two significant dispute settlement cases in the 1980s, reflecting no doubt the increasing importance of IP issues in international trade relations.

The primary thrust of GATT rules of relevance was (and remains) to ensure that IP laws and regulations do not discriminate against or between imported goods, while not preventing compliance with them. Given that IP laws and regulations have been held to be "internal" for GATT purposes, the most important provision is Article III:4; this requires that IP laws and regulations (like other internal laws and regulations) accord imported products no less favourable treatment than that accorded to national products. This requirement is tempered by the general exception provision of Article XX(d), which ensures that GATT trade rules do not stand in the way of measures necessary to ensure compliance with IP laws and regulations, subject to a number of safeguards to ensure such measures are not used as a disguised restriction on trade. There are also some specific rules aimed at ensuring that balance-of-payments import restrictions do not prevent compliance with IP procedures (Articles XII:3(c)(iii) and XVIII:10).

The only GATT provision that specifically promotes the protection of IP is that in Article IX:6 on the protection of distinctive regional or geographical names – what we would now call geographical indications (GIs). This does not lay down specific standards of protection of GIs but calls on GATT contracting parties to cooperate with each other on their protection. It was included in the Havana Charter (on part of which the original GATT was based) at the instigation of the French and the Cubans.

Both the dispute settlement cases were complaints by the European Communities (EC) about aspects of United States (US) IP law claimed to be unjustifiably trade restrictive or discriminatory. As the desk officer for IP matters in the Secretariat, I was the secretary of each of these panels. One of these cases concerned the so-called Manufacturing Clause of the US Copyright Act, which prohibited the importation into the United States of certain copyright works and penalized them in other ways unless they had been manufactured (i.e. printed) in the United States. The issue was not the GATT inconsistency of the import restriction but whether such inconsistency remained grandfathered by the Protocol of Provisional Application, under which the GATT had been originally applied, even though the United States had prolonged it after fixing an expiry date. The Panel, which reported in May 1984, found that the Protocol of Provisional Application had to be understood as a "one-way street" towards GATT conformity and that the US action constituted an unjustifiable reversion away from GATT conformity.[1]

The other dispute settlement case concerned Section 337 of the US Tariff Act, under which producers in the United States could obtain orders excluding the importation into the United States of goods found to be infringing US patent and other IP rights. This was an issue giving rise to considerable tensions at the time in US trade with not only the EC but also some other countries, including Japan, Canada and the Republic of Korea. The task of the Panel was to (i) interpret the national treatment standard of GATT Article III:4, (ii) examine whether the special remedies and procedures applicable under Section 337 when imported goods were challenged on grounds of IP infringement constituted less favourable treatment than that applicable under the US federal district court procedures when like products of US origin were similarly challenged, and (iii) consider whether any instances of less favourable treatment could be justified under the exceptions provision of Article XX(d). In what I believe was a seminal set of findings, the Panel found that six features of Section 337 did constitute less favourable treatment of imported goods inconsistently with Article III:4 and that most, but not all, of these inconsistencies could not be justified under Article XX(d). The Panel reported in January 1989 shortly after the Montreal mid-term ministerial meeting of the Uruguay Round.[2] While the Panel went out of its way to avoid impacting on the negotiations, the case demonstrated the ability of the GATT dispute settlement system to handle complex IP issues and highlighted the role of the GATT as a forum for preventing the abuse of IP rules as trade restrictive measures.

Work in the GATT on trade in counterfeit goods, 1978–85

The first initiative in the GATT framework to go beyond what was in the General Agreement in addressing IP matters was a proposal put forward by the United States in 1978, towards the end of the Tokyo Round of multilateral trade negotiations, 1973–9.[3] This was for a code, or a plurilateral agreement, on trade in counterfeit goods, roughly corresponding to what is now in Section 4 of Part III of the TRIPS Agreement on border measures (although limited at that stage to counterfeit trademark goods, not addressing pirated copyright goods). By the end of the Tokyo Round in 1979, only the United States and the EC supported the proposed code and it was not included in the results of the Round.

The matter was reverted to in 1982 when a ministerial meeting was held to agree on the post-Tokyo Round work programme. In the preparations for this, a revised proposed code was tabled, this time with support from the so-called "Quad" (Canada, the EC, Japan and the United States).[4] No agreement was reached on either the draft or pursuing work on the basis of it. But the Ministerial Declaration did include an instruction to the GATT Council "to examine the question of counterfeit goods with a view to determining the appropriateness of joint action in the GATT framework on the trade aspects of commercial counterfeiting and, if such joint action is found to be appropriate, the modalities for such action, having full regard to the competence of other international organizations".[5]

At the time, I was a relatively junior official in a division of the GATT Secretariat dealing with non-tariff measures. For no particular reason that I can recall, responsibility for servicing these consultations was given to me, as one of a number of files that I was tasked with. So began for me 25 years of work on IP issues in the GATT/WTO Secretariat on behalf of the GATT contracting parties and later the WTO members.

Pursuant to the 1982 Ministerial Declaration, consultations with GATT contracting parties were held by the then Deputy Director-General, M.G. Mathur, and background documentation prepared by the Secretariat.[6] It was decided at the end of 1984 to set up an expert group, including the participation of an expert from WIPO, to help the Council take the decisions which the ministers had instructed it to take.[7] In its report at the end of 1985, the expert group considered that there was a growing problem of trade in counterfeit goods and that there was a case for enhanced international action, but did not agree on whether the GATT was the appropriate framework for such action.[8] The further consideration of this issue then became caught up in the preparations for what would become the Uruguay Round.

Evolution of the Uruguay Round TRIPS mandate

The driver behind the inclusion of IP in the Uruguay Round was the United States. The background was that, in the years following the end of the Tokyo Round, large parts of US industry as well as the US Government became increasingly of the view that what they saw as inadequate or ineffective protection of US IP abroad was unfairly undermining the competiveness of US industry and damaging US trade interests. These concerns went beyond the issue of border controls to prevent the importation of counterfeit goods, to the substantive standards of IP protection in other countries and the effectiveness of means for their enforcement, internally as well as at the border. This, in turn, was part of a wider perception of many in the United States that the GATT system, while doing quite a good job in regard to standard technology manufactured goods where the United States was losing international competitiveness, was doing a bad job, or none at all, in the areas of agriculture, services and IP where US competitiveness increasingly lay. It should also be remembered that this was a period when the international value of the US dollar increased enormously, almost doubling between its low point in 1978 and high point in 1985 according to the DXY index (US dollar relative to a basket of foreign currencies); this greatly exacerbated concerns in the United States about the country's international competitiveness.

The US Trade and Tariff Act of 1984 made inadequate or ineffective protection of IP explicitly actionable under Section 301 as an unjustifiable or unreasonable trade practice that could lead to trade retaliation by the United States. It also explicitly made the pursuit of adequate foreign IP protection a major US objective in trade negotiations. Against the background of these and other trade provisions, the United States pursued its IP objectives through intensive bilateral consultations and also in the preparations under way from late 1985 for a new GATT round of multilateral negotiations.

As regards future GATT negotiations, in April 1986 the US Administration made a major policy statement setting its goals, not only to complete an anti-counterfeiting code but also to conclude a more far-reaching IP agreement, building on pre-existing WIPO standards. Later that month, the United States got some measure of support from other Organisation for Economic Co-operation and Development (OECD) countries when their ministers agreed that the new round should address IP, provided it concerned the "trade-related aspects".

In the Preparatory Committee for a new round meeting in Geneva, it was evident that, while the United States was fairly clear about what it wished to achieve, other developed countries were less so and many developing countries continued to oppose both a GATT anti-counterfeiting code and more ambitious ideas. The compromise text for the Uruguay Round TRIPS mandate that was eventually adopted at Punta del Este, Uruguay in September 1986 was a modified form of language developed in the parallel informal preparatory process of smaller developed countries and less hard-line developing countries under the auspices of Colombia and Switzerland.

TRIPS negotiations, 1986–April 1989

The Uruguay Round TRIPS negotiating mandate

The Uruguay Round was launched with agreement on a Ministerial Declaration in Punta del Este in September 1986. The TRIPS mandate appeared as one of 13 subjects for negotiation in Part I of the Declaration dealing with trade in goods (Part II dealt with trade in services). It read as follows (emphasis added):

> Trade-related aspects of intellectual property rights, including trade in counterfeit goods
>
> In order to reduce the distortions and impediments to international trade, and taking into account the need to promote effective and adequate protection of intellectual property rights, and to ensure that measures and procedures to enforce intellectual property rights do not themselves become barriers to legitimate trade, *the negotiations shall aim to clarify GATT provisions and elaborate as appropriate new rules and disciplines.*

> *Negotiations shall aim to develop a multilateral framework* of
> principles, rules and disciplines *dealing with international trade in
> counterfeit goods*, taking into account work already undertaken in
> the GATT.
>
> These negotiations shall be without prejudice to other
> complementary initiatives that may be taken in the *World
> Intellectual Property Organization* and elsewhere to deal with these
> matters.[9]

The only reasonably clear part of the mandate was the second paragraph, which
represented an agreement that some sort of code or agreement on trade in
counterfeit goods would be negotiated along the lines that had been discussed in
past GATT work on this matter. The first paragraph opened up the possibility of
going further if this were found to be appropriate, but this appeared to remain
anchored in the world of the GATT and of trade in goods. This sentence was quite
similar to the mandate agreed for negotiations on trade-related investment
measures (where the eventual results essentially took the form of a codification
of pre-existing GATT jurisprudence). The third paragraph reflected concerns about
the competences of other intergovernmental organizations, notably WIPO.

Work of TRIPS Negotiating Group, 1987–8

In its first two years, the TRIPS Negotiating Group organized its work under
agenda items corresponding to the three paragraphs of the mandate. In almost
any GATT/WTO negotiation, the first tasks are to assemble necessary factual
information and to get to understand the concerns and objectives of the
negotiators. Accordingly, the Group had the Secretariat prepare some factual
background material and also received a major contribution from WIPO in the form
of a paper on the existence, scope and form of generally internationally accepted
and applied standards/norms for the protection of IP.[10]

As regards the concerns raised by delegations, these were summarized in a
compilation paper prepared by the Secretariat under the following headings:

    I.   Issues in Connection with the Enforcement of Intellectual Property
        Rights:
        (a)   Enforcement at the border:
            (i) Discrimination against imported products
            (ii) Inadequate procedures and remedies at the border
        (b)   Inadequate internal enforcement procedures and remedies

II. Issues in Connection with the Availability and Scope of Intellectual Property Rights:
   (a) Inadequacies in the availability and scope of intellectual property rights
   (b) Excesses in the availability and scope of intellectual property rights
   (c) Discrimination in the availability and scope of intellectual property rights

III. Issues in Connection with the Use of Intellectual Property Rights:
   (a) Governmental restrictions on the terms of licensing agreements
   (b) Abusive use of intellectual property rights

IV. Issues in Connection with the Settlement of Disputes between Governments on Intellectual Property Rights:
   (a) Inadequate multilateral dispute settlement mechanisms
   (b) Excessive national mechanisms for dealing with disputes with other countries.[11]

In the TRIPS Negotiating Group's first two years, much of the discussion revolved around disagreements about the scope of its negotiating mandate, in particular its second paragraph. Whereas the United States was clear from the outset that it wished to negotiate on substantive standards of protection of IP and internal enforcement as well as border enforcement, it took some time for other developed countries to join the United States in this. It was not until mid-1988 that the EC came to this position. For all negotiating parties to come to this position involved, in addition to consideration of economic interests, finding a sometimes difficult accommodation between governmental agencies, in particular the IP offices and the ministry responsible for foreign trade. In the EC, there was the added complication that negotiations on IP issues, previously an essentially EC member state responsibility, would have almost inevitable consequences for the distribution of competences between member states and EC institutions, given that the latter had exclusive competence for GATT matters. Many developing countries continued to oppose the negotiations getting into issues of internal enforcement and especially substantive standards: they considered them as matters where a balance between domestic interests had to be found and, as such, only marginally trade-related, and they could not see how the GATT could negotiate on them without prejudicing work in WIPO and elsewhere.

Montreal mid-term ministerial meeting, December 1988

The Uruguay Round was originally scheduled to last for four years. A so-called mid-term review meeting was held at ministerial level in December 1988 in Montreal. In reporting on the work so far, the Chair of the TRIPS Negotiating Group made it clear that there were still wide divergences in the Group and that guidance from ministers was needed.

The meeting in Montreal was a tense affair, not least in the TRIPS area. What was at stake in the negotiations was becoming increasingly evident to ministers, including those from developing countries hitherto opposed to a major TRIPS outcome. Without a successful result to the Uruguay Round, it was not clear that the multilateral trading system, and the market access it secured, could survive as a functioning system, and a major agreement on TRIPS was increasingly seen as a necessary part of a successful result to the Round. Refusing to negotiate on IP matters in the Round would not mean that the issues would disappear; rather, they would have to be dealt with in an essentially bilateral framework, against the background, in the case of the United States, of a newly introduced Special Section 301 on IP. At the same time, the scope of the potential benefits that could flow to developing countries from the Round in such areas as textiles, agriculture, tropical products and tariffs was becoming clearer. All this meant that some developing countries, especially those with more export-oriented and market-based economic development policies, began to move their positions in TRIPS matters.

This was reflected in the tabling of new ideas on TRIPS in Montreal and their embodiment in a text from the Friend of the Chair conducting the consultations on TRIPS matters, Minister Yusuf Ozal of Turkey. All this was moving too fast for some delegations and no agreement was reached in Montreal on TRIPS, and neither was it on three areas of great interest to many developing countries – agriculture, safeguards and textiles. The specific cause of the meeting breaking down was that the main Latin American agricultural exporters came to the view that not enough was going to be on the table on agriculture. The outcomes achieved in 12 other areas were put "on hold" and the GATT Director-General, Arthur Dunkel, was tasked with holding consultations to secure agreement on a complete package. Overall agreement was reached in April 1989, with the TRIPS decision based closely on the Montreal Ozal text.

The TRIPS mid-term review decision

The April 1989 decision on TRIPS was a critical step in the negotiations. If the original Punta del Este Ministerial Declaration was characterized by a lack of clarity, the mid-term review decision was noteworthy for the precision of the guidance it gave to the negotiators. The key parts were in paragraphs 3 to 6, which read as follows (emphasis added):

> 3.   Ministers agree that the outcome of the negotiations is not prejudged and that these negotiations are *without prejudice to the views of participants concerning the institutional aspects of the international implementation of the results* of the negotiations in this area, which is to be decided pursuant to the final paragraph of the Punta del Este Declaration.

> 4.   Ministers agree that negotiations on this subject shall continue in the Uruguay Round and shall encompass the following issues:
> - (a)   the applicability of the *basic principles* of the GATT and of relevant international intellectual property agreements or conventions;
> - (b)   the provision of *adequate standards* and principles concerning the availability, scope and use of trade-related intellectual property rights;
> - (c)   the provision of *effective and appropriate means for the enforcement* of trade-related intellectual property rights, taking into account differences in national legal systems;
> - (d)   the provision of effective and expeditious procedures for the *multilateral prevention and settlement of disputes* between governments, including the applicability of GATT procedures;
> - (e)   *transitional arrangements* aiming at the fullest participation in the results of the negotiations.

> 5.   Ministers agree that in the negotiations consideration will be given to concerns raised by participants related to the *underlying public policy objectives of their national systems* for the protection of intellectual property, including developmental and technological objectives.

> 6.   In respect of 4(d) above, Ministers emphasise the importance of reducing tensions in this area by reaching *strengthened commitments to resolve disputes on trade-related intellectual property issues through multilateral procedures.*[12]

The basic deal in the TRIPS decision, as part of the wider trade-offs in the mid-term package as a whole (including textiles and agriculture), was between paragraph 4, on the one hand, and paragraphs 3, 5 and 6, on the other. Paragraph 4 represented a readiness to negotiate on the full range of issues that developed countries wished to see addressed. Paragraphs 3, 5 and 6 contained some key provisos or safeguards that made it possible for developing countries to accept the agenda in paragraph 4. Paragraph 3 made it clear that what became referred to as the "GATTability" of the results would not be prejudged, that is whether the results would be implemented in the GATT or some other framework; in some respects this put the TRIPS negotiations on a similar footing to the negotiations on trade in services where there had been a similar consideration since the outset of the Round. Paragraph 4 represented an acceptance that developing country concerns about the underlying public policy objectives of their national IP systems would be taken into account. Paragraph 6 reflected concerns about the absence of a functioning multilateral rule of law in the IP area, in particular, tendencies in the United States towards unilateral approaches to the resolution of disputes, and was important not only to developing countries but also to most other developed countries, especially Japan.

TRIPS negotiations, April 1989–90

Proposals and synoptic tables

The task facing the Negotiating Group, now that broad agreement had been reached on what should be addressed in the negotiations, was how to get all participants up to speed on what was at stake before the real negotiating phase was entered into. The main vehicle for this were proposals from delegations and Secretariat "synoptic tables" on standards and enforcement setting out side-by-side these proposals and relevant provisions of existing international conventions on each topic.[13] Specific proposals (not yet in legal form) were received for this exercise from nine developed, or groups of developed, countries (Australia, Austria, Canada, the EC, Japan, New Zealand, the Nordic countries, Switzerland and the United States) and seven developing countries (Brazil, Chile, Hong Kong, India, Korea, Mexico and Peru) as well as more general contributions from Thailand, Hungary, Chile and Bangladesh on behalf of the least-developed countries.

The detailed discussion of the proposals and the synoptic tables during the second half of 1989 and early 1990 was, I believe, essential for laying a basis of knowledge of the issues and understanding of each other's positions and concerns, which made possible the subsequent negotiating phase. This was particularly important for trade negotiators, who were generally not experts in IP, and for developing country participants who did not have the same depth of national expertise to draw upon as most developed countries had. It was also useful for virtually all active participants in getting national agencies to work together on a range of issues where this had not necessarily been required in the past. This was not just the trade and IP (patent, trademark, copyright, etc.) people, but also other affected ministries/agencies in areas such as agriculture (GIs, plant variety protection), justice (enforcement), finance and customs (border enforcement), culture/education/information/broadcasting (copyright and related rights), development, technology and competition/anti-trust.

Draft legal texts and Chair's texts, June–December 1990

Perhaps the most difficult transition in any international negotiation on rules of general application is that between exploratory work of the sort I have just described and actual negotiations on the basis of a common text. One way that this is sometimes done is for a group of delegations representing a critical mass in the negotiations to work out among themselves and put forward a common draft legal text that becomes *de facto* the basis. Such an approach can be effective but risks further polarizing the negotiations if the text comes from essentially one side. There was some effort made in this direction among the major *demandeurs*, in particular the Quad countries, but they found that, although sharing a broadly common objective in the negotiations, their positions on many specific issues were too far apart to make feasible a common draft. In the end, five comprehensive draft legal texts were tabled in the spring of 1990, by the EC, United States, 14 developing countries jointly (Argentina, Brazil, China, Chile, Colombia, Cuba, Egypt, India, Nigeria, Pakistan, Peru, Tanzania, Uruguay and Zimbabwe), Switzerland and Japan, followed by a draft from Australia on GIs.[14]

The Negotiating Group was under some pressure to find a negotiating basis, because the overall timeframe agreed at Punta del Este for completing the negotiations by the end of 1990 was still being adhered to and, given this, the superior negotiating body, the Group of Negotiations on Goods, had instructed all negotiating groups to have such a basis by July 1990. In the end, the Chair informed the TRIPS Negotiating Group of his intention to prepare, with the assistance of the Secretariat, a composite draft text, based on the draft legal texts submitted by delegations and without attempting to put forward compromise formulations where there were differences of substance between positions.

This composite draft text was circulated as an informal document in mid-June 1990.[15] With some minor modifications of a non-substantive nature, it proved possible to produce a usable document that incorporated all the different proposed formulations, using square brackets and alternatives to set out all the differences. The continuing disagreements on structure, reflecting different positions on the GATTability question, were described in the introduction.

Starting in June 1990 on the basis of the composite draft text, the Chair held a series of intensive informal consultations with delegations. After each of these rounds of consultations he circulated a revised draft, six in total in the latter part of 1990.[16] While the texts highlighted points of difference with square brackets and alternatives, they were circulated on the Chair's responsibility and on the basis that they did not commit any participant; indeed, it was the general understanding in the Round as a whole that nothing would be agreed until everything was agreed. Initially the consultations focused on getting rid of non-substantive differences and thus simplifying the text. They then sought to find compromise language on more substantive points. Sometimes the compromise would be worked out in the consultations themselves. Sometimes the Chair would make a suggestion in the next draft to see if it would fly. The first two of the drafts were characterized as compilations of options for legal provisions rather than draft agreements. The following four looked increasingly like draft agreements.

Brussels ministerial meeting, December 1990

The draft TRIPS text of 23 November was forwarded to the ministerial meeting held in Brussels in December 1990,[17] avowedly to complete the Round in accordance with the timetable agreed at Punta del Este. This text, which was forwarded on the Chair's own responsibility and did not commit any delegation, contained what could nevertheless be described as common language for large parts of the text, for example most, but not all, of the sections on general provisions and basic principles, trademarks, industrial design, enforcement and IP procedures (Part IV); but the text, and its covering letter, also highlighted continuing differences on the GATTability question and about 25 key issues of substance.

On the GATTability question, there were some delegations that advocated a single comprehensive agreement implemented as an integral part of the GATT, while some other (developing country) delegations wanted only the part on border enforcement against trade in counterfeit and pirated goods implemented in the GATT, with the remainder implemented in the "relevant international organization".

Linked with this were three different approaches to dispute settlement: one was the application of GATT rules and procedures *tel quel* (as it is), favoured by the major *demandeurs*; a second was a free-standing mechanism, with more emphasis on conciliation and no provision for retaliation, favoured by those with concerns about GATTability; and a third was a modified GATT system with special provisions to take account of IP, which was a compromise approach developed by New Zealand, Colombia and Uruguay.

As regards matters of substance, outstanding points on copyright included moral rights, computer programs, rental rights and exceptions, and there was also a range of differences on related rights. Most issues on GIs remained to be decided. While on patents a framework of language had been developed, most of the key questions still had to be resolved. The principle of the inclusion of provisions on the protection of undisclosed information remained to be settled as well as the content of possible rules in this area and in regard to anti-competitive practices. Further work was required on transitional periods and the question of the extent to which the new rules would apply to pre-existing IP (now Article 70).

Hopes to conclude the Round in Brussels proved wildly premature and the meeting broke up with, once again, the Latin American agricultural exporters believing that not enough was being achieved on agriculture. The first thing that the Argentinian minister did after the collapse of the agriculture negotiations was to burst into the room where the TRIPS negotiators were meeting to prevent further work in that area. Before this, some useful work had been done on TRIPS, for example on GIs, which was not lost when the work resumed in the second half of 1991, but no major breakthroughs had been made.

The final phases, 1991–4

Autumn 1991

Intensive work in the Round resumed in the autumn of 1991. This work was aimed at the Chair of the Trade Negotiations Committee (TNC), Arthur Dunkel, in conjunction with the chairs of the individual negotiating groups, tabling by the end of the year a revision of the texts that had been sent to Brussels. In the TRIPS area, this meant, especially in the later phases, more or less continuous negotiations, both in direct contacts between participants and under the auspices of the Chair. For these consultations, the Chair used, in addition to a so-called "10+10" group (i.e. 10 developed and 10 developing countries, but in practice open to any interested delegation), "5+5" groups with variable membership, especially on the most difficult issues. After these smaller group meetings, the Chair made detailed reports to meetings of all participants, which were also made available in writing, to ensure transparency and give all participants an opportunity to react.

The result of this work was a text forwarded by the Chair for inclusion in the Draft Final Act – sometimes referred to as the Dunkel Draft – that was circulated by Arthur Dunkel, in his capacity as Chair of the TNC, on 20 December 1991.[18] It aimed to offer a concrete and comprehensive representation of the results of the Round. Negotiations had continued on the TRIPS text until the small hours of the morning of 19 December, with exhaustion (Article 6) the last issue to be resolved, perhaps aptly. Agreement could not be reached on all issues, but participants had seen and discussed all the texts that the Chair planned to put forward, with only three outstanding points on which he had to arbitrate afterwards: the inclusion of spirits in additional protection for GIs, the duration of the transitional arrangements, and some details of the special transitional arrangements for pharmaceutical and agricultural chemical product patents.

In the autumn 1991 consultations, copyright and related rights, which for some participants had become linked with concurrent negotiations on market access for audiovisual services, continued to be difficult. Differences persisted on various matters: moral rights; the need to specify special exceptions on computer programs; the definition of "public" for the purposes of public performance and communication to the public rights under the Berne Convention for the Protection of Literary and Artistic Works; the scope of national treatment in respect of related rights; and a possible provision calling for respect of contractual arrangements on the allocation of rights. The approach adopted by the Chair to most of these difficulties was to exclude them from the text.

On GIs, the most difficult questions were providing additional protection for products other than wines – in particular spirits, as mentioned above – and how to find a proper balance between providing legal security for those who had been using foreign GIs in good faith and not legitimizing forever their loss (Article 24).

However, the key set of issues facing participants was the so-called patent complex, in particular the situation of countries that did not provide patent protection for inventions of pharmaceutical products and were relying on the production, or importation, of generics. The basic question facing delegations was: if the TRIPS agreement were to include an obligation to provide patent protection in virtually all areas of technology, including pharmaceuticals, how would a number of related provisions concerning the scope of patent rights, the ability of countries to take into account underlying public policy objectives and the timing of the economic impact of the new obligations need to be treated? In other words, what would be the TRIPS rules on such matters as exhaustion, compulsory licensing, test data protection, anti-competitive practices, the protecting of existing subject matter (Article 70) and transitional arrangements? It was not possible for participants to reach explicit agreement on all these matters – which for many would depend in any case on progress in other areas of the Round of vital interest to them – but the text sent forward by the Chair on these matters was that which had been developed in the negotiations, with only certain aspects of transition arrangements having to be filled in.

The TRIPS GATTability issue and the related dispute settlement issues were resolved through parallel negotiations on institutional questions that led to a text providing for the creation of a new organization, then proposed to be called the Multilateral Trade Organization (MTO), with an integrated dispute settlement system. Under the MTO, the TRIPS Agreement would sit alongside the GATT and a new agreement on trade in services (the GATS). The integrated dispute settlement system would include special provisions to regulate such matters as cross-retaliation and appropriate expertise on panels that had previously preoccupied TRIPS negotiators.

Autumn 1993

The tabling of the Draft Final Act was a major step forward, but it was done on the responsibility of the Chair of the TNC and it remained to be seen how acceptable it would be to participants. Moreover, the arduous process of negotiating specific schedules of tariff, agriculture and services commitments still had to be completed, as did the legal drafting clean-up of the texts. On matters of substance, the most controversial parts were agriculture, anti-dumping and the concept and details of the proposed MTO, which had been drawn up rather rapidly in the last days before the circulation of the Draft Final Act. It was not until the autumn of 1993 that the time was ripe to attempt to resolve outstanding difficulties in the draft texts and complete the Round.

The new GATT Director-General and Chair of the TNC, Peter Sutherland, asked Michael Cartland of Hong Kong, acting as a friend of the Chair, to take on the task of resolving any outstanding TRIPS issues. One feature of these consultations was five proposals from the United States, on rental rights and respect for contractual arrangements in the area of copyright and related rights, pipeline and test data protection in regard to pharmaceuticals, and shorter transition periods in regard to enforcement obligations. While many other delegations, developed and developing, would also have preferred some changes to the TRIPS text in the Draft Final Act, they took the view that they could live with it as part of a balanced outcome to the Round and that any reopening would be dangerous. Some developing countries (Egypt, India and Indonesia) indicated what sorts of changes they would like to see if the draft were to be reopened. In the final days of the negotiations, the United States' priorities switched to limiting the scope for compulsory licensing in the area of semiconductor technology.

The other major issue was a concern raised, notably by Canada and many developing countries, about the applicability of so-called non-violation dispute settlement cases in the TRIPS area. These delegations argued that they were not reopening the TRIPS text, but were putting forward their proposals pursuant to a footnote to the TRIPS dispute settlement provision in that text that said that it might need to be revised in the light of the outcome of the work on the integrated dispute settlement system; this had been included because work had been still under way on the proposed integrated dispute settlement system up until the tabling of the Draft Final Act.

In the end, two changes were agreed: the addition to Article 64 of paragraphs 2 and 3 on non-violation disputes and the addition of the language in Article 31(c) in regard to semiconductor technology. Otherwise, the final TRIPS Agreement text was in substance that tabled in the Draft Final Act of December 1991.

Some observations on the negotiations

The actors

Let me start with the least important of the actors, the Secretariat, only because that was my role. In the Uruguay Round, I was the senior Secretariat official working full time on TRIPS. Above me was the Director of the Secretariat division responsible, David Hartridge, who played a major role, including in chairing consultations on behalf of the Chair. My TRIPS team included a number of talented officers, notably Matthijs Geuze (now with WIPO), Arvind Subramanian (now Chief Economic Advisor to the Indian Government) and Daniel Gervais (now in academia).

The Secretariat's role obviously included typical secretariat functions such as the recording of the results of meetings and the preparation of background studies.

It also entailed advising the Chair on ways of making progress and equipping him with speaking notes and other material to help him do this. While the successive drafts of the Agreement were circulated on the Chair's responsibility, they were inevitably prepared initially by the Secretariat. Carrying out these roles required an understanding of the legal systems being dealt with, in both international and national law, and of national negotiating positions, including the factors affecting those positions. The GATT Secretariat did not have a stake in the specifics of the outcome of negotiations, but it did have a stake in doing what it could to facilitate an outcome and, in that outcome, whatever it might be, being as legally and systemically coherent as possible.

Let me now turn to the Chair. We (by which I mean delegations as well as the Secretariat) were very fortunate to have had Ambassador Lars Anell of Sweden in this capacity. Among the qualities which Lars brought were an intellectual capacity and energy that enabled him to master complex matter and to handle it with confidence, a Nordic concern for fairness and transparency that inspired confidence, a great sense of humour and a readiness to take decisions and initiatives when necessary.

But of course, what the Secretariat and even the Chair saw was only the tip of the iceberg of the work of the delegations and, more generally, of the governments participating in the negotiations. Much of this work was carried out in capitals. Whereas, in traditional GATT negotiations, national objectives had been often fairly easily defined (in mercantilist terms) and needed to involve only a limited number of people, the TRIPS negotiations differed in both respects. Apart from the number of ministries, agencies and interests involved, to which I have already alluded, the TRIPS negotiations entailed each participant government reassessing the myriad of balances in its IP system and judging to what extent they could be modified to take account of the interests of its trading partners.

Even in Geneva, the formal and informal meetings of the Negotiating Group were only a small part of the activity of delegations. Much of this was in groupings where delegations would seek to agree or coordinate positions in advance, ranging from the fairly permanent and well-structured groups such as the Quad, the Nordic countries, the Association of Southeast Asian Nations (ASEAN) group, the Andean group, the African group, the developing countries and the least-developed countries (not to mention the EC internal meetings), to subject-specific groups such as the Friends of Intellectual Property and the group of 14 developing countries, and ad hoc groups reflecting coalitions of interest on specific points, sometimes only for a limited time. In those less puritanical times, much of this provided good business for the restaurants of Geneva.

Unlike today when bilateral and regional work is favoured, multilateral trade negotiations during the Uruguay Round attracted the best and the brightest, and the TRIPS negotiations were no exception. They were blessed with a great many gifted delegates, from both developed and developing countries, who were able to be constructive as well as hard headed in the pursuit of their national interests. The negotiating teams typically included both trade and IP people and I would like, in particular, to pay tribute to the IP experts who contributed so much with their expertise and were able to win the confidence of others by their professionalism, including often delegates who did not share their negotiating objectives.

Some negotiating dynamics

Because so much of the post-Uruguay Round TRIPS literature has focused on the North–South aspects of the negotiations, there has been a tendency to underestimate the North–North components. It is important to remember this not only for its own sake but also because, once the negotiations got to specifics, developing countries quickly appreciated the room for manoeuvre this gave them, in particular the scope for North–South alliances. This was evident from the time the work on standards began in 1989 after the mid-term review decision; this started with copyright, an area where North–North issues were particularly acute (especially as, at that stage, the United States was not basing its proposals on the Berne Convention, which it had yet to sign).

Copyright and related rights continued to be an area dominated by North–North differences even after the United States had joined the other main proponents in advocating a Berne-plus approach. Moreover, even on computer programs and the protection of audiovisual works, where North–South differences predominated, there were some developing countries, notably India, that had interests and positions closer to those of the main *demandeurs*. GIs were not a North–South negotiation but essentially one between the "old world" and the "new world", with developed and developing countries on each side. In regard to the protection of technology, there were also major North–North differences. On pharmaceuticals, Canada and, to a lesser extent, some of the Nordic countries, Australia and New Zealand were generally on the defensive. Even among the major *demandeurs*, there were important differences on such matters as the patentability of plant and animal inventions, the limitation of the grounds for the grant of compulsory licences, government use, first-to-file, discrimination against foreign inventions and pipeline protection.

One feature was that developed and developing Commonwealth countries, which shared the common law legal tradition and in many cases much substantive law, would often have similar concerns. This was evident in particular in the areas of enforcement and copyright, but also in regard to some aspects of trademarks, GIs, patents and undisclosed information. On some issues, the United States (also a common law country) would be an ally. Sometimes these countries would find themselves opposed to the United Kingdom, where law was evolving by virtue of its membership of the EC.

How was TRIPS possible?

With the passage of time and in the light of the difficulties that the WTO has since had in making headway in its negotiating agenda, the scale of the TRIPS Agreement seems the more remarkable. The pre-existing public international law no longer provided the basis for a functioning multilateral rule of law in the IP area, especially in the field of industrial property where it was silent on most of the key parameters of a minimum standard of protection (protectable subject matter, rights, exceptions and term), not to mention enforcement. Building on and incorporating the key WIPO conventions, the TRIPS Agreement provided for minimum standards in these areas and made the whole Agreement subject to a functioning system for the resolution of disputes between governments, for the first time in the IP area.

The Agreement has continued to form the centrepiece of the multilateral rule of law in an area where there had been marked signs of this breaking down with resort to unilateral withdrawals of trade commitments. It is precisely because there were strong perceptions of divergences of interest that it was essential to achieve a multilateral consensus on how far governments could be expected to go, when setting their domestic IP regimes, in taking account of the interests of their trading partners. The TRIPS Agreement, including the WTO dispute settlement system as applied to it, has stood the test of the last 20 years relatively well. While worked on from both sides (to interpret the flexibilities as broadly as possible and to seek TRIPS-plus commitments through international negotiations in other contexts), no effort has been made to reopen the basic balances found in the Agreement, except on one relatively small but important point in regard to the compulsory licensing of pharmaceutical products – where a solution was agreed.

So how was all this possible?

As indicated earlier, it was generally recognized that at stake in the Uruguay Round was the very existence of a multilateral system of international trade relations. Indeed, the reality of this was recognized in the fact that the WTO Agreement provided for a new GATT, not the incorporation of the pre-existing GATT, and that any government that decided not to join it would lose its pre-existing trade rights. As also indicated earlier, developed countries became increasingly convinced, as the negotiations progressed, of the central importance to their future international competitiveness of the technology, creativity and reputation incorporated in the goods and services they produced and thus of the TRIPS negotiations, and developing countries came to accept that a successful outcome to the Uruguay Round would require a major result on the TRIPS negotiations.

But it was not just in the area of TRIPS that the results of the Uruguay Round exceeded what could have been reasonably envisaged at the outset. This was also the case in some areas to which developing countries attached importance, including as trade-offs for TRIPS: agriculture, which went from being largely excluded from trade commitments to being arguably more comprehensively covered than other areas (although often at higher levels of protection); textiles and clothing, where the previous system of trade restrictions was phased out by 2005 (not by chance the same timeframe as for key developing country obligations under the TRIPS Agreement); and the bringing of emergency safeguard measures under effective multilateral rules, including the end of so-called grey-area measures (such as voluntary export restraints). In other areas, the results also exceeded Punta del Este expectations: the very concept and structure of the WTO, including the multilateral application of virtually all agreements; the greatly strengthened and more juridical dispute settlement system; the establishment of a comprehensive framework for the liberalization of trade in services; and the preference for price-based balance-of-payments restrictions, to name only some. In broader terms, the Uruguay Round represented a major evolution in the basic character of the multilateral trading system, from one focused on border measures applied to goods to one dealing with a spectrum of laws and regulations governing the conditions of competition between the goods, services and persons of contracting parties.

Underlying the dissatisfaction with the pre-existing trading system and creating the conditions for these Uruguay Round achievements was a changing view of the role of trade and international markets in economic and social development, especially in developing countries and the countries of the eastern bloc. The failure of economic planning and import substitution policies followed by many developing countries and the success of the east Asian "tiger" economies and some ASEAN countries and Chile, which were following more export- and market-oriented policies, was not only influential in other developing countries but also meant that there was a growing kernel of developing countries committed to a major strengthening of the multilateral trading system from the outset. The dramatic collapse of the communist systems in Eastern Europe after the fall of the Berlin Wall in 1989 was both a reflection of the *Zeitgeist* and a great stimulus to it. Although the TRIPS Agreement went further and faster than some would have decided by themselves, much that was in it was going with the grain of economic policy thinking and reform under way at the time in many developing and Eastern European countries, where there was growing interest in the role of IP systems in promoting domestic innovation and creativity and facilitating the transfer of technology and foreign direct investment.

Another major consideration for developing countries in accepting the TRIPS Agreement was the international recognition they secured in it of important elements of balance and flexibility in IP systems, to safeguard their right to modulate their IP regimes to meet their national developmental, technological and public health objectives. The alternative of negotiating bilaterally with major trading partners, where developing countries would find it more difficult to use their collective weight and to exploit the differences between the major *demandeurs*, could not be expected to yield as much flexibility or give it the same degree of legitimacy.

When one considers how unusual were the circumstances that made the TRIPS Agreement – and, more generally, the results of the Uruguay Round – possible, one can also understand more readily the difficulties that the WTO has since had in making headway. Paradoxically perhaps, it may be that the comparative success of the WTO in "holding the ring", even at a time of severe international economic difficulties, has made making progress more difficult: on the whole, the prospect of new benefits is a weak incentive compared with the prospect of the loss of existing ones when it comes to the willingness of governments to expend the political capital necessary for change. Moreover, it may be that the very size of the Uruguay Round results, especially in the TRIPS area, and the lack of appreciation of the special nature of the circumstances that made them possible, has made some governments unduly cautious.

There are also other factors complicating progress. One may be the rigour of the WTO dispute settlement system. This has obvious advantages in providing an expectation of greater security of the benefits being negotiated, but it does the same also for the obligations being entered into. This can make negotiators more cautious and perhaps lead to a greater role for lawyers at the expense of deal-makers. A further factor has been the increasing political importance of non-governmental organizations, especially those that claim to represent the public interest and that have a synergetic relationship with the media. While they are a positive force in ensuring that some aspects are fully taken into account, they also increase the political cost of making the compromises necessary in any international negotiation. But perhaps most fundamentally, the WTO and its members are faced with making a transition to a world where a wider spectrum of countries must take the initiative if progress is to be made. Fortunately, its structures do not need modifying to take account of the changing importance of countries in the international trading system (unlike in the cases of the International Monetary Fund and the World Bank, or even the UN), but attitudes do, in both countries that formerly assumed leadership and those that now need to. These changes began in the Uruguay Round, but have still some way to go before the multilateral system can once more play its proper role.

Endnotes

1 GATT document L/5609, United States Manufacturing Clause – Report of the Panel, 1 March 1984.

2 GATT document L/6439, United States – Section 337 of the Tariff Act of 1930 – Report by the Panel, 16 January 1989.

3 GATT document MTN/NTM/W/204, Multilateral Trade Negotiations – Group "Non-Tariff Measures" – Sub-Group "Customs Matters" – Commercial Counterfeiting – 11 December 1978.

4 GATT document L/5382, Agreement on Measures to Discourage the Importation of Counterfeit Goods, 18 October 1982.

5 GATT document L/5424, CONTRACTING PARTIES – Thirty-Eighth Session – Ministerial Declaration adopted on 29 November 1982, 29 November 1982.

6 GATT document C/M/183, Council – Minutes of Meeting – Held in the Centre William Rappard on 6–8 and 20 November 1984, 10 December 1984.

7 GATT document L/5758, CONTRACTING PARTIES – Fortieth Session – Trade in Counterfeit Goods – Action Taken on 30 November 1984, 20 December 1984.

8 GATT document L/5878, Report of the Group of Experts on Trade in Counterfeit Goods, 9 October 1985.

9 GATT document MIN.DEC, Multilateral Trade Negotiations – The Uruguay Round – Ministerial Declaration on the Uruguay Round, 20 September 1986.

10 GATT document MTN.GNG/NG11/W/24, Negotiating Group on Trade-Related Aspects of Intellectual Property Rights, including Trade in Counterfeit Goods – Existence, Scope and Form of Generally Internationally Accepted and Applied Standards/Norms for the Protection of Intellectual Property – Note Prepared by the International Bureau of WIPO, 5 May 1988.

11 GATT document MTN.GNG/NG11/W/12, Negotiating Group on Trade-Related Aspects of Intellectual Property Rights, Including Trade in Counterfeit Goods – Compilation of Written Submissions and Oral Statements – Prepared by the Secretariat, 11 August 1987.

12 GATT document MTN/TNC/11, Uruguay Round – Trade Negotiations Committee – Mid-Term Meeting, 21 April 1989.

13 GATT documents MTN.GNG/NG11/W/32, Negotiating Group on Trade-Related Aspects of Intellectual Property Rights, Including Trade in Counterfeit Goods – Synoptic Tables Setting Out Existing International Standards and Proposed Standards and Principles – Prepared by the Secretariat, 2 June 1989; MTN.GNG/NG11/W/33, Negotiating Group on Trade-related Aspects of Intellectual Property Rights, Including Trade in Counterfeit Goods – Synoptic Table Setting out Proposals on Enforcement and Corresponding Provisions of Existing International Treaties – Prepared by the Secretariat, 7 June 1989; and their revisions. These documents contain references to the national submissions.

14 GATT documents MTN.GNG/NG11/W/68, Negotiating Group on Trade-Related Aspects of Intellectual Property Rights, Including Trade in Counterfeit Goods – Draft Agreement on Trade-Related Aspects of Intellectual Property Rights, 29 March 1990; MTN.GNG/NG11/W/70, Negotiating Group on Trade-Related Aspects of Intellectual Property Rights, including Trade in Counterfeit Goods – Draft Agreement on the Trade-Related Aspects of Intellectual Property Rights – Communication from the United States, 11 May 1990; MTN.GNG/NG11/W/71, Negotiating Group on Trade-Related Aspects of Intellectual Property Rights, including Trade in Counterfeit Goods – Communication from Argentina, Brazil, Chile, China, Colombia, Cuba, Egypt, India, Nigeria, Peru, Tanzania and Uruguay, 14 May 1990; MTN.GNG/NG11/W/73, Negotiating Group on Trade-Related Aspects of Intellectual Property Rights, including Trade in Counterfeit Goods – Draft Amendment to the General Agreement on Tariffs and Trade on the Protection of Trade-Related Intellectual Property Rights – Communication from Switzerland, 14 May 1990; MTN.GNG/NG11/W/74, Negotiating Group on Trade-Related Aspects of Intellectual Property Rights, including Trade in Counterfeit Goods – Main Elements of a Legal Text for Trips – Communication from Japan, 15 May 1990; and MTN.GNG/NG11/W/75, Negotiating Group on Trade-Related Aspects of Intellectual Property Rights, including Trade in Counterfeit Goods – Draft Text on Geographical Indications – Communication from Australia, 13 June 1990, respectively.

15 Restricted GATT document, 12 June 1990.

16 GATT document MTN.GNG/NG11/W/76, Negotiating Group on Trade-Related Aspects of Intellectual Property Rights, Including Trade in Counterfeit Goods – Status of Work in the Negotiating Group – Chairman's Report to the GNG, 23 July 1990; restricted GATT document, 1 October 1990; restricted GATT document, 25 October 1990; restricted GATT document, 13 November 1990; restricted GATT document, 20 November 1990; restricted GATT document, 23 November 1990.

17 GATT document MTN.TNC/W/35/Rev.1, Uruguay Round – Trade Negotiations Committee – Draft Final Act Embodying the Results of the Uruguay Round of Multilateral Trade Negotiations – Revision, 3 December 1990.

18 GATT document MTN.TNC/W/FA, Uruguay Round – Trade Negotiations Committee - Draft Final Act Embodying the Results of the Uruguay Round of Multilateral Trade Negotiations, 20 December 1991.

4

Working together towards TRIPS

Thomas Cottier[1]

Introduction

The negotiations on IP during the Uruguay Round of multilateral trade negotiations of the GATT (1986–94) were able to build upon a large body of existing law, both international and domestic. The main disciplines and notions of IP protection were already well established at the inception of the negotiations in 1986, with the adoption of the Ministerial Declaration in Punta del Este and its compromise that meant that negotiations would be conducted only on so-called trade-related aspects of intellectual property rights. The Paris Convention for the Protection of Industrial Property of 1883, and the Berne Convention for the Protection of Literary and Artistic Works of 1886 – both amounting to the very first multilateral agreements in the field of international economic law, long before the advent of the GATT in 1947 – provided the underpinnings in international law. More recent conventions, in particular the International Convention for the Protection of Performers, Producers of Phonograms and Broadcasting Organizations (Rome Convention) of 1961 and the more recent Washington Treaty on Intellectual Property in Respect of Integrated Circuits, adopted in 1989 but which never entered into force, added to these foundations. In domestic law, IP protection amounts to a mature field of commercial law in industrialized countries. This body of law strongly informed the IPR negotiations in the Uruguay Round. In addition, those engaged in the effort were able to benefit from extensive experience in the field of competition policy in these countries, in particular the experience of the United States (US) and the European Communities (EC) – later the European Union (EU) – which was one of the tools to curb excessive recourse to exclusive rights enabling dominant market positions and risk of abuse of these rights.

To some extent, building the TRIPS Agreement was an effort to bring these prior agreements and disciplines into the realm of the GATT and trade law and to further refine and expand them to global law, yet without seeking full harmonization. It was also an effort to extend the application of IP rules and safeguards to new and emerging economies and to extend established principles of domestic law to this group of countries. Patenting pharmaceuticals and chemicals is a case in point. It was one of the main objectives of industrialized countries. It was certainly the main goal for Switzerland, given its strong pharmaceutical and chemical industry, which is one of the pillars of its export industry. To a considerable extent, however, it was also a matter of introducing new disciplines and of seeking new ground. For example, relying upon protection against unfair competition, new disciplines on geographical indications (GIs) and the protection of undisclosed information emerged and were adopted. Foremost, negotiations developed novel disciplines on enforcing IPRs, which had previously been completely absent from international law. The provisions on fair and equitable procedures, addressing civil, administrative and penal provisions, amount to the first GATT and WTO agreement on regulatory convergence. Based upon the traditions of Anglo-American law and continental European law, a set of procedural requirements and obligations were negotiated that were entirely new to public international law.

The results achieved exceeded the much more modest expectations that were held at the outset of the process. The concept of minimal standards reminds us of these modest beginnings. It is somewhat at odds with the high level of standards achieved by the end of the negotiations and which today is increasingly being questioned from a trade and competition policy angle. The negotiations produced an impressive set of detailed rules and established the base code for international IP for decades to come.

In the 20 years since its adoption, the Agreement has faced much criticism for its uniform and detailed high standards of protection, which are largely applicable irrespective of the levels of social and economic development and the needs of developing countries. The debate on access to essential drugs, leading to waivers and modifications of the provisions on compulsory licensing, or the debate on appropriate levels of protection for goods in transit, show that the quest for a proper balance and calibration of IPRs has not ended, but was just opened up with the adoption of the TRIPS Agreement in 1995. The forum shift towards preferential agreements in recent years, adding additional standards of increased IPR protection (TRIPS plus) shows that the battle is far from won. It takes place today mainly in other fora on the basis of a very substantial TRIPS Agreement with largely universal and uniform standards different from the philosophy of progressive advancement (in this case, progressive liberalization) otherwise found in the GATT and the General Agreement on Trade in Services (GATS).

The reasons for this remarkable, albeit controversial, result are manifold. It has been argued that the outcome is mainly due to the effort of private lobbies, in particular in the United States.[2] While these efforts were critical, in particular at the outset, they alone do not explain the results achieved. In hindsight, the geopolitical changes of 1989, with the fall of the Berlin Wall and the collapse of the Soviet Union, changed the rules of the game and countries were obliged to turn to market economy precepts, including appropriate levels of IPRs, in order to attract foreign direct investment, which was much needed at the time. It was the time of "the end of history" (as stated by Francis Fukuyama). Progress made in laying new foundations for liberalizing textiles, services and agriculture offered internal, albeit eventually unsuccessful, balances within the GATT during the negotiations and greater willingness to engage in negotiations on the part of developing countries. But in addition to these endemic factors, and perhaps more importantly, there were a number of endogenous factors which allowed the negotiations to move forward. It is to these that I turn in this chapter commemorating the twentieth birthday of the TRIPS Agreement. They relate to the process of mutual learning, the building of mutual trust, and the negotiating techniques used to build a common and comprehensive treaty text. While the literature discussing the substance and the implications of the TRIPS Agreement is vast,[3] much less has been written about the process by which the Agreement actually came about.[4]

The learning process

The work of the Negotiating Group 11 assigned to trade-related IPRs (TRIPS) on the basis of the Punta del Este Declaration, at its inception and during the first years, may be well-characterized as a *dialogue de sourds* (a dialogue of the deaf). Discussions were based on introducing basic interests. Developed countries, led by the United States, and eventually joined by the EC, Japan and Switzerland, focused on the need for enhanced protection and the implications of insufficient protection observed around the world. In an early submission, Switzerland, for example, argued in favour of a strong linkage between trade and IPRs. "Proper protection of property is an essential precondition for trade at both national and international levels. In other words, if property is not protected, trade cannot expand and thrive."[5] Developing countries, on the other hand, stressed the risks of monopolization, the resulting South-to-North transfers and the detrimental effects on the building of their own technology base. Neither camp was able to provide solid evidence in support of its views. They were essentially dominated by doctrines adopted and developed in the Organisation for Economic Co-operation and Development (OECD), and United Nations Conference on Trade and Development (UNCTAD), respectively. Early proposals made the case for establishing IPRs in the trading system, or argued on the other hand for the need to minimize the effect of such rules in defence of domestic policy space and the need for flexibility commensurate with levels of social and economic development.

Eventually, engagement and discussions began. Many of the trade officials and diplomats assigned to the topic were new to IPRs, as the field was new in the context of the GATT, beyond unsuccessful discussions on combating counterfeiting and piracy held towards the end of the Tokyo Round. It was only at a later stage, if at all, that these officials were accompanied by specialists from their capitals. The Negotiating Group 11 was required to engage in a mutual learning process. This was a matter of becoming fully acquainted with the intricacies of IP and the various forms of protection, and with their functions and implications for the economy and international trade. But, most of all, it was a matter of fully understanding the interests and needs of others with a view to creating a common foundation upon which negotiations could eventually take place. It was here that I learned about the particular preoccupations of contracting parties, for example those with a strong generics industry, or the fear of abuse of rights, or the need to combine enhanced protection with enhanced transfer of technology and job creation. It was here that I learned about the importance of bringing about a proper balance while defending Switzerland's core interests, which lay mainly in the pharmaceutical and chemical sectors, machinery industry and extensive watch industry, all depending on patents and trademarks. Others would understand why patenting of pharmaceuticals and chemicals was of the utmost importance to Switzerland, as well as the introduction of effective protection of undisclosed information not only among private operators but also in the context of submitting test data in the process of drug approval before government agencies. Also, they would understand why a country like Switzerland depends upon enhanced protection of its specialty foods. It was thus that the protection of GIs eventually emerged as an important prerequisite for liberalizing trade in agriculture, but also laid the foundation for a larger coalition on offering protection beyond agriculture, in particular handicrafts, textiles and watches (see Thu-Lang Tran Wasescha, chapter 9). Next to enhanced market access in services, and thus negotiations on the GATS, IP amounted to the most important negotiating subject for the country. Defensive interests focused on agriculture and absorbed most of the governments' political capital. Without substantial results in services and IPRs, the Uruguay Round package as a whole was difficult to defend, given its potential negative implications, in particular on agriculture.

Learning on the job at this stage was one of the most rewarding experiences for me. The learning process took place in formal and informal meetings held throughout the negotiating process. Discussions increasingly resembled academic seminars, starting with a problem and the search for a common solution. I still recall, for example, the discussions on basic principles, the process of accommodating countries in the field of exceptions from patent rights, the development of disciplines on government use and compulsory licensing, and on developing transitional arrangements in patent law, combining special and differential treatment with the need for legal security and predictability. The same holds true, in particular, for negotiations on GIs or undisclosed information, and the new disciplines on enforcement of IPRs, combining common and civil law principles.

The input of the private sector was, as mentioned at the outset, of paramount importance. Interests and goals defined by contracting parties were largely influenced by domestic lobbies working with delegations. Direct influence was particularly strong in the US delegation. US interest groups also actively lobbied other delegations in Geneva in a concerted effort. Crucial in its importance and impact was the trilateral paper and draft proposal jointly submitted by the US, EC and Japanese industry associations in 1988.[6] Many of the formulations drafted therein influenced or even found their way into formal submissions of the respective contracting parties. They had a lasting influence, shaping the Agreement in its subsequent stages.

Internal preparations by the Swiss delegations were based upon regular internal meetings and briefings by the Swiss industry association (today Economie Suisse, represented by Thomas Pletscher and Otto Stamm) and interested circles, in particular relating to patents and trademarks (the chemical, machinery and watch industries) and copyright protection (collecting societies). Yet there was virtually no contact with individual companies, and finding out about the specific problems confronting them, beyond anecdotal evidence, was a particular difficulty the Swiss delegation faced. Companies were not willing to fully disclose the problems they faced abroad for fear that the information could be useful to competitors who were members of the same association. Non-governmental organizations (NGOs), other than those representing generic industries, defending developing country interests in the maintenance of low levels of IP protection, were not yet fully organized at the time and were not included in the process of defining negotiating interests and directions to be taken. The role of parliamentary committees was not yet developed in the field of international trade and the international dimension of IP. The Uruguay Round, however, created increasing awareness and the Swiss

Government and delegation was repeatedly called upon to address questions relating to the negotiations raised in parliament and by the public at large. The dialogue contributed to emphasizing and supporting reservations in the negotiations for the protection of environmental concerns and human dignity, and to the idea of a *sui generis* system of protecting plant varieties. In hindsight, a stronger influence of NGOs would have been beneficial in preparing an overall balanced result. I recall internal staff meetings held in May 1987 when arguments in favour of stronger disciplines on transfer of technology and on addressing restrictive business practices within the TRIPS negotiations were not taken up in further preparations for negotiations. Regular discussions were held among different governmental departments, in particular between the office responsible for external economic affairs at the Ministry of the Economy, responsible for overall GATT-related matters, and the Office for Intellectual Property at the Ministry of Justice and Police. Relating to enforcement and border measures, consultations were mainly held with the Customs authorities of the Ministry of Finance. Coordination among these different departments benefited from the fact that the people concerned within the Swiss Federal Administration and the GATT delegation were all well acquainted. Within the general and specific goals set, the negotiating team was given ample leeway. The business was conducted by setting objectives. No micro-management by the heads of the Swiss delegation, Secretary of State Franz Blankart or Ambassador David de Pury, took place.

Building mutual trust and inclusiveness

Understanding problems, issues and interests and conceptual work towards commonly accepted solutions did not happen on its own. It was accompanied by a process of building mutual trust among delegations and the Secretariat. It was characterized by inclusiveness of all those who had a strong interest in the subject and were willing to engage and participate in the negotiations. Not all of those who were active participants in the Negotiating Group can be mentioned here, but a few stood out and essentially formed the inner circle of the operation. The Chair of the Negotiating Group, Ambassador Lars Anell of Sweden, enjoyed the trust of all. He was impartial and open to all concerns alike. He was supported by a very able and neutral Secretariat with David Hartridge, eventually led by Adrian Otten and his staff, including Daniel Gervais, Arvind Subramanian and Matthijs Geuze. The Chair and Secretariat in the TRIPS negotiations operated an open and inclusive process. All contracting parties who were interested were able to participate if they so wished. There were only a few instances when interested parties, even among the Friends of Intellectual Property group, were deliberately excluded, for example while discussing restrictive business practices (informal meeting, 10 and 11 September 1989). Trust in the work of the Chair and the Secretariat was crucial and essential in running a largely informal, inclusive negotiating process in which all those voicing an interest were able to participate. Importantly, the composition of key delegations was stable and did not substantially change over time. As Gervais later noted, "Participants were more or less the same people at all meetings and got to know one another quite well."[7]

Trust was essential in compiling the proposals and developing the textual negotiating documents and subsequent versions of the composite text discussed below. The process was ably steered by the Chair and supported by the Secretariat; this also facilitated the gradual building of trust among delegations. Negotiators worked in an environment which allowed them to put problems and issues on the table in a frank and open manner. Negotiations were actively followed by some 25 contracting parties, with Argentina, Australia, Brazil, Canada, Chile, the EC, Hong Kong, India, Japan, Malaysia, New Zealand, Switzerland and the United States playing the most active parts. Discussions among these contracting parties were largely held in an open and transparent manner. There were, at least until the very last moments of the negotiations, no behind-the-scenes deals. Rather, the body of the text, together with all the brackets, was drafted in a joint effort.

The US delegation, led by Bruce Wilson, Michael Kirk, Michael Hathaway and Catherine Field, played a crucial role in offering transparency. In a series of bilateral meetings, delegations were able to react to proposals made and accommodations were sought to the utmost extent possible, taking up concerns voiced. The EC delegation, led by Mogens Peter Carl, Christoph Bail, Jean-Christophe Paille, Jörg Reinbothe and Hansjörg Kretschmer, mainly focused on coordinating EC member states and consolidating their varied interests and goals. The fact that, at the time, IP was not an established field of legal harmonization in European internal market law (apart from the case law of the European Court of Justice) rendered it a matter of extensive internal consultations, which often led to other delegations being kept waiting until meetings could start with GATT delegations. The position of the Commission, owing to the constitutional set-up of the EC at the time, was a challenging one of having to navigate between external and internal negotiations, between Charybdis and Scylla. Contracting parties sometimes double-checked information with delegations of other GATT contracting parties in order to get the full picture, in particular European Free Trade Association (EFTA) countries. The setting of what eventually qualified the TRIPS Agreement as a mixed agreement under EU law in Opinion 1/94 of the European

Court of Justice rendered negotiations more demanding than under today's powers granted under Article 207 of the Treaty on the Functioning of the European Union, including IPRs in European trade policy powers. Clear internal allocations of powers facilitate transparent modes of negotiation.

Canada, another member of the "Quad" (Canada, the EC, Japan and the United States) and led by John Gero, assumed an important role in bridging interests between industrialized and developing countries, given its strong interest at the time in defending a generics-based pharmaceutical industry. Japan, the fourth member of Quad, with its large delegation led by Shozo Uemura and Kazuo Mizushuma, actively intervened in formal meetings and played a discreet but important role in informal discussions, in particular among Quad members. India, the leading voice of the developing countries, led by A.V. Ganesan and Jayashree Watal, together with Argentina, led by Antonio Gustavo Trombetta, and Brazil, represented by Piragibe dos Santos Tarragô, were the main representatives of the developing countries present at the negotiating table. African countries, except Egypt, Nigeria and Zaire (in the early phases), were largely absent at the time, certainly from the inner circle of negotiations. This was particularly true of South Africa, which at the time was under a regime of anti-apartheid economic sanctions, and essentially silenced. Among the other Asian countries that participated actively, to the extent that they were already GATT contracting parties at the time, Korea, Thailand, Malaysia, Singapore, Indonesia, the Philippines and Hong Kong come to mind. Developing countries, except for the larger ones, faced the problem of understaffing and the challenge to cover all the subjects discussed in the Round, including IP. The voice of China, while a candidate for accession, was not heard during the talks. BRICS (the major emerging national economies of Brazil, the Russian Federation, India, China and South Africa) did not exist at the time.

It would, however, be wrong to assume that the TRIPS negotiations were essentially limited to the Quad and the leading developing nations, in particular Argentina, Brazil and India. Smaller countries made important contributions to the debate. In addition, Australia, represented by Patrick Smith, played an active part in the negotiations, in particular in relation to industrial property, in particular patents, and design protection for textiles. Together with Chile, Australia was most active and persistent in the field of GIs, wishing to ensure protection of its growing wine industry using traditional European names. New Zealand was represented by Adrian Macey, a thoughtful and active diplomat, Hong Kong by Peter Cheung, John Clarke and David Fitzpatrick, with his unique Welsh sense of humour, and Malaysia by the articulate Umi Kalthum Binti Abdul Majid. Switzerland was represented by Thu-Lang Tran Wasescha, Luzius Wasescha, William Frei and myself, and enjoyed the privilege of having its additional Bern-based staff members Pietro Messerli, Carlo Govoni, Philippe Baechtold, all of the Federal Office of Intellectual Property (today the Swiss Institute of Intellectual Property), and Hermann Kästli of Customs Administration close by. The combination of generalists and specialists worked out very well and formed a strong team. The Nordic countries had a strong voice in the field of copyright with Jukka Liedes and Hannu Wager from Finland, but otherwise there was little coordination among EFTA countries due to a divergence of interests.

Indeed, the diverse interests and varied goals opened the door for flexible coalitions which varied among different subjects and even forms of IP protection. Such variable geometry and flexibility allowed progress to be made and avoided stalemate. Beyond the early stages, the alignments among the Group of 77 (for developing countries) and the B group (for developed countries), paramount in WIPO and other UN agencies, did not materialize in GATT talks. Each of the contracting parties would, at some point, find itself in agreement with another contracting party despite having divergent views on other subjects. This largely contributed to the building of mutual trust on the one hand and a rational distinction of diverging interests, goals and mutual confidence on the other hand. For these reasons, the TRIPS negotiations, contrary to the usual public perception, were much less a North–South negotiation than a negotiation among a divergent group, often with major difficulties to be solved, among industrialized countries. (The subsequent record in TRIPS-related dispute settlement confirms this point. Most of these cases have been filed by industrialized countries against other industrialized countries; only a few have been filed against or between developing countries).[8]

Of particular importance in building trust were informal meetings held outside the premises of the GATT over the weekends. The Swiss delegation and its Geneva-based mission under the auspices of Luzius Wasescha and William Frei, organized and chaired a series of meetings of the Friends of IP,[9] with gradually increasing participation. Meetings were held in Coppet (7 February 1990, organized by the Japanese mission) and during two weekends in Gruyères (14 and 15 September 1989) and in Zug (28 and 29 October 1989); the latter one also included the delegations from interested developing countries, in particular Brazil, India and Thailand. These informal meetings organized by the Swiss were crucial, not only to advance common thinking towards solutions, but also to deepen acquaintances with colleagues and to learn more about the needs of contracting parties and delegations in a relaxed atmosphere and in circumstances of mutual respect. These were good moments, often with a helpful sense of humour. Understanding and mutual respect, sometimes even friendship, did not run counter to defending interests in an open and transparent manner; quite the contrary. These encounters greatly facilitated work back in Geneva and paved the way for making progress on the texts.

A further meeting was organized by the EC, and the French delegation in particular, in Talloires (12 December 1989), and later on meetings were held among extended Quad members, including Switzerland, in Choully (17 May 1990) and in Geneva (21, 22 and 26 June 1990). Delegations met in different discussion groups throughout the heyday of the negotiations in 1989 and 1990: the Boeuf Rouge Process,[10] and the Anell Group, which consisted of the "most interested participants", known as 10+10,[11] included, in particular, Brazil and India.[12] The Association of Southeast Asian Nations (ASEAN) Group on Enforcement, the Andean Group, and bilateral talks between different parties, in particular the EC and the United States, further characterized the architecture of the process.

These groupings (and perhaps additional ones not on my record) were crucial not only for mutual understanding and resolving outstanding issues, but also in forming flexible coalitions and advancing negotiations. It is impossible to recall and list all the informal activities that were going on at the time. Many will remain unrecorded in the history of the TRIPS negotiations. But overall, relations among negotiators were conducted in a spirit of transparency and openness, creating mutual trust. They were more important than the formal meetings that were regularly held in Geneva for the record.

The fact that many of the TRIPS negotiators met at the WTO 20 years after the entry into force of the TRIPS Agreement[13] reflects the level of understanding and trust which the core group was able to create. In hindsight, it amounts to the most valuable asset and explains much of the success to the extent that it was in the hands of negotiators and delegations.

Building the TRIPS Agreement

The TRIPS Agreement amounts to the most comprehensive international treaty in the field of IPRs. Incorporating the Paris and Berne Conventions, it provides the basis for the additional commitments eventually made in preferential trade arrangements (PTAs), subject to the national treatment and most-favoured nation (MFN) obligations of the TRIPS Agreement. In addition to the factors mentioned above, the methodology for building the Agreement through the process of consultations and negotiations deserves highlighting.

The different stages of the process are aptly described in the paper by Adrian Otten in this volume (see Adrian Otten, chapter 3). Reviewing different generations of submissions, the process started with conceptual papers, emphasizing the interaction between trade and IP and establishing the latter as a proper subject for GATT talks. The Swiss delegation initially proposed to build a TRIPS agreement on the basis of GATT disciplines of nullification and impairment, developing normative principles and an indicative list of types of conduct considered detrimental to international trade.[14] The idea of an indicative list was not considered sufficient and was eventually replaced by proposals for minimal standards, in the second generation of submissions. The submissions at the time were all strongly influenced by the trilateral paper jointly prepared by the industry associations of the EU, Japan and the United States, as well as other inputs.[15] Further efforts resulted in the submission of a complete draft agreement in May 1990.[16]

The Chair and the Secretariat compiled these proposals in a systematic manner, first indicating the source of the proposal in a composite draft text,[17] and later deleting its authorship and provenance.[18] Negotiators started a process of condensing and refining by means of eliminating and combining different proposals of which the origin was no longer transparent. A checklist of issues and open questions, prepared by the Secretariat, was a most helpful aid to this process.[19] The negotiations led to a sequence of draft texts still containing a considerable amount of brackets, which were mainly addressed in informal sessions. The technique of using compilations and draft texts compiled, but also structured, by the Chair and the Secretariat amounts to one of the most remarkable features of the process of building up a complex agreement. The work resulted in a second and almost complete draft by the December 1990 ministerial meeting in Brussels.[20] The draft was further negotiated in 1991 and the so-called Dunkel Draft of December 1991 found its way, with minor amendments and upon legal checking and integrating a separate draft agreement on counterfeiting, into a single TRIPS instrument, inserting it into the dispute settlement system and into the overall package deal completed in 1993.[21] The TRIPS Agreement was completely negotiated within the Negotiating Group and no arbitrage was required in the so-called Green Room, i.e. horizontal talks among Geneva-based ambassadors chaired by the Director-General of GATT.

It is fair to say that, without these complex and gradual steps, the TRIPS Agreement could not have been achieved, with its comprehensiveness and overall structure, nor organized into general provisions, standards relating to the different forms of IP, enforcement and due process, and transitional arrangements. The result was due to a well-structured negotiating process, clearly dedicated to different issues, which also allowed experts to be flown in from the capitals to deal with specific issues.

Conclusions

Perhaps once in a lifetime a negotiator meets a window of opportunity comparable to that afforded by the TRIPS negotiations. Endemic and endogenic factors were matching at the time, allowing for results which today are unlikely to be achievable. Lessons to be learned need to take into account the geopolitical changes that have come about in the meantime: they only allow for very limited conclusions. Yet lessons relating to the learning process – the need to primarily understand the needs of partners and what they are compelled to bring to the table and to bring home – remain valid today. A deliberate process to build mutual trust and run an open, transparent and inclusive process in close cooperation with the Secretariat of the WTO remains an important prerequisite to success in regulatory matters. Transparency and building trust does not exclude informal meetings. To the contrary, they are essential to making progress. Of course, there were also confidential meetings among different partners in the flexible and changing coalitions. Yet, to the extent that they existed, they were not able to destroy mutual trust. Never was there a climate of profound distrust, despite all the different interests and goals at stake. The techniques employed, with conceptual papers, comprehensive and selected proposals, compilations and composite texts, and regularly updated negotiating texts that no longer indicate the source, are most suitable for addressing complex regulatory issues of the kind the WTO will face in its future work. These lessons from the TRIPS negotiations deserve to be learned and remembered.

A look back at the process of the TRIPS negotiations cannot be concluded without a critical note. In hindsight, the process failed to address the problem of maximal standards and to properly balance exclusive rights beyond fair use and compulsory licensing. When the levels of protection unexpectedly increased and were refined, ceilings and a closer link with competition policy safeguards would have been warranted. In fact, negotiations should have extended into disciplines of competition policy relevant to IPRs, much as they could be partially observed in the reference paper on telecommunications in the GATS. Instead, the TRIPS Agreement left its parties with policy space to address competition policy in domestic law, ignoring the fact that most countries at the time would have had competition law and policies in place. Perhaps the subsequent debate on access to essential drugs and the changes to the law of compulsory licensing could have been prevented if a broader approach had been adopted. The concept of minimal standards opened the door for ever-increasing levels of protection when fora eventually shifted to PTAs. No ceilings were built into the Agreement. The implications of national treatment and MFN, lifting global standards by means of these agreements, were not sufficiently anticipated at the time. Except for least-developed countries, most of the rules applied across the board, irrespective of levels of social and economic development. Special and differential treatment was not properly settled and subsequently led to proposals on graduation and a return to more flexibility based upon economic indicators built into a future revised TRIPS Agreement.[22] These deficiencies of the TRIPS Agreement are perhaps also due to the fact that, at the time of the Uruguay Round, there was insufficient debate with NGOs. Except for Greenpeace, globally active organizations such as Oxfam or Médecins Sans Frontières were not yet active in the field as they are today, and protests were anecdotal. Also, the linkages to WIPO and the World Health Organization (WHO), or the human rights bodies of the UN were not sufficiently developed, and the TRIPS negotiations were largely perceived at the time as a matter of unfriendly takeover of, instead of cooperation and joining forces with, other international organizations and bodies. The input to the negotiations largely came from industries and professional organizations interested in enhanced protection of IPRs. Governments and negotiators were not always able to arbitrate and establish a proper balance between right owners and users in the respective fields. These are also lessons which can be learned from the experience of negotiating the TRIPS Agreement in the Uruguay Round.

Endnotes

1 I am deeply indebted to Thu-Lang Tran Wasescha for sharing her memory, and to her and Jayashree Watal for valuable comments on the chapter. I am grateful to Erich Gehri, Swiss Intellectual Property Institute, for checking a number of dates in the official Swiss negotiating record.

2 Susan K. Sell, *Private power, public law: The globalization of intellectual property rights* (Cambridge: Cambridge University Press, 2003), 2, 164, 171 and passim.

3 The author's contributions to the topic include: "The Agreement on Trade-Related Aspects of Intellectual Property Rights", in Patrick F.J. Macrory, Arthur E. Appelton, and Michael G. Plummer, eds., *The World Trade Organization: Legal, economic and political analysis*, volume I (New York: Springer, 2005): 1041-1120; *Trade and intellectual property protection in WTO law: Collected essays* (London: Cameron, 2005); *International intellectual property in an integrated world economy*, with Frederick M. Abbott and Francis Gurry, 3rd revised edition (The Netherlands: Wolters Kluwer, 2014); *Concise international and European IP law: TRIPS, Paris Convention, European enforcement and transfer of technology*, editor with Pierre Véron, 3rd edition (The Netherlands: Kluwer, 2014).

4 For an analysis of the TRIPS negotiating history, see Daniel J. Gervais, *The TRIPS Agreement: Drafting history and analysis*, 3rd edition (London: Street and Maxwell, 2008), 10-26. For a paper contemporary to the negotiations, see Thomas Cottier, "The prospects for intellectual property protection in GATT", *Common Market Law Review* 28 (1991): 383-414.

5 GATT document MTN.GNG/NG11/W/7/Add.2, Negotiating Group on Trade-Related Aspects of Intellectual Property Rights, including Trade in Counterfeit Goods – Submissions from participants on trade problems encountered in connection with Intellectual Property Rights – Switzerland, 5 August 1987.

6 Intellectual Property Committee (US), Keidanren (Japan), Union of Industrial and Employers' Confederations of Europe (UNICE), (June 1988), *Basic Framework of GATT Provisions on Intellectual Property: Statement of Views of the European, Japanese and United States Business Communities.*

7 Supra note 3 at 21 footnote 74.

8 Matthew Kennedy, *Dispute settlement and the WTO TRIPS Agreement: Applying intellectual property standards in a trade law framework* (Cambridge: Cambridge University Press, 2015).

9 The Friends of Intellectual Property group included Australia, Austria, Canada, the EC, Finland, Hong Kong, Japan, New Zealand, Norway, Sweden, Switzerland and the United States.

10 The Boeuf Rouge group of medium-sized countries included Argentina, Australia, Austria, Canada, Colombia, Finland, Hong Kong, Hungary, Israel, Malaysia, Mexico, New Zealand, Nigeria, Norway, Singapore, Sweden, Switzerland, Thailand and Uruguay. Boeuf Rouge refers to a restaurant, the Bistrot du Boeuf Rouge, located in the Paquis district in Geneva, where these negotiators met.

11 Gervais note 3 at 23.

12 The Anell Group (named for the Ambassador and Chair of the TRIPS Negotiating Group) included, with varying composition depending on the subject matter, Argentina, Australia, Austria, Brazil, Canada, Chile, the EC, Hungary, Hong Kong, India, Indonesia, Japan, the Republic of Korea, Malaysia, New Zealand, Norway, Peru, the Philippines, Sweden, Switzerland, Thailand, Turkey and the United States.

13 The TRIPS Symposium organized by the WTO Secretariat on 26 February 2015 brought together many contributors to this volume.

14 GATT document MTN.GNG/NG11/W/15, Negotiating Group on Trade-Related Aspects of Intellectual Property Rights, including Trade in Counterfeit Goods – Suggestion by Switzerland for Achieving the Negotiating Objective, 26 October 1987; GATT document MTN.GNG/ NG11/W/23, Negotiating Group on Trade-Related Aspects of Intellectual Property Rights, Including Trade in Counterfeit Goods – Compilation of Written Submissions and Oral Statements – Prepared by the Secretariat, 26 April 1988.

15 GATT document MTN.GNG/NG11/W/38, Negotiating Group on Trade-Related Aspects of Intellectual Property Rights, including Trade in Counterfeit Goods – Standards and Principles concerning the Availability, Scope and Use of Trade-Related Intellectual Property Rights – Communication from Switzerland, 11 July 1989; GATT document MTN.GNG/NG11/W/38/ Add.1, Negotiating Group on Trade-Related Aspects of Intellectual Property Rights, including Trade in Counterfeit Goods – Standards and Principles concerning the Availability, Scope and Use of Trade-Related Intellectual Property Rights – Communication from Switzerland – Addendum on Proprietary Information, 11 December 1989.

16 GATT document MTN.GNG/NG11/W/73, Negotiating Group on Trade-Related Aspects of Intellectual Property Rights, including Trade in Counterfeit Goods – Draft Amendment to the General Agreement on Tariffs and Trade on the Protection of Trade-Related Intellectual Property Rights – Communication from Switzerland, 14 May 1990.

17 GATT document MTN.GNG/NG11/W/12/Rev.1, Negotiating Group on Trade-Related Aspects of Intellectual Property Rights, Including Trade in Counterfeit Goods – Compilation of Written Submissions and Oral Statements – Prepared by the Secretariat – Revision, 5 February 1988; restricted GATT document no. 1404, Composite Draft Text, 12 June 1990; GATT document MTN.GNG/NG11/W/33/Rev.2, Negotiating Group on Trade-Related Aspects of Intellectual Property Rights, Including Trade in Counterfeit Goods – Synoptic Table Setting Out Proposals on Enforcement and Corresponding Provisions of Existing International Treaties – Prepared by the Secretariat – Revision, 1 February 1990.

18 GATT document MTN.GNG/NG11/W/12/Rev.1, Negotiating Group on Trade-Related Aspects of Intellectual Property Rights, Including Trade in Counterfeit Goods – Compilation of Written Submissions and Oral Statements – Prepared by the Secretariat – Revision, 5 February 1988; restricted GATT document, 12 June 1990; GATT document MTN.GNG/ NG11/W/33/Rev.2, Negotiating Group on Trade-Related Aspects of Intellectual Property Rights, Including Trade in Counterfeit Goods – Synoptic Table Setting Out Proposals on Enforcement and Corresponding Provisions of Existing International Treaties – Prepared by the Secretariat - Revision, 1 February 1990.

19 GATT document MTN.GNG/NG11/W/76, Negotiating Group on Trade-Related Aspects of Intellectual Property Rights, Including Trade in Counterfeit Goods – Status of Work in the Negotiating Group – Chairman's Report to the GNG, 23 July 1990; restricted GATT document, 1 October 1990; restricted GATT document, 25 October 1990; restricted GATT document, 13 November 1990; restricted GATT document, 23 November 1990.

20 GATT document MTN.TNC./W/35/Rev.1, Uruguay Round – Trade Negotiations Committee – Draft Final Act Embodying the Results of the Uruguay Round of Multilateral Trade Negotiations – Revision, 3 December 1990.

21 GATT document MTN.TNC/W/FA, Uruguay Round – Trade Negotiations Committee – Draft Final Act Embodying the Results of the Uruguay Round of Multilateral Trade Negotiations, 20 December 1991, Annex III; restricted GATT document, 21 June 1992; restricted GATT document, 27 June 1992.

22 See Thomas Cottier, "From progressive liberalization to progressive regulation in WTO law," *Journal of International Economic Law* 9 (2006): 779-821.

5

Why we managed to succeed in TRIPS

John Gero

There have been many books and articles written about the TRIPS Agreement. Most go into great detail over the costs and benefits of the various provisions of the Agreement. As one of the negotiators of the Agreement, I will not attempt to debate such an analysis. Rather, this chapter will provide brief, personal reflections of my experiences during the negotiations, which have had a significant impact on the rest of my career as a Canadian diplomat focusing on trade issues.

The most important aspect of these negotiations for me was that people matter and, more particularly, one's interpersonal relationships with people matter a lot. These relationships played a significant role, not often truly recognized, in the successful conclusion of the TRIPS Agreement. The TRIPS Negotiating Group was blessed to have a superb group of negotiators, but so did many of the other negotiating groups. We were also blessed with two other aspects. We had a phenomenal Chair in Ambassador Lars Anell, who exhibited the finest traditions of Swedish diplomacy and knew how to push us, pull us back a little bit and get the best out of us. I am personally convinced that this Agreement would not have happened without his chairmanship. We also had a superb Secretariat team, led by David Hartridge and Adrian Otten. Importantly, we got to know them and trust them. We recognized that the Secretariat was not our enemy, although, at the beginning of the negotiations, we were all very hesitant about letting the Secretariat do anything. Ultimately, we learned that we had a Secretariat who knew how to listen, who knew how to think, who knew how to be fair in reflecting conflicting viewpoints and who knew how to write, and we used those skills to maximum advantage. Therefore, the first answer to the question of why the TRIPS Agreement happened is that it was the people who were involved and the relationships of trust that they established that made it happen.

At the time, all we knew was the GATT, and we had 40 years of experience of knowing how to put square pegs into square holes. However, the Uruguay Round of multilateral trade negotiations was different. All of a sudden, we were required to deal with circles and octagons, in areas such as services and IP. When we tried using square pegs (i.e. the GATT concepts), they did not always fit. Therefore, the second aspect that led to a successful TRIPS Agreement was the ability of the negotiators to think on their feet, using new methodologies and new perspectives. Many of the concepts that we had learned over the past four decades as trade negotiators, concepts that were totally unfamiliar to our IP colleagues in our national capitals, had to be adapted or even discarded in the context of the TRIPS negotiations. The GATT had largely dealt with border measures. Services and TRIPS were creating a new kind of international regulatory agreement that was walking a very fine line between international obligations and the right of countries to regulate their national economies, as we were actually establishing new global societal norms. This led us towards negotiating not traditional trade policies but domestic economic policies that had an impact on trade. We had to look at this prism from a new angle.

For example, one of these concepts was the non-violation provisions of the GATT. They had worked well as part of the GATT, but here was an example of trying to make a square peg fit into a round hole and, for the longest time, we did not know what to do with it. Some felt that the concept should not be a concept in a TRIPS agreement, while others felt that it was absolutely necessary. We finally agreed on a compromise, which placed it in the text but also waived its application, leaving it to future generations to come to grips with its ultimate effect. Canada can be blamed or thanked, depending on your perspective, as being one of those that emphasized that this square peg would not fit into the round hole of the TRIPS Agreement. In the case of non-violation, there was the important issue of policies that governments could follow that did not violate the TRIPS Agreement but that could still be the subject of a non-violation case. At that point in time, Canada was specifically concerned about pharmaceutical price controls that would not be contrary to any provision of the TRIPS Agreement but could conceivably be subject to a nullification and impairment case under a non-violation clause. In today's context, it would be interesting to contemplate what the Australian tobacco case would have been if recourse to a non-violation, nullification and impairment clause had been available.

There can be a tendency among negotiators to pass the buck, by either pushing it upwards to politicians or entrusting it to some third-party arbitrator. This way, it is easier to stick to firm negotiating positions and blame someone else if a compromise to a national position is made. There has been a mythology created, in the context of the Uruguay Round, that this methodology was followed by the negotiators. The so-called Dunkel Draft is being perceived as a message from God that descended upon the office of Arthur Dunkel, Director-General of the GATT, late in December 1991, which Arthur Dunkel then delivered to the multitudes, as a third-party arbitrator. The third reason that the TRIPS Agreement happened is that this is a false perception. In the case of the TRIPS negotiations, the Dunkel Draft, in essence, had been 95 per cent thoroughly and utterly negotiated and vetted by the contracting parties. Under Ambassador Lars Anell, the Negotiating Group was a very hard-working group. The negotiators were meeting in all sorts of dingy corners of Geneva, poring over the nuts and bolts of the agreement. Furthermore, the term "negotiated by the members", meant that all negotiators were under very close political guidance from their capitals, given the political sensitivity of many of the issues involved. This close link between the negotiators and their ministers was vital to the ultimate success of the negotiations. In the Canadian context, agreeing to the TRIPS Agreement involved a number of significant policy and legislative changes to the Canadian patent system. As negotiations were going on in December 1991, the Canadian delegation sat in sessions as late as 1 a.m., waiting for instructions from our capital, because the Canadian Cabinet was meeting in Ottawa where it was only around 7 p.m. The Canadian delegation had to keep open a constant line of communication between Geneva and Ottawa to determine whether it could agree to the Chair's latest text, which used certain language more acceptable to Ottawa but which still implied significant changes for the Canadian patent system. This was an important dimension of the TRIPS negotiations at a crucial stage. While, in the end, there was a certain amount of give and take, to a large extent, it was the blood, sweat and tears of the negotiators talking, working things through, negotiating and coming to solutions based on compromises that led to an agreement. There was no shortcut to sitting down with one's colleagues and negotiating, spending the time and effort to understand each other's problems and trying to figure out solutions by trusting each other.

There seems also to be a mythology that the TRIPS negotiations were a North–South negotiation. It was not. In fact, most of the negotiations were North–North in nature. The developed countries were split as badly as were the developing countries. All countries' IP laws attempt to find a societal balance between inventors or creators and users. Each party to the negotiation had been trying to find such a balance in a national context for the past 100 years. Interestingly, these balances are constantly shifting according to developments within a society. Not surprisingly, therefore, in attempting to find global balances, each country attempted to enshrine its own laws, balances and interests. Where we got lucky in the TRIPS Agreement, is that we were having approximately a dozen negotiations in parallel. We all had offensive and defensive interests. Since countries negotiate in their national interests, alliances were formed, but, given the multifaceted nature of the TRIPS negotiations, there were always shifting alliances. India and Canada may have had differences with the United States and the European Communities (EC) on patents, but India and the United States shared similar interests on copyrights. On the subject of geographical indications, India and the EC had differences with Canada and the United States. These shifting alliances forced the development of trust and cooperation among the negotiators, since they changed from being allies to adversaries, and vice versa, as they moved through the various parts of the text. As a result, TRIPS negotiations were not a simple "theological" negotiation or rift between developed and developing countries.

Finally, negotiators of the TRIPS Agreement had to learn not to underestimate the value of finding simple solutions. Given the complexity of the subject matter, it was not unusual to have lengthy "theological" discussions based on one's own policies and laws, but such discussions could not yield negotiated solutions. The negotiations on the enforcement section of the Agreement featured lengthy treatises on the benefits of civil law versus common law, and vice versa. Ultimately, the simple solutions that were found were based on the common principles underlying both types of law. Another example was the discussions on the patentability of life forms. The Harvard mouse, that famous little mouse, had been patented in the United States and there were substantial "theological" arguments about whether one should or should not be able to patent life forms. Countries took widely varying positions in that regard. All negotiators were bombarded by various interest groups that were either scared of, or in favour of, such patents. There were heated discussions about how such a practice would lead to the patenting of cows, and how that would enhance or destroy the whole agricultural sector. Ultimately, negotiators began to examine what countries actually did. When we looked at our own national practices, we found that they all used very similar language. In essence, differences arose because courts had interpreted these provisions differently in different jurisdictions. Ultimately, we found that, if we went back to the language that existed in some of our practices, a solution could be found. That is why the section on the patentability of life forms is a very close parallel to the actual Canadian practice at that time.

What this brief chapter demonstrates is that there was no magic or divine guidance in reaching an agreement on TRIPS. All that it took was a number of skilled and dedicated people working together in trust in the right global political environment. Fortunately for me, I was present when it happened.

6

Evaluating the TRIPS negotiations: a plea for a substantial review of the Agreement

Mogens Peter Carl

The historical context

The successful conduct and conclusion of the TRIPS negotiations can only be understood if they are seen in their historical context.

The late 1980s and early 1990s saw the peaceful disappearance of what seemed like an everlasting East–West confrontation. Then, in the space of a few years, starting with Mr. Gorbachev's tenure in power in the USSR, the autocratic systems were overturned peacefully from within, ending with the disappearance of the USSR itself and the simultaneous appearance of democratically elected governments in the Eastern bloc, for the first time in decades.

This also led to the disappearance of the East–West confrontation by proxy in third countries.

In parallel with this, we witnessed the replacement of autocratic regimes in other countries, especially in Latin America, by democratically elected governments.

No one who has had the privilege of living during that period will forget it. It was as if a window had been opened to let air into a stuffy room, destroying in the process the nightmare of nuclear war. For the first time in nearly half a century, there was a feeling, not that this was "the end of history" but that it was a new beginning, not only for Europe but also for the rest of the world. In Europe, all this coincided with the creation of the single, open market and with the establishment of the political basis for the euro. There seemed to be no limits to what could be done.

Some thought that this was a return to some sort of "normalcy", to the possibility of resolving problems or conflicts through dialogue and negotiation. If only this were still true today …

I believe that it was this unique political and psychological context that, more than any other factor (of which there were many), created a favourable context for the Uruguay Round of multilateral trade negotiations in general and helped bring about the successful conclusion of the Round and of the TRIPS negotiations. In that sense, we, the negotiators of the Uruguay Round, were translating into binding international obligations the *Zeitgeist* of the early 1990s. This *Zeitgeist* has now disappeared into the mist of history.

The mandate and the objectives

The Uruguay Round, launched in 1986, was the specific context for the negotiations, and was based on the notion of "reciprocal concessions", which were supposed to result in a comprehensive, balanced agreement of sufficient advantage to all. In reality, as any negotiator knows, this objective of a "comprehensive, balanced agreement" is unquantifiable, much more psychological than mercantilist and much more "political" than economically measurable.

At the outset, the aims of trade-related negotiations were expressed in very general terms. This also applied to the TRIPS negotiations:

> Trade-related aspects of intellectual property rights, including trade in counterfeit goods:
>
> In order to reduce the distortions and impediments to international trade, and taking into account the need to promote effective and adequate protection of intellectual property rights, and to ensure that measures and procedures to enforce intellectual property rights do not themselves become barriers to legitimate trade, the negotiations shall aim to clarify GATT provisions and elaborate as appropriate new rules and disciplines.
>
> Negotiations shall aim to develop a multilateral framework of principles, rules and disciplines dealing with international trade in counterfeit goods, taking into account work already undertaken in the GATT.
>
> These negotiations shall be without prejudice to other complementary initiatives that may be taken in the World Intellectual Property Organization and elsewhere to deal with these matters.[1]

If anything, this is the definition of an open-ended mandate which, depending on the numerous other variables entering into play, could have resulted in a much more modest outcome than the result that materialized after several years of trial and error.

One could, however, say the same about virtually all other aspects of the negotiations. For example, the radical modification of the dispute settlement system does not appear in the very prudent text agreed at Punta del Este.

Is this a lesson for future negotiations? Should one avoid the wordy mandates that often restrict, indeed pre-negotiate, the eventual outcome by circumscribing the negotiations with excessive detail? The question is perhaps not whether one "should" but whether one "could": to return to the argument made at the beginning of this chapter, the atmosphere back then was one, if not of trust, at least of openness to discussion and experiment. Is that the case today? Probably not, but the recurrent theme of this chapter is that we should *try* for this, in the absence of which the multilateral system of the WTO will not evolve to meet the preoccupations of today and tomorrow.

The European context

At the outset, few, if any – certainly on the European side – had a clear idea of what our objectives should be and the European Commission itself, at Punta del Este, was quite reluctant to accept the text reproduced above. Ideas, objectives, and ways and means of expressing our interests, largely "offensive", emerged over time, and our level of ambition grew in step with the understanding that these issues were of major importance for our future and an important element in the overall economic and political equation of the Round. This was, naturally, also influenced by those in the private sector who discovered that here was a process of interest to them.

The European producers of pharmaceuticals were, at the time, the world's biggest investors in research and development (R&D) (and so they have remained, but are now close behind US producers), but their attitude towards the GATT negotiations in general and any TRIPS agreement in particular was hardly one of great enthusiasm, nor was there, initially, much of an interest in other IP-intensive sectors. Their home market was enormous and securely funded by the world's most generous social security systems, access to other developed markets was largely unfettered and exports were significant. Exporting, let alone imposing, European Communities (EC) standards of IP protection to developing countries was seen as a useful addition to an already healthy profit margin by the pharmaceutical industry, but hardly as a major objective. In any event, there was a general feeling that one should not overdo the level of ambition in respect of these countries – an attitude shared by the EC member states. Without much exaggeration, the basic principle was "live and let live" and this was the reflection of a general attitude towards the development of the "third world" shared by most in European society. Paradoxically – or typically, for the Europeans – there were strong pressures from those with a position of principle to promote without much economic significance, for example, on "moral rights". However, it is also true to say that, when EC industry and other sectors came to understand the extent of the potential agreement as it developed, their support for the negotiations grew exponentially, and the inclusion of the TRIPS Agreement in the WTO became politically essential for the EC.

We were also in the strange situation where relatively little harmonization of IP legislation had taken place at the European level and where the Commission did not have the "exclusive competence" to negotiate externally that it later obtained in a Treaty revision. Consequently, every six months, under each new Presidency of the Council, member states would make solemn declarations to the effect that IP matters were of national, not EC competence, to make sure that the Commission did not forget it … This has now changed completely and "trade-related IP" issues are firmly anchored in the Treaty as a competence.

Despite these internal complications (which never created any significant problem), from the first to the last day, the EC negotiating positions were led from inside the Commission, aiming at what we thought should become a "reasonable" result for all participants. There were useful contributions made by some member state IP experts and by a a few companies with a strong stake in IP, but these inputs were largely of a general nature. What made our situation different from that of other participants was that pressures exercised by private interests on the negotiators were limited and, in any event, less important than might be the case today, however incredible this may seem to negotiators from other countries.

To an outsider, this may be difficult to grasp, but the EC system was and is such that the Commission is much less directly exposed to external pressures than are its member states, and it is the Commission that negotiates. Member states can, of course, then blame the results on the Commission and they rarely hesitate to do so. The Commission has an obligation to "consult" member states, and it does so having in mind the need to obtain their support at the end of the negotiations. Nevertheless, the involvement of private parties, industry or non-governmental organizations (NGOs), was far removed from the experience of other negotiators. The internal EC decision-making system was also much less rigid than it is today, without any formal, written negotiating mandate, and with no obligation to submit the results for the acceptance of the European Parliament. I am not arguing that this was "better" than what has emerged through subsequent changes in EC and European Union (EU) treaties and practice, but it worked. For such a system, or "non-system", to work in the public interest, it does, however, require that those in charge are imbued by what they consider to be in that same public interest and capable of promoting it against opposition, internal or external. Many now argue that international negotiations must be conducted much more openly, allowing non-governmental parties to be informed at all stages of the negotiations in order to allow them to intervene to influence the conduct of the negotiations. Right or wrong, this may have undesired or undesirable effects: (i) opening up to pressures from party A by definition also opens to pressures from party B; the relative strengths of the two may lead to an outcome that is not in the public interest, unless you adopt a Darwinian-type interpretation of the latter (i.e. the victory of the strongest); (ii) alternatively, this may lead to a stalemate or defeat the very purpose of the negotiations; (iii) it raises the question of legitimacy: who is "legitimate" to pursue the public interest – democratically elected governments and their representatives or private pressure groups? (The latter will, of course, argue that their governments are wrong and/or have sold out to another pressure group, but from what do they derive their own legitimacy?).

These questions are highly relevant to the question of a possible revision of important parts of the TRIPS Agreement, as suggested below.

One final remark on the European context: 30 years earlier, we had embarked on a unique historical experiment, trying to put behind us 2,000 years of civil war by creating what has become the EU, abolishing age-old barriers and adopting a *de facto* federal approach to most economic legislation. In this process, we hardly made a difference between the opening up to fellow European nationals and to those outside the EC and the whole thrust of this historical experiment was to "transfer competence" (i.e. ever-growing bits and pieces of sovereignty) to "Brussels". Therefore, the notion of abandoning national sovereignty to international bodies became much less of a taboo than in other countries. To some, it became an objective of its own. Many Europeans were therefore enthusiastic "rule globalizers" at that time and quite a few have still not understood that this enthusiasm is hardly shared outside our borders.

North vs South, West vs West?

As the negotiations developed and their aims began to become more clearly defined, at least from the perspective of the *demandeurs* in the industrialized countries, it became increasingly obvious that some developing countries would be asked to make important changes to their IP regimes. However, it would be wrong to imagine that the negotiations were of a classic North–South character. The differences in legal tradition between continental Europe and the United States were such that we must have spent as much time in protracted arguments about the virtues of EC vs US approaches and legal philosophy as we did in "North–South" negotiations. The latter were, in any event, never monolithic. Temporary alliances would be struck between participants on specific issues, without such alliances setting a precedent for cooperating on other issues.

Some believe that the market access concessions dangled in the air by the developed countries helped persuade developing or other developed countries to accept an outcome of the TRIPS negotiations that would require important modifications of their IP regimes. I remember using the argument on occasion, referring mostly to the negotiations on agriculture which, rightly or wrongly, were seen as the holy grail by many developing countries. Did this argument have any real impact? Perhaps, by underlining the general atmosphere of give and take, that this was a global negotiation of interest to all. To suggest that there was a more specific trade-off would be a crude, mercantilist but also unrealistic view of our microcosm. In any event, when a negotiator makes a concession, he or she persuades themselves that it is in their own interest … If there were any "crude, mercantilist exchanges of concessions", they were very limited and probably more to be found between developed countries. Indeed, in my view, ultimate success was the result of many other factors.

In addition, some of my fellow negotiators from developing countries mentioned during our meeting in February 2015 that they were under pressure of the risk of "unilateral" measures threatened or taken by the United States, in particular with regard to the protection of pharmaceutical inventions. This may or may not have been an important consideration (it obviously was not a concern on the EC side) but it is certainly true that the negotiations on dispute settlement were seen as essential to remove the risk or threat of unilateral action from international trade. This happened as a result of the negotiations on the new dispute settlement system, from my perspective *the* other great achievement of the Uruguay Round.

The "radical" aspects of the new WTO

I have already mentioned the background music of the peaceful revolutions in Eastern Europe and elsewhere and the impression that we were entering a new era of international cooperation (the word "globalization" had not yet become the buzzword it is today), a "return to" and not an "end to" history. Other unquantifiable aspects of the Uruguay Round negotiations were radical in nature, seen as very positive by those who believed in a law-based system for international trade, for example, the creation of the powerful system of dispute settlement referred to above and a reinforcement of agreements in virtually all areas of GATT rule-making (such as trade defence, sanitary and phytosanitary rules, standards, etc.). These were seen as being in the interest of all contracting parties and, if possible, even more so to the advantage of developing countries, supposedly at a disadvantage in terms of defending their interests as compared with the major industrial countries.

What is indisputable is the fact the new GATT, the WTO system, has created the only comprehensive set of rules of virtually universal application, backed up by law and sanctions-based enforcement through the potential withdrawal of "mutual concessions" in the case of non-compliance with the conclusions of the dispute settlement body. The question of the impact of this on "globalization" and the virtues or vices of this phenomenon, is a much broader question, for another symposium.

One last remark on the historical and economic context: these were, generally speaking, years of relative economic optimism. World trade was growing and there were no major crises of the type that one has experienced over the past ten years. There was no mass unemployment in the "West", no financial crisis, no overnight disappearance of whole swathes of industry due to imports.

The atmosphere and conduct of the negotiations, give and take

These are, I believe, the reasons why a group of about 20 or so officials, crammed into various small meeting rooms in the GATT building, could reach agreement on issues that had defied others for many years. Add to this the psychological compatibility of the negotiators and the invaluable contributions made by the Chair of the Negotiating Group, Ambassador Lars Anell, and two exceptionally able and sympathetic staff of the GATT Secretariat, David Hartridge and Adrian Otten. Without their assistance and support, we would not have succeeded.

Another reason why the negotiations succeeded was the calibre of the participants, the fact that the negotiators got to know each other, that they engaged in an open debate aimed at persuasion rather than a classic trade negotiation, and that the discussions came to focus on what was seen as "good" or "bad", "persuasive" or "reasonable". Some of us were legal or IP experts. Others, like myself, were professionals otherwise engaged in conducting international economic relations and negotiations. Arguably, the mixture of these two very different professions provided the yeast missing in other fora. This does not, of course, detract from the fact that the delegates from parties with much to gain from increased patent protection (such as the EC) had important economic interests to promote (see also below, on the patent negotiations) but the discussions quickly moved away from the question of "whether" to the question of "how", with what qualifications or restrictions, including the overarching question of compulsory licences.

This was light years away from my experience of other negotiations where the main, if not only, argument was "what will you give me in exchange?" This kind of approach works, and should not be despised, when you are trying to reduce classical trade barriers. It would have been counterproductive in the context of the TRIPS negotiations, and has turned out to be incapable of bringing about agreement in the international climate negotiations.

It could be argued that there was one important conceptual exception in the TRIPS negotiations to the absence of the classic approach of barter or "reciprocal exchange of concessions", at least in conceptual terms. As we all know, or should learn, "more" is not always synonymous with "better". This axiom in certainly true for IP, where public interest requires that the monopoly rights attributed to the owner of IP should be subject to certain exceptions or restrictions, especially in case of abuse, although this naturally applies more to certain types of rights than to others. The recognition of this by the participants put confidence, and political and intellectual flexibility, into the discussions and helped bring about a balanced outcome, in the sense that the interests of users as opposed to those of producers were explicitly, indeed strongly, recognized and protected, at least in some areas. It also took the sting out of a potential North–South disagreement: such public policy considerations are common to all countries; we are almost all both "users" and "producers" of IPRs, taking into account the whole gamut of rights, including not only patents but also copyright, designs, trademarks, geographical indications (GIs) and so on.

GATT/WTO vs WIPO: WTO+?

This brings us to the thorny question (at the time) of the relation between our work and that of WIPO, which had tried and failed for years to reach agreement on issues of major importance that were finally settled in the GATT/WTO context. What was done in the TRIPS context was a *de facto*, time-limited takeover bid. Whether this takeover bid was "reasonable" or "trade related" or not is now largely beside the point: it happened and it succeeded. Why qualify the words "beside the point" by the adverb "largely"? The reason is that one may ask whether other "trade-related" issues dealt with by other international bodies should be addressed by the WTO. What comes to mind are questions of labour rights and conditions and questions regarding the protection of the environment and climate, and the impact on and relations between these issues and international trade. This is, of course, of a philosophical and therefore political character: what should be the relative importance attributed to cheap production and imports compared with the conditions of work and life of those engaged in such activities and the future of our physical environment and climate? How many more disasters of the Rana Plaza type (when more than 1,000 workers were killed in the collapse of a garment factory in Bangladesh) will it take before exporters and importers agree to take preventive or remedial concerted action? For me, the limitation of the WTO rulebook to areas that are largely economic is a major weakness in terms of the long-term credibility and success of the WTO system. This view is, however, not shared by most members of the WTO, and the degree of mutual confidence is such that few would be prepared to contemplate negotiations aiming at the inclusion of such issues in the WTO.

Extending the coverage of the WTO system to such other issues is, in the current circumstances, illusory, but then the unexpected can happen when the wheel of history decides to turn. Who would have believed in 1986 that the world would change as rapidly as it did? And who could argue that the world has not changed so much over the past 20 years that a thorough review of the rulebook is becoming overdue?

These negotiations were probably also the last to be conducted and concluded without much publicity or so-called "transparency". Critics might say that this was one of the reasons for the popular backlash, at least by the "anti-globalization" forces, whose violent protests were to accompany international meetings over the coming years. This is, however, doubtful. The TRIPS Agreement changed little in terms of IP protection in the developed countries and the main change for developing countries was arguably positive: the introduction of patent protection for pharmaceuticals came after a ten-year transition period, leaving substantial time for producers of generics to review their business model. Furthermore, the introduction of legislation fighting trade in counterfeit goods, of which inhabitants in developing countries are the first victims (counterfeit goods kill more citizens in developing than in developed countries). Patent protection for pharmaceuticals was, of course, a very major change but of limited immediate impact post the TRIPS Agreement, if it had not been for the precipitation and excessive greed of certain non-European pharmaceutical producers on the markets of at least two developing countries, South Africa and Brazil. I have always attributed the controversy over "access to drugs" (resolved at Doha in 2001) more to the provocative behaviour of these producers than to the text of the TRIPS Agreement itself. The proof of this lies in the fact that the Doha Declaration on the TRIPS Agreement and Public Health did *not* call for any amendment to the text of the TRIPS Agreement, except to introduce additional flexibility in terms of compulsory licences for exports. It is also possible that its very adoption led the companies (potentially) tempted to overdo their profit maximization to mind their ways.

The demise of the only post-TRIPS Agreement attempt to agree on additional international rules on IP enforcement, the Anti-Counterfeiting Trade Agreement (ACTA),[2] was due to much more complex reasons. On the one hand, there was an unusual coalition among major companies with an interest in preserving their dominant position on the Internet and that feared that effective rules would be introduced to combat copyright and trademark infringements essential to their business model; on the other hand, there was a populist backlash against protecting any form of IP, and various NGOs purported to defend access to cheap medicines for patients in poor countries, not to speak of their extraordinary level of incomprehension (more on this below).

A review of the TRIPS Agreement?

All this is relevant to the future of the TRIPS Agreement.

Back in 1990, there was a general consensus that innovation, and its protection, were "a good thing". That consensus is now being battered by the emergence of not only "patent trolls" in the United States but also huge companies that are investing relatively little in R&D and that draw largely on the efforts made by others, which they then translate into assembling very successful consumer products while doing everything possible to minimize the royalties due to the original inventors. The fight against the trade in counterfeit goods or copyright violations on the Internet is also assuming a very different dimension and is subject to much less consensus.

No major international negotiation today escapes from public or parliamentary scrutiny or "oversight" by self-appointed critics. This probably implies that negotiations concerning any change to the TRIPS Agreement of any significance would have to be conducted in a very different way. In any event, they would be much more difficult. This would be a pity because any agreement needs to be brought up to date. No agreement is perfect and it would be useful, indeed necessary, to review the substance of the TRIPS Agreement and its pertinence to the world of the twenty-first century, but also the extent to which it is being faithfully implemented by all parties, including some of the major economies.

Five specific issues

Finally, I wish to speak more specifically about five areas of the negotiations, focusing on what I believe was exceptionally important, what went wrong, what has turned out to be insufficient, and therefore also on what should be done now, 20 years subsequently.

1. Copyright

The negotiations on copyright assumed little of the intensity or controversy common to those on patents and GIs. There were relatively few North–South issues, since most developing countries had adopted European-type approaches, but there was more of a confrontation between the United States and the EC over certain specific aspects of copyright protection, such as neighbouring rights and moral rights, where emotions ran high.

What could or should have been the focus of much more discussion was the question of how to protect software. Quite early in the negotiations, there was a lively and friendly discussion between the Europeans and some Latin Americans on the question of whether a specific regime should be envisaged for software (as was the case in France, for example). I was preoccupied by the question because I thought that copyright protection was too absolute, unqualified and without the checks and balances referred to above, and this for something that was increasingly important in economic life. I found, and indeed still find, it unconvincing that the result of an intellectual process in terms of writing a book or a piece of music should be treated in the same manner as the result of another intellectual process such as the creation of software aimed at producing something which serves an "industrial" purpose. This is not intended to underrate the complexity or intellectual challenge of the latter. The difference, rather, resides in the use and the context of the use of the product of this intellectual process. Software serves an economic purpose and should therefore, in my view, be treated as an industrial invention, through a *sui generis* regime. Such a system should then include the same types of checks and balances that have been created by lawmakers in other areas in order to counteract abuse by right holders.

This general statement needs to be qualified in order to be more precise and practical about the definition of the real, "industrial" problem. Thus, copyright protection only applies if there has been actual (direct or indirect) copying. Also, copyright only protects the actual, detailed expression of an idea or concept, not the idea or concept itself. In other words, even if someone "copies" the general idea or concept of a particular piece of software, but arrives at the same or similar software independently without copying the source code, there is no copyright infringement. So far, so good. The problem, as I understand it, is not with the protection of "software" in the general sense of the term but with the refusal by some right holders to allow access to the source code, such access being indispensable, *inter alia*, for reasons of interoperability or further development and improvement of proprietary software. If the refusal to allow access to the source code is justified by its owner by invoking copyright, the problem of potentially excessive anti-competitive protection raised in the preceding paragraph becomes real, and of major importance, as demonstrated by a number of major antitrust cases in the EC. The problem may actually be less with copyright protection as such than with the denial of access to the source code. This may, therefore – as has been demonstrated in Europe – be subject to intervention by the competition authorities.

In any event, I found myself in the minority of one, in both the EC and the Negotiating Group, and I therefore regretfully had to drop the attempt to advance the idea of a specific software regime.

Should one envisage a reopening of the question? There seems to be an important problem with respect to the management of the protection of software, especially the source code and access thereto, which may, in any event, be blocked by technical means. The importance of this has expanded manifoldly since the 1990s, accompanied by continued accusations of abuse of dominant position. This should *not* be misunderstood as a plea in favour of the adoption of patent protection for software, but as a plea for an unprejudiced discussion of what is really in the public interest, to the extent that this is still possible in today's very different political environment. Is this not the quintessence of a "trade-related" problem?

The question of the protection of copyright and related rights on the Internet has also become of great relevance and of great concern to right holders who find themselves pitted against the interests of the major companies and the insistence on full, unfettered, free-for-all access. In view of the truly globalized nature of the phenomenon, would this not be an area suitable for WTO discussion and action?

2. Patents

The biggest contribution of the TRIPS Agreement towards the adoption of a high, but carefully circumscribed, common level of IP protection was, without any doubt, in the area of patents.

The agreement on patents, five pages in the 1994 collection of legal texts, still reads well today, 20 years later. One could even say that it is a model of relative clarity and economy of words. If negotiated today, it would probably be ten times longer and much less comprehensible.

In a nutshell, what preoccupied the negotiators was how to adopt a quasi-common basis for patent protection, including for pharmaceuticals, while qualifying these rights by a long list of special provisions qualifying and circumscribing these rights, including, in particular, compulsory licences, which came to represent 40 per cent of the total text, but also numerous other issues like exhaustion, patentability and so on.

Once this basic balance had been achieved, the only important variable left, that of time, became the political question that would make or break the negotiations.

Compulsory licences

It would be difficult to over-emphasise the importance of the question of balance between the exclusive rights of the patent owner and the provisions on compulsory licences. Was the balance that emerged from the negotiations right and sufficient? We thought so at the time and it has, to my knowledge, not been questioned since, except in the context of the controversy over "access to medicines" which I believe would never have come about but for the excessive greed of a couple of non-European companies that sought to exploit a specific situation.

The text says in substance that the public authorities may grant exceptions to the exercise of patent rights, for example, if these rights are being abused or if there is an overriding public interest (e.g. national emergency, extreme urgency). However, and very importantly, the right holder is not deprived of his property: "Due process" is obligatory, and so is an "adequate remuneration".

This is, of course, an extremely condensed summary of the provisions on which we laboured for weeks, in what was a very friendly and intellectually interesting discussion, where many let themselves be pulled into a challenging comparison of arguments of "right" and "wrong".

Has it reached its objectives in terms of ensuring the right balance in terms of protecting private property rights and the public interest?

Partly yes, in those countries where the political and administrative systems are such that the business conduct of private right holders is influenced by the realistic expectation that their rights may be affected by the grant of a compulsory licence if they go too far in terms of exploiting their monopoly rights.

And partly no, in many (most?) other countries with a weaker administrative apparatus. Governments are responsible: it is up to them to implement the TRIPS Agreement in detail, both in terms of undertaking the necessary scrutiny of patent applications and of applying the provisions on "use without authorization" of the right holder.

Has this been done by all governments? Undoubtedly no, and some actors, such as the United Nations Development Programme, argue that even some developing country governments with a high level of administrative capacity (such as that of South Africa) have failed to do so.

Clearly, the TRIPS Agreement cannot be held responsible for imperfect national implementation or inexistent innovation or inefficient public health policies, but it is also a timely reminder of the dangers of drafting and adopting *de facto* international law identical for all parties, regardless of their political and administrative capacities, even if accompanied by the usual references to "special treatment of least-developed countries", if for no other reason that even some advanced developing countries face, and have faced, similar difficulties in implementation.

Balanced texts, drafted in good faith, can only be successfully applied according to the letter and spirit of their authors if those who are supposed to ensure their implementation are willing and capable of doing so. If they are not, the high, but also carefully balanced, level of protection agreed on paper will not be applied in practice. To argue that this becomes a question of "technical assistance", the easy paper panacea for resolving all problems, is not persuasive. In any event, IP protection cannot be separated from the overall emphasis on, and respect for, the rule of law, or lack thereof.

Does this mean that we went too far? More on this below … but, before that, a few words on "exhaustion", which was hotly debated.

Exhaustion

The main question was whether one could agree on common rules on international exhaustion – a very important issue, especially, but not only, in terms of allowing parallel imports of pharmaceuticals (i.e. unauthorised by right holders). Manufacturers have a clear commercial interest in segmenting markets. Users have a clear interest in the opposite – a classic issue for the GATT/WTO. Suffice it to say that the compromise found was of a Solomonic character: each WTO member may decide on its parallel import regime, provided that it applies the basic GATT/WTO principles of national treatment and most-favoured nation treatment to all right holders.

I still believe that this was the right compromise on this very sensitive political and economic issue. It allows those countries with a predominant "user" interest to adopt international exhaustion, and it allows those with important producer interests to refrain from doing so, if they believe that this would serve to achieve the right balance between domestic producers and consumers.

Another question is, of course, whether the choice is really made on the basis of such a careful examination of what constitutes public interest, but at least this can be done on the basis of a sovereign decision by the governments concerned.

Patentability

The adoption of a universal principle that "patents shall be available for any inventions … in all fields of technology " (TRIPS Article 27) constitutes the basis for an international community of interest in promoting invention, a belated recognition of the importance of science and technology for our societies. But let us not be hypocritical: it was also of major economic interest to those countries whose industries had a significant interest in promoting universal protection of their inventions.

On the other hand, let us not draw erroneous conclusions from this recognition of self-interest: if one wants to promote and protect R&D, the cost has to be borne by someone. To me, at least, at the time, it seemed obvious that there would be little privately funded investment in research to develop treatment of tropical or "orphan" diseases unless such investment was supported by the prospect of reaping some return on investment, by definition risky and uncertain. I realise now that this view is not shared by all and that some attribute the lack of investment in combating such diseases to the lack of purchasing power in the less affluent countries. Right or wrong, this was my personal motivation at the time.

Has the adoption of a quasi-universal basis for patent protection had the hoped-for impact on R&D to combat such diseases? It is difficult to find conclusive answers. Some companies have indeed invested, sometimes massively, to find remedies for such diseases. Have they done so because they could expect to receive patent protection for their inventions and recoup their investment or simply because they thought that it was right? Furthermore, some "orphan diseases" may be doubly "orphan" in that they concern such a limited, or poor, population that the cost of developing protection or treatment may be out of proportion to any potential return. In such circumstances, it is up to the public authorities to step in and provide the necessary impetus and financial support. This has begun. Is it enough? Certainly not, yet.

The final compromise

Finally, by the time that the negotiators had reached what they thought was a reasonable balance between qualified monopoly rights and the exercise thereof, some national governments woke up to the fact that there was a risk of their opposition on principle being swept away. Political pressures on negotiators grew by the day from 1991 onwards.

As in many other negotiations, this political problem was resolved by introducing the question of time into the equation. The end result was a mixture of substance and a play of mirrors. In substance, the "statesman-like" decision by India to accept to protect product patents for pharmaceuticals allowed the negotiations to succeed. This was expressed in the TRIPS Agreement as an obligation to "provide as from the date of entry into force of the WTO Agreement a means by which applications for (protection for pharmaceutical inventions) can be filed" and to "apply to these applications, as of the date of application of this Agreement, the criteria for patentability as laid down in this Agreement as if those criteria were being applied on the date of filing … and provide patent protection in accordance with this Agreement as from the grant of the patent and for the remainder of the patent term, counted from the filing date in accordance with Article 33 of this

Agreement …" (note the heavy syntax which, while somewhat inelegant, was very precise).

To an innocent bystander, this looks like gobbledygook. It has to be understood against the background of (i) the existence of a transition period of ten years for the introduction of product patent protection for the countries that wanted it (Art. 65), (ii) the fact that it normally takes about ten years from the start of patent filing to complete the clinical tests and obtain marketing approval in that jurisdiction, by which time only ten years remain to enjoy the associated rights on the market, and (iii) an unsuccessful attempt by certain pharmaceutical lobbies to obtain immediate protection for existing subject matter through "pipeline protection".

The essential elements of the final result were unusually "intelligent" – intelligent not only because of the complexity of the concepts employed and their intricate interrelationship but also because of the unambiguous nature of the result. This also took a lot of courage on behalf of some negotiators, because of the high level of political controversy surrounding the question of patenting medicines, especially, but not only, in India. To their credit, my own political authorities, and European industry, finally accepted and agreed to what I was convinced was a fair deal.

Twenty years after the event, can it be convincingly argued that the interests of developing countries have been prejudiced by the outcome of the negotiations on pharmaceuticals? The contrary is probably the case. At least in some major developing countries, local producers have grown beyond recognition, leaving behind the limited scope of activity of producing generics ("generic" in terms of pre-TRIPS Agreement national law) by copying inventions made elsewhere. This growth has been encouraged by the confidence created by the establishment of an effective level of protection, the great progress made in reliable manufacturing methods, to the point where a substantial proportion of the active ingredients of pharmaceuticals consumed in Europe is now imported from state-of-the-art laboratories located, for example in India.

The main exception to this optimistic conclusion may be the phenomenon mentioned above, the absence of local, national administrative and/or political capability to apply all relevant aspects of the TRIPS Agreement, including its balancing elements, such as compulsory licences. The least-developed countries have been granted several exemptions or transition periods, the latest one being further extended until July 2021. However, if a country with the administrative and political capacity of certain "intermediate" developing countries has difficulties in applying the carefully drafted balance of rights and exceptions, how can one expect one of the least-developed countries to do so? Would common sense not suggest that at least an additional, substantial transition period be granted to the least-developed countries, falling short of exempting them completely from applying this part of the Agreement? If not, what credible, effective action could be taken to encourage full implementation? Granting a blank cheque, or an overdraft without a time limit, is also unlikely to generate a climate conducive to productive investments – much needed in least-developed countries.

Important problems have, however, emerged in major developed countries and in China. In the United States, the litigation system has allowed the emergence of the destructive phenomenon of "patent trolls" and the previous consensus in favour of those who undertake major R&D efforts is frayed at the edges and made very complex and expensive. As to China, its implementation of the TRIPS Agreement in general and of the patent chapter in particular still leaves much to be desired, because of strategies of favouring "national champions" and a general lack of judicial enforcement – particularly when a foreigner challenges a Chinese company. Do these developments militate in favour of a review of the patent chapter? Perhaps not, with at least one exception, but they do at least suggest that the chapter on enforcement should be substantially strengthened in all relevant respects.

The "one exception" concerns that notion of what constitutes "fair, reasonable and non-discriminatory" (FRAND) terms for licensing IP, especially in the context of international standard-setting. Major disagreements are emerging between key participants and decisions should not be made without a thorough public debate, and international negotiation, of what is in the global interest.

3. Geographical indications

The time and energy spent on discussing GIs was proportionate to the profound disagreement on the very principle of introducing such protection. This was a disagreement that existed not only between Europe (writ large) and Canada, the United States and Australia but also between the EC and a number of other countries to which European emigrants had brought with them the names (but not the *terroirs*) of the places from which they came.

Although economically important, the question was deeply "political" in the sense that the importance attached to protecting GI, or not, assumed the nature of a question of principle, on both sides of the fence.

I could, of course, make the argument for the European approach and position in my sleep, but this is hardly the place for partisan presentations, 20 years after the event. Suffice it to say that the controversy, for the Europeans at least, came to be seen as the fight of the small against the big producers, of traditional methods against industrial processes, even of "good food and drink" against what in French is called *malbouffe* ("junk food" would be the closest translation). To my counterparts, it became a political headache because Europe was trying to obtain a roll-back of existing (ab)uses of European origin appellations, or "usurpations", as we would somewhat poetically refer to them. This would have compelled producers using such names in those countries to abandon their use and adopt other ways of distinguishing their products.

The mixture of a question of basic principle with important commercial interests made the negotiations exceedingly difficult. For those on the other side of the fence, it was, naturally, very difficult to persuade, let alone force, private producers to abandon names that they had been using, sometimes for many years.

The final outcome, which I have just re-read after many years, looks like a sound compromise and was seen as such at the time. In substance, it introduces the principle of protecting GIs in all members of the WTO, defines what this means and then largely "grandfathers" existing use, or misuse as the EU would say, of what are mainly European origin appellations. To my mind, this is a convincing example of a reasonable compromise. It was also seen as the foundation for pursuing an ambition that the EU has subsequently tried to realize, and often succeeded in realizing, in bilateral negotiations, most recently in the free trade area negotiations with Canada.

Ironically, it should also be mentioned that more and more "New World" producers have adopted the concept. Hence, for example, Napa Valley wine producers have registered a GI.

4. Implementation

Has the TRIPS Agreement been implemented by all parties and is it being enforced? The short answer is no.

Days and weeks were spent on the "enforcement" section, which, in terms of WTO-type agreements, is probably a model of comprehensiveness and balance, not to speak of its successful compromise between principles of law enforcement prevalent in continental European civil law and those of the common law tradition.

There are two basic questions that arise in this context: are the basic provisions on substance faithfully implemented by all parties, and are the enforcement provisions, indispensable for the application of the former on the ground, put into effect?

The superficial impression is positive. The great majority of WTO members have put the provisions of the TRIPS Agreement into effect by adopting or adapting national law. Reality is, however, somewhat different.

One could argue that five important problems have emerged:

- As pointed out in the context of the patent protection section above, even advanced developing countries seem to have problems in administering some of the most essential provisions of the patent section, not necessarily to the detriment of the right owners, but to the detriment of their own population.

- Major problems of "real" implementation have been identified in countries such as China that have no tradition of protecting IP, often combined with prejudiced or corrupt law enforcement.

- Other problems have developed over the past two decades, especially in the field of patents, where the emergence of a new profession, that of "patent trolls", was certainly not foreseen at the time (it could, of course, be argued that this problem is not only one of enforcement or administration of rights but rather a problem of the US system of litigation).

- The consensus surrounding the basic principle of IP protection is being battered by the emergence of Internet service providers with opposing interests and other major companies with little investment in R&D and much investment in marketing and lobbying.

- The ever-growing importance of counterfeiting (see also below).

These are questions of major importance to which no answers have yet been found and which the members of the WTO should address, and soon.

5. Trade in counterfeit goods

Trade in counterfeit goods, and its repression, was, at the outset, one of the main objectives of the negotiations: "Negotiations shall aim to develop a multilateral framework of principles, rules and disciplines dealing with international trade in counterfeit goods, taking into account work already undertaken in the GATT."[3]

The outcome was an apparently impressive section on border enforcement, which should, of course, be read together with the provisions on enforcement, not to speak of the substantive standards regarding trademarks, copyright and so on.

Why is it, then, that trade in counterfeit goods and other forms of violation of IP rights, for example, on the Internet, have grown exponentially since 1990? Briefly, because the TRIPS Agreement turned out to be a small barrage against an unforeseen tsunami of very powerful interests.

The economic, social and political contexts then were very different from those of today. The Internet was in its infancy, and therefore, by definition, so were violations of rights, especially of trademarks, copyright and related rights. China was not yet a member of the WTO, nor did it occupy the predominant place as a country of origin of counterfeit goods. Twenty or 30 years ago, the use of physical border controls was significantly higher than today. At the European level, there were still physical borders at which goods could be controlled. Today, the EU has become a single entity without internal borders.

The Brave New Globalized World of today makes the fight against counterfeiting much more difficult than when the TRIPS Agreement was drafted, from both the political and a practical perspective: physical border controls have been reduced to a minimum, under pressure from consumers and importers; speedy and low-cost customs procedures have become of the essence. The profits reaped from trade in counterfeit goods have increased immensely, exceeding those derived from drugs trafficking for less risk, with an ever-growing involvement of criminal or even terrorist associations. Trade in counterfeit medicines, pesticides and fertilizers is jeopardizing the health and safety of millions of people. The growth of the Internet and violations of copyright have become virtually institutionalized, the political clout of certain Internet service providers being such that efforts to impose effective controls are being blocked at the level of the public authorities. Add to this a heady mixture of populism, such as the iconic status of a virtually totally unregulated Internet, sheer ignorance of the health impact of counterfeit medicines, and a short-sighted insistence on obtaining the lowest possible price for products at the expense of other objectives. Last, but not least, there has been a decline in the authority of governments, at least in most countries with democratically elected governments, in front of self-appointed "grassroots" NGOs, some of which have intervened in favour of major Internet companies.

Since it soon emerged that the enforcement section of the TRIPS Agreement was clearly insufficient to resolve these problems, a number of countries launched the

ACTA negotiations that led to the adoption of a text that was initialled by the negotiators, but its ratification was subsequently blocked in the EC and the United States, under the pressure of the forces summarized above. It is essential to underline that nothing in the ACTA text changed the substantive balance of the TRIPs Agreement (e.g. there was nothing on patents and *a fortiori* on public health, nothing on duration of copyright protection, etc.). ACTA focused exclusively on the enforcement aspects of commercial-scale violations of the TRIPS Agreement, which could be much improved.

This perpetuates an intolerable situation that, apart from its impact on innovation and creation, puts the lives of millions at risk. One phytosanitary product out of five is counterfeit and/or inherently dangerous. An unknown but also very high proportion of medicines is equally dangerous, even much more so in developing countries, where law enforcement and distribution channel controls are weaker.

This is not the place to propose concrete remedies. There is nothing wrong with the existing provisions of the TRIPS Agreement, but they have clearly become completely insufficient to combat, for example, new channels provided for counterfeiting, such as Internet sales – they represent a small barrage against a huge tsunami. We need a major effort by the WTO members to launch and complete negotiations on an anti-counterfeit treaty that would effectively address these problems, which are the responsibility of all public authorities and the result of a certain *laissez-aller* approach by all – governments, producers, exporters and importers alike.

Conclusions

Ever since the conclusion of the Uruguay Round, there have been attempts to relaunch a comprehensive negotiating process in the WTO. Most of these endeavours have met with failure or have been substantially delayed.

There has been much speculation and discussion surrounding the question of why this has been so. Many have argued that some of the key participants were not willing to accept the necessary compromises and concessions for classic economic reasons, and this remains, apparently, the majority view.

I believe that the reasons are much more fundamental.

First, as argued in the opening paragraphs of this chapter, the Uruguay Round was launched, conducted and concluded in an exceptionally favourable political, intellectual and economic environment. This environment no longer exists.

Second, there has emerged the political and psychological impact of globalization and the social upheaval caused by rapidly expanding international trade, which, by definition, means the reduction or elimination of production and employment in some sectors in some countries, hopefully, but not always, to be compensated by the growth of others.

Third, we have seen the growth of the opposition in many countries to any further international rule-making, perhaps in part as a reaction against the very ambitious outcome of the Uruguay Round. This also explains why most attempts at introducing new areas of rule-making or reviewing existing agreements have met with failure. (The notable, but very partial, exception to this is the Doha Declaration on the TRIPS Agreement and Public Health and the agreement reached in August 2003 to make it easier to export pharmaceuticals covered by a compulsory licence to an importing member that is unable to manufacture the product itself. This happened, however, more than ten years ago).

Fourth, the huge profits made on Internet sales have created a powerful lobby against IP enforcement of both copyright and trademarks. This lobby has been successful in intimidating legislators.

The Doha Round has now largely become focused on classic market access issues. The lack of progress has been presented as a major risk for the WTO system. Nevertheless, the very fact that the rulebook, as adopted in 1994, continues to apply, as witnessed by the dispute settlement system that is being actively used, means that the WTO is still alive and well.

Can this continue? In my view, yes, for several years to come, but rules adopted 20 years ago are beginning to show the signs of age and important gaps have emerged. The mistakes made inevitably by the negotiators, and the strains surrounding the application of certain agreements, all militate in favour of a major review. If this does not eventuate, the WTO agreements will continue, like Snow White, to hibernate until a prince arrives to wake them up. The question is whether that prince will be a harbinger of universal common sense and an understanding of shared interests, or will assume the guise of major upheaval, putting the achievements of the past in jeopardy.

We still have the choice.

Endnotes

1   GATT document MIN.DEC, Multilateral Trade Negotiations – The Uruguay Round – Ministerial
     Declaration on the Uruguay Round, 20 September 1986.

2   ACTA, the 2007–10 attempt to agree on IP enforcement rules. The parties were Australia,
     Canada, the EC and its member states, Japan, the Republic of Korea, Mexico, Morocco, New
     Zealand, Singapore, Switzerland and the United States.

3   GATT document MIN.DEC.

7

Some memories of the unique TRIPS negotiations

Matthijs Geuze

The invitation to contribute to this book was certainly a pleasant surprise. The question for me was what I should write about: I had not been one of the negotiators and the chapter on the TRIPS negotiations from the perspective of the GATT Secretariat is dealt with by Adrian Otten, who was the Secretary of the TRIPS Negotiating Group. Several suggestions were made by my co-authors and, upon reflection, I decided to contribute with just a short compilation of some memories in respect of a diverse set of aspects, whether trade-related or not.

No one from the IP world would have believed you in 1986, if you had said that, within ten years, a treaty would be in force among more than 100 countries and territories establishing international norms and standards for IP protection in respect of all main areas of IP. People would even have laughed at you. Yet, in 1995, the TRIPS Agreement entered into force, establishing definitions, scope of protection, duration, permissible exceptions to protection and enforcement procedures in respect of copyright and related rights, trademarks, geographical indications (GIs), industrial designs, patents, layout-designs of integrated circuits and undisclosed information.

Before I joined the GATT Secretariat, in July 1989, I had worked as a legal officer at the Dutch Patent Office since 1981, involved in opposition and appeal procedures, which had allowed me to get insights into procedural as well as substantive law aspects of patent law. The job had also, however, allowed me to gain some experience in legislative work in the area of patents, trademarks and industrial designs, as well as in international negotiations, in particular in the area of trademarks – as I was part of the delegation of the Netherlands in the negotiations on the European Community Trademark Regulation and Directive, and in the negotiations in WIPO on the Madrid Protocol concerning the international registration of marks.

This experience was definitely a helpful background for the job in the GATT Secretariat during the TRIPS negotiations, in particular in respect of the nitty-gritty IP law aspects. For example, in June 1990, the Secretariat was entrusted by the TRIPS Negotiating Group to prepare a composite draft text of the various draft texts that had been tabled by delegations. This composite draft text was prepared by a Secretariat team that reported to David Hartridge and consisted of Adrian Otten, Arvind Subramaniam, Daniel Gervais and me. It was not an easy task, to decide on the approach to take in reflecting the various policy and legal aspects in a balanced way. I remember very well that, once the composite draft text had been put together by the four of us, Daniel and I went through the document for a final check, using, as Adrian called it, a very fine comb. The composite draft text became the starting point of a textual negotiation that resulted, a year and a half later, in the draft TRIPS agreement that formed part of the Draft Final Act of the Uruguay Round of multilateral trade negotiations dated 20 December 1991, the so-called Dunkel Draft. As explained elsewhere in this book, that draft of the TRIPS Agreement functioned, as of 1992, as a draft treaty establishing *de facto* international standards for IP protection. The text was adopted with very few changes as part of the Marrakesh Agreement Establishing the WTO (WTO Agreement) in 1994.

Another remembrance relates specifically to Article 27.3(b) of the TRIPS Agreement. The text of this provision was presented to the Chair of the TRIPS Negotiating Group, Ambassador Lars Anell, at some point late in the negotiations, as the result of negotiations between the "Quad" – Canada, the European Communities, Japan and the United States – and several developing countries, among which were Brazil and India. The text differed from earlier drafts that had been on the table in the Negotiating Group. When the Chair enquired about these differences, at the time that the group presented the text to him, John Gero of the Canadian delegation responded that this text was acceptable to all who had negotiated it. No explanations were given. The text found its way into the Dunkel Draft without any change. Article 27.3(b) allows for exceptions to patentable subject matter in respect of living matter, while, at the same time, requiring certain types of inventions in this category to be protectable under patent law or, as far as plant varieties are concerned, alternatively, an effective *sui generis* system or any combination of the two. Questions have since been asked as to how Article 27.3(b) should be interpreted, in particular as the provision was negotiated at a time when there were also other negotiations taking place relevant to aspects addressed in Article 27.3(b), that is, those that led to the revision of the International Convention for the Protection of New Varieties of Plants (UPOV

Convention) and those resulting in the adoption of the Convention on Biological Diversity. In this regard, the TRIPS negotiators seem to have opted for constructive ambiguity.

There are more provisions of this kind in the TRIPS Agreement, and the interpretation of several of these has meanwhile been addressed in proceedings under the WTO dispute settlement system. I may refer to the provisions of Articles 13, 17 and 30; the negotiators chose to model all three on Article 13 of the Berne Convention for the Protection of Literary and Artistic Works, despite the textual differences that were necessary in view of the different nature of the rights conferred under copyright law, trademark law and patent law, respectively. Article 20, which could also be mentioned in this regard, could not be modelled on a provision of one of the pre-existing IP conventions. The provision deals with the issue of special requirements encumbering the use of a trademark in the course of trade. Two real-life issues had been mentioned during the negotiations, namely, (i) a requirement in some jurisdictions to the effect that goods or services of a foreign company – and their trademark for these goods or services – could only be used in these countries and territories through a local company and together with the trademark of the local company; and (ii) a requirement that trademarks for pharmaceuticals could only be used together with the generic name of the pharmaceutical, in such a way that the generic name would predominantly appear on the packaging, for example, three times the size of the trademark. These two situations are reflected in Article 20, in a more general way – "use with another trademark" and "use in a special form" – and together with other criteria of a more general nature.

Of course, I would like to address here also a recollection from the negotiations concerning the provisions of the TRIPS Agreement on GIs. However, in view of my current position in WIPO, I cannot do so without the necessary restraints. Let me just say that I cannot imagine that anybody would have thought that the membership of the Lisbon Agreement for the Protection of Appellations of Origin and their International Registration would grow after the entry into force of the TRIPS Agreement. Rather the contrary. In 1995, the Lisbon Agreement had 17 member states and no new accessions had taken place since 1977. Then the TRIPS Agreement entered into force in 1995 (as part of the WTO Agreement), among more than 100 WTO members, requiring them – albeit subject to transitional periods – to provide, *inter alia*, for the protection of GIs. When preparing the implementation of their obligations under the TRIPS Agreement, many WTO members have taken initiatives that have resulted in the establishment of GIs for local products from their territories. Apparently, several have also looked at the Lisbon Agreement in this connection, as the Lisbon Union has welcomed 11 new accessions since 1997 and about 25 per cent of the current registrations were filed after 1995. True, the number of members of the Lisbon Union is still modest, but interest in the Lisbon System is growing, in particular in view of the revision process that the Lisbon Union initiated in 2008, with the objective of refining and modernizing the legal framework of the Lisbon System and, thus, of allowing for accession by the largest possible number of countries or entities, including intergovernmental organizations administering regional systems for the registration of GIs. This revision process was finalized in May 2015 with the adoption of the Geneva Act of the Lisbon Agreement on Appellations of Origin and Geographical Indications.

In its section on copyright and related rights, the TRIPS Agreement excludes, in Article 9.1, the protection of moral rights under Article 6*bis* of the Berne Convention from rights and obligations under the TRIPS Agreement. During the negotiations, it was clear that obligations existing under the Berne Convention itself in respect of moral rights should be safeguarded from this exclusion. In the decisive debate on how this should all be reflected in the TRIPS Agreement, an attempt was made to draft the provision in such a way that it would not exclude the protection of moral rights from rights and obligations under the TRIPS Agreement but, instead, incorporate the norms and standards of Article 6*bis* of the Berne Convention, while allowing any WTO member to make a reservation in that regard. In the end, the exclusion provision was retained. As regards obligations in respect of moral rights under the Berne Convention, these should be understood to be safeguarded by Article 2.2 of the TRIPS Agreement. An interesting question in this regard is, of course, whether the violation of a safeguard provision can be the subject of dispute settlement under the TRIPS Agreement.

Let me finish this brief contribution with an anecdote from one of the meetings of the TRIPS Negotiating Group. It concerns a debate on one of the issues on which the delegations of India and the United States had diametrically opposed positions. The debate had already taken much of the Negotiating Group's time that morning, when the Chair announced that only a few minutes were left before the meeting had to be interrupted for lunch and that it was his intention to close the debate on the issue before lunch. However, he still had two requests for the floor – from the delegations of India and the United States. With these words, he gave the floor to A.V. Ganesan of the Indian delegation, who said: "Would you like us to make a joint statement, Mr. Chairman?"

Part III

Perspectives from the developed world

8

Negotiating for the United States

Catherine Field[1]

Introduction

The TRIPS Agreement introduced a new foundation for IP agreements. Through the TRIPS Agreement, WTO members established minimum standards for the protection of the broadest range of IP ever addressed in a single agreement and broke new ground with the acceptance of norms for domestic enforcement of IPRs. The Agreement forged new and stronger connections between trade policy and other domestic policies, including enforcement and competition policy, and, for the first time, IP issues were subject to an effective international dispute settlement mechanism.

The negotiations on the TRIPS Agreement presented significant challenges for the trade and IP communities. Negotiators tackled a wide array of new and difficult issues, for example, defining and recognizing rights in "undisclosed information" and establishing norms on domestic enforcement of IPRs. Trade negotiators and IP experts had to learn each other's policy perspectives and language, and officials from some United States (US) agencies became participants in a trade negotiation for the first time. Congress and private sector groups were key drivers in the US negotiating process.

During the negotiations, developed countries, including Canada, Japan and the United States, as well as the European Communities (EC), pursued objectives between themselves, including major issues related to copyright, such as rental rights, moral rights and contractual rights, patentability of agricultural chemicals and pharmaceuticals, and trademarks and geographical indications (GIs). Often, the most difficult issues to resolve in the negotiations were those arising between these major trading partners. For their part, developing countries sought recognition of the need to achieve transfer of technology and prevent abuse of IPRs, and some developing countries, such as India, pursued affirmative objectives in the negotiations on issues such as copyright and GIs.

As discussed below, the TRIPS Agreement reflects pragmatic compromises with regard to achieving various objectives and the timing for implementation of results. While negotiators were able to produce an agreement that achieved key objectives for many participants, some issues remained to be resolved. Time and technology have diminished the significance of some of the issues that were left outstanding from the TRIPS negotiations, others have been addressed in other negotiations, but some still remain and many new issues involving the interface of IP with other issues have arisen.

This chapter sets out a personal perspective on the negotiations – the initiation of negotiations in the context of the GATT, US objectives for certain issues, the negotiating process and the results of that process. The TRIPS Agreement has now been in effect for 20 years. WTO members face new issues, such as the connection between IPRs and standards-setting and licensing practices and whether too much protection can prevent innovation, prompting policy makers to consider maximum as well as minimum levels of protection. The chapter concludes with a few brief observations on the IP issues that are currently demanding the attention of policy makers.

Accepting IP as an issue for negotiation in the GATT

A patchwork of multilateral obligations and increases in trade in counterfeit goods

Prior to the TRIPS Agreement, multilateral disciplines on the protection and enforcement of IPRs were the subject of international treaties, most of which were negotiated and administered under the aegis of WIPO. Texts of the two principal treaties, the Paris Convention for the Protection of Industrial Property (Paris Convention) and the Berne Convention for the Protection of Literary and Artistic Works (Berne Convention), dated back to the nineteenth century. As of 1986, some GATT contracting parties did not participate in these and other IP treaties or adhered to an early version of the relevant treaty. The United States, for example, did not become a party to the Berne Convention until March 1989. Chile, Colombia and India – and several other contracting parties – were not parties to the Paris Convention, and Canada applied the 1938 version of Articles 1–12 of that Convention.[2] These and other international IP treaties were based in part on national treatment and, in some cases, permitted parties to require reciprocity as a condition for a particular right. The scope and terms of protection for new technology, such as computer programs and biotechnology, had not been established. While the GATT (1947) included a few references to IP, for example,

Articles, IX, XVIII and XX, these provisions did little to address core IP issues, such as lack of consistency in the level of protection, weak standards and uncertainty over the protection of new technologies.

During the 1970s and 1980s, governments saw a surge in both the development of new technologies – such as computer software and biotechnology – and international trade, including trade in counterfeit and pirated goods (counterfeit goods). IP owners faced significant difficulties in enforcing IP rights, in particular in obtaining remedies that deterred infringement.

During the Tokyo Round (1974–9), the United States and some other GATT contracting parties began negotiations on an Agreement on Measures to Discourage the Importation of Counterfeit Goods (Anti-Counterfeiting Code). Participants failed to conclude negotiations on the Anti-Counterfeiting Code during the Tokyo Round, but intensified efforts before the 1982 GATT ministers' meeting. Faced with resistance from some developing countries regarding whether the GATT was the appropriate forum for negotiating and concluding an Anti-Counterfeiting Agreement, ministers instructed the GATT Council to:

> [E]xamine the question of counterfeit goods with a view to determining the appropriateness of joint action in the GATT framework on the trade aspects of commercial counterfeiting and, if such joint action is found to be appropriate, the modalities for such action, having full regard to the competence of other international organizations.[3]

The draft Anti-Counterfeiting Code included requirements for parties to provide owners of trademarks the means to initiate procedures to protect rights against imported counterfeit goods, and some of the principles and language of the draft Anti-Counterfeiting Code can be found in the border enforcement section of the TRIPS Agreement. While the United States considered the draft Anti-Counterfeiting Code ready to conclude in 1985, action on the Code and addressing IP more generally in the Uruguay Round of multilateral trade negotiations continued to face resistance from some delegations as ministers met at Punta del Este to decide on initiating the Round.

Developments in the United States

In the 1980s, a wide spectrum of US industries that rely on IP protection were working to strengthen the link between access to the US market and whether a country provided adequate and effective protection and enforcement of IPRs.

The first tangible result of their efforts was seen in the Trade and Tariff Act of 1984 (1984 Act). That legislation included protection and enforcement of IP as a criterion for evaluating whether a country should receive preferential market access under the US Generalized System of Preferences (GSP). The 1984 Act also spelled out that denial of adequate and effective IP protection and enforcement was an unreasonable act, policy or practice within the meaning of Section 301 of the Trade Act of 1974. That provision authorizes the President (and subsequently the US Trade Representative) to take action to address unreasonable acts, policies or practices that burdened or restricted US commerce.

In 1985, President Reagan delivered remarks endorsing the initiation of a new round of negotiations, including on IPR. Subsequently, the Reagan Administration issued a White Paper on IP and initiated investigations under Section 301 in regard to the Republic of Korea's IP regime and Brazil's treatment of computers and computer software (Informatics). The United States was sending a strong message that maintaining access to its market was linked to having adequate IP protection.

Achieving a strong agreement on IPR in the Uruguay Round negotiations was a top offensive objective for the United States. The United States saw IP as the future for US high-tech industries and economic growth, and industry was able to identify significant economic harm resulting from lack of protection and enforcement of IPRs. In addition, US policy makers believed that including IP in the Uruguay Round negotiating package and achieving an outcome that set the stage for increased trade in IP-based goods would build support for the results of the Round as a whole, and help overcome domestic objections to a result that addressed sensitive issues for the United States, such as textiles, safeguards and anti-dumping.

In 1988, after a three-year effort, Congress enacted the Omnibus Trade and Competitiveness Act of 1988 (1988 Act), which provided guidance to US negotiators on objectives for the Uruguay Round negotiations, including on IP and dispute settlement.[4] The 1988 Act also included a provision known as Special 301. Based on a statutory requirement to identify countries that denied adequate and effective protection and enforcement of IPRs or market access for goods embodying IPRs, the Office of the US Trade Representative and other agencies developed a process for reviewing IP regimes of other countries and used it as a mechanism to organize and prioritize bilateral engagement on IP issues.

Starting in 1989, the United States began an intensive process of review and engagement with its trading partners on trade-related IP issues. US objectives in the TRIPS negotiations were one of the benchmarks used in evaluating partners' IP standards and enforcement. Before and during the Uruguay Round negotiations, the United States successfully engaged with its trading partners as part of its GSP process and under Special 301 to obtain improvements in IP protection in other countries. For example, Singapore enacted improvements to its copyright law and Korea strengthened its protection of copyrights, patents and trademarks. In the TRIPS negotiations, Special 301 was the target of repeated objections and claims of unilateral action intended to improve the negotiating position of the United States. Special 301, and actions the United States took under it, provided motivation for those delegations seeking to prevent unilateral trade actions as reflected in proposals in the TRIPS and dispute settlement negotiations.

Status of TRIPS in the Uruguay Round negotiations

The early years, 1987–8

The mandate for the TRIPS negotiations was one of the last elements of the Punta del Este Ministerial Declaration to be resolved. The TRIPS negotiating mandate consisted of three paragraphs, including the instruction that the "negotiations shall aim to clarify GATT provisions and elaborate, as appropriate, new rules and disciplines". Negotiations were to aim to develop a multilateral framework of principles, rules and disciplines dealing with trade in counterfeit goods, taking into account work already undertaken in the GATT. Finally, the negotiations were not to prejudice other "complementary initiatives" in WIPO.[5]

Under the TRIPS work plan that the GATT Council adopted in February 1987,[6] the Negotiating Group spent innumerable hours debating the scope of the Group's mandate. At the same time, however, many delegations engaged in an internal process of determining objectives and educating trade experts on IP issues. In the early stage of the negotiations, the United States, the EC, Switzerland, Thailand, the Nordic countries, Brazil and other delegations submitted general papers setting out views on the scope and nature of negotiating objectives and how they should be achieved. The GATT and WIPO Secretariats produced documents on the status of protection of various IPRs and enforcement.[7] Reflecting its view that the Anti-Counterfeiting Code was ready to sign in 1987, the United States proposed that GATT contracting parties sign the Code and reap an "early harvest" for the negotiations. Delegations did not take up that proposal, and the debate continued until April 1989 over whether it was appropriate to include anything more than provisions related to importation of counterfeit goods in the GATT and, if so, what types of provisions should be subject to negotiation.

In October 1988, the United States submitted to the TRIPS Negotiating Group a detailed proposal on standards for IP protection and enforcement to be included in a TRIPS agreement.[8] The proposal included legal text on standards for the protection of patents, trademarks, copyrights, trade secrets and integrated circuits, as well as on civil and criminal enforcement of those rights. Descriptive language addressed the issues of dispute settlement, national and most-favoured nation (MFN) treatment as well as international cooperation. Other delegations also submitted general proposals. This proposal and those from other delegations, including from the EC, Japan, and Switzerland,[9] which followed in 1989, provided the necessary building blocks for the substantive negotiations.

After the mid-term review, 1989–93

In April 1989, as part of the Montreal mid-term review, ministers resolved that negotiations could include substantive provisions on IP protection and enforcement. Ministers agreed, *inter alia*, that negotiations would continue and encompass:

- the applicability of the basic principles of the GATT and of relevant international IP agreements or conventions;

- the provision of adequate standards and principles concerning the availability, scope and use of trade-related IPRs;

- the provision of effective and appropriate means for the enforcement of trade-related IPRs, taking into account differences in national legal regimes;

- the provision of effective and expeditious procedures for the multilateral prevention and settlement of disputes between governments, including the applicability of GATT procedures;

- transitional arrangements aiming at the fullest participation in the result of the negotiations.

Ministers also agreed that the negotiations would include consideration of the "underlying public policy objectives" of national systems for the protection of IP, "including developmental and technological objectives".

In addition, negotiations were to include the development of a multilateral framework of principles, rules and disciplines dealing with international trade in counterfeit goods.

Another key element of the Ministerial Declaration was agreement that the negotiations were without prejudice to views concerning the institutional aspects of the international implementation of the results and that this would be decided at the end of the negotiations. The TRIPS Negotiating Group maintained work on international trade in counterfeit goods as a separate agenda item until the end of the negotiations, which resulted in duplicative and often overlapping drafts on this issue.

Work done in parallel with the TRIPS negotiations

The delay in reaching a consensus to engage in detailed, text-based negotiations had both immediate and longer term benefits for the negotiating process. Trade and IP experts had the opportunity to become familiar with their respective IP regimes and policies, assess other participants' objectives for the TRIPS negotiations and identify their own objectives and sensitivities. The EC, for example, needed the time to obtain a mandate on negotiating IP standards and thus focused its initial efforts on enforcement, where it had competency.

During this period, the WTO Secretariat produced a number of factual papers that informed the negotiations and helped identify gaps in IP protection and enforcement under existing international IP agreements. The Chair of the Negotiating Group, Ambassador Lars Anell of Sweden, began a process of meeting with individual delegations and groups of delegations to encourage candid exchanges of views, and then providing reports on those meetings to the broader group to provide transparency in the negotiations.

Delegations began meeting in various groups to exchange views and build support for proposals. At the early stages of the negotiations, a group of like-minded contracting parties (the Friends of Intellectual Property group) started meeting and discussing core issues. Switzerland and the United States hosted seminars on existing IP standards and domestic enforcement regimes, which improved the negotiators' level of knowledge on IP and related trade issues. All of these initiatives built confidence in the process and strengthened relationships between negotiators as well as with the Chair and Secretariat. As the negotiations progressed and delegations tackled the many "hard" issues between them, groups often formed and reformed based on the particular issue under negotiation. During the later stages of the negotiation, work among the "Quad" countries (Canada, the EC, Japan and the United States) was often the most contentious. On some issues, one or more of the Quad countries would share the views of some developing country delegations and form the core of support for, or opposition to, a particular proposal. For example, the United States and India shared views on aspects of copyright protection, while Canada and India opposed some of the US proposals on patents.

During 1987–8, industry groups engaged intensively with their counterparts in other countries to reach a consensus on the substance of a comprehensive agreement on IP in the GATT. Independent groups, such as the Intellectual Property Committee and the IP Task Force of the US Chamber of Commerce, produced specific recommendations for negotiators. In particular, the Intellectual Property Committee, the Keidanren of Japan, and the Union of Industrial and Employers' Confederations of Europe (UNICE) issued a common statement of views in their *Basic Framework of GATT Provisions on Intellectual Property: Statement of Views of the European, Japanese and United States Business Communities*, in June 1988. While this statement assumed that an IP agreement in the GATT would be a code, many of the principles and ideas expressed in this document provided useful guidance on the business communities' perspective and what disciplines they could support, thus providing a better foundation for the intensive negotiations that commenced in earnest in the spring of 1989.

Summary

As of April 1989, negotiations on IP standards and enforcement requirements began in earnest after more than 10 years of debate over whether even more limited disciplines could be appropriate to include in the GATT. A multitude of reasons, ranging from progress on other trade issues to domestic politics, likely contribute to the explanation of why delegations agreed to negotiate a broad, substantive IP agreement. Among those reasons, I would highlight the growing concern of governments and industry regarding IP issues and the determination of some, in particular the US Government, to take trade action to address those concerns. Further delay or refusal to negotiate on issues such as IP meant risking market access. The emphasis that some delegations placed on dispute settlement —generally, and in regards to the TRIPS Agreement – also supports the view that some participants in the TRIPS negotiation now recognized that enforceable disciplines could provide a shield against unilateral action. Changes in IP or more general economic policies have been mentioned as reasons for the change in position on IP negotiations. That said, while GATT contracting parties agreed that negotiations on substantive standards and enforcement requirements could move forward, delegations reserved the right to assess the entire package and what, if any, IP disciplines would be implemented in the GATT.

Objectives, negotiations and results

General observations

With over half of the announced negotiating period for the Uruguay Round having expired, TRIPS negotiators engaged in intensive work in the run-up to the ministerial meeting in Brussels in December 1990. In May 1989, delegations asked the Secretariat to produce a synoptic table of submissions from delegations regarding substantive standards for the protection of IPRs. This approach was replicated with enforcement issues, as well as for proposals focused on addressing trade in counterfeit goods. At the participants' direction, the Secretariat left nothing out of the synoptic table and its revisions. This provided a good format for delegations to see the degree of divergence on each issue and encouraged drafting that narrowed that divergence.

In the spring of 1990, the EC, the United States, a group of 14 developing countries, Switzerland, Japan and Australia each submitted detailed proposals including specific standards for the protection and enforcement of IPRs.[10] The US submission was the product of months of internal work, including input from a wide range of agencies that had a direct or indirect stake in protection or enforcement of IPRs. While the United States had consulted intensively with the EC and other delegations, significant divergences existed on several subjects, including copyright and neighbouring rights, GIs and some aspects of patent protection.

In June 1990, the first consolidated text was produced for discussion. Six successive bracketed texts were produced between June and November 1990, along with countless "room documents" that delegations circulated as part of the discussions. Negotiators made progress on areas where delegations agreed in principle on substance and wording was the main issue. With essential guidance from the Chair, the process of reaching agreement on language that delegations could "live with" ensued. Based on these intensive negotiations, in November 1990, the Chair of the TRIPS Negotiating Group provided a text that was incorporated into the comprehensive text for the Brussels ministerial meeting. The IP text was incomplete as several critical issues remained unresolved, including patent and copyright issues and dispute settlement. While the Brussels ministerial meeting concluded with an impasse on several issues, in particular on those related to agriculture, the Uruguay Round negotiations resumed in 1991. On TRIPS, delegations met almost non-stop to address the remaining issues, many of which were the most difficult and contentious. At the end of the year, the Chair circulated a proposed text that delegations were asked to evaluate and accept as part of the final Uruguay Round package. As with the other draft texts developed in the TRIPS negotiations, the Chair circulated it on his own responsibility. In some cases, the Chair proposed solutions, such as the language in Article 27.1 on non-discrimination in enjoyment of patent rights and the transition periods, and asked delegations to decide whether they could live with the proposal. The text that the Chair circulated at the end of 1991 became the TRIPS Agreement with only two changes. In 1992, negotiations on the overall Uruguay Round package were suspended until delegations were able to address key obstacles in the agriculture negotiations. In 1993, when the TRIPS and other Uruguay Round negotiations resumed, the United States presented five proposals to address concerns expressed in the United States about the text, which were not accepted. The Negotiating Group did adopt two US proposals to limit the grounds for issuing a compulsory licence on a patent for semiconductor products and to adopt a moratorium on non-violation disputes on IP issues.

Comments on the negotiating process

The negotiations concerning the TRIPS Agreement and the text that evolved from those negotiations reflect certain axioms that, in my view, apply generally. The fact that the TRIPS Agreement and its negotiating process are consistent with these axioms may help explain why the TRIPS Agreement changed the IP landscape and became an important part of the WTO Agreement.

The first axiom is that all participants in the negotiations need to benefit from something in the package. In this case, that package could be within the TRIPS Agreement itself or the larger Uruguay Round package. In the Uruguay Round package, these benefits varied, but most were linked to market access, such as increased market access for textiles and agriculture, improved protection and enforcement of IP, which would promote exports of IP-based goods and licensing of IP, or market access for services. The package also included a mechanism to enforce rights and obligations, which helped induce implementation and provided some safeguards against unilateral action.

Second, each participant needs to prioritize its objectives and be willing to make changes in its own regime – even somewhat difficult ones. That was certainly the case for the United States in the context of the TRIPS negotiations. Some of the changes that the United States made to implement the TRIPS Agreement were controversial. For example, in the copyright area, changes to US law related to Article 18 of the Berne Convention were the subject of domestic litigation that was not resolved until 2014, when the US Supreme Court decided that the relevant change in US law did not violate the US Constitution.[11] The legislation implementing Article 33 (Term of Patent Protection) as applied to pre-existing patents also provoked controversy and litigation in the United States. The United States also amended Section 337 of the Tariff Act of 1930, which involves enforcement of IPRs at the border, in the legislation implementing the results of the Uruguay Round negotiations. These changes had been subject to intensive debate for nearly five years.

At an appropriate point in the negotiations, delegations need to engage in a realistic assessment of potential outcomes. With regard to "must achieve" objectives, the successful pursuit of such an objective likely depends on its nature. Does the objective require a change to a country's domestic law or practice that is consistent with the overall direction of a country's system and its longer term goals, or would the objective require a change to a core principle of that country's IP or other regime? As seen in the TRIPS negotiations, the former may be achieved, while the latter may be unattainable or not implemented as envisioned.

Finally, flexibility is essential and with it negotiations can make progress in achieving even difficult objectives. Progress can occur through a text that encourages certain action, through the development of norms in other fora, for example, regional agreements, which can provide ideas and approaches that may be adopted later on a multilateral basis, and through continued domestic debate and further experience with particular issues.

In 1989, some delegations raised major systemic issues for negotiation that had eluded resolution in other fora, for example, requiring parties to adopt a first-to-file patent system and enhanced protection of GIs, as well as particular trade irritants, for example, procedures for enforcement of IPRs at the border through Section 337. Other delegations sought to "safeguard" the ability to protect against abuse of IPRs (patent licensing), promote transfer of technology and maintain space for pursuing other policy objectives. During the negotiating process for the TRIPS Agreement, each delegation had to prioritize its objectives and decide how to address "deal-breaker" issues (both offensive and defensive) for it and other delegations. The resulting text had to be acceptable at each level, that is, particular article, IP topic, agreement and as part of the overall Uruguay Round results. This was achieved through hard work, flexibility and pragmatism, and good will on the part of all participants.

Observations on how the negotiations played out on specific topics

1. The patent complex (patents, undisclosed information and transitional provisions, including exclusive marketing rights)

General observations

The negotiations on the patent complex involved two major elements: (i) general aspects of patent protection, such as term and scope of protection and conditions for compulsory licensing, and (ii) issues related to the unavailability of product patents for pharmaceuticals and agricultural chemicals in some countries and protecting otherwise undisclosed data that must be submitted to obtain government approval for marketing pharmaceuticals and agricultural chemicals. Often these issues, along with proposals on use of a patent without the authorization of the right holder, were considered as a package with "trade-offs" proposed among the various provisions. Proponents of addressing the data protection issues, including the United States, focused on the diminished "effective" term of patents for pharmaceuticals and agricultural chemical products, and providing a means for applicants for product patents for pharmaceuticals and agricultural chemicals to secure some benefit under the TRIPS Agreement in the near term. The United States and other proponents noted that, unlike other IPRs, obtaining a patent for a pharmaceutical took several years and marketing approval additional years and required large expenditures of time and resources.

The negotiations on rights and obligations related to patents presented some of the most complex and contentious issues in the negotiations. Among developed countries, the general standards for patent protection, such as the term of protection, varied widely. While many countries provided a term of 20 years from the date a patent application was filed, some countries provided a shorter term, for example, 16 years. When the TRIPS negotiations started, Canada and the United States calculated the term of protection from the date of grant of the patent. In 1989, Canada moved to a term of 20 years from the date the application is filed. Additionally, product patents for pharmaceuticals and agricultural chemicals were not available in all developed countries. Spain, Portugal and Greece had agreed to provide product patents for pharmaceuticals after a transition period that ended in 1992, and Canada did not provide product patents for pharmaceuticals until 1993.

Objectives and results for patent standards

As of 1989, the main negotiating objectives for the patent section related to patentable subject matter, rights conferred, term of protection, limitations and exceptions, patent-related procedures including first-to-file and reversal of burden of proof in cases involving process patents, and provisions on "Other Use without the Authorization of the Right Holder" (compulsory or non-voluntary licensing). At least one objective – requiring a party to adopt a first-to-file patent system – would have required a basic change in the US patent system. This objective was not achieved.

The key objective for the United States and several other delegations was to ensure that product patents would be available for pharmaceuticals and agricultural chemicals. This objective was achieved, but with flexibilities provided in other provisions in the patent complex.

Most delegations had to deal with various exceptions in their respective domestic laws. Common exceptions were included in proposals on the matter made by the EC, Switzerland, Japan and a group of developing countries.[12] For some delegations, exceptions such as the one relating to patenting humans were based on moral as well as legal grounds. The exception for plants or animals other than micro-organisms and essentially biological processes for the production of plants or animals (other than non-biological and microbiological processes) reflected the state of domestic law for many participants in the negotiations.

Contrary to the US proposal,[13] the TRIPS Agreement explicitly enumerates exceptions from patentable subject matter. Given the overwhelming support for exceptions, the United States worked to craft text that could prevent their abuse. The exception for exclusions from patentable subject matter necessary to protect *ordre public* or morality, for example, is conditioned on the requirement that the party prohibit the commercial exploitation of the invention.

The EC's initial proposal also included a provision on "Exceptions to Rights Conferred".[14] That proposal included examples of certain acts that could be excepted from a patent holder's rights provided that the exception took into account the legitimate interests of the patent holder and third parties. Many delegations welcomed this proposal and initially engaged in a debate on the list of actions mentioned in the text. Not surprisingly, that list grew to include the exceptions from each participant's domestic law. After extensive debate, negotiators adopted general language drawn from the Berne Convention that included the elements relating to normal commercial exploitation of the patent, the interests of the patent holder and those of third parties. This approach preserved flexibility and addressed concerns that an excepted act would be omitted from the list.

Another element of flexibility in the patent text related to "other use without the authorization of the patent owner" (compulsory licences). The discussion of this matter was intertwined with the debate on elimination or maintenance of a requirement in domestic law to "work" (manufacture domestically) the patent within a certain period from its grant or face a compulsory licence, if requested. Elimination of the so-called "working requirement", that is, a requirement for use of a process or manufacture of a product in the country granting the patent within a certain time period, was a major objective of the United States and the EC. Industry support for approval and implementation of any IP agreement required a good outcome on this issue.

While governments seldom granted compulsory licences for non-working, governments used these provisions more often as a threat to induce a "voluntary" licence or investment in domestic production. During the negotiations, some developing countries sought an explicit obligation for a patent holder to work the invention in the country granting the patent within the time period specified in national legislation. While the Paris Convention recognizes the possibility for a party to grant a compulsory licence for failure to work the patent in that party, the Convention does not require parties to include such requirements in domestic law.[15]

Building on the trade concept of non-discrimination, the Chair of the Negotiating Group proposed compromise language that, subject to the transitional provisions in the agreement, "patents shall be available and patent rights enjoyable without discrimination as to the place of invention, the field of technology and whether products are imported or locally produced". Delegations were asked if they could live with this compromise, taking into account the provisions on limitations and exceptions and compulsory licences. This language now appears in the TRIPS Agreement.

The TRIPS Agreement also needed to deal with those cases in which a party's domestic law provided for a compulsory or non-voluntary licence. These provisions could be found in laws on a variety of subject matter, including government or sovereign use provisions and competition law. The United States recognized that its domestic law had provisions under which the government or others on behalf of the government could use a patent upon payment of full compensation. In addition, a compulsory licence, in theory, could be part of a settlement or remedy in a competition matter.

The United States, the EC, Japan and Switzerland, among others, shared the objective of a transparent process of decision-making on the grant of a compulsory licence, with recourse to judicial review of that decision available to the right holder, and payment of appropriate remuneration. Limitations on the use, for example, scope and duration, of compulsory licences also had strong support. After considerable discussion, negotiators were able to propose conditions that applied to compulsory licences generally and which relied on concepts of "public non-commercial use", "national emergency" and other "circumstances of extreme urgency" to provide flexibility and serve as the basis for a waiver of the requirement for prior negotiations on a voluntary licence. The United States and others also proposed language to deal with the special case of a compulsory licence to address anti-competitive behaviour. This language permitted competition authorities to pursue remedies resulting from actions to address anti-competitive practices such as abuse of IPR licensing, subject to other provisions of the Agreement, including Article 40.

With regard to other patent issues, such as rights conferred and term of protection, negotiations focused on the development of a consensus on the details rather than agreement on basic principles. Reversal of the burden of proof in civil actions for infringement of a process patent was a widely held objective, since proof of infringement required information uniquely in the hands of the alleged infringer. Although reaching a consensus on how to achieve this objective required detailed discussions of the various legal mechanisms that were available and flexibility on the part of all, negotiators reached a consensus on the conditions that would give rise to a presumption of infringement, thus providing an incentive for the alleged infringer to provide the necessary information on the process it used.

Objectives and results on protection of undisclosed test and other data submitted to obtain marketing approval

In addition to achieving recognition of undisclosed information as a form of IP and reaching agreement on a basic standard for its protection, the EC, Switzerland and the United States sought disciplines on the use of undisclosed test and other data submitted to governments to obtain marketing approval for pharmaceuticals and agricultural chemicals. Difficult discussions ensured, reflecting the differing policy perspectives among delegations. At the later stages of the negotiation, the EC, Canada and India presented the Negotiating Group with a package proposal to resolve the patent complex, which covered compulsory licences, protection of undisclosed information to obtain marketing approval of pharmaceuticals and agricultural chemicals, and transitional provisions linked to the availability of product patents for pharmaceuticals and agricultural chemicals.

The United States had significant difficulties with this package proposal, in particular with regard to protection of undisclosed data submitted to obtain marketing approval and the transitional provisions. Although the final text of Article 39.3 includes some elements of the initial proposals from the United States, several limitations were included and specific references to the duration of the protection were deleted. Article 39.3 refers to "new chemical entities", and requires considerable effort in the development of the relevant data and the protection of that data against "unfair commercial use" (which is not defined) for an unspecified period of time. While parties are required to protect the data against disclosure, except where necessary to protect the public, or unless steps are taken to ensure that the data are protected against "unfair commercial use", again, this second obligation is for an unspecified period of time. The absence of a definition of "unfair commercial use" and the open-ended nature of the obligations have led to a continuing debate over the meaning of the obligation.

Certain transitional provisions (Article 70.8 and 70.9): Objectives and results

While inventors of pharmaceutical or agricultural chemical products could apply for product patents when a party implemented the relevant provisions of the TRIPS Agreement, it would be many years before that patent holder could realize benefits from the patented product due to the time taken for patent examination and obtaining marketing approval for these types of products. In its early submission, the United States had proposed a form of transitional protection for products which were not previously patentable subject matter. Under this proposal, India, for example, would have provided protection for certain foodstuffs as well as pharmaceuticals, agricultural chemicals and any other categories of products excluded from patent protection, unless one of the exceptions set out in the chapter, such as that for diagnostic, therapeutic and surgical methods for the treatment of humans or animals, applied. In such cases, if the product was the subject of a patent in another party prior to entry into force of the TRIPS Agreement and the product had not been marketed in the relevant country, the party providing transitional protection would limit the right to make, use or sell the relevant product to the owner of that patent for the remaining term of the relevant product patent. The party seeking exclusive rights under this proposal would need to submit a patent on the product granted in another party. The term of protection would be limited to the remaining term of the product patent submitted to the party providing transitional protection. This proposal for what was known as "pipeline protection" was the most ambitious of the proposals on transitional provisions and became part of the patent complex discussions.

During the course of negotiations, the Swiss delegation presented a proposal that was limited to pharmaceuticals and agricultural chemicals and set up a mechanism for accepting applications as of the date the TRIPS Agreement became applicable in that country, and examining those applications based on the date of receipt of the application. This would address the issue of whether an invention was "new" or "novel" at the time of examination. The proposal also required the party to provide exclusive marketing rights in that party for a period of five years after obtaining marketing approval or until the product patent is granted or rejected. This proposal focused on the most important technologies that some parties had excluded from patentability and provided the possibility for patent applicants to reap some economic benefit during the transition period. At the time the Swiss made this proposal, the actual transition periods for implementing the obligation to make product patents available was not known.

Assessment

The proponents of a broad scope of patentable subject matter achieved their main objective. Members must make product patents available for pharmaceuticals and agricultural chemicals. The results of negotiations on the patent complex were a very mixed bag for the United States. The combination of long transition periods and the limitations on the form of transitional protection that were included gave parties that needed to implement product patent protection for pharmaceuticals and agricultural chemicals a long period for adjustment. These provisions provoked significant complaints from the US pharmaceutical industry about the potential ten-year delay in actually realizing the benefit of patent protection for its products. WTO members continue to debate the details of the obligations set out in Article 39.3. Some WTO members, including the EU and the United States, have used negotiations on the accession of countries to the WTO as an opportunity to add specific details on the substance of this obligation. The matter has also been addressed in various free trade agreements (FTAs).

With regard to other patent issues, such as term of protection, rights provided to patent holders and shifting the burden of proof that had created uncertainty about the level of patent protection that would be provided, the TRIPS Agreement sets out clear disciplines. On compulsory licensing, a member must meet specified conditions, including transparency, review of decisions and payment of remuneration if it grants a compulsory licence. Such actions can no longer be by fiat and for entire categories of technologies, for example, all pharmaceuticals. A member also has obligations to maintain the confidentiality of undisclosed information submitted to it to obtain marketing approval of pharmaceuticals and agricultural chemicals and to prevent unfair commercial use of such information. While the patent provisions set out significant improvements in the level of protection for inventions, those provisions also have proven to include the flexibility necessary to address specific concerns that have arisen.

2. Trademarks and geographical indications

Trademarks: Objectives and results

The major objectives for the United States regarding the protection of trademarks related to defining the scope of protectable subject matter in as broad a manner as possible, for example, to potentially include marks consisting of a colour, sound or scent; maintaining the ability of parties to require use of a mark as a condition for obtaining and maintaining protection; clarification of the requirements for establishing that a mark is "well known" and thus subject to special treatment; extending Paris Convention provisions on trademarks to service marks; setting the parameters for exceptions to the rights provided; and establishing a minimum term of protection.

The negotiations on standards for trademarks were somewhat less contentious than those for patents and GIs. Implementing the TRIPS Agreement section on trademarks does not require a party to make major changes to foundation principles of its trademark system. Thus, parties whose systems included use requirements to obtain or maintain a registration or the possibility for a sign to obtain trademark status through use rather than registration were able to maintain those elements of their respective systems. Conditions and limitations were, however, placed on any requirements for use.

With regard to the standard for determining whether a mark was well known, negotiators were able to agree on some clarifications: that the standard continues to be subjective and authorities apply various criteria. Among those criteria, parties were required to recognize efforts to promote the mark, such as through advertising, rather than use of the mark in the relevant territory. In addition, language was included to address some participants' particular requirements on how a trademark is presented or used. Overall, however, participants applied basic trademark principles, such as distinctiveness and likelihood of confusion, in drafting the text, and showed flexibility on issues such as term (seven years was adopted rather than ten, as many developed parties proposed) and scope of protection. Enforcement of trademarks was more of a critical issue for delegations, and the provisions on civil and criminal remedies and enforcement at the border reflect the desire for strong disciplines to address an issue that had adverse effects on consumers and businesses in many countries.

Geographical indications: Objectives and results

If the negotiations on trademark standards were comparatively uncontentious, the opposite was the case for GIs. The EC's submission on standards for GIs included a broad definition of protected indications (that included appellations of origin as a subcategory and covered all types of products); restricted use, *inter alia,* based on "susceptibility to mislead"; and, "where appropriate", required protection for appellations of origin, "in particular for products of the vine, to the extent that it is accorded in the country of origin."[16] The proposal required parties, *inter alia*, to provide a means for "interested parties" to prevent a GI from becoming generic and declared that "products of the vine shall not be susceptible to develop into generic designations." Finally, the EC proposed the establishment of an international register to facilitate the protection of GIs, including appellations of origin.[17]

While some delegations, such as Thailand and India, welcomed the fact that the EC's proposal covered products other than wine and distilled spirits, since they had an interest in GIs for certain beverages and food products, many questioned the need for a special regime for GIs. To the United States and several other delegations, it seemed that the main issue was that those using GIs did not want to go through the time and expense of litigating rights provided through trademarks. Instead, the EC's proposal would have required many developed and developing countries to establish a form of *sui generis* protection for GIs, modify core provisions of their respective trademark regimes, including provisions related to generic terms, and invalidate existing trademarks. Despite strong opposition to its proposal, the EC indicated that including obligations in respect of GIs, in particular on wines and distilled spirits, was a "must have" element of any TRIPS Agreement.

Australia submitted a counterproposal on GIs, and delegations worked intensively on a package that reinforced requirements to protect against trademark infringement and unfair competition, including acts which mislead the public as to the true origin of a good. These protections would apply to all GIs. Since many parties had special regimes in place relating to GIs for wines and spirits, the text includes additional provisions related to protections for GIs for wines and spirits. Article 23.4 refers to negotiations for a multilateral system for notification and registration of wines. The further elaboration on those negotiations set out in Article 24 reflects a hard-fought balance between proponents of GIs and those seeking to defend and preserve trademark principles and the continued use of trademarks with geographical elements. The negotiations on a possible GI register have consumed the time of the TRIPS Council and special sessions for years and appear to remain stalled.

Since the TRIPS Agreement entered into force, the EU and the United States have concluded FTAs with provisions on GIs that take divergent approaches to protection of GIs. EU agreements tend to include lists of products that are to be protected if used in accordance with the relevant laws of the EU and products of the other party that are used in accordance with that party's relevant laws.[18] The US approach requires a party to provide certain procedural safeguards, such as cancellation or opposition proceedings, to address concerns, *inter alia*, regarding protection of generic terms and trademarks.[19] Although some countries have agreements with both the EU and the United States, it remains to be seen whether the divergent approaches can be reconciled.

3. General provisions on national treatment, most-favoured nation treatment and exceptions

National treatment and most-favoured nation treatment

Until the later stages of the negotiations, the United States, the EC and others worked on the basis that the TRIPS Agreement would be a plurilateral Tokyo-Round-style code, such as the Anti-dumping Code, with no requirement that all GATT contracting parties become party to the Agreement. The proposals on national treatment and MFN and the final text of the Agreement were an amalgam of IP and trade principles, with the IP community unwilling to give up existing exceptions to national treatment and the trade community seeking to avoid "free-riders."

As noted, certain IP agreements, including the Berne Convention, Paris Convention and International Convention for the Protection of Performers, Producers of Phonograms and Broadcasting Organizations (Rome Convention of 1961) require a party to provide national treatment in respect of certain rights. Thus, if a party decides to limit the rights it accords to its nationals, that party is not required to provide those rights to foreign owners of IP. This principle is maintained to some extent in Article 3 of the TRIPS Agreement, which maintains the exceptions to national treatment included in the three previously mentioned Conventions and in the Treaty on Intellectual Property in Respect of Integrated Circuits. Furthermore, the national treatment obligation in respect of performers, producers of phonograms and broadcasting organizations applies only in respect of the rights covered under the TRIPS Agreement. The exceptions to national treatment related to enforcement of IPRs, however, are subject to a classic trade limitation, that is, that they not be applied in a manner that would constitute a disguised restriction on trade. The overall effect of maintaining these exceptions, however, is diminished in the TRIPS Agreement, because under the TRIPS Agreement members must provide their nationals the rights specified in the Agreement.

US right holders were particularly disappointed that WTO members could maintain the exceptions from national treatment provided in the Rome Convention. Under these exceptions, US performers, producers of sound recordings and broadcast organizations received less favourable treatment than those of Rome Convention parties, and this could continue.

MFN treatment in the context of IP requires a party to provide the same treatment to owners of IP from all other parties and addresses those infrequent cases where a party provides better treatment to foreign right owners than to its nationals. The EC was the principal proponent of including MFN provisions in the TRIPS Agreement. While recognizing that exceptions to MFN would be necessary, the EC wanted to ensure that higher levels of protection granted under bilateral agreements would be accorded generally. This objective was due to provisions in a bilateral agreement between the United States and the Republic of Korea concerning "pipeline protection" of certain pharmaceutical products covered under US patents. Products covered under a patent granted by a member state or the European Patent Office did not qualify for such protection.

Commentators have raised an interesting question about the application of the MFN principle in the context of regional or bilateral FTAs and customs unions. The TRIPS Agreement does not include an exception from MFN for advantages or benefits relating to protection of IP under such agreements, that is, it does not contain a counterpart to Article XXIV of the GATT 1994. Since most IP laws are drafted and administered on an MFN basis, the issue has arisen principally in the context of agreements related to the protection of GIs. To date, members have chosen not to challenge such provisions as denial of MFN treatment.

Exceptions: General exceptions

Article 73 of the TRIPS Agreement sets out the security exception to the provisions of the Agreement with language taken from Article XXI of the GATT, thus avoiding any question as to whether measures permitted under Article XXI of the GATT (1994) could be contrary to the TRIPS Agreement. Article XX (d) of the GATT 1994 provides an exception from the obligation of the Agreement for measures "necessary to secure compliance with laws or regulations which are not inconsistent with the provisions of this Agreement, including those relating to ... the protection of patents, trade marks [sic], and copyrights, and the prevention of deceptive practices;"[20] The TRIPS Agreement does not include a "general exceptions" article corresponding to Article XX of the GATT 1994. The need for a counterpart to Article XX was considered and rejected.

The TRIPS Agreement takes a different approach in providing for exceptions. It includes specific, limited exceptions to national and MFN treatment and, within Part II, the Agreement sets forth specific provisions on exceptions or limitations to rights for each form of IPR in the Agreement.[21] This approach permitted exceptions tailored to each right. With regard to enforcement, which is the focus of the GATT Article XX(d) exception, the TRIPS Agreement sets out the specific disciplines. Indeed, Article 1 of the TRIPS Agreement recognized that members could provide more extensive protection than provided in the Agreement provided that it did not contravene the Agreement. A general exception from the enforcement obligations would be inconsistent with the principle that the Agreement expresses the minimum standards for enforcement.

4. Dispute settlement

Application of GATT/WTO rules

Achieving the application of GATT/WTO dispute settlement procedures to rights and obligations on IP was a top-level objective for the United States before and throughout the negotiations, and was coupled with ambitious objectives for modifying the dispute settlement procedures in place at the time the Uruguay Round negotiations began.[22] Negotiators often remarked that strong standards for IP protection meant little if disciplines requiring effective enforcement of IPRs were not included. The same could be said of government-to-government enforcement. The lack of an effective government-to-government enforcement mechanism in existing IP treaties was a significant factor in deciding to initiate negotiations in the GATT. Initial proposals from both the United States and the EC were in the form of an additional GATT article with detailed provisions included in an Annex to GATT (1947). As such, GATT dispute settlement procedures, as negotiated in the Uruguay Round, would have applied.

While the United States favoured application of GATT dispute settlement rules, including any modifications agreed during the Uruguay Round, India and some other delegations proposed procedures that focused on consultations without retaliation. New Zealand led a group of countries putting forward a middle-ground proposal that would authorize the TRIPS Committee to endorse sanctions only after a period of non-compliance.

Those delegations, such as the United States, that sought application of new dispute settlement rules to IPR had to address a number of questions, including whether to include some special rules, for example, on recourse to experts, and what trade actions could be authorized after a finding of violation of IP obligations and subsequent non-compliance. The Draft Final Act issued in December 1990, for example, included three texts as options for consideration once the institutional issues were decided.[23]

During the hiatus in negotiations during 1992 and part of 1993, thinking evolved on the formation of what was proposed to be the Multilateral Trade Organization (MTO). An organization, which eventually was named the World Trade Organization, would be established and the results of the Uruguay Round negotiations would be agreed as part of a "single undertaking". This would assure that a participant could not "opt out" of a sensitive part of the Uruguay Round package and that those accepting the single undertaking would know the entirety of the deal and decide whether it was sufficient and acceptable.

Ultimately, ministers decided to include the TRIPS Agreement as Annex IC to the Marrakesh Agreement Establishing the WTO (WTO Agreement) and subject it to the rules and procedures set out in the Understanding Governing the Rules and Procedures on the Settlement of Disputes. The only special rule that applies to matters under the TRIPS Agreement is the moratorium on complaints of the type provided for under paragraphs 1(b) and 1(c) of Article XXIII of the GATT (1994), that is, non-violation and other matters.

Cross-retaliation

One key reason for industry and government support for the application of GATT/ WTO dispute settlement to the TRIPS Agreement was the potential for authorized trade action against imported goods. The IP community in the United States was comfortable with the link between market access for goods and IP, as seen in the criteria for its GSP and Special 301. Taking action against IP owned by nationals of a member found in violation of an IP obligation was considered neither practicable nor fair. Numerous questions were presented. Would the action need to be against the same form of IP? How would the affected member and ultimately the WTO value the violation and the resulting trade action? The results of the Uruguay Round negotiations included cross-retaliation and, to date, three members have received authorization to take action with regard to IPRs for violations in agreements related to trade in goods and services.[24]

Non-violation complaints

As mentioned above, negotiators agreed to two changes to the draft TRIPS text that was proposed in December 1991 as part of the Draft Final Act. The delay in finalizing the negotiations had provided contracting parties time to examine and socialize the text. Most contracting parties found it acceptable without change as part of the overall Uruguay Round package. The United States, however, proposed a handful of changes to the patent, copyright, transitional and dispute settlement provisions of the draft TRIPS text. Since most delegations considered that the current text was acceptable, any changes had to be by consensus.

In addition to these changes, the United States proposed to establish a five-year moratorium on so-called "non-violation" complaints as part of a package that included limiting the grounds for issuing compulsory licences on semiconductor technology. During the five-year moratorium, the TRIPS Council was to study the scope and modalities for bringing such complaints and make its recommendations to address these issues or to extend the moratorium to the ministerial meeting. Several, but not all, delegations supported elimination of "non-violation" complaints due to uncertainty over the scope of the provision and how it would apply in the context of IPRs.

GATT contracting parties and WTO members have brought only a handful of disputes that include a non-violation complaint. The elements of such a dispute differ from a violation complaint, *inter alia*, because nullification or impairment of rights is not presumed and must be established and, even if the complaint is successful, the respondent member is not required to modify the relevant measure. Thus, to a large extent, non-violation complaints have been used to bring the respondent member to the table to address an issue.

As noted, the United States was motivated to propose the moratorium on non-violation complaints to obtain a consensus in support of another of its proposals, which would limit the application of compulsory licences to patents on semiconductor technology to cases of public non-commercial use or to remedy anti-competitive practices. Since it was difficult to predict what type of measure might be actionable under a non-violation complaint and the remedy was limited, policy makers thought that the value of the provision was also limited. Moreover, the moratorium was intended to end in five years. Members, however, have repeatedly decided to extend the moratorium. The United States, with little support, has urged an end to the moratorium. The option of bringing a non-violation complaint would provide a useful tool to address new issues that have arisen since the TRIPS Agreement entered into force.

Observations on evolving issues related to IP

The TRIPS Agreement broke new ground with regard to multilateral disciplines on the protection and enforcement of IPRs. That said, it has been more than 22 years since the text was negotiated. Since then, new multilateral IP agreements, such as the WIPO Internet Treaties and the Patent Law Treaty, have entered into force. New technologies and products have been developed and the Internet provides unprecedented access to information. Indeed, information has become a good that is gathered and traded.

Governments must address a wide range of issues with implications for IP protection. One such issue is how to provide access to patented technology used in interoperability standards for various products, such as smartphones, that must interface with complex and growing networks. Standards-setting organizations in the telecommunications area that require participants in the standards-setting process to license standards and essential patents on fair, reasonable and non-discriminatory (FRAND) terms present a potential model that could be strengthened and emulated in other situations. A key element in that process is that the right owner makes the initial decision on whether to participate in the process and accepts both its positive economic consequences (many licences) and other consequences (limits on the level of royalties and possibly on other terms of the licence).

Practices of those who purchase patent rights for the sole purpose of licensing them (so-called patent trolls) have raised concerns that patent rights are not serving the purpose of promoting innovation. Addressing the objectionable practices, rather than weakening patent protection generally, would seem to be the better approach. Members of the US Congress, for example, have proposed measures to address some of the more egregious practices of patent trolls.

Concerns about potential abuse of patents or copyrights have led some to urge use of competition law as a means to investigate and prevent such abuse. This is a longstanding concern with regard to patents. In the United States, the intensity of application of antitrust law to those asserting patent rights has varied over decades. The TRIPS Agreement recognizes a member's right to apply appropriate measures to address abuses of IP by a right owner, including licensing practices that may adversely affect trade or impede the transfer of technology, but any measures taken must be consistent with the TRIPS Agreement. From an IP perspective, the lack of a common approach or international standards for application of antitrust or competition law leaves a right holder vulnerable. Currently, application of competition law lacks transparency and predictability.

Whether any of these or other IP-related issues is appropriate for international negotiations is an open question. Maintaining the integrity of systems for the protection of IP, which have their foundation in the TRIPS Agreement, should be a major consideration in deciding next steps. The solution worked out on access to medicines is an example of the flexibility of the TRIPS Agreement and the IPRs provided under that Agreement. Members adopted a solution without making major changes to the Agreement or to IPRs generally. In my view, a similar approach needs to be taken to address the "new" IPR issues that are arising.

Endnotes

1   The US delegation had various "chief negotiators" during the period 1986–93, and officials from the US Patent and Trademark Office, and Copyright Office, among others, had significant responsibilities in the negotiations. For the United States, this was a quintessential team effort. I thank the US Uruguay Round negotiating team, the TRIPS team, my colleagues from other delegations and the GATT Secretariat who participated in the TRIPS negotiations for a proud highlight of my career and many fond memories of them.

2   See www.wipo.org and GATT document MTN.GNG/NG11/W/13/Rev.1, Negotiating Group on Trade-Related Aspects of Intellectual Property Rights, Including Trade in Counterfeit Goods – International Conventions Regarding Intellectual Property and Their Membership – Note by the Secretariat – Revision, 19 June 1989.

3   GATT document L/5424, CONTRACTING PARTIES – Thirty-Eighth Session – Ministerial Declaration adopted on 29 November 1982, 29 November 1982. The contracting parties requested the Director-General (DG) to consult with the DG of WIPO to clarify the legal and institutional aspects involved. Those consultations occurred and work continued through 1985. NB: "Joint Action" pursuant to Article XXV of the GATT refers to the mechanism by which the contracting parties took decisions.

4   Section 1102(b)(10) of the Omnibus Trade and Competitiveness Act of 1988.

5   GATT document MIN.DEC, Multilateral Trade Negotiations – The Uruguay Round – Ministerial Declaration on the Uruguay Round, 20 September 1986.

6   GATT document MTN.GNG/5, Uruguay Round – Group of Negotiations on Goods (GATT) – Fifth Meeting of the Group of Negotiations on Goods – Record of Decisions Taken, 9 February 1987.

7   See, for example, GATT documents MTN.GNG/NG11/W/24/Rev.1, Negotiating Group on Trade-Related Aspects of Intellectual Property Rights, including Trade in Counterfeit Goods –- Existence, Scope and Form of Generally Internationally Accepted and Applied Standards/ Norms for the Protection of Intellectual Property – Note Prepared by the International Bureau of WIPO – Addendum, 15 June 1988, and MTN.GNG/NG11/W/31, Negotiating Group on Trade-Related Aspects of Intellectual Property Rights, including Trade in Counterfeit Goods – Proposal by the European Community for the Negotiations on the Enforcement of Trade-Related Intellectual Property Rights, 30 May 1989.

8   GATT document MTN.GNG/NG11/W/14/Rev.1, Negotiating Group on Trade-Related Aspects of Intellectual Property Rights, including Trade in Counterfeit Goods – Suggestion by the United States for Achieving the Negotiating Objective – Revision, 17 October 1988.

9   See, for example, GATT documents MTN.GNG/NG11/17, Negotiating Group on Trade-Related Aspects of Intellectual Property Rights, Including Trade in Counterfeit Goods – Meeting of 11, 12 and 14 December 1989 – Note by the Secretariat, 23 January 1990 (Japan); MTN.GNG/ NG11/25, Negotiating Group on Trade-Related Aspects of Intellectual Property Rights, Including Trade in Counterfeit Goods – Meeting of Negotiating Group of 10–21 September 1990 – Note by the Secretariat, 8 October 1990 (Switzerland); and MTN.GNG/NG11/26, Negotiating Group on Trade-Related Aspects of Intellectual Property Rights, Including Trade in Counterfeit Goods – Meeting of Negotiating Group of 8 and 18 October 1990 – Note by the Secretariat, 31 October 1990 (the EC).

10 GATT documents MTN.GNG/NG11/W/68, Negotiating Group on Trade-Related Aspects of Intellectual Property Rights, Including Trade in Counterfeit Goods - Draft Agreement on Trade-Related Aspects of Intellectual Property Rights, 29 March 1990; MTN.GNG/NG11/W/70, Negotiating Group on Trade-Related Aspects of Intellectual Property Rights, including Trade in Counterfeit Goods – Draft Agreement on the Trade-Related Aspects of Intellectual Property Rights – Communication from the United States, 11 May 1990; MTN.GNG/NG11/W/71, Negotiating Group on Trade-Related Aspects of Intellectual Property Rights, including Trade in Counterfeit Goods – Communication from Argentina, Brazil, Chile, China, Colombia, Cuba, Egypt, India, Nigeria, Peru, Tanzania and Uruguay, 14 May 1990; MTN.GNG/NG11/W/73, Negotiating Group on Trade-Related Aspects of Intellectual Property Rights, including Trade in Counterfeit Goods – Draft Amendment to the General Agreement on Tariffs and Trade on the Protection of Trade-Related Intellectual Property Rights – Communication from Switzerland, 14 May 1990; MTN.GNG/NG11/W/74, Negotiating Group on Trade-Related Aspects of Intellectual Property Rights, including Trade in Counterfeit Goods – Main Elements of a Legal Text for Trips – Communication from Japan, 15 May 1990; and MTN.GNG/NG11/W/75, Negotiating Group on Trade-Related Aspects of Intellectual Property Rights, including Trade in Counterfeit Goods – Draft Text on Geographical Indications – Communication from Australia, 13 June 1990, respectively.

11 US Supreme Court case Golan v. Holder, 565 U.S. (2012).

12 The group of developing countries comprised Argentina, Brazil, Chile, Colombia, Cuba, Egypt, India, Nigeria, Peru, Tanzania, Uruguay, Pakistan and Zimbabwe. Twelve of them (Pakistan and Zimbabwe joined the group later) submitted MTM.GNG.NG11/W/71 with specific proposals on IP standards, consultations, and trade in counterfeit goods. (China also signed on to the submission, but was in the process of accession during the Uruguay Round negotiations).

13 GATT document MTN.GNG/NG11/W/70.

14 GATT document MTN.GNG/NG11/W/68.

15 See Article 5 of the Paris Convention.

16 GATT document MTN.GNG/NG11/W/68.

17 Ibid.

18 See, for example, the EU–Korea Free Trade Agreement Article 10.19.

19 See, for example, the United States–Korea Free Trade Agreement Article 18.2 paragraphs 8, 14, and 15.

20 In addition to meeting the requirements set out in subparagraph (d), a member asserting an Article XX exception must establish compliance with the conditions set out in the chapeau to that Article.

21 For undisclosed information, the limitations are in the form of conditions on what information qualifies for protection, that is, language in Article 39.2 subparagraphs (a) through (c) and 39.3.

22 See, for example, GATT documents MTN.GNG/NG11/W/14, Negotiating Group on Trade-Related Aspects of Intellectual Property Rights, including Trade in Counterfeit Goods – Suggestion by the United States for Achieving the Negotiating Objective, 20 October 1987, and MTN.GNG/NG11/W/70.

23 GATT document MTN/TNC/W/35/Rev.1, Uruguay Round - Trade Negotiations Committee – Draft Final Act Embodying the Results of the Uruguay Round of Multilateral Trade Negotiations – Revision, 3 December 1990.

24 Action against IPRs has been authorized in three disputes to permit the following: Ecuador to take action against the EC in connection with the bananas dispute; Antigua and Barbuda to take action against the United States in connection with the General Agreement on Trade in Services (GATS) dispute involving online gambling; and Brazil to take action against the United States in connection with the dispute regarding subsidies for upland cotton.

9

Negotiating for Switzerland

Thu-Lang Tran Wasescha[1]

Introduction

Learning is a continuing process in one's life. Some lessons are well archived on our "personal hard disk", with learning by doing being the most efficient method of saving those lessons. Negotiating the TRIPS Agreement was "unforgettable", to cite a famous American TV series. Indeed, it is one of the most well-archived and prominent learning experiences of my career. Having been born and grown up in a developing country, namely, Viet Nam (south), with its realities printed in my DNA, I came a long way, eventually working at representing a small developed country. Switzerland, which is characterized by an economy based on free enterprise, innovation and exports of manufactured goods and services, as well as by a compromise-oriented "culture" in terms of policy, law-making and negotiating, set the stage for this learning experience in the field of IP, prior, during and after the Uruguay Round of multilateral trade negotiations under the GATT.

As a law student, I worked part time in a small private trademark bureau, which specialized in trademarks and applications for drugs marketing authorization by the Interkantonale Kontrollstelle für Heilmittel (IKS, Intercantonal Office for the Control of Medicines), now called Swissmedic. It was bureaucratic and technical work but educative. I joined WIPO, first as a trainee, and finally moved up as Senior Legal Officer in the Industrial Property Division.[2] There, I learned the complex and subtle art of combining substance and diplomacy – at both internal and external levels. In 1987, I joined the Federal Office of Intellectual Property in Bern – now the Swiss Federal Institute of Intellectual Property – to deal with international affairs. This covers WIPO, the GATT, the World Health Organization, the United Nations Educational, Scientific and Cultural Organization, the International Labour Organization, the Organisation for Economic Co-operation and Development (OECD) and the Food and Agriculture Organization. I also dealt with environmental issues (notably, biodiversity), human rights, bilateral and regional affairs and negotiations, for example EFTA,[3] the EU and third countries. After 14 years, the most challenging period for me as a civil servant, I joined the WTO Secretariat (Intellectual Property Division). It was a great school of intellectual rigour for navigation in waters with cross currents. I served as Secretary to the Special Session of the TRIPS Council, the negotiating group on the establishment of a multilateral system of notification and registration of geographical indications (GIs) for wines and spirits. I would not have been able to live through all these interesting experiences without all those who gave me that opportunity. The Uruguay Round experience is, for me, "unforgettable", not only for its various processes of high intellectual and negotiating complexity but also for this unique human touch, formed by colleagues, delegates, a very professional Secretariat led by Adrian Otten, and a brilliant Chair, Ambassador Lars Anell. That human touch greatly facilitated dialogue, set alight sparkles of ingenuity and led to success.

This chapter does not have the ambition of being a rigorous scientific work. It is a mere recollection of experiences and observations, a mix of anecdotes, remembrances and descriptions of the Swiss approaches. It cannot but be an individual and subjective perception of the landscape of that time.[4] This, I hope, may help the reader understand the Swiss role, in addition to chapter 4, by Thomas Cottier.

This chapter first gives an overview of considerations that made Switzerland embark on a long journey of some eight years to the very end of the negotiating round. It gives a brief list of the areas of focus for Switzerland. It will then address some specific aspects of TRIPS Article 27 (patentability), and Articles 22–24 (GIs). Finally, this chapter offers some reflections on the future if lessons learned from the past could at all help avoid errors, and if future and creative thinking by the new generations of negotiators or Secretariat staff could ensure a coherent development of the TRIPS framework, and not disrupt a delicate balance.

Overview of considerations before the Uruguay Round negotiations

The pre-Uruguay Round phase

Globalization hit market economies, the "peak" being in the 1970s to 1980s. While it had not reached today's dimensions, it was the first challenge for economic players and governments, particularly newly independent countries facing the challenges of political change, and for other governments needing to step outside the comfort zone of uninterrupted economic development and business models. It changed the market access conditions for entrepreneurs. New technology acceleration implied adjustments, sometimes drastic, for many small and medium-sized entrepreneurial businesses, including the loss of markets, bankruptcy and job losses. As a civil servant – both international and national – I unfortunately witnessed a number of such casualties. But, as the old saying goes, there are two sides to every coin. Technology also facilitated easier counterfeiting and piracy. This phenomenon was not easy to combat due to mobility, that is, the capacity of counterfeiters – producers and distributors – to move from one place to another: closing down a counterfeit-producing premise, even if such enforcement action was taken in a country, rarely resolved the problem. Judicial or administrative costs discouraged actions abroad. In any event, they were beyond the reach of small and medium-sized enterprises. At the same time, technology made it easier to engage in useful activities, for example, reverse engineering, which also helped genuine invention.

In the GATT context, attempts to contain counterfeiting had already been made in the Tokyo Round (see Adrian Otten, chapter 3). This would rather contradict the belief that the TRIPS negotiations were malevolently introduced into the GATT by industrialized countries. It is well known that economic actors affected by counterfeiting tried to find a forum to resolve it; this was true as well for their opponents, who would use the channels they could find.

During the TRIPS negotiations, the GATT Secretariat issued a summary of "Activities in Other International Organizations of Possible Interest in Relation to Matters Raised in the Group".[5] This gave a comprehensive view of the landscape and the issues addressed or being debated elsewhere. It listed work undertaken in WIPO: Committee of Experts on Measures against Counterfeiting and Piracy, revision of the Paris Convention on the Protection of Industrial Property, Stockholm Act 1967 ("Paris Convention"), and patent law harmonization.

The revision of the Paris Convention addressed complex and controversial topics, such as compulsory licences and GIs, and faced many difficulties, not least due to the varying but rigid alliances among the contracting parties. Compulsory licences faced a North–South divide, with some developed countries, such as Australia, Canada, New Zealand, Portugal and Spain, occupying the "middle ground". GIs was a New World–Old World battlefield, each group including developing and developed countries. The two issues, as well as the one relating to inventors' certificates, opposing market and planned economies, did not offer enough diversity to create a real coalition-building potential. It was difficult to make trade-offs. While developed market economies formed a relatively united front against proposed rules on inventors' certificates, the "non-voluntary" licences pitted developed countries against developing ones, with some developed countries, such as Canada, which had a strong generic industry, taking positions closer to those of some developing countries. Government use, or "Crown use", a common law "legacy" to former Commonwealth countries, was not clearly put on the table, as was done later in the TRIPS negotiations. The revision might, in my view, have been beset by birth defects. It was too difficult for negotiators to reconcile and agree.

In 1985, WIPO launched a process to address the issues of counterfeiting. Ideas such as some stronger implementation and monitoring systems, for example, a mention of the lack of protection or enforcement in the General Assemblies' meetings, drew a blank with the strong opposition from developing countries, led by Brazil. The exercise eventually turned into a process for the adoption of model provisions for national laws.

The above-mentioned GATT Secretariat summary also mentioned the work of the United Nations Conference on Trade and Development (UNCTAD) on technology transfer. Patents for inventions were at the heart of the controversy: for some, patents benefit society at large and stimulate innovation; for others, they create monopolies, which could lead to monopolistic abuses to the detriment of competitors and consumers. Eventually, UNCTAD did not alleviate the tension surrounding the dichotomous perception of the role of patents. In hindsight, in my view, the burden of the debate on whether or not IPRs, in particular patents, were good or bad shifted to WIPO. Not surprisingly, it was a massive offensive. What struck me was the organization of discussions and negotiations on the basis of regional groups within the UN system: Group B (developed countries), Group D (socialist or planned-economy countries) and the Group of Developing Countries (G77 and other developing countries), with relatively rigid operating rules; while there had always been bilateral, regional or subregional alliances or "sympathies", the position-taking was rather straight-jacketed. As is underlined elsewhere in this publication, the GATT operated differently. Delegations seemed to have more leeway to negotiate according to their best interests, which varied depending on the topic. And, more importantly, the GATT had a relatively prompt and efficient system for resolving disputes between parties.

As far as Switzerland was concerned, the pharmaceutical and chemical industries' interest in protecting their innovations was at the forefront of TRIPS negotiations, but exporting companies also had strong interests in other IPRs: trademarks for products and services, in particular, the protection of well-known marks; industrial designs; know-how; GIs, notably "Swiss Made" for watches; and, of course, enforcement. It was believed that, without actual enforcement, the best of substantive standards would remain a dead letter. Switzerland, although a small country – that is, not the size of the "Quad" countries (Canada, the European Communities (EC), Japan and the United States) and other developed ones – had adjusted its legislation to the latest international developments, notably in the area of patents for inventions. Switzerland had joined the European Patent Organisation in 1977. This relatively late adherence to the community of pro-product patent countries did arouse curiosity, which was not always friendly, I assume. How could Switzerland demand from developing countries higher levels of protection when it had itself introduced such protection only in 1977? On a similar note, why did Switzerland deny to developing countries the right to imitate and build up its industry as it had itself done at the beginning of the twentieth century? Similar observations were made regarding Japan during the Meiji era. The questions were not simple to respond to, in particular, if the interlocutor's agenda were political, which was often the case. The suggestion I received from the then Director-General of the Swiss IP office was illuminating: transition periods could be envisaged for structural adjustments but they should be short, taking into account technological advances available worldwide and other considerations. The suggestion was clear and politically helpful for a "newcomer" in the negotiating team.

The "Swiss spirit"

In Switzerland, amendments to the Federal Constitution, acceptance of certain agreements or adherence to certain international organizations are subject to the so-called "mandatory referendum", requiring a double majority of votes, that is, a majority of the total population vote as well as a majority of the 26 cantons of Switzerland. New or revised laws, certain federal ordinances and certain other international agreements are submitted to a nationwide referendum, if 50,000 electors or eight cantons so request. For this category of referendum, called "optional", only a majority of the population's votes is required. With the Damocles' sword of referendum, even the single-majority one, hanging over TRIPS negotiators' heads, embarking on negotiations with the aim of arriving at an international treaty was an exercise that required extreme prudence. This special feature of the Swiss system explains, in my view, the Swiss propensity to internal (administration) and domestic consultation, task forces, dialogues, step-by-step process and mid-way solutions. This takes time and efforts but proves eventually rewarding because it is transparent enough and is propitious to a wider acceptance of the result. This holds true for my "TRIPS journey" during the Uruguay Round.

As was pointed out by Thomas Cottier, negotiators were fortunate enough to have a certain leeway, working with objectives-setting and without micromanagement by the "big bosses" of the negotiating team. Implementing the Uruguay Round results in 1994 was limited to the minimum necessary for the purposes of submitting the whole package, which was subject to an optional referendum of the Swiss people. On the TRIPS front, the biotechnology-related provisions were the most critical ones for such a request for referendum, if added to the concerns of certain circles opposed to the liberalization of services and agriculture.

A task force gathering together federal administration "départements" (ministries, with several portfolios) was set up. Each department and its offices (agencies or even ministries in some other countries) have their own channels of information flows and consultation within the ambit of their activities, that is, among interested circles. For example, the Department of Economy covers, *inter alia*, the Federal Office for External Economic Relations (now the State Secretariat for Economic Affairs), dealing with the GATT, UNCTAD, EFTA and OECD on any trade agreements, and the Agriculture Office, which is responsible for agriculture matters and plant varieties protection. The Department of Interior has under its aegis the Office of Culture, the Office for Science (in charge of biotechnology) and the Health Office. Within the State Secretariat for Economic Affairs, the former Federal Department for Exports has a technical cooperation division and the Department of Foreign Affairs is responsible for, *inter alia*, international organizations, international law and the Swiss Agency for Development and Cooperation, which has its channels of information and consultation, for example, with Swiss non-governmental organizations (NGOs), such as La Déclaration de Berne, Swissaid and Pain pour le prochain. Customs matters are under the aegis of the Department of Finance. Finally, during the Uruguay Round, the Department of Environment, Transport, Energy and Communications was handling the work undertaken on environmental issues, including biodiversity in the context of the Rio Summit of 1992. The cantons were kept informed, notably on enforcement issues. The Swiss IP office was placed under the Department of Justice. Unlike many other countries' IP offices, its tasks covered both copyright and industrial property. Coordination and information flows were therefore facilitated.

Of course, the Swiss delegation did not suffer from jetlag and capital-based experts were readily able to come to Geneva. This advantage of capital-based assistance was not available to all delegations and, for those who had it, it could not be available at each and every meeting, in particular, when the negotiations entered into the critical phase and decisions on the drafting of a provision, a sentence, a term, or the deletion of square brackets had to be agreed to. It was of paramount importance to be part of the small, informal groups, but it was not a free lunch. Delegations that insisted on participating just for the sake of it and could not demonstrate the usefulness of their participation by contributing to the negotiations would endanger the process and, for example, incite the most interested ones to meet outside the group and strike a deal. The Chair's authority in arbitrating a carefully balanced and meaningful distribution of seats was of utmost importance. It was rarely challenged.

It was in certain moments of the Uruguay Round that I fully measured the meaning of the "solitude" of the negotiator in small delegations. It was more comfortable to be a team of two, to consult each other and take decisions quickly. Leaving the room to make a telephone call for instructions could be costly as that meant missing an opportunity to approve or oppose a proposal. *"Les absents ont toujours tort"* ("Those who are absent are always in the wrong"). If silence could mean acquiescence, repeating a position *ad nauseam* could irritate and, since it did not bring anything new or helpful, could mean eviction from the group at the next meeting. It was also there that I learned the GATT process and negotiating peculiarities, for example, what a "1+1" meeting was – a head of delegation plus an expert, if available, of course; and why minutes or hours seemed so long while one was waiting in the corridors next to rooms F, D and E when two, or a small group of, delegations met with the Chair and the Secretariat to remove the stumbling block from the path to consensus. The expert had therefore to brief his or her boss well, and bear the burden of ill or good advice. The head of delegation in turn did not have an easy task: he or she had better have taken the right approach and been able to justify the outcome *vis-à-vis* his or her superiors. You can be two and feel alone. As others have said in this volume, the process was masterfully and creatively handled by the Chair, and the Secretariat facilitated our work.

Another lesson: a failure to explain a position and to convince others generally produces the effect of having the interlocutor digging in his or her heels. That said, Switzerland did not always have time to explain and convince. Maybe today's generation is living through the unfinished business of clarifications and convincing with regard to some parts of the TRIPS Agreement. We might have accepted "constructive ambiguity" for the sake of achieving a package of results, assessing the win–win elements in the whole Agreement. The balance in the TRIPS Agreement was delicately struck. Its core is like a house of cards. If a card is removed or added, the house risks falling apart; the core should remain untouched. In retrospect, I remember thinking that when no one was happy with the result it must mean that the text is somewhere mid-way. The TRIPS Agreement was a text no one was entirely happy with – this, in itself, could be an achievement.

The TRIPS Agreement being such a comprehensive agreement on IPRs, delegations could find provisions they had defended to the maximum, depending upon their mandate. All were interested in patents and trademarks; some were more interested in copyright and related rights, industrial designs, undisclosed information or GIs. The alliances varied depending on the category of IPR. To cite a few examples, we shared the same concerns as did Japan with regard to the system of equitable remuneration of copyright and related rights vs rental rights, and we had a similar system of dependent inventions. In the area of patents, we were certainly closer to the United States, except for certain aspects of the patent system: the first-to-invent approach and government use. While Austria – not yet a member of the EC – and India did not object to Switzerland defending a wider scope of protection of GIs for products, the Swiss delegation had to repeat *ad nauseam* its negotiating mandate for the protection of GIs for all products, in particular industrial products. Moreover, defending GIs for services was, in retrospect, terrifying. There, I felt the loneliness of the unarmed soldier advancing on a battlefield. Maybe we were too "visionary". Or, more humbly put, Switzerland, not blessed with natural resources, was already relying on tertiary sector activities, in addition to manufactured goods.

Bilateral IP arrangements were flourishing, even in the late 1970s and 1980s, presaging an invasive comeback of reciprocity endangering the national treatment principle in existing IP conventions. The straw that broke the camel's back was the retroactive "pipeline protection" accorded by the Republic of Korea to US pharmaceutical companies in 1985–6. Switzerland was not able to invoke the national treatment of the Paris Convention. The pipeline protection privilege was given to US – and later, to European – companies. I remember that we also envisaged exploring the most-favoured nation (MFN) clause in the Swiss–Korean bilateral investment agreement but did not pursue that path very far. In any event, the discrimination convinced Switzerland that the GATT MFN might be an avenue to explore further, in order to ensure better treatment of Swiss IP interests outside its frontiers, thus avoiding a repetition of discrimination. It was Switzerland's firm conviction that a multilateral framework was the best shield for a country of its size, however successful it was in economic and trade sectors. The Korean experience led to the Swiss proposal for inclusion of the MFN provision in the TRIPS Agreement.

In spite of its top innovation ranking at that time (and today), Switzerland was (and remains) a medium-sized economy relying on exports with its added value being in the form of IP. IP became an objective of world trade policy to correct several situations, namely: (1) the lack of adequate international legal instruments against counterfeiting and piracy, resulting in commercial losses for innovative and creative enterprises; (2) excessive or too complex a protection, which could be a disguised trade barrier to the extent it discouraged market access; and (3) the lack of effective non-discrimination obligations (national treatment and MFN). There was a need to recalibrate the multilateral framework.

Not only for IP-related matters but also for the wide gamut of disciplines, Switzerland was active on almost every front of the Uruguay Round package. Not surprisingly, IP was among the most important. The delegation covered all the discussions on a road that was initially foggy and muddy, with only the Punta Del Este Ministerial Declaration as a map and, later, with greater visibility shed by the results of the Montreal mid-term review in 1988. Nonetheless, the road remained winding and full of obstacles.

I remember that the first formal meetings were strongly divided between the pro-IP and anti-IP delegations in GATT, with some developing countries, in particular the Asian "dragons", which had started modernizing their IP systems, in the pro-IP camp or in a neutral, observation mode. Most debates had an air of *déjà vu* and, to be frank, this pertained to both camps, including Switzerland. I remember, for example, how statistics published by the Swiss IP office were interpreted by the Colombian delegation to support the following point: since, at the peak of the curve, the duration of patent renewals was ten years, the duration of patents should therefore be limited to ten years, and not, as requested by industrialized countries, 20 years from the date of filing the patent application. My response was not the best one of my life: "There are three categories of lies: the big ones, the small ones and statistics": *déjà vu*, as someone more famous than I had said that. Fortunately for me, I was supported by the fact that companies would not pay progressive annual fees if the patented invention proved not to be a successful one. Of course, there could be cases of abuses, that is, where a company might want to pay fees for the sake of preventing competitors from entering the market. Such cases could, under a rules-based system, be corrected and should not be used as an example to undermine the role of patents by throwing the baby out with the bath water. But that is another story.

After a heated internal discussion, the small team in Berne, based on comments made by some delegations and individuals, agreed to make a soft take-off by proposing an approach more familiar to the GATT but alien to IP, that is, to "build TRIPS on the basis of GATT disciplines of nullification and impairment, developing normative principles and an indicative list of types of conduct considered detrimental to international trade ..."[6] (see Thomas Cottier, chapter 4). The idea of an indicative list approach, alien to IP thinking, was not considered sufficient and was eventually replaced by proposals for minimum standards, in the second generation of submissions. The prize for that was a cartoon posted in an American paper, with a cat (WIPO) stuck in the branches of a tree and a firefighter (Switzerland) climbing to rescue the animal. Never mind, we had broad shoulders: the classic approach of standards as known in the IP world was, in any event, easier for drafters.

This was how we slowly came to the Communication from Switzerland of 14 May 1990, discussed by Adrian Otten, Thomas Cottier and Jayashree Watal in this volume.[7] I shall limit myself to a few points on which the Swiss delegation was particularly active in dialoguing, or asking for or providing clarifications.

The journey down the long, winding road of TRIPS negotiations was slowed down not only for substantive reasons but also due to the pressure put on delegates by their own mandates, leading to misunderstandings, and sometimes to acrimonious mutual hints of bad faith. On the process itself, Switzerland (Luzius Wasescha) played the go-between the EC and the United States. I queried India (Jayashree Watal) about the real difficulties it had in accepting the incorporation of Paris Convention provisions when India and the EC were log-jammed on this issue. I also asked Thailand why it opposed the patenting of life forms, notably micro-organisms. Thomas Cottier patiently built up the dialogue with Hong Kong and Singapore on exhaustion, with Argentina on pharmaceuticals patents, and with many others, such as the EC, India and the United States. I also remember the bilateral discussions on price controls for pharmaceuticals, under the trees of the parking lot at 2 a.m.; that is a veteran's memory.

Paris, Berne and Rome Conventions and the IPIC Treaty

The incorporation of the substantive provisions of the two fundamental IP Conventions, Paris and Berne, was – in terms of international law legal drafting – a bold new step. On the one hand, it faced objections from some developing countries and quarters because of the possibility of making applicable the GATT dispute settlement system, or simply because they were not yet party to those Conventions. On the other hand, it would be impossible to take up each and every provision of the Conventions again. The incorporation of the Paris Convention also absorbed a great deal of time and energy to convince Brazil, which had not accepted the latest Acts of Lisbon and Stockholm. For copyright (or *droit d'auteur*), the incorporation of the Berne Convention was less controversial for one of the main developing countries, India. The Indian movie industry – the appellation "Bollywood" was not yet coined in the 1970s and early 1980s – was doing well in many parts of the world, including South-East Asia. On a personal note, in Viet Nam (south), after the diplomatic freeze with France, the entertainment treat in my youth was divided between (old) French and (newer) Indian movies.

Another intriguing but fascinating consequence from a purely legal drafting point of view was the 1989 Treaty on Intellectual Property with Respect to Integrated Circuits (IPIC or Washington Treaty). Designed as a *sui generis* system, it has never reached the required number of ratifications to enter into force. Some of its substantive provisions are still "living" due to their incorporation into the TRIPS Agreement. This was a result of creativity under time pressure, necessity and using the systemic approach of the incorporation technique. The 1961 International Convention for the Protection of Performers, Producers of Phonograms and Broadcasting Organizations (Rome Convention – or "Super Rome", as David Fitzpatrick from Hong Kong once called it) was a difficult piece of meat to chew on. Most Commonwealth countries and the United States accepted only some parts of the Rome Convention; rental rights for phonograms were introduced with a special grandfather clause on equitable remuneration for Japan and Switzerland. That said, the partly incorporated Rome Convention provisions later formed a useful basis for many countries (Switzerland) or groups of countries (EFTA) to ask for, in their bilateral agreements with third countries, a commitment to join the Rome Convention. It was still not an easy task, as some of our partners knew that the TRIPS Agreement did not require a full Rome Convention adherence. The world has evolved since then: there is better acceptance nowadays as countries are well aware of the importance of related rights, for example, performers' rights.

TRIPS Agreement

There is no hierarchy between the TRIPS Agreement and the aforementioned WIPO Conventions, corresponding to the classic rules of *lex posteriori* or *lex especialis*; they were all considered to be on an equal footing. This political and legal outcome is the best one that could be envisaged. That said, it is not an easy task for lawyers and panelists to analyse a measure. Maybe the following simplified illustration of the IP universe could help, to a limited extent, with understanding the relationship between the WIPO Conventions, the TRIPS Agreement and other texts, bilateral, regional or multilateral (figure 1). The blue colour indicates what the provisions negotiated were meant to do: to fill the gaps, complement or clarify other treaties. That said, the degree of creativity in interpreting IP and the TRIPS Agreement in accordance with the Vienna Convention on the Law of Treaties is sometimes high. In principle, the equilibrium struck in the TRIPS Agreement should not be disrupted and the acquis should not be eroded.

Figure 1: The IP Universe

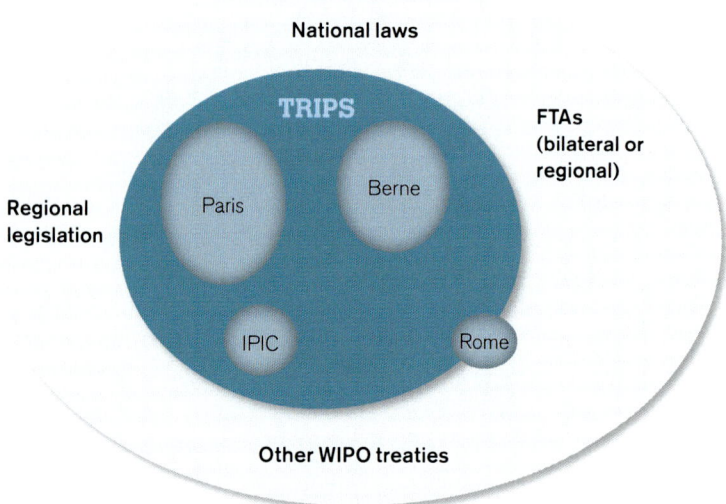

MFN was introduced in TRIPS Article 4, with very limited exemptions listed in 4(d), and in Article 5 with regard to registration treaties administered by WIPO. The TRIPS Agreement is different from the GATT and the General Agreement on Trade in Service (GATS), which provide for an *en bloc* (i.e. per category) exception to MFN with regard to free trade agreements (FTAs). A member granting higher protection "to the nationals of any other country" must grant MFN "immediately and unconditionally" to the nationals of other members, provided they do not fall into the above-mentioned exemptions. *De facto* and *de jure*, any IP privilege granted by a treaty is, in principle, transposed – unless directly applicable – into national legislation and applied to its nationals. Other WTO members could therefore get the same advantage by invoking national treatment. The additional requirement for MFN in the TRIPS Agreement – and other FTAs – should not, in practice, be a major obstacle or give rise to fears. MFN only adds to national treatment in situations where a contracting party does not give the advantage to its own nationals. It is, however, a reality that the effects of MFN in those contracting parties that accept a higher level of IP protection would be greater than for their counterparts in the negotiations who are the strong IP *demandeurs*. Switzerland fought to the very end of the negotiations for an additional exemption under Article 4. Switzerland's proposal read as follows:

> Any advantage, favour, privilege or immunity deriving from bilateral agreements related to the protection of geographical indications, including appellations or origin, provided that the PARTIES to that agreement are prepared to enter into negotiations in good faith with other interested PARTIES in order to expand such recognition of respective geographical indications and appellations of origin with a view to avoid arbitrary and unjustifiable discrimination of competing products or disguised restrictions on international trade (…)[8]

The ground for such rejection was that protection granted to GI is name by name, and by this very nature is on a reciprocal basis and not amenable to MFN. I am convinced that there could be cases where our concerns would materialize, or have already materialized. But this would be the topic of another article. "At ten minutes before midnight" – that is to say, at the last moment, just before the deal was closed – the Swiss felt the extreme loneliness of the isolated negotiator on this issue.

Industrial designs were one of our areas of focus after patents and trademarks. There was a long, difficult discussion on the criteria for protection, namely "new and/or original", and I learned there the role of the written slash, which, in my view, was not advisable in a legal text. It did, however, help move the discussions. The final text eventually resolved the problem, to a great extent. There was another issue: once the application for protection under the category of designs was published, the design was quickly copied and produced, well before the original was put on the market. Another obstacle for producers of original designs was a too-long period for examination under certain countries' systems, which Swiss producers considered as impairing the possibility of seeking and obtaining protection for products that have to respond swiftly to fashion or seasonal imperatives. Costs for protection could be very high, in particular in multiple applications (textiles and watches). Thomas Cottier and I spent some time explaining our proposals to some partners, including the EC. Most of Switzerland's objectives were attained, except for a point dear to our heart: Australia proposed that copyright protection should be an alternative avenue, in particular for textiles and wall painting designs (if my recollection is correct). We were a bit disappointed by the final wording, as copyright protection would, at least in my view, not ensure the same degree of business security. To the best of my knowledge, most WTO members have modernized their legislation to comply with the TRIPS design section, in particular the industrial-type protection, thus showing the increasing economic importance of this sector.

Patents

The negotiators' work was facilitated to some extent by the fact that the Swiss legislation already had higher levels of protection. With the objective of reaching out to a great number of countries, we could not but be realistic and expect a lower common denominator. Whether this latter is already too high or unrealistic for some quarters is another matter, addressed in other chapters. As has been indicated, Switzerland was party to the European Patent Convention (EPC) and to the WIPO registration agreements. But what is more relevant was the fact that Switzerland and other EFTA countries were negotiating the European Economic Area with the EC, and were, in principle, permanently negotiating the *acquis communautaire*. For example, the protection of test data in Switzerland was an issue between Switzerland and the EC for reasons to do with its compatibility with the legislative trend in the EC, and not a matter of TRIPS minimum-level protection. Some quarters, including industry and some federal colleagues in Switzerland, erred when they analysed the implementation of the Uruguay Round, which did not cover test data protection, and thought that the implementation package missed mentioning the duration of protection. It was time and energy consuming for the Swiss IP office and IKS/Swissmedic to explain that we already had provisions under revision to match the European standards.

The Swiss economic operators signalled several issues or problems that clearly showed that the patent area was not, as often alleged, limited to a South–South divide but included North–North divergences as well as those between continental law and common law. This is ably described by Jayashree Watal (chapter 16). I, rather, delve into the contributions of, or issues raised by, the Swiss negotiators on the basis of information, requests, clarifications or concerns by interested circles, in particular economic and industry sectors, and parliamentary interventions. It is worth mentioning that some TRIPS provisions have been developed *au fur et à mesure* ("progressively") in the negotiations. The following list is not exhaustive.

- Exhaustion of rights: Pharmaceutical and chemical industries, in particular, had strong interests in the national exhaustion for patents.

- First-to-file (all countries except the United States) vs first-to-invent: We were fully aware it would be difficult to obtain reform of a well-anchored system, not only for legal and judicial reasons but also for domestic, political ones. For both Swiss and European industry, the complexity and costs of US judicial proceedings, including the discovery procedure and the ensuing legal and business insecurity, were too high.

- The issue of government use in general and in the United States in particular.

- The issue of compulsory licensing for local working and the realities of modern trade and GATT concepts (quantitative restrictions to imports and comparative advantages for countries): The local working requirement in the old approach would consist in requiring production of the products *"sur place"*, which would not make sense for small market countries such as Singapore, or even Switzerland, particularly in the case of products the demand for which would be too low. I learned a lot of these GATT aspects from Thomas Cottier, Luzius Wasescha and John Gero (on exports), even if, intuitively, I had the same thinking on the obligation of local working. Put in GATT terms and concepts, it was perhaps more palatable to others.

- There was the unexpected setback of an EPC provision, Article 53 (exceptions to patentability) (see below on TRIPS Article 27.2).

- Better protection of biotechnological inventions.

- Environmental issues.

On the prohibition of discrimination between imported and locally produced products, one of my recollections was that the old United Kingdom Patent Act, which was using working as a ground for compulsory licensing, was amended before the entry into force of the Marrakesh Agreement Establishing the WTO) to expressly provide that importation would equal working. This change, made by an important player in the IP world, may have inspired other, similar changes in the laws in former Commonwealth countries.

TRIPS Article 27.2 is one of the provisions on which the Swiss delegation had invested much of its energy and efforts. It reads:

Members may exclude from patentability inventions, the prevention within their territory of the commercial exploitation of which is necessary to protect ordre public or morality, including to protect human, animal or plant life or health or to avoid serious prejudice to the environment, provided that such exclusion is not made merely because the exploitation is prohibited by their law.

It is a combination of the EPC provisions, with additional wording regarding environmental concerns and the Paris Convention. To refresh our memory, here is the text of the Article 53(a) and (b) of the EPC (1973):

European patents shall not be granted in respect of:

(a) inventions the publication or exploitation of which would be contrary to "ordre public" or morality; such exploitation shall not be deemed to be so contrary merely because it is prohibited by law or regulation in some or all of the Contracting States;

(b) plant or animal varieties or essentially biological processes for the production of plants or animals; this provision shall not apply to microbiological processes or the products thereof;

The practical and legal problem encountered by the Swiss pharmaceutical industry was as follows: a patent application could be rejected because the publication thereof could be considered by a country's authorities as against *ordre public* or morality. Such exclusion from patentability had the unexpected outcome that the invention that was the subject matter of the rejected application could, nevertheless, be used by others, as it had no protection and was therefore in the "public domain". The example of the abortion pill in a European country was put forward. The EC member states were bound by the EPC, and the EC had some leeway to negotiate, but not to negotiate the kind of change the Swiss delegation was requesting and which would require an insurmountable round of negotiations among the EC member states. What we proposed was to go a step further, that is, to deal with the prevention of commercial exploitation only. Not only did we have to defend the Swiss ideas *vis-à-vis* those of developing countries, but also those of other developed countries. Here again, the message delivered by some quarters that the TRIPS Agreement was a conspiracy of the evil against developing countries is ill founded.

It took some time for the Swiss delegation to explain its position in various fora, for example, the Swiss Federal Parliament, and clarify its proposal to reflect the practical concerns of industry and also the concerns expressed by some interested circles, notably the anti-biotechnology and pro-ethics circles. Thus, the concept of "human dignity", which would discourage the creation of chimeras or human clones, might be encompassed in the concept of *ordre public* or morality. Animal dignity, a very hot issue in Switzerland, was discussed too. But like *ordre public*, morality is subject to the perception of the people living in a country or region. Protection of the environment was already a topical issue, and the delegation explained as much as it could the need to reflect on problems in a relatively unchartered area, but presaged by discussions in scientific circles and the UN in the context of the Rio Summit 1992 process. In hindsight, the wording negotiated in Article 27.2 is the best we could have. Albeit a bit convoluted, it has all the ingredients: the territoriality principle, the GATT necessity test and other GATT terms, and the reflection of the idea that the patent is neutral and should not be confused with other considerations in domestic law. It should be noted that the refusal of an application or the cancellation of a patent in this paragraph 2 must be made on a case-by-case basis. I believe, in the present circumstances, that this provision will remain untouched for some time, thanks to the flexibility it offers. That having been said, I confess that I am amazed that sensitive issues, which terrified me, have now been well accepted by a large section of the Swiss public.

Paragraph 3(a) of Article 27 relates to optional *en bloc* exclusions from patentability. As a minimum level of protection, the subparagraph did not present any major obstacle. Contracting parties may provide or not provide for the patentability of certain methods of treatment.

My recollection is that the Swiss delegation tried, in the drafting committee, to advance the wording it had initially proposed, that is, the words "human and animal body" instead of "humans and animals". Like several attempts by other delegations to change the final text here and there (e.g. the EC regarding spirits in Article 23.4), this was flatly turned down – rightly so, in retrospect. If it had been accepted, others would also have demanded different changes. Good soldiers have to give it a try and know when to retreat.

As regards Article 27.3(b), I simply refer to the contributions of other authors (see Jayashree Watal, chapter 16, and Matthijs Geuze, chapter 7) and to the Secretariat's paper on the matter.[9]

I would like to simply add some comments. In the course of negotiations leading to the Brussels ministerial meeting in December 1990, the Swiss team had to face questions from the Swiss Federal Parliament, Swiss NGOs and internationalized NGOs such as Greenpeace. The latter, in a spectacular action, sent climbers to the top of the GATT building in Geneva to hang a banner protesting against the "patenting of life". The deal struck on Article 27.3(b) in particular within a small group of delegations left the Swiss delegation with some frustration at that time. The long-term impact is difficult to measure. In any event, those quarters that feared the TRIPS Agreement could be reassured. The TRIPS Agreement is about minimum levels of protection.

Article 27.3(b) is flexible enough. Eventually, it is a policy matter left to the contracting parties. As a delegate, I had to endure for quite some time the difficulties of the constructive ambiguity of a provision as part of an "agreed" TRIPS package, almost fully fleshed out but not yet agreed in the overall package. The negotiation of the future Convention on Biological Diversity (CBD) before the Rio Summit was one of most difficult experiences. The process was different from the one in the GATT, at least from my point of view: there was a lack of real dialogue, lack of transparency and defensive positions taken by all sides (plant variety circles, patent circles, biodiversity experts, NGOs, industries, etc.). Evidently, the lack of time did not permit a clarification process to alleviate concerns about the role of patents. At the end of the conference – actually midnight – it was in the area of technology transfer that we felt we should and could intervene as it was too late to negotiate or correct anything else. This was why the adoption of the CBD by Switzerland was accompanied by an interpretative declaration on technology transfer. I felt lonely, but Thomas Cottier helped me from Bern, over the phone and by fax. It reads:

> *Declaration:*
>
> *Switzerland wishes to reaffirm the importance it attaches to transfers of technology and to biotechnology in order to ensure the conservation and sustainable use of biological diversity. The compliance with intellectual property rights constitutes an essential element for the implementation of policies for technology transfer and co-investment.*
>
> *For Switzerland, transfers of technology and access to biotechnology, as defined in the text of the Convention on Biological Diversity, will be carried out in accordance with article 16 of the said Convention and in compliance with the principles and rules of protection of intellectual property, in particular multilateral and*

bilateral agreements signed or negotiated by the Contracting Parties to this Convention.

Switzerland will encourage the use of the financial mechanism established by the Convention to promote the voluntary transfer of intellectual property rights held by Swiss operators, in particular as regards the granting of licences, through normal commercial mechanisms and decisions, while ensuring adequate and effective protection of property rights.[10]

The overall question I keep asking – and Thomas Cottier has posed it in different terms in another context – is: if we had had more time, or the process had been different, would we have a different text, and could biodiversity conservation – a visionary issue – have been more promptly operationalized?

On both paragraphs 2 and 3 of Article 27, the jurisprudence developed by the European Patent Office is of great importance. That said, I would like to pay tribute to our successors in the Swiss IP office for having revised the patent law, in full consideration of a fundamental requisite, that is, the balancing of rights and obligations, of interests and of all parameters – legal, sociopolitical and Swiss entrepreneurs' competitiveness – not only on the domestic front but, as importantly, on the international plane. What will remain a great challenge is to arrive at an interpretation of what is a "plant" or an "animal", parts thereof and so on, matching the developments of science and the legal framework (laws, regulations, practices and jurisprudence). The legislator went through a long and purposeful exercise of adjusting the Swiss legislation, ensuring some legal and business security, preserving innovative initiatives and, at the same time, appeasing the concerns about trespassing a certain ethical line.[11] In any event, this area will keep the next generation of lawyers busy.

Geographical indications

Every part of the TRIPS Agreement had provoked heated debates during negotiations. All other categories of IP follow, with slight differences, the following pattern: definition, if possible; protection requisites; rights granted; exceptions to rights; duration of protection; and other issues. The structure of the text for GIs slightly differs. The TRIPS Agreement contains a definition of GIs, provides for a first, general level of protection for all products, and provides for a higher level of protection for wines and spirits, with a series of exceptions authorizing members to continue certain uses of the geographical name on their territory and, *de facto*, to export into third country markets.[12]

It was not a North–South confrontation, or a North–North one. It was a New World–Old World divide, with, on one side, the Old World – mostly European countries at the time of the negotiations – and, on the other side, the New World – that is, those countries with population composed of migrants from Europe who used names they knew for the same products in their country of origin. There are, of course, other reasons, notably, the branding business model consisting in using certain signs and/or names evoking a geographical place. There was the feeling and posture among some Old World countries that these signs or names were used in an unfair manner, either by misleading consumers as to the true origin of the product or for "free-riding" purposes, that is, taking advantage of the existence or reputation of a geographical name or sign.[13]

For one side, countries of the Old World, the export of products to some New World countries faced market access barriers with regard to the product itself and to objections posed by the New World producers – for example, that there was a prior trademark containing the geographical name or that the name had become generic. For the other side, market access to some Old World countries was more difficult, not only on the grounds of production rules but also because there was a GI protected by a *sui generis* system. The wave of bilateral agreements on GIs concluded by certain European countries with neighbouring countries had occurred in the twentieth century. Switzerland concluded agreements with (in chronological order): Germany, Czechoslovakia (now the Czech Republic and the Slovak Republic), France, Spain, Portugal, Hungary and, in the post-Uruguay Round period, the EC (later validated for the EU), the Russian Federation and Jamaica.[14] I also remember a delegate attempting to find in Geneva a certain branded beer from his country. In conformity with a bilateral agreement with a third country, Switzerland could not let in any product bearing a name that was protected under the bilateral agreement and not coming from that third country. I would like to make a general comment here: this is an area where business circles concerned sometimes strike deals between themselves that governments would not be able to do, sometimes, genuinely, because they may be obliged to stick to a wider picture of cross trade-offs.

The Swiss system

Why was Switzerland so active in this field of the TRIPS negotiations? To be able to be so, there must be legal background. The Swiss trademark law then in force provided for the protection of *indications de provenance or Herkunftsangaben* (GIs). As has already been mentioned, Switzerland is attached to free enterprise. This means that, in sectors where there is a need for production rules, producers would favour self-regulating and to agreeing on the rules. The *indications de provenance* system works relatively well within the general federal framework of the trademark law. The only sector in which there were specific provisions concerned "Swiss Made" for watches, showing – if need be – the importance of the sector for the Swiss economy. Names of a locality or a region were, in principle, entitled to protection. There was no special registry under the trademark law.

In addition to the legal framework of the trademark law and of cantons, the pre-Uruguay Round bilateral agreements provided for extremely detailed protection with geographical names negotiated and listed in annexes. The main body of the bilateral agreements contained, in general, provisions on the following points (this is a non-exhaustive list; there are variations of the list depending on the partner):

- Protection of "Confédération suisse", "Suisse" and its variations in adjectival form, as well as its emblems (e.g. the cross)

- Protection of the canton's names and emblems

- Protection of names listed in annexes

- Provisions on free-riding or unfair competition and on dilution of the GI name

- Protection against use of terms such as "type" or "imitation", translations or the mention of the true place of production

- Rules on homonymous GIs for wines, spirits and other products

- Enforcement provisions.

The scope of products is very wide in several agreements, that is, from names of countries to GIs for agricultural products and foodstuffs to handicrafts and industrial products. The more recent agreement, with Jamaica, includes GIs for services. As regards the relationship between the Swiss–EC agreement and EC members' agreements concluded, the first replaces the latter, except for any aspect not covered by the Swiss–EC text; the individual bilateral agreement will remain within the purview of the EC member. In the EC agreement, there is no annex for industrial products, as there is not yet any EC regulation thereon. In that regard, one may conclude that Swiss handicrafts and industrial products remain protected in those EC members concerned. Implementation and enforcement seemed to work well. Under the bilateral agreement with France, the Swiss producer of a sparkling wine changed the labels, abandoning the use of "champagne" as a common term. For the sake of transparency, I should mention the case of the Swiss village of Champagne (Canton de Vaud) which, under the Swiss–EC treaty, had to renounce the use of its own name on still wine. This shows that bilateral agreements may entail some risks if GIs are subject to trade-offs regarding market access in other areas.

It is worth mentioning that, apart from these agreements specifically devoted to GIs as a category of IP, there are a number of bilateral arrangements on market access – preferential tariffs – for a product bearing a GI. The most advanced agreement with market access features for products bearing GIs is the Swiss–Japan FTA, by which Switzerland obtained market access for a number of cheese products.

It is against this background of a mix of the trademark law, cantonal rules and the pre-Uruguay Round bilateral agreements that we embarked on an adventure, sometimes in an agitated state. One of Switzerland's main objectives was to ensure market access, in particular for small and medium-sized enterprises. It is worth mentioning that, for quite a long period, Switzerland had no specific protection at the federal level for the category of "appellations of origin". Foreign appellations of origin were mainly covered in bilateral agreements with those EC members that had such systems.

One of the main instructions for the Swiss negotiators was to cover industrial products in GI-related provisions of the TRIPS Agreement. Not covering them would entail the risk that Switzerland could be attacked under, for example, technical barriers to trade. The watch industry was facing great structural and economic difficulties and it was of utmost importance to avoid job losses, in particular in the Jura region, where a myriad of small and medium-sized enterprises were facing difficulties. The fact that other GATT contracting parties were using Swiss watch movements and called the final products "Swiss Made" was a hurdle to surmount. The brave soldiers that we were spent much energy and time to explain and convince. The result, the definition in Article 22.1, was a good one, covering all products. We are grateful to those who understood our position and accepted to reflect parts of our expectations. We failed on one point of principle, GIs for services.

Initially, the EC made an ambitious proposal for the protection of GIs. At a certain point in time, Switzerland was the main advocate for GIs. To be frank, I did not pay much attention to GIs for foodstuffs, being preoccupied by the scope of definition. The link was made later, I believe, at a higher level and also when the higher level for wines and spirits was accepted. The Swiss delegation had to convince countries outside the group meetings. Should there have been the possibility to spend more time, we might have rallied some supporters, or calmed down some vocal opponents. I do remember a question posed bilaterally in coffee breaks on whether or not "Gruyère" could be used as a trademark for bicycles. I shall never know whether or not my explanation on the specialty principle in trademark law and other points had actually convinced my interlocutor. Another concern was whether restaurants specialized in Chinese cuisine could continue to use names such as Hong Kong, Shanghai and so on. The problems dividing the EC member states – the feta/Feta case and the Torres case – did not help facilitate the negotiations. I also remember an anecdote from some years later: the delegation of a developing country interested in the production of ewe's or cow's milk cheese in brine informally asked me whether producers could call the cheese "feta". I reminded the delegate of the TRIPS section on GIs and the ongoing discussions. It was not a difficult task; the points made by the two camps were reflected in the minutes and reports and so on for example, bilateral agreements with third countries and costs of re-renaming. In the mid- or long term, it would be better, right from the beginning, to use a new name or one's own geographical name.

Another point, which was later developed by opponents to the *sui generis* system, was the claw-back of generic names, in particular by the EC. Australia and South Africa reported that negotiations on wine GIs undergone with the EC were traumatizing. Some countries of the New World felt they had sufficiently paid the price for accepting the inclusion of GIs in the TRIPS Agreement, but would not agree to go beyond that line, should other members ask for extension. In that regard, I would like to recall a post-Uruguay Round statement made by a developing country interested in agriculture, at an open-ended informal TRIPS consultation meeting: "Tell me what you are ready to give my country in agriculture and I will discuss extension." The call was addressed to the EC, Switzerland and other delegations. It gives a good picture of the emotional pressure on all delegations.

The acceptance by the US of a higher level of protection for wines and spirits was, to a great extent, due to the fact that the US Bureau of Alcohol, Tobacco and Firearms had a list of names. To my great surprise, the names of many Swiss wines were on the list. Thus, it was on the basis of a text outside the purview of IPRs that the deal on Article 23 was struck.

GIs was perhaps the most emotional topic of the negotiations, not only for its economic and trade impact but also for the sociocultural and historical aspects involved. While it is feasible to deal with one's own market, the fear relates to the possibility of losing third markets. Imagine one million Asians importing and consuming only Swiss Gruyère – a dream for the Swiss Gruyère producers. It is also the TRIPS GIs section which contains the highest incidence of constructive ambiguity, at least from my point of view. The built-in agenda of Article 23.4, complemented in Singapore to cover spirits, can be endlessly interpreted in different ways. While parties to the Agreement are lost in rhetorical debates, business circles may have found their own solutions. And more FTAs with a GI component have been concluded.

One important point recurrently raised is the freedom of countries to determine the appropriate method of implementing the TRIPS provisions within their own legal system and practice. Certification and collective marks are one possible way and a *sui generis* system another avenue. There are some differences between the two, explained by both camps.[15] To date, no camp has convinced the other of its choice. Both continue to pursue the path of FTAs. We get either a spaghetti bowl or, more optimistically, a lasagne plate.

Back to the future

There are many challenges and open issues. One is what would have been the current landscape if negotiators had agreed on certain issues in the Uruguay Round. Thomas Cottier has suggested that establishing a five-year period in Article 39.3 might have better protected countries from being pressured to adopt an even longer term of protection. As regards this specific issue, developing countries may continue availing themselves of the point that the TRIPS Agreement is about minimum levels of protection and they could protect themselves behind this shield to alleviate the pressure. But would this retracting posture be a long-term viable choice? Would Switzerland be the first-ranking country it is in terms of innovation if it had not voluntarily opted for an outward-oriented policy of investment? Would Singapore have been chosen by a Swiss multinational as a biotech hub in South-East Asia if it had not voluntarily opted for an outward-oriented policy and created an environment propitious for foreign direct investment? Would the CBD be more promptly operational if patents were not considered as the target to shoot at, as having the main responsibility for biodiversity reduction or loss?

As regards patents, I still believe that this IPR, compared with others, is the most precise and effective protection system for the right holder as well as for competitors. I still do not believe in the straight-jacket perception of patents as being fully monopolistic. During the 20 years of protection, there are many safeguards for competitors; abuses, if any, can be corrected. Moreover, the WTO case law as well as the Doha Declaration on the TRIPS Agreement and Public Health have demonstrated or confirmed the TRIPS Agreement's flexibilities. To some extent, the TRIPS Agreement is the best we could arrive at. In a similar vein to Thomas Cottier's remarks at the TRIPS Symposium (February 2015), I do not believe that compulsory licences are the best way to obtain actual technology transfer. That said, one consequence of TRIPS Article 31 is that the mere threat thereof had produced some effects, for example, lowering of prices and more cooperation. This in itself is an achievement. Curiously enough, there does not seem any modern, comprehensive paper analysing the current situation, at least to the best of my knowledge.

I have – maybe a bit presumptuously – suggested food for thought from the lessons learned. I strongly believe that the issues of IP remain basically the same; it is only the clothes which have changed and need more efforts and creative thinking. I have cited the achievements made by the Swiss IP office regarding biotechnology. At the risk of repetition, I am perplexed that, currently, biotechnology is not raising the same emotional concerns as it did at the time of the Uruguay Round. Are there other fronts on which civil society is focusing, or are biotechnological advances better accepted? Should this be the case, there would be a need to reflect on a possible revisiting of our current thinking and postures. Should the TRIPS Agreement not be flexible enough to cover future technological developments? In any event, biotechnology will keep the next generation of lawyers and policy makers busy, if not at the WTO or WIPO, then at least at the national level. Should the TRIPS Agreement be flexible enough to cover future developments, we could then be content.

Reflecting on this chapter, I believe the younger generation has talent. Should they follow what we experienced in the Uruguay Round? The Uruguay Round process and ingredients have been efficiently used in the course of the negotiations of the Doha Declaration on the TRIPS Agreement and Public Health. Attempts to use the same way of proceeding were made for the register of GIs for wines and spirits. The Doha Declaration on the TRIPS Agreement and Public Health was an exceptional case due to the unchallenged urgency aspect of a humanitarian problem. Otherwise – and this is my personal opinion – we need to create the same conditions for a wider landscape, propitious for negotiations, namely, with possible trade-offs across the board. Maybe a repetition of the Uruguay Round would not be possible, but some results are likely to be achieved by gathering persons with goodwill in a similar magic constellation.

I would add, on a personal note, that we negotiators often met during rest days, between two meetings or in the evenings, to get the pressure off our chests. I have fond memories of many – Lou Flaks, Sivakant Tiwari, Emery Simon, Larry Nelsen and David Hartridge, to name a few. Even the sandwiches and the one litre bottles of red wine offered by the GATT Secretariat were, in retrospect, not too bad. I have fond memories of a group of women (Alice Zalik, the Nordic delegates, Umi K.B.A. Majid from Malaysia and Jayashree Watal from India, among others). We did not talk about TRIPS negotiations but about families and frivolous things. Friendship is fully compatible with the defence of national interests and, in some cases, "shouting" at each other – as delegates – when we disagreed. I also have fond memories of a dedicated and skillful Secretariat and a very wise Chair.

Finally, I would like to paraphrase the vibrant call of a respected emeritus professor of sciences to new graduates and doctorates in Berne some time ago, and say: "Have a good state of mind, be patient and be cheerful" (*Haben Sie Mut, Geduld und Fröhlichkeit*, in German).

Endnotes

1   My thanks go to Felix Addor (Swiss Federal Institute of Intellectual Property), who helped me write and defend the TRIPS part in the implementation message relating to the results of the Uruguay Round. But, foremost, I am indebted to Thomas Cottier, my former superior, who made me discover the arcane GATT. I value his deep knowledge of constitutional and international law, his humanist mind and his genuine and respectful attitude *vis-à-vis* all delegations while tenaciously defending the Swiss positions, unless they were proven ill founded by the opponents. I am deeply indebted to him as well as to Adrian Otten and Jayashree Watal for their comments and corrections – enlightening as usual – and for sharing their memories. Anything the reader considers as historically erroneous inaccurate, substantively wrong or incomplete should be attributed to a fading memory.

2   I worked there under the able guidance of Ludwig Baeumer and François Curchod.

3   EFTA stands for the European Free Trade Association.

4   Certain parts or sentences on the Swiss system and legislation have been extracted or translated from the following sources: www.amtsdruckschriften.bar.admin.ch/viewOrigDoc. do?id=10107965&action=open (Message relatif aux modifications à apporter au droit federal dans la perspective de la ratification des accords du GATT/OMC (Cycle d'Uruguay) (Message 2 GATT), du 19 septembre 1994, FF 1994 IV 995; www.ipi.ch; www.parlement.ch (all sites last accessed 8 July 2015).

5   GATT document MTN.GNG/NG11/W/20, Negotiating Group on Trade-Related Aspects of Intellectual Property Rights, Including Trade in Counterfeit Goods – Activities in other International Organizations of Possible Interest in Relation to Matters raised in the Group – Note by the Secretariat, 8 February 1988.

6   GATT document MTN.GNG/NG11/W/15, Negotiating Group on Trade-Related Aspects of Intellectual Property Rights, Including Trade in Counterfeit Goods – Suggestion by Switzerland for Achieving the Negotiating Objective, 26 October 1987.

7   GATT document MTN.GNG/NG11/W/73, Negotiating Group on Trade-Related Aspects of Intellectual Property Rights, Including Trade in Counterfeit Goods – Draft amendment to the General Agreement on Tariffs and Trade on the Protection of Trade-related Intellectual Property Rights – Communication from Switzerland, 14 May 1990.

8   GATT document MTN.GNG/NG11/W/73, Article 102 (2).

9   WTO documents IP/C/W/273/Rev.1, Council for Trade-Related Aspects of Intellectual Property Rights – Review of the Provisions of Article 27.3(b) – Illustrative List of Questions – Prepared by the Secretariat – Revision, 18 February 2003, and IP/C/W/369/Rev.1, Council for Trade-Related Aspects of Intellectual Property Rights - Review of the Provisions of Article 27.3(b) - Summary of Issues Raised and Points made - Note by the Secretariat - Revision, 9 March 2006.

10 See https://treaties.un.org/pages/ViewDetails.aspx?src=TREATY&mtdsg_no=XXVII-8& chapter=27&lang=en#EndDec (last accessed 7 June 2015).

11 See www.ipi.ch; www.ige.ch/fileadmin/user_upload/Juristische_Infos/f/j10010f.pdf (last accessed 7 June 2015).

12   For a more detailed description of the GI section of the Agreement, I refer to *A handbook on the WTO TRIPS Agreement* (Cambridge, UK; Geneva: Cambridge University Press; WTO, 2012).

13   In this respect, I would like to refer to: the minutes of the TRIPS Council meetings up until the end of 2002 (the date by which the Council should make a report on the discussions on implementation issues, as instructed by ministers) (WTO document series IP/C/M); the minutes of the Doha ad hoc negotiating body entrusted with the negotiations on a register of GIs for wines and spirits (WTO document series TN/IP/M); WTO document WT/GC/W/546 – TN/C/W/25, Compilation of Issues Raised and Views Expressed – Note by the Secretariat, 18 May 2005; and the reports by former Director-General Pascal Lamy on implementation issues (WTO document WT/GC/W/591 – TN/C/W/50, 9 June 2008), (WTO document WT/GC/W/633 – TN/C/W/61, 21 April 2011).

14   See www.ige.ch/fr/indications-de-provenance/indications-de-provenance-et-indications-geographiques/traites-bilateraux.html (last accessed 7 June 2015).

15   For the most recent discussion, see former WTO Director-General Pascal Lamy's reports at www.wto.org/english/tratop_e/trips_e/ta_docs_e/5_2_wtgcw546_e.pdf (last accessed 7 June 2015).

10

Negotiating for the European Communities and their member states

Jörg Reinbothe

Introduction

The focus of this chapter

This chapter will focus on the substance of the TRIPS negotiations. I will explain what was at stake, how the negotiations went and what the outcome was for the substance of IP – all from my own personal perspective and based on my own previous and subsequent experience in this field. It follows that this chapter is not designed to provide a comprehensive assessment of the TRIPS Agreement, nor will it embark on the political environment of the Uruguay Round of multilateral trade negotiations in general and of the TRIPS negotiating mandate in particular. But let me present the flavour of what we, the negotiators, were up against and what we eventually achieved in the area of IP.

My starting point will be an explanation of where I came from when I joined the TRIPS negotiating team and what my role was during the negotiations. As background information, I will also present the status quo of IP protection in the European Communities (EC) and its member states in the late 1980s and early 1990s and its interface with the treaty now known as the Treaty on the Functioning of the European Union (hereinafter the ECT) – that is, the substance of IP protection at the time from an EC perspective. Subsequently, I will cover the main challenges for the EC in the TRIPS negotiations, which will be followed by a presentation of some selected achievements of the TRIPS Agreement, which strike me as being particularly important. Finally, I cannot help looking beyond the TRIPS Agreement: I have personally witnessed its major impact on the further development of international law on IP.

My role in the TRIPS negotiations

Shortly after I had taken up my position in the European Commission in summer 1988, I joined the EC team in the TRIPS negotiations of the Uruguay Round of the GATT. At that time, pure trade negotiations were new to me, but the substance of, and international negotiations on, IP were not. As a lawyer by training, I had previously served in the Ministry of Justice of the Federal Republic of Germany, dealing with IP issues and participating in international negotiations within the framework of WIPO and the United Nations Educational, Scientific and Cultural Organization (UNESCO). In addition, immediately prior to coming to Brussels in 1988, I had served for two years as a Counsellor at the Permanent Representation of the Federal Republic of Germany to the UN in New York.

All this helped me to pursue my responsibilities in the EC TRIPS negotiating team, which was headed by Mogens Peter Carl from the European Commission Directorate General responsible for trade. My tasks in our team were mainly twofold: due to my IP expertise and as an official of the European Commission Internal Market Directorate General (which was responsible for the domestic EC aspects of IP), I had to coordinate the substance of IP within the Commission services and give input on such substance to the EC negotiating team; and, to fulfil this task, I had to cross-check our input on substance with IP experts in EC member states and assure their feedback. Needless to say, I shared these tasks with other members of our team, notably Tony Howard, whose expertise, particularly on industrial property issues, was crucial throughout the negotiations. Both Tony and I came from the substance of IP when we joined the EC TRIPS negotiating team. We were so fascinated by the negotiating targets, the process and the progress, that we could not resist, already in 1991, sharing our impressions on the state of play of the TRIPS negotiations with a wider audience.[1]

Intellectual property within the framework of the European Communities

At the outset, let me shed some light on a rather particular, if not unique, challenge that we in the EC delegation had to face: the features and state of play of IP protection in the EC at the time of the TRIPS negotiations. Why would our internal situation in this respect be so special, and why would this be relevant for the negotiations? The main reason is that the EC then, as well as the European Union (EU) today, was not, and still is not, a state. Other delegations represented states and their national interests, with their own national legal order and economy in mind. As the EC delegation, we had to carry an even bigger backpack, or at least one with more complex contents: there was hardly any genuine EC law in place on IP, but, at the same time, we had to keep in mind all the - at the time – 15 rather different legal systems and economic orientations of the EC member states.

Having a closer look at these differences makes sense. After all, with IP law at EC level in the making in parallel with the TRIPS negotiations, and with IP and intra-EC trade also being an issue within the EC, we could easily draw on our own domestic experiences when negotiating a TRIPS agreement. We were busy building bridges in both the TRIPS negotiations and the EC.

The interface between intellectual property law and the European Communities treaty

In fact, at the time of the TRIPS negotiations, EC law on IP was still pretty much in its infancy and presented a rather scattered picture: from the outset, the EC had left the protection of IP to its member states. While topics such as agriculture, competition or the EC internal market had always been core policies for the EC, IP protection was not an active EC policy. Rather, the ECT addressed IP only in a defensive manner: under Article 36, EC member states were allowed to maintain their IP protection to the extent such protection did not unduly interfere with the functioning of the EC internal market. In this respect, the concept of Article 36 of the ECT was very similar to that of Article XX(d) of the GATT.

Nevertheless, the interface between IP, on the one hand, and two other major EC policies (namely, competition and the internal market), on the other, had already been an issue for a long time before the TRIPS negotiations. Since the early 1960s, the European Court of Justice had marked the territory and the dividing lines in several decisions. And from the 1970s, the EC legislator began taking on an active role in the structuring of IP protection through the harmonization of EC member states' laws and, in some cases, the creation of EC-wide titles. The focus was, in particular, on industrial property, such as patents (biotechnology) and trademarks, whereas copyright harmonization was not initiated until the late 1980s.

The EC law (acquis communautaire) on intellectual property during the TRIPS negotiations

EC member states and their different economic realities

A closer look reveals that the state of play with respect to IP protection in the EC member states at the time of the TRIPS negotiations was not homogeneous, to say the least. In most of the 15 member states of the EC, different cultures, different languages, different economic realities and, in some cases, different legal traditions prevailed.[2] Also, some EC member states were net exporters; others were net importers of IP-based products, such as pharmaceuticals, brand-named products, such as cars or consumer electronics, products with a link to a geographical indication (GI), music and films; and member states' views on the protection of IP were not always identical. However, they were all trading partners with respect to goods and services protected by IP and had to find common ground on the parameters of protection. Note the similarities with the TRIPS negotiations!

The EC *acquis communautaire* on intellectual property in the early 1990s

At the time of the TRIPS negotiations, the EC had harmonized its member states' laws only to a certain extent: in the area of patents, the European Patent Organization was in place, though it was not an EC institution; one aspect of patent law, namely, the treatment of inventions in the field of biotechnology, was harmonized by Directive 98/44/EC only after the TRIPS Agreement, and there was no EC patent office; trademark law was harmonized through Directive 89/104/EEC in 1989, but Community Trademark Regulation 40/94 was only adopted in 1993, and the European Trademark Office had not yet taken up its work; the harmonization of design law was in the making; the harmonization of copyright had just taken off with the adoption of a first Directive on the protection of computer programs in 1991, followed by three other Directives in 1992 and 1993 (the Database Protection Directive was adopted in 1996 and the other EC/EU copyright Directives followed even later); the Directive on the protection of topographies of semiconductor layouts was adopted in 1986; and no comprehensive EC legislation yet existed on the protection of GIs.

All this demonstrates that, at the time of the TRIPS negotiations, there was no settled *acquis communautaire* on IP in place. As a result, in WIPO as well as within the TRIPS framework, the EC negotiating team always had to take into account the to some extent rather different approach of EC member states to IP. The progress that we were after on IP had to pass the acceptability and sustainability tests with respect to both EC member states and the international community.

During the TRIPS negotiations, we could also draw upon something else that was very familiar to legislation within the EC internal market framework: the principle of subsidiarity. We have always been bound to limit EC legislation to what was absolutely needed for the functioning of the EC internal market; the rest was to be left to EC member states' own legislation. Indeed, this principle was (and still is) relevant in the TRIPS context, too: the TRIPS Agreement, like any other multilateral framework of IP rules, addresses (only) those issues that are relevant for the functioning of international trade on IP – not more, and certainly not less.

The challenges of the TRIPS negotiations regarding the substance of intellectual property

In addition to the respect for these general principles of acceptability, sustainability and subsidiarity, which we were very familiar with against our EC experience, there were some truly IP-related principles, crucial for legislating on IP protection, at no matter which level, that we had to keep in mind – and, I believe, we respected – in the TRIPS negotiations.

General objectives

The balance of rights and interests

In preparing and negotiating any legislation on IP, be it in national parliaments, within the EC framework, or with international partners, one has to face a fundamental challenge: how to balance the IP rights of right holders and give them a strong and meaningful protection of their property while protecting the interests of users, consumers and the society at large in the access to protected goods and services at low prices, and within competitive markets. It did not come as a surprise that the search for a fair balance of these rights and interests – something I had already experienced on so many occasions – was also an important issue in the TRIPS negotiations. But, also, the need for finding a balance between the often very different interests and traditions of states was all too familiar: the differences in the approach to IP protection of the GATT contracting parties were mirrored, albeit on a smaller scale, by the situation within the EC.

The interface between intellectual property protection and free trade

Similarly, and again due to my previous experience with domestic and regional IP legislation, I was not surprised by the presence of another challenge, which is inherent in the very nature of IP protection: how to reconcile the monopoly protection that IP grants with open competition and free trade. When I joined the TRIPS negotiations, it was already clear to me that both competition and free trade, on the one hand, and IP protection, on the other, serve very similar, if not identical, objectives, namely, fostering high quality and stimulating inventions, creations and investments for the benefit of the society at large. So for me, these are not contradictions in terms but, rather, very valuable policies and instruments that have to be seen together in perspective; this is also reflected in Article XX(d) in the GATT and Article 36 of the ECT mentioned above, which were designed to do justice to all these policies and strike an appropriate balance among them.

TRIPS negotiations and the existing international intellectual property framework

For the Uruguay Round negotiations, IP might have been considered the new kid on the block – but was it really? While IP had already been an issue raised in the GATT (previously, mainly through Article XX(d) and the project of an Anti-Counterfeiting Code), it had been addressed in other international fora, such as the Organisation for Economic Co-operation and Development (OECD), UNESCO and the United Nations Conference on Trade and Development (UNCTAD), and, of course, in WIPO. It was, in particular, the comprehensive WIPO framework of international IP protection, with its more than 20 international treaties, that had to be taken into account. But we were determined to do more than that, to respect the treaties administered by WIPO, build upon them and prove that a meaningful and balanced IP protection is a legitimate part of international trade – beneficial for all countries and territories, irrespective of their state of development.

Also, those familiar with the existing international IP framework and coming from that side of the spectrum, like me, shared the strong feeling that the time was ripe to integrate IP into the framework of international trade. Commerce with IP had already become an indispensable part of world trade, so that IP experts, too, could no longer afford to turn a blind eye to the successful and operational set of GATT rules and mechanisms. So why not try to engage together, we felt, in a new endeavour – without abandoning the fundamental principles of IP protection? This truly created a common spirit between IP experts and trade negotiators.

Overview of some selected issues at stake

Copyright

Apart from these general or, as one may call them, horizontal, challenges described above, each area of IP presented its own challenges on substance. As far as copyright is concerned, the principal reference point was the Berne Convention for the Protection of Literary and Artistic Works, with its then over 80 contracting parties.[3] Here, the main focus was on issues on which the Berne Convention or other conventions could benefit from clarification or where gaps had to be filled with a view to providing for more legal certainty.

The Berne Convention had last been revised in 1971. Further revisions would have been called for in view of the rapid progress of technology, such as in computers, but revising the Berne Convention directly through a diplomatic conference at WIPO had apparently not been a realistic option. Such a revision would have required unanimity among all Berne Convention contracting parties. The GATT, with its more pragmatic decision-making mechanism, was therefore the obvious route to take. At the same time, we had to be aware of Article 20 of the Berne Convention. It provides that any other agreements by Berne Convention contracting parties outside the Berne Convention must not reduce the level of IP protection granted by the Berne Convention. So, agreeing on a lower level of protection than provided by the Berne Convention was not an option, supported also on legal grounds.

From an EC perspective, this translated into the following main objectives in the field of copyright: a clarification that computer programs (an issue on which the EC itself had only in 1991 adopted its very first Copyright Directive) and compilations of data (creative databases), both areas where new technology had become relevant for trade, are protected as literary works; granting explicit rental rights; providing certain neighbouring right holders with at least basic protection; clarifying the scope of the national treatment obligations; respecting in all of that Article 20 of the Berne Convention, the provision "safeguarding" the Berne level of protection, as explained above; and, finally, integrating the substantive provisions of the Berne Convention into the TRIPS Agreement. In the copyright area, it turned out to be particularly difficult to bridge the cultural differences and the different legal traditions inherent in most, if not all, of these issues (see Hannu Wager, chapter 17).

Patents

In the field of patents, clarifications were sought regarding the term of protection (duration), the required minimum level of protection and the conditions for protection. One of the major challenges here was to agree on exclusions from patentability.

Trademarks, models and designs

On trademark protection, the desired clarifications included the conditions for protection, the rights conferred, permitted use requirements and the term of protection of trademarks. Regarding design protection, the issues were rather similar to those in the field of trademarks. However, a particular challenge here was to determine the borderline between protectable designs and designs following technical requirements or functions. In fact, this was an almost classic dispute about the scope of IP protection: should the monopoly held by car manufacturers, which is based on their IP protection, extend to spare parts, if the shape and design of the latter is merely dictated by their function?

Semiconductor layouts

Agreeing on the protection of topographies of semiconductor layouts presented specific problems, because attempts to define such protection at international level had so far been unsuccessful; the Treaty on Intellectual Property in Respect of Integrated Circuits (IPIC or Washington Treaty) of 1989 had never come into force, so that, actually, no specific international treaty covered this type of subject matter. The objective was, therefore, to arrive – for the first time internationally - at common ground on the protection of semiconductor layouts by way of drawing upon the IPIC Treaty, but redefining a self-standing, appropriate balance of all rights and interests.

Geographical indications

The existing international treaty on the protection of GIs (the Lisbon Agreement for the Protection of Appellations of Origin and their International Registration) had a rather limited membership. And yet, trade in goods with a reputation based on their geographical origin, such as wines, spirits, other foodstuffs or industrial products, had gained a worldwide dimension. Protecting the producers as well as consumers against unfair trade in such products was, therefore, an important negotiating objective of the EC. However, several challenges surrounded this issue throughout the negotiations, and they all had a lot to do with different cultures, outlooks and traditions. Still, we felt that a line had to be drawn between indications that have a link to a certain region and its reputation for quality (and that are purposefully (ab)used on non-original products with a view to benefiting from the reputation of the original product), on the one hand, and generic names that no one would confuse as referring to a region in the first place, on the other hand. We would believe that the latter category was fairly small, as are the sometimes claimed differences in the perception of consumers worldwide.

Unfair competition and trade secrets

Originally, the objective behind this issue was to arrive at a clarification of the protection against unfair competition, dishonest practices, misconception and passing-off as it is contained in Articles 10*bis* and 10*ter* of the Paris Convention for the Protection of Industrial Property. But even with these Articles of the Paris

Convention as a basis, the challenges attached to this issue were the rather different concepts of protection against unfair competition – again, even within the EC.

Enforcement

One may say that, in general, legislating on the substance of IP protection is of little use without meaningful provisions on its domestic enforcement – and the same holds true for reaching a level playing field at international level. In fact, the quality and scope of IP protection depends on its enforcement. The problem we had to face here was that, apart from the rather general provisions in the Berne Convention or the Paris Convention, with their adjudication left to the International Court of Justice, which had never been applied, no multilateral discipline or agreement existed with rules on the domestic enforcement of IP. Putting together an operational and, at the same time, balanced text on enforcement in the TRIPS Agreement was thus a major challenge – and an uphill battle: while we all agreed that such rules would be needed, many negotiators had different views on what they should look like; and even within the EC, finding a valid common denominator of all the civil procedure concepts with their many different features was not an easy call.

This survey could only present a selection of the different challenges. Yet it only goes to show that, on each of these issues, the cards on the TRIPS negotiating table were shuffled anew. The views differed, even controversies occurred, according to the varying features of IP topics, cutting across geographical and political boundaries, be they North–South, North–North, between different regions or even within the same region. Nevertheless, we were all dedicated to arriving at good and sustainable results. And I have only the best memories of the constructive and always fact-oriented spirit of these, at times, rather tough discussions.

Some selected achievements and value additions

Despite all these difficulties, differing conceptual views and the implied challenges, we succeeded. Yes, personally, I believe that the TRIPS Agreement does represent a success for all states, rights and interests involved. All negotiators were winners in the sense that all elements of added value contained in the TRIPS Agreement – and there are quite a few – remain faithful to the general objectives of international IP protection that any national, regional or international legislator has to keep in mind: providing for an appropriate balance of rights and interests;

doing justice to the interface between IP protection and free trade; and respecting, and building upon, the existing international IP obligations. Let me highlight in the following some of the features of added value that we accomplished.

Copyright

There are plenty of such added-value elements already in the area of copyright. We settled the dispute about the "work" character of computer programs and creative databases by (i) clarifying that computer programs, by definition, and databases, on condition that they are "intellectual creations", are protected as literary works within the meaning of the Berne Convention's terminology, and (ii) drawing explicitly the borderline with the public domain in Article 9(2). For the first time in an international IP agreement, rental rights were explicitly granted for certain works and under certain conditions, the term of protection for legal persons' rights was clarified, and some basic protection was provided for performers, producers of phonograms and broadcasting organizations. In addition, and again for the first time, the copyright section contains several general principles of copyright protection: it states explicitly the general principle that copyright protection extends to "expressions and not to ideas, methods of operation or mathematical concepts as such" – an important clarification on the limits of protection; it clarifies that the protection of databases ("compilations") does "not extend to the data or material itself"; and it establishes the "three-step test" (drawn from the Berne Convention where it applies only to exceptions from the reproduction right) as a general, generic test for the application of any exception to copyright.

Moreover, it should not be forgotten that this TRIPS section on copyright and related rights very elegantly confirms the substantive provisions of the Berne Convention and includes them into the TRIPS Agreement through the "compliance clause" in Article 9(1) – a new method and a breakthrough in international law-making: it *de facto* overcame the requirement of unanimity for the revision of the Berne Convention.

Semiconductor layout-designs

The "compliance clause" that was already applied for copyright protection in Article 9(1) was used again for the protection of semiconductor layouts. But, as neither the IPIC Treaty nor any other international treaty had come into force in this field of IP, the "compliance clause" was simply, and in a very pragmatic manner, applied as a reference to those provisions of the IPIC Treaty that all negotiators were in a position to agree on. In addition, several other provisions were adopted to fill gaps or overcome controversies that were left by the IPIC Treaty. For my taste, the added value of this section stems from both its contents on substance and the chosen method of international law-making, namely, the particularly interesting use of the "compliance clause" – referring to a treaty that never came into force.

Trade secrets

The common ground on the understanding of the notion of unfair competition within the meaning of Article 10*bis* of the Paris Convention turned out to be limited. Part II Section 7 is called "Protection of Undisclosed Information" and provides, basically, for the protection of trade secrets and certain test data. Still, the reference to the Paris Convention was maintained, so that this Section does serve as a clarification of a very important aspect of unfair competition.

Geographical indications

Admittedly, Part II Section 3 on GIs does not go as far as the EC would have wanted (or as would have been appropriate, in my view). However, with its structure of a general protection of all GIs, a more explicit protection of indications used for wines and spirits, and the explicit promise to enter into negotiations on a reinforced protection, this Section was at least a good start. It was certainly a valid and constructive way out of the international deadlock on this topic that we could witness in the late 1980s.

Enforcement

Last, but not least, a word on Part III of the TRIPS Agreement on the Enforcement of Intellectual Property Rights. When we worked on our first draft proposal of this Section, but also throughout all the negotiations that followed, we were painfully aware that we entered new territory. Internationally, we were in "no man's land"; we could not draw upon any existing multilateral international agreement in this respect. But, on the other hand, this area was densely populated by national laws and, being a lawyer myself, I know that lawyers tend to be convinced that their own country's system is the best. It was a bit like exploring new uninhabited territory with an overly heavy backpack filled with preconceptions.

This is how we went about this task that appeared to be an attempt to square the circle: we closely cooperated with other delegations; we discussed with the EC member states (which have plenty of differences among themselves in their legal enforcement systems, including civil law and common law concepts); we consulted experts, judges and customs officials; we cross-checked our ideas with the interested circles concerned; and we relied on advice from WIPO.

I think Part III is a particularly successful result of our negotiations. Even if it may appear to be too detailed for some and too general for others, it does reflect the common ground among all negotiators – and, as I am convinced, it was a balanced breakthrough based on common sense.

TRIPS and beyond: The impact of the TRIPS Agreement on international intellectual property law and EU law

I just described Part III of the TRIPS Agreement, on enforcement, as a breakthrough, and, indeed, it had a significant impact on international IP protection and its future. In fact, not only did this Part of the TRIPS Agreement open doors and lead to further international progress in this field, many other features of the TRIPS Agreement were subsequently adopted by international law-makers and included in other IP treaties. Indeed, other elements of the TRIPS Agreement were further elaborated on in international, national and EU law: had we called some of the TRIPS provisions on copyright "Berne plus", we can now find TRIPS provisions and "TRIPS-plus" elements elsewhere.

Let us take the copyright provisions in Part II Section 1 and Part III on enforcement as examples. The provisions on the protection of computer programs and on the non-protectability of ideas found their way almost verbatim into the WIPO "Internet Treaties" (WIPO Copyright Treaty (WCT) and WIPO Performances and Phonogram Treaty (WPPT)) of 1996. These Treaties also provide for rental rights, albeit more explicitly than TRIPS and, therefore, constitute an example of TRIPS plus. The "three-step test", for the first time introduced as a general test for all copyright exceptions by the TRIPS Agreement, has now become the international standard: it is not only reiterated in the WCT and the WPPT, as well as in the more recent WIPO treaties (Beijing Treaty on Audiovisual Performances, 2012 (BTAP) and Marrakesh Treaty to Facilitate Access to Published Works for Persons Who Are Blind, Visually Impaired or Otherwise Print Disabled, 2013), but also included in Directive 2001/29/EC on the harmonisation of certain aspects of copyright and related rights in the information society. The legal technique of the "compliance clause", introduced by the TRIPS Agreement in the field of copyright, has become established international practice when classic conventions that can only be formally revised unanimously are to be amended. It has already been used in several IP treaties, notably in the WCT and the BTAP.[4]

Finally, Part III of the TRIPS Agreement, on enforcement, has been the pacesetter for, and/or is referred to, in several more recent IP treaties, including the WCT and the WPPT. The fact that, to date, the TRIPS provisions on enforcement have remained unrivalled, and no other more detailed international rules have been put in place, amply proves their quality. In the EU, the very first Directive on the enforcement of intellectual property rights (Directive 2004/48/EC) clearly draws on, and was inspired by, the TRIPS provisions.

Conclusion

Accomplishing the TRIPS Agreement was proof of the possibility of reaching, and the will to reach, common ground, despite all the initially rather strong North–South, North–North or other divergences in the field of IP. On substance, the TRIPS Agreement has managed to accommodate the needs and interests of countries with different backgrounds and different economic realities. This was even the case within the EC and, subsequently, the EU; and I believe it is fair to say that this aspect has added to our negotiating team's credibility. Moreover, the TRIPS Agreement has also given an incentive and a push, in a balanced way, to the economies of such countries as Bulgaria, Hungary, Poland and Sweden, which were not yet members of the EC at the time of the TRIPS negotiations.

The protection of IP has always been an evolving scenario. And the positive impact of the TRIPS Agreement on a balanced IP protection regime and on trade with IP-based goods and services has also been taken further into the future. Not only has the TRIPS Agreement been the solid basis for many other international agreements in this field, it is itself "alive and kicking" and nowadays an indispensable part of the international IP environment.

No, negotiating the TRIPS Agreement was not easy. But I am proud to have been part of it. After all, EC officials are used to bridging gaps. We are used to squaring circles, to persuading experts not to focus exclusively on their own national systems. But once a Directive is in place, once we have overcome the hurdles and been successful in arriving at a balanced outcome, once there is satisfaction with and co-ownership of the result, we know that it was worth all the effort. All this greatly resembles the TRIPS negotiations.

What was very rewarding for me was the constructive climate of the TRIPS negotiations, which I remember well – the common spirit among so many different nations and those with different outlooks, from around the world. The TRIPS negotiations and their result have shown how much we have in common. It is our responsibility not to put these achievements at risk.

Endnotes

1 See Jörg Reinbothe and Anthony Howard, "The state of play in the negotiations on TRIPs (GATT/Uruguay Round)", *European Intellectual Property Review*, 13(5) (1991), 157-64.

2 This was the number of EC member states between 1986 and 1995.

3 In 1990, the Berne Convention had 83 contracting parties.

4 More details on the extent to which these new WIPO treaties have drawn upon the TRIPS Agreement are provided in Jörg Reinbothe and Silke von Lewinski, *The WIPO treaties on copyright: A commentary on the WCT, the WPPT and the BTAP,* 2nd edition (Oxford: Oxford University Press, 2015).

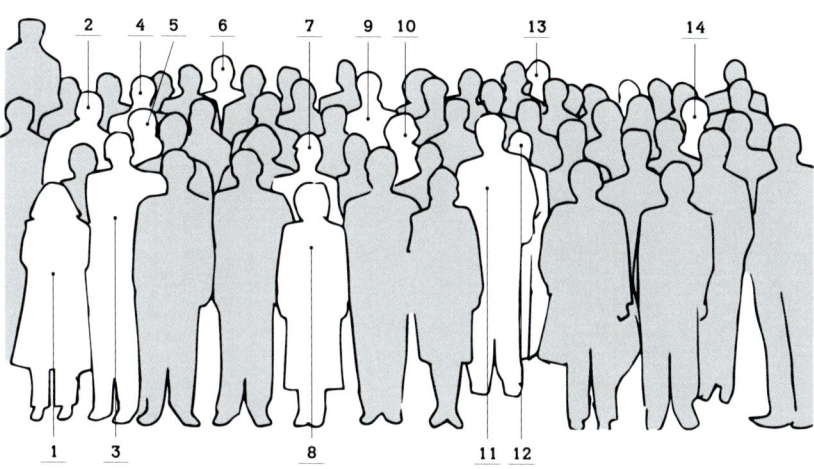

TRIPS negotiators in 1990 at the Centre William Rappard (authors in the volume shown below).

1 Thu-Lang Tran Wasescha (Switzerland)
2 Thomas Cottier (Switzerland)
3 Adrian Macey (New Zealand)
4 Adrian Otten (GATT Secretariat)
5 Piragibe dos Santos Tarragô (Brazil)
6 Matthijs Geuze (GATT Secretariat)
7 Catherine Field (USA)
8 Umi Kalthum Binti Abdul Majid (Malaysia)

9 Antonio Gustavo Trombetta (Argentina)
10 Jayashree Watal (India)
11 Lars Anell (Sweden; Chairman of the TRIPS Negotiating Group)
12 Jagdish Sagar (India)
13 Jörg Reinbothe (European Commission)
14 John Gero (Canada)

Symposium on the TRIPS Agreement, 26 February 2015,
at the WTO headquarters in Geneva, Switzerland.

Many of the contributors to this book, attending the
Symposium on the TRIPS Agreement in February 2015.

Ambassador Lars Anell, Chair of the Swedish Research Council, speaking at the Symposium. He chaired the TRIPS Negotiating Group during the Uruguay Round TRIPS negotiations.

Jayashree Watal, Counsellor in the Intellectual Property Division of the WTO, speaking at the Symposium.
She represented India during the Uruguay Round TRIPS negotiations.

Antony Taubman, Director of the Intellectual Property Division of the WTO, speaking at the Symposium.

Adrian Otten, former Director of the Intellectual Property Division of the WTO, speaking at the Symposium. He was Secretary of the TRIPS Negotiating Group during the Uruguay Round TRIPS negotiations.

Thomas Cottier, Emeritus Professor of European and International Economic Law at the University of Bern, speaking at the Symposium. He represented Switzerland during the Uruguay Round negotiations, first on dispute settlement and subsidies, and he later led Swiss negotiations on TRIPS.

John Gero, former Canadian Ambassador to the WTO, WIPO and UNCTAD in Geneva, speaking at the Symposium. He represented Canada during the Uruguay Round TRIPS negotiations.

Mogens Peter Carl, former European Commission Director-General for External Trade, speaking at the Symposium. He represented the European Communities during the Uruguay Round TRIPS negotiations.

Matthijs Geuze, Head of the International Appellations of Origin Registry in the Brands and Designs Sector of WIPO. He assisted the Uruguay Round TRIPS negotiations as a member of the GATT Secretariat.

Catherine Field, consultant and former Deputy General Counsel of the US Trade Representative, speaking at the Symposium. She was an Associate General Counsel and legal adviser to the United States delegation during the Uruguay Round TRIPS negotiations.

Thu-Lang Tran Wasescha, Counsellor at the Swiss Federal Institute of Intellectual Property, speaking at the Symposium. She was deputy head of the Swiss TRIPS negotiating team during the Uruguay Round TRIPS negotiations.

Jörg Reinbothe, Professor at the European Institute of the University of Saarbrucken, is the former head of the "Free Movement of Capital Unit" in the Directorate General of Internal Market and Services of the European Commission. He was part of the European Communities delegation during the Uruguay Round TRIPS negotiations.

A.V. GANESAN

A.V. Ganesan, former Commerce Secretary of India and former member of the WTO Appellate Body, speaking at the Symposium. He represented India during the Uruguay Round negotiations, including on TRIPS.

Piragibe dos Santos Tarragô, Ambassador of Brazil in the Netherlands, speaking at the Symposium. He represented Brazil during the Uruguay Round TRIPS negotiations.

Antonio Gustavo Trombetta, Ambassador of Argentina in Switzerland, speaking at the Symposium. He represented Argentina during the Uruguay Round TRIPS negotiations.

Umi K.B.A. Majid, a judge of the Court of Appeal in Malaysia, speaking at the Symposium. She represented Malaysia during the Uruguay Round TRIPS negotiations.

David Fitzpatrick, barrister, solicitor and occasional academic lawyer, speaking at the Symposium. He was legal adviser to the delegation of Hong Kong during the Uruguay Round TRIPS negotiations.

Hannu Wager, Counsellor in the Intellectual Property Division of the WTO, speaking at the Symposium. He represented the Nordic countries during the Uruguay Round TRIPS negotiations.

Adrian Macey, Senior Associate at the Victoria University of Wellington Institute for Governance and Policy Studies, speaking at the Symposium. He represented New Zealand during the Uruguay Round negotiations, on both dispute settlement and TRIPS.

Part IV

Perspectives from the developing world

11

Negotiating for India

A.V. Ganesan

Background to the TRIPS negotiations, including the mandate

In this chapter, I venture to walk down memory lane and try to recall my experiences with the negotiation of the TRIPS Agreement nearly 25 years ago. I had the honour of representing India at some of the important stages of the negotiations between 1987 and 1993: first, as Additional Secretary, Ministry of Industry, when the administration of patents, trademarks and industrial designs in India was under my charge; then as Special Secretary, Ministry of Commerce and Chief Negotiator of India for the Uruguay Round of multilateral trade negotiations; and finally, as Commerce Secretary of the Government of India, from which position I retired from civil service on 30 June 1993. I hope my memory does not fail me in recalling my experiences with some degree of accuracy at this distance in time.

The focus and thrust of this chapter is on the Indian approach and attitude towards the TRIPS negotiations and the main reasons behind it. To be sure, domestic economic and political compulsions, as well as domestic policies towards foreign trade and investment, lay at the heart of that approach at all stages of the negotiations, more so as divergent pulls and pressures had to be accommodated in the vocal democratic polity of India. These are reflected in this chapter to the extent possible. It is my conviction that domestic economic policies, as well as domestic economic strength and confidence, tend to influence a country's attitude towards the recognition and rewarding of IPRs. This is well exemplified by India, and therefore, the chapter does not stop at merely looking at the past but also touches upon how India looks at IP protection now and how it could leverage this to achieve its economic and technological goals. Now that the TRIPS Agreement is firmly in place, the chapter also points to the way forward, to gain wider acceptance of the Agreement and of IP protection in general.

The Uruguay Round marked a defining moment in international economic and trade relationships. It is said with modesty that the WTO of 1995 had "evolved" from the GATT of 1947, but if the ambit and authority of the WTO is recognized, it is perhaps no exaggeration to say that the WTO is as different from the GATT as homo sapiens is from a Neanderthal. With the establishment of the WTO, multilateral trade no longer means trade in goods only, and multilateral trade rules no longer means only rules that stop at national borders and that do not intrude into the domestic policy space of members. Three factors, in particular, changed the complexion of the multilateral trade rules and they all had an impact on the negotiation of the TRIPS Agreement: first, the extension of the trade rules to the areas of services, investment and IPRs (besides subjecting agriculture and textiles also to multilateral trade disciplines); second, the adoption of the concept of "a single undertaking", which, *inter alia*, paved the way for exchange of concessions and commitments across sectors and induced countries to look at the Uruguay Round package as a whole; and third, the dispute settlement undertaking that made it obligatory for members to resolve trade disputes only through the dispute settlement mechanism of the WTO and to seek multilateral authorization before any retaliation or cross-retaliation across sectors was undertaken. It is therefore important that the negotiation of the TRIPS Agreement is viewed not in isolation but as part of a larger package of agreements under the Uruguay Round.

When the idea was mooted in the early 1980s to launch a new round of multilateral trade negotiations, it lay in the logic of things that the industrialized countries, led by the United States, would insist upon the inclusion of services, investment and IPRs in the purview of multilateral trade rules. The industrialized world was fast losing its competitive edge in world trade in the manufacturing sector, especially in respect of standard technology goods. But its strength and supremacy in capital- and technology-intensive services, in various high-technology fields, and in areas where protection of IPRs was crucial for market dominance, was intact and needed to be preserved and promoted. Market access, market protection and market penetration for such goods and services across the world were critical for industrialized countries, to advance the interests of their big transnational companies. Such interests were represented by a formidable array of companies whose operations ranged from banking, insurance and telecommunications in the services sector to pharmaceuticals and chemicals, films and music, computers and software, and seeds and biotechnology in manufacturing and other fields.

At the commencement of the Uruguay Round, Japan and the United States were in the forefront for the inclusion of IPRs in the mandate of the negotiations. The other industrialized countries, including Australia, Canada, New Zealand, the Nordic countries and Switzerland, joined the fray later. As for the European Communities (EC), it had an ambivalent stand at the beginning of the negotiations about the extension of GATT rules to IPRs, probably because it was unsure of its impact upon the legislation of its member states. But, as the negotiations proceeded, the EC became an equally staunch advocate for the protection of IPRs under multilateral trade rules. Its approach has sparked the perceptive comment that the EC could have lived without a TRIPS Agreement at the beginning of the negotiations, but could not have done so at the end of it.[1] I should hasten to point out, however, that, although the industrialized countries were united on the issue that substantive norms and standards for the protection of IPRs should form an integral part of the multilateral trade rules, there were a number of differences among them, at least on two counts: first, they had their differences on the scope or form of protection of some of the IPRs, such as computer software, broadcasting and television rights, geographical indications (GIs), life forms and so on; and second, they had differing views on how developing countries with special problems needed to be accommodated, especially with respect to transition periods, "pipeline protection" and compulsory licensing in the pharmaceuticals and food sectors. But these differences among them were of a different class and character.

On their part, the developing countries, including India, were least enthusiastic on the extension of the authority of the GATT to new areas such as services, investment and IPRs. They had both philosophical and practical reasons to oppose the enlargement of GATT's jurisdiction: first, their long-held conviction that the role and reach of the GATT ought to be limited to the goods sector and that the GATT was best equipped to deal only with "border measures"; second, their apprehension that such an extension would seriously intrude into their domestic policy space and constrain their freedom to pursue economic and social policies best suited to their individual needs; and third, from a purely practical point of view, they had nothing to gain but much to lose from undertaking obligations and commitments in these new areas. In short, they saw themselves not as *demandeurs,* but as hapless defenders in these new areas, with no *quid pro quo* for them from any agreements on these subjects.

With respect to IPRs in particular, they had the additional reservations that the protection and enforcement of IPRs was not trade-related, that WIPO was the appropriate forum in which to deal with IP issues, and that, as the industrialized countries were the owners of nearly 99 per cent of global patents and other forms of IP, any agreement for their protection would only favour them at the cost of developing countries. In particular, they were concerned that stringent patent protection would emaciate their capacity to provide affordable health care to their poor. They were also apprehensive that, as they were not familiar with all the technical issues involved in the protection of IPRs, especially in the case of newer technologies, they might be negotiating from a lack of both strength and knowledge on the subject.

It was against this contentious backdrop that the mandate for the inclusion of IPRs in the agenda of the Uruguay Round was negotiated and formulated in Punta del Este in September 1986. The text of the mandate read in part:

> In order to reduce the distortions and impediments to international trade, and taking into account the need to promote effective and adequate protection of intellectual property rights, and to ensure that measures and procedures to enforce intellectual property rights do not themselves become barriers to legitimate trade, the negotiations shall aim to clarify GATT provisions and elaborate as appropriate new rules and disciplines.

> Negotiations shall aim to develop a multilateral framework of principles, rules and disciplines dealing with international trade in counterfeit goods, taking into account work already undertaken in the GATT.

> These negotiations shall be without prejudice to other complementary initiatives that may be taken in the World Intellectual Property Organization and elsewhere to deal with these matters.[2]

The mandate is certainly not an epitome of clarity, coherence or consistency. Given the divergent positions of the industrialized and developing countries on the mandate, it was not surprising that it took another two and a half years for the content of the mandate to be settled. The industrialized countries laid emphasis on the two phrases "taking into account the need to promote adequate and effective protection of intellectual property rights" and "elaborate as appropriate new rules and disciplines". According to them, it was the lack of adequate protection of IPRs that led to "distortions and impediments to international trade". On the contrary, developing countries placed their faith in the three phrases "In order to reduce the distortions and impediments to international trade", "to ensure that measures and procedures to enforce intellectual property rights do not themselves become barriers to legitimate trade" and "the negotiations shall aim to clarify GATT provisions", as well as in the clear-cut provisions of the second subparagraph, and the reference to WIPO in the final subparagraph. Both sides insisted that the texts that they relied on warranted the inclusion of substantive norms and standards for protection of IPRs within the mandate, or, oppositely, their complete exclusion. When the scope of the mandate was finally settled in April 1989 in favour of the inclusion, it was not so much because the developing countries came to see clarity or conviction in the mandate as because of other factors, including, in particular, the pressures exerted on them by the United States through unilateral action under its Trade Acts, changes in the internal policies and negotiating approach of some developing countries, the trade-off perceived by some developing countries from the inclusion of agriculture in the negotiations, and the hope that sufficient flexibilities could be negotiated to balance protection with their own policy objectives.

India's approach to the TRIPS negotiations

Let me now turn to India's approach to, and attitude towards, the TRIPS negotiations, which, as I stated earlier, is the focus of this chapter. There were three distinct phases in India's approach, each guided by the dominant economic policies followed by the country at the relevant time. The first phase was from the Punta del Este mandate of September 1986 until the meeting of the Trade Negotiations Committee (TNC) of the WTO in Geneva in April 1989. The second phase was from April 1989 until the issue of the so-called Dunkel Draft in December 1991, when the specific provisions for substantive norms and standards for the protection of IPRs were discussed in the TRIPS Negotiating Group. The third phase was after the issue of the Dunkel Draft, when efforts were made by India to seek improvements in the provisions relating to transition period and pipeline protection for pharmaceutical patents. In each of these phases, there were shifts in India's stand based on its own examination of what changes it would have to make in its laws, what would be their impact on domestic policies, how those changes could be made politically acceptable and how much time would be needed to gain such acceptance.

The first phase, from the Punta del Este mandate until the TNC meeting of April 1989

From the beginning of the negotiations until the TNC meeting of April 1989, India was firmly opposed to the inclusion of substantive norms and standards for the protection of IPRs within the negotiating mandate. It must be admitted that, in the wide-ranging and gruelling negotiations that took place in Punta del Este in September 1986 on various issues, India spent more of its energy and resources on the negotiating mandate for services and on advocating a "twin-track approach" to the implementation of the results of the negotiations, than on the formulation of the negotiating mandate for IPRs. The extension of the jurisdiction of the GATT to the services sector was then considered by India to be more inimical to its interests than anything else on the agenda. (Oh, how times have changed! The services sector now accounts for nearly 55 per cent of the country's gross domestic product (GDP) and India is riding on the back of a vibrant computer software industry to manage its external balance of trade. No one seems to be worried now in India over the General Agreement on Trade in Services (GATS) and its inclusion in the WTO). That India's participation in the Negotiating Group on IPRs was not as robust and active as it might have been was revealed, to some extent, by the fact that, at the concluding session of the Punta del Este negotiations on 20 September 1986, India made a weak statement: that its understanding of the scope of the mandate on IPRs was that it was limited to trade in counterfeit goods and anti-competitive practices of the right holders, and that the mandate did not extend to substantive norms and standards for the protection of IPRs.[3]

Be this as it may, India stuck to the position until April 1989 that substantive norms and standards for the protection and enforcement of IPRs went beyond the scope of the negotiating mandate and could not therefore be considered by the TRIPS Negotiating Group. Apart from the philosophical and practical grounds that I have referred to earlier, there were two India-specific factors that prompted it to adopt this stand.

First was the inward-looking and non-market-oriented economic policies that India was pursuing at the time. Excessive government control over the economy and the "Licence Permit Raj" were still in their heyday. Foreign investment and foreign trade were shunned as either unnecessary or anti-self-reliance. Far from inviting foreign investment, in the late 1970s, India implemented an aggressive policy directing foreign companies operating in India to divest or dilute their foreign shareholdings. Although the philosophy of leaning to the left of centre on economic and social issues is always endemic in India, at the time, there was considerable opposition to globalization and India's integration into the global economy among academics and activists, as well as from the political classes. India's foreign trade (exports and imports) was less than 10 per cent of its GDP and it was considered to be good for India to stand on its own feet. In this milieu, the extension of the GATT's jurisdiction to new areas such as services, investment and IPRs was anathema to India. For India, the GATT had been established solely to deal with tariffs and trade remedy measures in the goods sector and its jurisdiction must remain such. Its extension to the new areas was seen as an attempt on the part of the industrialized world to impose its hegemony on developing countries to further the interests of its multinational companies. It may sound strange that such views flourished in a country with a vibrant and vocal democracy that allowed for every kind of freedom except economic freedom. That the economy was consequently operating far below its true potential was, unfortunately, missed.

But the more important factor behind India's opposition to TRIPS was the character of the Indian Patents Act 1970 and the Indian pharmaceuticals industry that it had spawned. Under British rule, India had the Patents and Designs Act 1911, which granted product and process patents in every sector and prohibited compulsory licences without the involvement of the patent holder. Local pharmaceutical production by Indian companies was therefore at a standstill and imported medicines held sway in the marketplace, albeit at unaffordable prices. This situation led to the formation of the Indian Drug Manufacturers Association in 1961 and it lobbied strongly for the enactment of a new patent law that would encourage local production of pharmaceuticals and thereby make them available to people at low prices. Following the recommendations of a committee appointed under the chairmanship of a High Court judge, a new law, namely, the Indian Patents Act 1970, was enacted, which repealed the 1911 Act insofar as it related to patents. The new Patents Act 1970 came into force on 20 April 1972.

The new law was truly a turning point for the domestic pharmaceuticals industry. Five features of the new law are worth noting here to show how far apart it was from the TRIPS Agreement. First, the Act provided for only process patents, and prohibited product patents, in the food, pharmaceutical and chemicals sectors. Second, the Act provided for a term of only seven years for process patents in the food and pharmaceuticals sectors, while for process patents in the chemicals sector, and for product or process patents in all other sectors, the term was 14 years from the date of filing. Third, compulsory licences could be granted liberally under the Act, including for non-working of the patents. Fourth, the Act allowed for automatic "licences of right" in the food, pharmaceuticals and chemicals sectors, under which anyone could produce and sell such products on payment of a royalty not exceeding 4 per cent. Fifth, in the case of process patents also, the owner of the patent had to prove the alleged infringement of his or her patent in a court of law. In a nutshell, the Indian Patents Act 1970 did not allow a patent worth its salt in the food, pharmaceuticals and chemicals sectors.

The Act was a shot in the arm for the domestic pharmaceuticals manufacturers. Thanks to the abundant skilled manpower available in India in chemical technology, especially in the synthesis of chemical molecules, the domestic pharmaceuticals industry started producing new patented chemical entities through reverse engineering, choosing pharmaceuticals that had proved their safety and efficacy in the industrialized world and that had also become commercial blockbusters there. In addition, governmental regulations that compelled the manufacture of medicines from the basic stage, prohibiting simply the transformation of intermediate products into bulk pharmaceuticals or formulations, as well as the setting up of public sector undertakings in the pharmaceuticals sector, also helped India acquire the necessary skills in the manufacturing of pharmaceuticals. Within three to five years of new drugs being introduced into the world market, they were introduced in India at a fraction of their world prices. Although this did not lead to new drugs being discovered in India for diseases relevant to India (a point to which I will return), it is not an exaggeration to say that, if India today is a major supplier of generic drugs to the world market, the seeds of it were sown by the Indian Patents Act 1970.

It was the combination of these two factors, the insular and inward-looking economic policies of the country and the growth and achievement of the domestic pharmaceuticals industry under the Patents Act 1970, that lay at the bottom of India's strident opposition to the inclusion of protection of IPRs within GATT disciplines. For India, such an extension of the GATT's jurisdiction would have required not marginal or incremental amendments but a complete and radical overhaul of its Patents Act 1970, which was an extremely difficult political proposition for the country. It must be noted here that the same advocates against the extension of the GATT's jurisdiction to IPRs were also dead against India joining the Paris Convention for the Protection of Industrial Property. Although India was arguing that WIPO was the appropriate forum for dealing with IP, India is one of the perhaps few countries that joined the Paris Convention after it had subscribed to the TRIPS Agreement.[4] Even though the Paris Convention allowed considerable discretion to parties in framing their patent laws and had no worthwhile enforcement mechanism against transgression, India was then opposed to joining it. The reason was that it would have entailed the acceptance of international obligations on patent protection that would diminish India's freedom to formulate and implement its patent law the way it wanted.

The second phase, from April 1989 until the Dunkel Draft of December 1991

The question then arises as to what caused India to change its stand and agree to the inclusion of substantive norms and standards for the protection and enforcement of IPRs within the scope of the TRIPS mandate in the TNC meeting of April 1989. I was a member of the Indian delegation that participated in the mid-term review meeting in Montreal in December 1988 and the TNC meeting in Geneva in April 1989. From my recollections of the pulls and counter-pulls that operated at the policy-making level at the time, and which made policy choices difficult and controversial, both politically and otherwise, I venture to say that three factors were prominent behind the change in India's stand.

The first of these, it must be admitted candidly, was the pressure exerted by the United States through its unilateral actions under Section 301 of the US Trade Act 1974 and the Special 301 provisions of the US Omnibus Trade and Competitiveness Act 1988. India had the distinction of being on the priority watch list of the United States from 1989 onwards, with the exception of the years 1991 to 1994, when its status was even worse, that of a Priority Foreign Country. This designation arose primarily due to the lack of pharmaceutical patent protection in India. Retaliatory action against Indian garment and other exports to the United States was looming large over India like a Damocles' sword, especially in the last few years of the Uruguay Round. Avoidance of trade friction with the United States was a necessity in order to safeguard the interests of the Indian exporters whose complaint was, why should they be penalized for no fault of their own? In this context, it is also worth noting that India had a number of scientific and technical cooperation relationships with the United States at both the academic level (e.g. between universities) and the level of government science departments. The need for adequate protection of IPRs in India was raised by the American side as well, if those relationships were to be sustained.

The second factor was the incipient beginning of a change in India's economic policies. Although a significant outward orientation in the policies was not yet on the cards, there was a clear move in the direction that India must attempt to integrate its economy into the global economy and that this must be an objective of India in the Uruguay Round negotiations as well. When I was appointed Special Secretary and Chief Negotiator for India for the Uruguay Round in July 1989, an instruction given to me was that I should make this objective of India clear in my bilateral meetings with other countries.[5] In the Summit Conference of Heads of State or Government of the Non-aligned Movement held in Belgrade in September 1989, which I attended, the Indian Prime Minister specifically stated that India wanted to integrate its economy into the global economy and that he hoped the Uruguay Round negotiations would help developing countries to do so on favourable terms. This shift in approach meant that India did not want to be seen in the negotiations as always being in a denial mode and that it tabled its own specific proposals of its demands on other countries or in defence of its position.

The third factor was a perceived shift in the approach of other developing countries to the inclusion of substantive norms and standards for protection of IPRs in the agenda. Some of them felt the pressure from the United States under Section 301 of its Trade Act 1974 in the same way as India did. Some in the Cairns Group thought that their interest in the agriculture sector should not be harmed by their intransigence on the TRIPS negotiating mandate. Some others thought that, rather than fight a losing battle, a better strategy would be to bargain that, while norms and standards might be included in the agenda, it should be on the basis that they would stop with those enshrined in the Paris Convention and the Berne Convention for the Protection of Literary and Artistic Works, but not go beyond them. I recall such a view being articulated in a subtle manner by an Association of Southeast Asian Nations (ASEAN) member state in the Montreal mid-term review group on TRIPS, in order to avoid deeper inroads being made by industrialized countries in patent and copyright protection. Whatever was the true state of play in this respect, there was reason for India to believe at the time that it was only a question of time before developing countries gave up their position that the Punta del Este mandate did not go beyond the issues of trade in counterfeit goods and anti-competitive practices of right holders.

India also thought that, once the substantive norms and standards for protection of IPRs was brought into the mandate, efforts could be made to balance protection of IPRs with the developmental, technological and policy objectives of the host countries, to carve out exceptions for the special needs of developing countries, and to obtain sufficiently long transition periods for switching over to the new regime. There were indications, at least from some developed countries, that differential treatment for developing countries in this manner could be worked out during the course of negotiations.

It is possible that, to an outsider, and to many in India as well, these reasons for a sudden shift in India's stand might appear to be specious or unconvincing, apart from the reason that India simply surrendered to the pressure exerted by the United States and gave up its principled position. That the pressure exerted by the United States, not only on India but also on some other developing countries was the prime reason is not disputed, but the shift in stand needs to be seen in the context of the entire gamut of the Uruguay Round negotiations, including the TRIPS mandate (which could not convincingly be interpreted to be limited only to trade in counterfeit goods) as well as the shift in India's internal policies.

Needless to say, there was sharp and extensive criticism in India, in both the press and the academic and political arena, over India's tamely agreeing to the protection of IPRs under pressure from the United States and thereby sacrificing the interests of both the domestic pharmaceuticals industry and the health care of the Indian poor. The Indian Government's explanation that efforts would be made in the further negotiations to have provisions that would balance protection of patents with public policy objectives, including the health care needs of the poor, carried little conviction. I still recall an article in a leading Indian newspaper, written by Inder Malhotra, a highly respected and widely read journalist in India, in which he called 5 April 1989, the date of the TNC meeting, a "Black Wednesday for India", excoriated the government for its abject surrender of vital national interests and called for the immediate sacking of the leader of the Indian delegation to the negotiations, the then Commerce Secretary of India (not me, fortunately, who was only a lesser fry in the delegation!).

After the finalization of the negotiating mandate in the TNC meeting of April 1989, India tabled, for the first time, a comprehensive document setting out its views on norms and standards for protection of various types of IPRs.[6] It did not suggest their formulation in legal terms but was about the principles that must inform them, from a developing country's perspective. With respect to patents, the document argued for freedom and flexibility for developing countries in the matter of grant of patent protection in sectors such as food and pharmaceuticals. For India, the value of the document lay not so much in its capacity to persuade the industrialized world to an opposite point of view, but in its conveying the message that India was interested in substantive engagement on the issues and that its chief concern was that protection of patents must be balanced by the host country's needs and public policy objectives. The document, widely reported in the Indian press, also helped allay the earlier criticism over India's having changed its stand on the negotiating mandate, as it showed that the government was committed to the issue of negotiating a balance between protection of patents and protection of the public interest.

The next important document from the standpoint of the developing countries was that tabled collectively by 14 developing countries, including India.[7] This document submitted specific proposals on all aspects of the negotiating mandate in legal language, dividing the subject into two parts: Part I dealing with "Intellectual property and international trade", including trade in counterfeit and pirated goods; and Part II dealing with the "Standards and principles concerning the availability, scope and use of intellectual property rights". As the first statement of the negotiating position of the countries concerned, it naturally took an extreme position on a number of issues, especially with respect to the obligations of the right holders and the scope of the protection granted. A few of the proposals in the document would illustrate this fact: it stated that, while patent protection will be available in all fields technology, a licence of right will also be automatically available to any person wanting to work the patent in the case of food and medicines; it is for each national legislature to determine the duration of patent protection it wants to grant; a patent owner has the obligation to work the patented invention in the territory of grant, failing which a compulsory licence is liable to be granted; a compulsory licence may also be granted, where necessary, in the public interest to secure free competition; and the agreement shall be implemented in the relevant international organization.

On their part, the industrialized countries had already tabled their proposals in early 1990, taking equally strident positions that focused only on watertight protection and enforcement of IPRs. According to them, a compulsory licence could be granted only in narrowly defined circumstances and certainly not for the non-working of patents. The negotiations therefore lingered on in this phase without any tangible meeting ground until the text was reached at the Brussels ministerial meeting in December 1990. That text merely put in brackets the contentious proposals of each side on issues such as duration of patents, obligation to work patents, exclusion from patentability of food, chemical and pharmaceutical products, and forum of implementation of the agreement. With the breakdown of the Brussels ministerial meeting for other reasons, this phase of the negotiations went into limbo.

There were, however, several silver linings in the Brussels text that proved useful at the later stage of the Dunkel Draft, as they gave policy options to developing countries to attenuate the adverse effects of protection of IPRs. One, in particular, stands out – it relates to compulsory licences (Article 34 of the Brussels text and Article 31 in the TRIPS Agreement). Of note, first, is the inclusion of the proposition that a compulsory licence could be granted on the individual merits of each case. This meant that the reasons for the grant of a compulsory licence were not circumscribed or conditioned, so long as the "merits" of the case at hand justified the grant of the compulsory licence. Second, in the case not only of public non-commercial use by the government but also of a national emergency or other circumstance of extreme urgency, a compulsory licence could be granted without prior negotiation with the right holder (Article 34(b) and (o) of the Brussels text and Article 31(b) of the TRIPS Agreement). Along with the support of some developed and developing countries, the Indian negotiators were able to get these important provisions included in the article on compulsory licences, while, at the same time, accommodating the viewpoint of the other side in the subsequent provisions of that article pertaining to the conditions that will be applicable once a compulsory licence is granted.[8]

The third phase, spanning the Dunkel Draft and thereafter

The famous Dunkel Draft came out in December 1991 but it had been a work in progress for quite some time beforehand. It was a child of the fatigue of the negotiators who, having gone around in circles over a long period and having reached an impasse on critical issues of the negotiations, entrusted the conundrum to Arthur Dunkel, the Director-General of GATT and a suave Swiss diplomat, for him to come out with a package that, in his personal view, reflected the agreements reached by the negotiators and possible compromises on the contentious issues still to be resolved. Arthur Dunkel produced such a package on the basis of the suggestions he received from the Secretariat and the chairs of the various negotiating groups, including the TRIPS Negotiating Group. With the benefit of hindsight, I venture to say that he did a fair and impressive job, with every country finding good and bad parts in his package, like the curate's egg. This was reflected by the fact that many countries, particularly from the developing world, wanted that the delicate package that he had so carefully worked out should not be unravelled lest the whole negotiations fell apart and the Uruguay Round sank into oblivion.

I was appointed as Commerce Secretary of the Government of India in November 1991 and my immediate responsibility was to deal with the Dunkel Draft, *inter alia*, in close consultation with developed and developing countries. A striking new development on the Indian scene was that the new government that had come into power in June 1991 had embarked on major economic reforms, necessitated as much by the dire economic straits the country had reached as by the conviction that the country needed a reversal of its economic policies. While everyone recognized that the country was operating far below its economic potential, the new government had the courage to decide that the solution lay in adopting outward-looking and market-oriented economic policies that were congenial to foreign investment and foreign trade. It is now an accepted fact that the seeds of economic reforms and of the reversal of inward-looking economic policies were sown in India in mid-1991. As the new policies yielded tangible gains to the economy, the pursuit of outward and market-reliant policies has gathered momentum in the subsequent years and such policies have not only come to stay but have become an integral and staple part of the economic landscape of the country.[9]

The Dunkel Draft was, naturally, considered by India in the light of its changing economic policies. Underlying that consideration was also the pragmatic approach that a multilaterally agreed set of rules, even if they were not in favour of India in every respect, was preferable to bilateral or other arrangements that might exact a higher price from India. It was therefore felt that the right course of action for India was to stay within the multilateral trading system, take a constructive and effective part in it, and try to seek improvements in the rules with the support of like-minded developing and developed countries. A system of compulsory multilateral resolution of disputes, according to an agreed set of rules, was also considered to be of advantage to India to withstand unilateral punitive actions on the part of other countries.

The Dunkel Draft on the TRIPS Agreement was also examined by India within this scenario. As that text and the final TRIPS Agreement did not differ much as far as India was concerned, I will refer now only to those aspects where India attempted to secure changes in the Agreement and failed. When it became clear to India that patent protection would be extended to all fields of technology and that the pharmaceuticals sector would neither be excluded from product patent protection nor would automatic licences of right be allowed for it, India chose to focus on the following five issues as the next best options: compulsory licensing provisions, transition period, flexibilities in the agreement, recognition of underlying public policy objectives and multilateral dispute resolution. Of these, India was largely satisfied with the kinds of provisions that came out in the Dunkel Draft, except for the transition period and the concomitant pipeline protection.

With respect to the contentious issue of compulsory licences, India was satisfied with the final provision that a country was free to grant a compulsory licence on the individual merits of each case. This implied that, while automatic or across-the-board grant of compulsory licences would violate Article 31(a), selective and judicious grant of compulsory licences would not fall foul of it. The grounds for the grant of a compulsory licence were not conditioned or circumscribed by that Article and were left to the judgment of the authority granting the licence, who had only to show that it was justified by the merits of the case at hand. The other conditions enumerated in Article 31 came into play only after a compulsory licence was granted. India had no serious problems with those conditions. Even without the provisions of Article 31, the legality of the grant of a compulsory licence or payment of adequate remuneration to the patent holder would have been subject to judicial review in India.

While on the subject of compulsory licences, I must also refer to the other contentious issue of "working of patents", as both an obligation of the patent holder and a ground for grant of a compulsory licence. A corollary issue is whether importation constitutes working of a patent or not. My own view has always been that this issue gets blown up out of context. If the manufacture of a product is economically, technically or commercially unviable or difficult in a country, because of the small volume of demand, regulatory approvals or any other reason, it is unfair to argue that it must still be produced in the country by the patent holder because there is a patent granted to it. If the country needs the product and the patent holder or his or her licensee imports it into the country, it is as good as working the patent. Conversely, even if an automatic licence of right is available, no one else is likely to produce it for the same reasons. They might, at best, try to import it from sources other than the patent holder. On the other hand, if a product is technically and commercially viable to be produced in a country, first, there is no a priori reason why the patent holder would not see that opportunity. Second, even if he or she does not do so, recourse to a compulsory licence is open to the country on the grounds that the product is widely needed to tackle a particular situation, that the market is not being served adequately or is being served by imports at very high prices and that a competitive source of production is considered necessary in the public interest. In other words, a compulsory licence could be thought of not because the patent is not worked in the country but because of the particular facts of the situation at hand. Given the open-ended nature of the compulsory licensing provision in Article 31(a), India felt that the working or non-working of patents was not an issue of serious concern to it. In any event, India had reason to believe that, given the size of its domestic market and its abundant technical skills in the manufacture of pharmaceuticals, it was unlikely that a patent holder would forego the opportunity of producing the product in India for the Indian market, if they found that it makes economic and commercial sense to manufacture the product in India.

I should also refer to another dimension of compulsory licences based on the Indian experience. It is the extent to which compulsory licences are actually used when they are freely available. As noted earlier, the Indian Patents Act 1970, which came into force in April 1972, did not grant product patents for pharmaceutical products and, furthermore, it allowed automatic licences of right for them. It was therefore a free-for-all situation for the domestic pharmaceuticals industry. Even in this era of freedom, during the 15-year period 1983–97, when 653 new drugs (new chemical entities) were introduced into the world market, India saw only 72 of them in its market. Typically, they were introduced into the Indian market by the domestic manufacturers within three to five years of their introduction into the world market, after their efficacy, safety and commercial success had been established elsewhere. Even of the 72 new drugs so introduced, only about ten to 15 could be considered to be top-selling drugs in the Indian market. The Indian experience, even in the halcyon days of the Patents Act 1970, was that only about 10 to 15 per cent of the patented drugs introduced into the world market were introduced into the Indian market by the domestic firms because they found only so few of them to be worth introduction for commercial reasons. This belies the lay perception that every patented drug that comes into the world market will automatically be introduced into the market of a developing country as well, if only licences of right for them were freely available. On this issue, there is thus much exaggeration by the protagonists on both sides of the fence – those who allege that compulsory licences will kill patent protection and those who claim that free compulsory licences is the panacea to ward off the injurious effects of the patent system. It will help informed debate if global data were collected on a country basis on the number of compulsory licences granted, the reasons for their grant and the commercial performance of those licences.

Turning to the other issues noted earlier, India was reasonably satisfied with the Dunkel Draft on the recognition of the underlying public policy objectives, as set out in the Preamble and Articles 7 and 8, and the flexibilities (i.e. the nature and extent of discretion allowed) embodied in some of the important provisions of the Agreement. India was conscious of the fact that the objectives and principles were too broadly worded, hortatory in nature and subject to compliance with the provisions of the Agreement. It is always a matter of debate in WTO law as to what weight and effect would be given to them by panels and the Appellate Body in the event of a dispute over a particular measure. Even so, their articulation under specific articles would be of value to the defence of a contested measure as they reflect what the negotiators had in mind to balance protection with other objectives, especially when the measure in question is not in breach of the basic structure of the Agreement.[10]

As regards the flexibilities embodied in the Agreement, the one with respect to "inventive step" is worth mentioning here in the Indian context. Under Section 3(d) of the amended Indian patent law, the tweaking of existing molecules or the dressing-up of a combination of existing molecules, with a view to the "evergreening" of patents, is not to be considered as an inventive step. The decision of the patent examiner is, of course, subject to judicial review, as all administrative and executive acts are under the Indian legal system. The existence of similar flexibilities in various other provisions of the Agreement is a matter of considerable importance, not only to India but to all developing countries as well. As long as a measure is consistent with the basic provisions of the Agreement, the flexibilities provide an important tool to the developing countries to balance the protection of rights with their needs and objectives.

As regards dispute resolution, by the time the Dunkel Draft came out, the basic architecture of the dispute settlement mechanism of the WTO had taken shape and came to be reflected in it. This was a subject of considerable importance, for not only the TRIPS Agreement but all the multilateral agreements covered by the WTO. In fact, the single undertaking concept of the Uruguay Round was underpinned, crucially, by the common dispute settlement mechanism for all the agreements, as embodied in the Dispute Settlement Understanding (DSU). Developing, and a number of developed, countries had demanded an outright prohibition of all unilateral measures and punitive actions, to shield themselves from actions such as those they consistently faced under Section 301 provisions of the US trade laws. They did not succeed beyond getting an anaemic text in Article XVI.4 of the Agreement Establishing the World Trade Organization (WTO Agreement) that "each Member shall ensure the conformity of its laws, regulations and administrative procedures with its obligations" under the covered agreements. However, in the DSU they substantially got what they wanted: first, all disputes arising out of the covered agreements shall be compulsorily and exclusively settled through the multilateral dispute settlement mechanism of the WTO; and second, no retaliatory or cross-retaliatory action shall be taken without the multilateral authorization of the Dispute Settlement Body. As the TRIPS Agreement was also covered by the DSU, and as this prevented cross-retaliation without following the multi-layered process incorporated in the DSU, India was reasonably satisfied with the outcome in this matter.

It was with regard to the transition period and pipeline protection that India was disappointed with the Dunkel Draft and the TRIPS Agreement. As India had to completely overhaul its Patents Act 1970 and had to cope with considerable political, academic, scientific and industry opposition to the new regime envisaged by the TRIPS Agreement, India lobbied for a clean transition period of at least ten years. No pipeline protection to patents in the transition period was acceptable to India. India gave a proposal to Arthur Dunkel, with the support of the EC, to the effect that "low-income economies", as defined by the World Bank, be allowed an additional transition period of five years (over the normal period of five years for all developing countries) to introduce product patents in the food, pharmaceuticals and agrochemicals sectors.

The Dunkel Draft did allow an additional transition period of five years to developing countries for all fields of technology in respect of which a developing country did not provide product patents as at the date of application of the agreement (Article 65.4 of the TRIPS Agreement). But it was qualified by the requirement to provide pipeline protection, namely, that such a country should provide a mechanism for receiving product patent applications as at the date of application of the WTO Agreement (1 January 1995) and keep them pending for examination until the expiry of the ten-year transition period. It must also grant exclusive marketing rights for the products covered by such pending applications, provided a product patent and a market approval had been granted to them in some other member in that ten-year period. This requirement of pipeline protection was applicable only to product patent applications filed on or after 1 January 1995 in respect of pharmaceutical and agrochemical products, not for foodstuffs, chemicals in general or any other product (Articles 70.8 and 70.9 of the TRIPS Agreement).

This form of pipeline protection was called the "Swiss pipeline protection" as it was proposed by Switzerland. There is no doubt it was less virulent than the form of pipeline protection advocated by the United States, which originally wanted such exclusive marketing rights to be given for all pharmaceutical and chemical products that were covered by product patents from 1986 onwards (from the launch of the Uruguay Round) and which later toned down its proposal to at least such product patents that were in force on the date of entry into force of the WTO Agreement (1 January 1995). India argued that neither form of pipeline protection was acceptable to it as it virtually eliminated any transition period for introduction of product patents for pharmaceutical and agrochemical products. The developed countries were under pressure from the United States, which would not accept any agreement without a pipeline protection. The thrust of the argument of the United States was that, if the TRIPS Agreement were to apply only to product patent applications filed after expiry of the ten-year transition period in the developing country concerned (i.e. on or after 1 January 2005), patent protection would be available only to new drugs that would come into the world market after 2002 or 2003, since it took at least seven to eight years for a drug to come into the market after patent grant and regulatory approvals. Such a prolonged waiting period for deriving benefit from the TRIPS Agreement was unacceptable to India. Switzerland was also interested in pipeline protection because of its own strong pharmaceuticals industry, but was willing to accept it being restricted to product patent applications filed on or after the entry into force of the WTO Agreement.

On behalf of India, I pointed out that there must be a tenable nexus for the grant of exclusive marketing right for a product and that such a nexus could not be that the product enjoyed patent protection elsewhere in the world, as patents have only national jurisdictions. Therefore, any grant of exclusive marketing rights for a product without a product patent application having been filed in India was most likely liable to be rejected by the judiciary in India. The EC appreciated both the arguments of India – that pipeline protection virtually eliminated any transition period for grant of product patents to these products, and that the American form of pipeline protection was liable to be struck down in India on judicial review – and therefore supported the Swiss form of pipeline protection as a compromise.[11]

I was not happy with even the Swiss form of pipeline protection. I tried to persuade my government that it would be better for India to go in for a clean transition period of only five years, like other developing countries and thereby restrict the applicability of the TRIPS Agreement to product patent applications filed in India on or after 1 January 2000. That would have enabled the Indian pharmaceuticals industry to continue to manufacture drugs that were patented elsewhere on applications filed there up to 31 December 1999, that is to say, the Indian pharmaceuticals industry would have had an extra period of five years and that would have meant freedom for it to choose from another 200 new drugs for domestic manufacture. But a shorter transition period of five years did not find favour with the political leadership as it was considered to be too short a period to bring about the necessary legislative changes. A longer transition period was considered necessary by the government to allay the apprehensions over the TRIPS Agreement and to explain the Uruguay Round package as a whole to the public and the parliament. As a consequence of the pipeline protection provisions in the TRIPS Agreement, the grant of product patents for pharmaceutical and agrochemical products is perhaps the only example of a WTO obligation for the acceptance of which a concerned developing country did not get a single day of transition period! The inequity of this extreme measure has escaped attention in the discussions on the TRIPS Agreement.

Other categories of intellectual property

Thus far, this chapter has been overly concentrated on patents because patent protection, especially in the pharmaceuticals sector, was the issue that caused much concern and controversy in the negotiations, not only for India but also for developing countries generally. Within the patents area, there was also concern over the patenting of micro-organisms and *sui generis* protection for plant varieties, but it was to a lesser degree because of the newness of the subjects and the flexibilities incorporated in the Agreement. Some of these concerns were outside the purview of the TRIPS Agreement, such as the ethical and moral aspects of patenting life forms and genes, harmony with the Rio Convention on Biological Diversity, prevention of biopiracy, recognition and rewarding of traditional knowledge of indigenous communities, compensation for the use of the biological resources of developing countries, farmers' and researchers' rights in plant variety protection and the like. But a general lack of understanding of all the issues involved and the broad wording of the provisions helped limit contentious negotiations in these areas.

As regards the other six categories of IP covered by the TRIPS Agreement, namely copyright, trademarks, GIs, industrial designs, layout-designs of integrated circuits and trade secrets, India did not have much of a problem because the Indian policies, laws, regulations, administrative procedures and judicial framework were either in conformity with the proposed obligations or the changes that might be required in them were minimal in nature. For example, in the area of copyright, computer programs and compilations of data were being protected under the Indian copyright law from 1984 onwards. The Indian film industry was as vociferous as Hollywood on the prevention of piracy of cinematographic works. Regarding trademarks, under both common law tradition and statutory law, trademarks, including service marks, were adequately protected under the Indian law to safeguard the interests of both the consumer and the owner of the trademark. India had a stake in the protection of GIs as it wanted such protection to be extended to products of Indian origin such as Darjeeling tea. The Indian Designs Act 1911 provided adequate protection to industrial designs and India was also interested in strengthening its indigenous design capabilities. With respect to layout-designs of integrated circuits, India was already a signatory to the Treaty on Intellectual Property with Respect to Integrated Circuits (IPIC or Washington Treaty) of May 1989 and was taking steps to enact the necessary legislation to implement it. Regarding trade secrets, subject to the owner of the trade secret or the know-how exercising due diligence and care in protecting its secrecy, theft of a trade secret was punishable under Indian criminal law as theft of any other property.

On the question of exhaustion of IPRs (parallel imports), India was in favour of international exhaustion of such rights and was therefore satisfied with the freedom allowed by Article 6 of the Agreement in this matter. With respect to the important issue of enforcement of IPRs, India had little difficulty in agreeing to the measures proposed because these were largely in conformity with its own laws, regulations, administrative procedures and judicial system. Judicial review is guaranteed in the Indian legal system against all executive or legislative acts and would have applied regardless of the WTO agreements. Also, on the question of reversal of the burden of proof, under the Indian Evidence Act, the philosophy is that the party which is in exclusive possession of a piece of relevant evidence is obligated to produce that evidence in a court of law to substantiate or defend its assertion.

The other six categories of IP did not, therefore, evoke much ire or attention in India. I have often felt (and sometimes written) that it is ironic and unfortunate that, despite protecting most IPRs in line with international standards, except for patents for pharmaceuticals, and despite adhering to the rule of law in such protection, India has unwittingly created an impression around the world that it does not respect or recognize IPRs. This is even more ironic because India has innate scientific and technological capabilities and is keen to build a knowledge- and technology-based society.

Reflections on India's approach to the negotiations

To conclude this negotiating history from the Indian perspective, the TRIPS Agreement was unusually contentious right from the beginning of the Uruguay Round negotiations and until their conclusion on the basis of the Dunkel Draft, especially with respect to the area of patents. Although the developed countries had internal differences in their positions on certain issues, there was a sharp cleavage on the fundamental issues of protection between developed and developing countries, more than under any other agreement of the negotiations, including the Agreement on Agriculture, the GATS and the Agreement on Trade-Related Investment Measures (TRIMS). It is undeniable that developing countries as a whole yielded more ground under the TRIPS Agreement than under any other agreement of the WTO, given the fact that such stringent protection of IP favoured only the industrialized world. The developing countries can only draw some consolation from the fact that the TRIPS Agreement formed part of a larger package from which they could derive benefits and advantages in other areas of interest to them. At times, there was more heat than light in the negotiation of the TRIPS Agreement, reminding one of the words of Winston Churchill that "the worst quarrels only arise when both sides are equally in the right and in the wrong". The TRIPS Agreement is now firmly in place, but it must not be overlooked that it addresses the concerns of the past. The technological changes that are taking place so swiftly and so sweepingly in almost every field may soon render these concerns obsolete and may throw up new concerns requiring a paradigm shift in the approach to deal with IPRs.

India's present approach to intellectual property rights

The TRIPS Agreement is no longer as emotive and explosive an issue in India as it was at the time of its negotiation. The main reason behind this change is the increasing outward orientation of India's economic policies and the growing strength and confidence of its economy. At present, economic reforms are being given a further hard push in India in order to raise steeply the levels of investment and economic growth. Foreign investment and foreign technology are being actively and openly courted under flagship programmes with titles such as "Make in India", "Skilled India", "Digital India", "Smart Cities", "Clean Energy Development" and the like. Pursuant to these programmes, foreign investors are being assured not only of stability and predictability in policies and of the "ease of doing business" in India but also of protection of their IPRs according to international standards. For the first time, foreign investment, foreign trade and foreign technology, as well as related economic policies, are being viewed in a holistic manner so that they complement and reinforce each other to realize these programmes. To signal a new approach towards IPRs, a think tank has recently been appointed by the government to make recommendations for the formulation of a national policy on IPRs. It has published its recommendations, suggesting a wide range of measures for adoption under the logo "Creative India; Innovative India". One of its recommendations is the setting up of a National Institute of Excellence on IPRs for enhancing the awareness of IPRs among all stakeholders, including, in particular, domestic innovators and creators of IP. The think tank has also stated that Indian laws are TRIPS compliant and that India would do well to join more international conventions on IP (e.g. the Madrid Protocol).

In this changed scenario, the TRIPS Agreement has almost become a blessing in disguise for India. Having become a signatory to it, and having a good track record of abiding by international agreements it has entered into, India can now confidently assure foreign investors and technology suppliers that their IPRs will be protected in accordance with internationally accepted standards as embodied in the TRIPS Agreement. The TRIPS Agreement can also help India avoid unnecessary trade frictions with other countries by suggesting that a grievance over protection of IP can be resolved through the dispute settlement mechanism of the WTO. Given the size of the Indian domestic market, and its projected growth rates, such an assurance of protection of IPRs (in addition to other supportive policies) may well encourage foreign investors to establish manufacturing facilities in India through subsidiaries and joint ventures or to license their technologies to domestic manufacturers.[12]

With respect to the pharmaceuticals sector in particular, according to a recent study by global consultants McKinsey & Company, the Indian pharmaceuticals market will more than double from the 2013 level of US$ 18 billion to more than US$ 45 billion by 2020, making India the sixth-largest pharmaceuticals market in the world.[13] The study says that it is not the lack of protection of IPRs but deficiency in infrastructure and the restrictive policy towards clinical trials that constrain global research and development (R&D) engagement with India. The study also points to new chemical entities beginning to come out of Indian R&D. Thus, with the rapidly growing size of the Indian pharmaceuticals market, and assurance of protection of IPRs according to the TRIPS Agreement, patent-owning companies are more likely to establish their own manufacturing (and even some part of their R&D) facilities in India to penetrate and protect the Indian market. Should this happen, the need for using compulsory licensing provisions is likely to diminish in the coming years. However, if the circumstances warrant it, India could use them selectively and judiciously to meet genuine public interest needs. As noted earlier, the grant of compulsory licences on the individual merits of each case is permissible under the TRIPS Agreement and is as much an integral part of the Agreement as the protection of patent owners' rights.

There are, however, two aspects relating to the pharmaceuticals sector that need India's close consideration. The first is that the Indian pharmaceuticals companies must be encouraged, through fiscal, financial or other incentives, to spend on R&D that would lead to discovery of new drugs for diseases specific to India. The pharmaceutical companies of the industrialized world concentrate their R&D on discovering drugs of significance to those countries because that market is lucrative to them. They have no incentive to focus on diseases afflicting the poor societies. As has been aptly remarked, the industrialized world suffers from "old age" diseases, whereas developing countries, such as India, still suffer from "age-old" diseases.[14] It is therefore argued that, while the West needs "lifestyle changes", the East needs "life-saving changes". This dichotomy cannot be solved by compulsory licences because they only lead to the production of drugs that have been discovered for the Western market. The Indian pharmaceuticals companies are not inclined to spend on R&D for diseases relevant to India, both because they do not have the financial muscle to spend large amounts of money on R&D and because they do not find the market for such drugs to be commercially attractive. Now that product patent protection would be available for drugs, they could be induced to change their strategy and make efforts to discover drugs for diseases afflicting the poor in India. The Indian Government must find ways and means to raise and allocate sufficient resources for the development of drugs, vaccines and diagnostic kits for diseases that are endemic to India, putting to use the scientific and technical talent available in the country for this purpose.[15] There is no easy alternative to self-reliance and self-determination for finding drugs to cure "diseases of poverty".

The second aspect is the attention to be paid to the introduction of generic drugs into at least the Indian market immediately on the expiry of their Indian patents. The application of Section 3(d) of the Indian patent law to prevent evergreening of patents is only a partial solution to this problem. For drugs that will be on patent protection in India for 20 years under the TRIPS Agreement, mechanisms must be put in place to ensure that generic versions of those drugs are placed in the Indian market (and also in the markets where patent expiry takes place simultaneously) immediately on the expiry of the patents in India. The limited exceptions provisions of Article 30 of the TRIPS Agreement could be prudently used to enable companies to prepare for, produce and stock such drugs for commercial introduction into the Indian market immediately on the expiry of the Indian patents.

The way ahead for the TRIPS Agreement

Now that the TRIPS Agreement is in place, after all the controversies that surrounded it when it was conceived, the way ahead lies in adopting measures that will enhance its acceptability not only among developing countries but also among academics and activists who are concerned over its impact on health care for the poor and the public interest in general.

The heart of the issue in this regard is the balancing of protection of IPRs with the protection of public health needs, especially in poorer societies. As Ambassador Lars Anell, Swedish diplomat and Chair of the TRIPS Negotiating Group put it recently, the question with respect to protection is "how much is too much",[16] or, put differently, "how much" is not "enough" or "adequate" protection. It is difficult to answer this question, but it highlights the imperative need for balancing protection with other public policy objectives and for regarding the balancing act not as a limited exception to protection but as an equally important and inseparable part of protection itself. Looked at this way, every act of compulsory licensing or parallel imports would not be viewed as an egregious erosion of the rights of the holder of the IP.

Second, the way the TRIPS Agreement is interpreted and implemented so as to respect this balance is critical to secure and enhance its fairness and credibility.

The preamble to the TRIPS Agreement emphasizes the need for "recognizing the underlying public policy objectives ... including developmental and technological objectives" of the host countries, and this is elaborated in more specific terms in Article 8.1 of the Agreement to indicate the kinds of measures that the host countries may adopt to realize these objectives. The TRIPS Agreement also consciously embodies certain flexibilities to enable countries to adopt measures that they may consider to be best suited to their individual needs. To secure a balance between protection and public interest, it is important that all these features of the Agreement are given full weight and meaning in the actual interpretation and implementation of the Agreement.

A third element that can help promote greater acceptability of the TRIPS Agreement is to avoid unilateral actions, either to pressure developing countries to refrain from using the flexibilities allowed under the Agreement, including the grant of compulsory licences, or to adopt levels of protection greater than those envisaged by it. The TRIPS Agreement itself goes far beyond the ambit of the Paris and Berne Conventions, and it is therefore unfair to put pressure on the developing countries to go farther than the TRIPS Agreement for protection of IPRs. In the same vein, if a dispute were to arise concerning compliance with any obligation under the TRIPS Agreement, the dispute must be resolved in good faith through the dispute resolution mechanism of the WTO and not through unilateral coercion or threat.

In addition, there must be increasing and purposeful efforts, based on global consensus, to make generic drugs available easily, to mitigate the possible abuses arising from patent protection. There are two facets to this problem. First, when the patents are still in force, the use of compulsory licences and parallel imports must be supported to create cheaper sources of generic drugs, especially to deal with epidemics and diseases that require global cooperation and action. The second aspect is to ensure that cheaper generic drugs come into the world market immediately on the expiry of patents and that this is not impeded by either the enhancing of the patent term or legal or regulatory hurdles. This is of significance even to the developed countries where consumers suffer from price gouging even more than in the developing world. To my mind, the credibility and sustainability of an agreement such as the TRIPS Agreement depends on how well it adapts itself to bringing generic drugs into the market, subject, of course, to protecting the legitimate rights of the patent owners and their receiving adequate remuneration for their patents. In this regard, it is also important that the 2001 Doha Declaration on the TRIPS Agreement and Public Health is not allowed to remain as a mere expression of noble intentions on paper, but is implemented in practice with purpose and sensitivity, whenever acute problems of public health arise and availability of drugs at affordable prices becomes a critical factor in dealing with them.

Lastly, there are academics and activists who argue that protection of IP is unnecessary because, even without such protection, inventions and investments in R&D would have taken place to the same extent for purely commercial reasons. It is difficult to say whether the evidence relied upon for this assertion is valid for all cases. Rather than base policy-making on such a risky assumption, a more prudent approach would be to accept the need for protection as a necessary incentive, but balance it with larger societal needs. The balancing act requires application of restraints, such as compulsory licences, parallel imports, avoiding extension of the term of protection, supporting generic drug production, curbing anti-competitive and abusive practices, and other measures that would prevent stifling of competition in the market place.

Conclusion

Let me return to the Indian story and conclude this chapter on a lighter note. I attended the ministerial review meeting held in Tokyo in November 1989. On its concluding day, the Japanese minister in charge of the meeting told the gathering that Japan was not bad at making pencils and that therefore he would like the audience not to disregard the pencils kept on their tables. The participants who until then had paid little attention to the pencils started looking at them more closely, and there was immediately a mad rush to collect them as souvenirs. This was because the pencils carried the logo "IN GATT WE TRUST". I have preserved a couple of them until today. Having come a long way from opposing the TRIPS Agreement, but looking now to leverage it for its own benefit, India could well adopt the motto "IN TRIPS WE TRUST" in its quest to attract foreign investment and technology and to ward off Section 301-type coercions!

Endnotes

1 See Appendix 1.

2 GATT document MIN.DEC, Multilateral Trade Negotiations – The Uruguay Round – Ministerial Declaration on the Uruguay Round, 20 September 1986.

3 It is my understanding that a few other developing countries, namely, Brazil, Cuba, Peru and Nicaragua, also made similar statements at the concluding session at Punta del Este.

4 India joined the Paris Convention in 1998.

5 Between July 1989 and September 1989, I had bilateral meetings with the EC in Brussels, Sweden in Stockholm, Norway in Oslo, Brazil in Sao Paolo and Thailand in Bangkok, when I indicated to those countries that a key overall objective of India in the Uruguay Round negotiations was to integrate the Indian economy into the world economy on beneficial terms and that India would put forward specific proposals of its demands from this standpoint.

6 GATT document MTN.GNG.11/W/37, Uruguay Round – Group of Negotiations on Goods (GATT) – Negotiating Group on Trade-Related Aspects of Intellectual Property Rights, including Trade in Counterfeit Goods – Standards and Principles concerning the Availability Scope and Use of Trade-Related Intellectual Property Rights – Communication from India, 10 July 1989. This document was presented by me in the TRIPS Negotiating Group immediately after my taking over as the Chief Negotiator of India for the Uruguay Round. In an interview with the Indian newspaper *The Hindu*, Julio Lacarte Muró, an acclaimed GATT warhorse and the then Uruguayan Ambassador to the GATT in Geneva, described the document as the most comprehensive and lucid articulation thus far of the viewpoint of the developing countries on IPRs. The *Financial Times* reported that India had submitted a comprehensive paper on the norms for IP protection from the perspective of the developing world.

7 GATT document MTN.GNG/NG11/W/71, Negotiating Group on Trade-Related Aspects of Intellectual Property Rights, including Trade in Counterfeit Goods – Communication from Argentina, Brazil, Chile, China, Colombia, Cuba, Egypt, India, Nigeria, Peru, Tanzania and Uruguay, 14 May 1990.

8 I must record here that Jayashree Watal, then a negotiator on behalf of India and now a Counsellor in the Intellectual Property Division of the WTO, played an important role in this negotiation. She referred to the consistent practice of the United States itself of its government agencies using patented inventions for a public purpose without the involvement of the patent holder. The reader is directed to her account (chapter 16) for more details on this subject.

9 An idea of the distance that India has travelled on the economic front can be had from the fact that, in 1991, when the changes in economic policies were ushered in, India's exports and imports were of the order of US$ 15 billion and US$ 17 billion respectively, and its foreign exchange reserves were only about US$ 2 billion. In 2014, exports were of the order of US$ 350 billion and imports US$ 480 billion. The foreign exchange reserves are now (March 2015) of the order of US$ 330 billion. The size of the Indian economy is now close to US$ 2 trillion and it is poised to exceed US$ 5 trillion within the next five years. India is now a major destination for foreign direct and portfolio investments.

10 The Doha Declaration on the TRIPS Agreement and Public Health, 14 November 2001, which sets out principles and objectives in the area of public health, must also be viewed in this light.

11 Even today, I have my doubts whether Articles 70.8 and 70.9 of the TRIPS Agreement would have survived judicial scrutiny in India had they been challenged. But the situation did not arise; as I understand it, there was only one case of exclusive marketing right application in India in the transition period of ten years.

12 The Indian economy is now close to US$ 2 trillion in size and is projected to grow at 8 per cent or more per annum from the next couple of years. The economy is therefore likely to reach US$ 5 trillion in size within a short period of time, perhaps five years. Given a favourable investment climate, including protection of IPRs according to international standards, such a market is bound to attract manufacturing facilities, including those with advanced technologies.

13 Narayanan Suresh, "McKinsey: Indian pharma to touch $45 bn in 2020", *BioSpectrum*, 28 June 2013.

14 Typically, these are infectious tropical diseases transmitted by mosquitoes, flies and parasites, and their prevalence and persistence in poor societies is mainly due to lack of sanitation infrastructure and hygiene. The World Health Organization has been urging national governments to increase their investments to prevent, control and treat such diseases, including certain neglected tropical diseases.

15 In this context, it is worth recalling that Médecins Sans Frontières has been advocating that the developed countries should support the formulation of an international "Neglected Diseases Drugs Act" for the development of drugs for diseases that are endemic to poor countries, and that they should provide publicly mandated resources for the discovery and development of such drugs.

16 See Appendix 1.

12

Negotiating for Brazil

Piragibe dos Santos Tarragô

The beginning

In the 1980s, intellectual property rights (IPRs) reappeared as one of the top items in discussions on international trade. In my view, some factors would explain this:

- the emergence of new technologies, especially computer programs, integrated circuits, biotechnology and new pharmaceutical products

- the interest of producers of high-tech products in obtaining enhanced market access by means of IPR protection

- the competition from producers and exporters in third-country markets from countries where the protection of IPRs was considered insufficient or not available

- the absence of an effective multilateral dispute settlement mechanism to address complaints for violation of IPRs, and the lack of adequate remedies in the treaties administered by WIPO against violations of IPRs or inadequate protection of IPRs

- the perceived economic value of technology as a means to gain access to international markets and beat competitors

- the need to recoup the high research and development (R&D) costs involved in the launching of new products, especially high-tech products and pharmaceuticals

- the fact that technology in itself had become a valuable asset in international markets; enhanced protection of IPRs would further increase its market value

- the perception of the technology producers that higher standards and more effective protection of IPRs would strengthen their predominant position in international markets of high-tech goods

- the view of the technology producers that the looseness of the international agreements on IPRs administered by WIPO facilitated non-authorized copying and was at the origin of the growth in international trade of counterfeit goods manufactured by low-cost producers

- the commitment by the *demandeurs*[1] to a strengthened international system of protection of IPRs as a part of the multilateral trading system, via an expanded GATT.

By that time, in the GATT, preparations had begun to launch a new round of trade negotiations. After extensive discussions and bargaining, IP was eventually included among the subjects to be negotiated in the new round, together with two other so-called new themes – services and investments. This represented a major departure from the pattern of trade rounds thus far undertaken. By encompassing subjects outside the traditional mandate of the GATT, the Uruguay Round of multilateral trade negotiations opened the way for the creation of the WTO, including under its coverage not only trade in goods but also trade in services, trade-related aspects of IPRs and trade-related investment measures.

In general, developing countries, such as Brazil, had misgivings about the inclusion of new themes in the GATT, as these would hardly bring benefits to the developing contracting parties. But, eventually, they accepted the inclusion of the new themes in exchange for negotiations aiming at enhancing market access, mainly for agricultural, textile and tropical products, improving rules on safeguards and strengthening the dispute settlement system against the use of unilateral measures. In accepting the new themes, they were clear that they would have to negotiate potential gains in sectors of their export interest against, *inter alia*, required changes in domestic rules and policies concerning industrial and technological development, services and investment.

Therefore, in approaching the TRIPS negotiations, Brazil and many developing countries formulated their respective negotiating positions in defensive terms. Particularly in the case of Brazil, the national authorities were aware that the country was targeted by the *demandeurs* on the subject, as the latter regarded Brazil's IP laws as obstacles to the higher rents their corporations would like to obtain from higher standards of IP protection.

In the main, Brazil's stance on negotiating an agreement on TRIPS derived from the consideration that the protection of IPRs afforded by the existing Conventions administered by WIPO (Paris Convention for the Protection of Industrial Property, Berne Convention for the Protection of Literary and Artistic Works and International Convention for the Protection of Performers, Producers of Phonograms and Broadcasting Organizations (Rome Convention)) was sufficient or adequate. If changes were to be introduced in those treaties, Brazil would have favoured, at the time, further flexibility in the application of rules regarding, for instance, compulsory licences and forfeiture for patents and the adoption of a *sui generis* protection for computer programs or, at best, including them in a category similar to that of applied art under the Berne Convention.

As the negotiations took a decisive turn after the mid-term review (1988–9), where it was agreed to include under the negotiating mandate higher standards of IP protection, as was the intention of the *demandeurs*, Brazil, as part of a group of developing countries, felt it necessary to submit the group's proposal in writing so as to demarcate its lines of defence in the negotiations on such a wide range of subjects.

In this personal account, I think a few selected topics are important in gaining an understanding of Brazil's concerns and approach to the negotiations.

The mid-term ministerial meeting, 1988–9

A mid-term review meeting at ministerial level took place in Montreal in December 1988, but it was concluded in Geneva in April 1989. It was a crucial moment in the negotiations, for it defined the terms under which we negotiators would work until the conclusion of the Uruguay Round (initially foreseen for December 1990).

At the Montreal meeting, Brazil and a number of developing countries still insisted on the inadequacy of the GATT to host negotiations on IPRs. They maintained that the treaties on IP were fundamentally about the protection of rights, whereas the GATT essentially concerned trade in goods. Delegations of some developed countries replied, in no ambiguous terms, that they considered a TRIPS agreement as part of the package on market access for goods. As many of us in the delegations of the developing countries thought that IPRs were, first and foremost, designed to reward inventors and creators and protect their works against undue copying, to us, WIPO was the most appropriate body to hold discussions on the matter. But for the developed countries, now acting almost in unison, since the European Communities (EC) had accepted to engage in full-fledged negotiations about TRIPS in the GATT, it became more and more difficult to block the holding of the TRIPS negotiations in the GATT.

In order to avoid the failure of the Uruguay Round and be subject to the unilateral application of trade sanctions against their exports, Brazil and other developing countries eventually did not block the rewriting of the mandate as the outcome of the mid-term review. Therefore, the *demandeurs* succeeded in having their approach to the negotiations prevail in the terms of the new mandate. It was then clear that it would cover new or higher standards of IPRs, including measures of enforcement. But definition on the lodgement of the eventual TRIPS Agreement was left open, to be decided at the end of the negotiations. It was, possibly, a concession to the developing countries' position (and perhaps to some European countries that still upheld WIPO against the GATT).

The agreement at the mid-term review was also possible because many developing countries softened their stance in view of the trade-offs in other areas. They entertained the expectation of receiving important concessions in other negotiating areas, such as agriculture and textiles, in exchange for agreeing to negotiate new standards in the TRIPS Agreement. In addition, and of no less importance, many were compelled to take a "more constructive attitude" in the negotiations in order to avoid being subject to trade sanctions by the United States, under its national legislation (in particular, Section 301 of the Trade Act 1974 and Special 301 of the Omnibus Trade and Competitiveness Act 1988).

The negotiations

The *demandeurs* soon made known their proposals, which were characterized by a high degree of ambition. They had particularly in mind the strengthening of IP holders' rights and further restrictions on the ability of governments to set conditions to grant those rights. If they could have their way entirely, it was possible that: the duration of patent protection would be uniformly applied and valid for a longer period (certainly more than the 20 years finally agreed, along with "pipeline protection"); the use without authorization of the right holder would be limited to a minimum (possibly only to national emergencies and to avoid anti-competitive practices); the enforcement measures would probably be stiffer and more intrusive than those that found their way into the agreed text; and the transition period for the actual application of the new standards, including for the existing IPRs unprotected prior to the TRIPS Agreement, would also be much shorter than that finally adopted.

The negotiations showed two quite distinct approaches. Whereas the developed countries aimed to raise, considerably, the international standards of protection of IPRs, including by submitting it to the GATT dispute settlement mechanisms, a group of developing countries (which were the equivalent of today's so-called emerging countries, including Argentina, Brazil, China and India – although China was still in the process of accession to the GATT), set for themselves the goal of preserving the current standards as much as possible. That group of countries could agree to insert into the TRIPS Agreement clauses that, for example, would allow them to continue to establish limitations to the protection of IPRs for public policies in general.

To my mind, the gap between the negotiating positions of these two groups was quite considerable, rendering almost impossible the attainment of a common ground. But through a process of "composite texts", first craftily elaborated in June 1990, taking into account the texts of the *demandeurs* as well as that of 14 developing countries,[2] the draft of the Agreement was being gradually built, first, around the common perceptions existing among the *demandeurs* and, later, around language that could count on the widest possible acceptance by the latter. The objections raised in the negotiations by the group of 14 developing countries to the draft proposals of the *demandeurs*, incorporated under the Chair's guidance in the "composite text", were, as the Chair used to state, "duly noted and to be addressed at a later stage". Actually, they were to be taken up only after the *demandeurs* had settled their differences and reached agreement. It was usually commented within the group of 14 developing countries that the Chair of the Negotiating Group was clearly bent on giving primacy to the big players' positions, for they represented the only possibility of giving substance to the mandate agreed in the mid-term review ("availability, scope and use"[3]), as the group of 14's positions were considered too limited or did not cover all the issues.

At the same time, and apparently under instructions by the Chair of the Trade Negotiations Committee (TNC), the then GATT Director-General, Arthur Dunkel, the Chairs of the various negotiating groups were to advance as much as possible in the drafting of the agreements, with a view to leaving to the political masters at the ministerial meeting in December 1990 only the most sensitive issues for possible cross-sector deals. That is why the Chair of the TRIPS Negotiating Group, with the help of the Secretariat, drafted (in practice, "arbitrated") certain portions according to what, in his view, could represent the closest to a balanced agreement.

The developing countries' proposal

By and large, the developing countries regarded themselves as the main targets of the major producers of goods subject to IP protection that alleged that the developing countries' national legislations did not provide for protection of IPRs for certain sectors, or did so in insufficient or inadequate manner. During the Round, some of those countries, such as Brazil, for example, were under unilateral trade sanctions by the United States for lack of patent protection for pharmaceutical and agrochemical products and for not applying "adequate" IP protection to software. In order to better express how they envisaged a possible final TRIPS agreement, and to have a voice in the negotiations, a group of 14 developing countries decided to draft a proposal.[4] It was elaborated in defensive terms, basically reflecting their national standards. But it meant to underline the relationship between the protection of IPRs and the socioeconomic, technological, development and public interest concerns prevailing in those countries.

The level of IP protection, as practised by those countries, reflected their low stage of development. They had not yet gone through the learning curve, unlike many developed countries that, just a few decades before, had benefited from "lower" standards of protection of IP that they now sought to raise. Underlying the position of many developing countries, in the TRIPS negotiations, one could distinguish considerations of public policies, such as the preservation of social benefits and the creation of conditions to set up a strong industrial and technological base, as opposed to purely commercial aspects or the need to recoup R&D expenditures, as transpired in the proposals of the developed countries. Distinct from the latter's proposals, the submission of the 14 developing countries envisaged a double-track approach – it consigned to GATT the negotiations of what the group deemed to be trade-related aspects of IPRs proper (basically, trade in counterfeit goods) and to "the relevant international organization" (i.e. WIPO) the negotiations of standards of IP protection.

Even in standards, the level of ambition of that group of countries was abysmally low as compared with that of the *demandeurs*. Nonetheless, the proposal provided the 14 developing countries with an opening to participate meaningfully in the negotiations and a chance to have some influence in the final outcome. It has to be noted that, in GATT/WTO negotiations, it is relatively common for a group of "like-minded" countries to jointly draft proposals, though the degree of substantial commitment to the proposals could vary according to the importance each country attaches to the subject matter. In the TRIPS negotiations, some developing countries added their support to a common proposal for tactical reasons, that is, in order to improve their chances of bargaining better deals in other sectors being negotiated in the Round. Among the group of 14 countries, that was evident in relation to certain delegations, which had their priorities set in areas such as agriculture or textiles, for example.

Patents

The TRIPS Agreement amplified considerably the scope of sectors subject to patentability. It rendered it mandatory to grant patents in all fields of technology. But it allowed national laws to exclude from patentability (which also means permission to "include", if desired) plants, animals other than microorganisms, and essentially biological processes.

The developing countries were unable to retain the possibility of invoking reasons of public health to exclude inventions from patentability. If that carried, they would have been able to continue not to grant patents to pharmaceutical products and processes, which, for many *demandeurs*, was their critical objective in the TRIPS negotiations. The 14 developing countries, with the possible exception of India, agreed not to insist on the issue as they were already in the process of changing their national laws to grant patent protection to pharmaceutical products.

I believe Brazil became more amenable to accepting patents for pharmaceutical and agrochemical products after a new government took office in early 1990, which coincided with the beginning of the crucial period in the TRIPS negotiations. Having embraced more market-friendly and privatization policies, and assuming the "inevitability" of changing the national law to grant patents to products hitherto not protected, the new Brazilian Government revised its TRIPS negotiating position. From then on, it took a more tactical approach to the TRIPS negotiations with a view to accumulating bargaining chips to strike more favourable deals in the negotiations on agriculture, then identified as the main sector of Brazil's interest in the Round. The Brazilian delegates were aware of the value of the concession Brazil was offering in accepting patents for pharmaceutical products. Estimates made by a Brazilian association of manufacturers of chemicals and pharmaceuticals indicated that, as an immediate consequence of the adoption of a new patent law, the country's import bill would increase by more than US$ 500 million. Though it is hard to attribute such an increase only to the changes in its patent law that Brazil had to enact as a result of the Uruguay Round accords, the fact is that, today, imports of pharmaceutical and agrochemical products in Brazil reach dozens of billions of US dollars annually.

Biotechnology

The question concerned the appropriation by patents of inventions involving living materials. In this case, even the developed countries could not agree on the extent to which that could be done. It was a difficult proposition, for many scientific and technical studies could not confirm the compatibility of inventions in this field with the criteria of patentability. It was especially hard to prove how the living materials in question could meet, for instance, the criterion of novelty. It was rather problematic to ascertain that a given microorganism was "created" in a laboratory and not "found" in nature. And even if it were "invented", how could the process of invention be described so that the microorganism could be reproduced by means of technical application? This, actually, was one of the strongest arguments, espoused by Brazil and others, to exclude from patents plant and animal varieties, as these can be reproduced by natural means. If a plant could be patented, how could it be possible to control its propagation and determine whether it has been reproduced by employing technical means or has been the result of simple natural reproduction?

The matter had clear and deep-seated economic implications, in particular for medicines, food and agriculture. Brazil is one of the world's largest agricultural producers, and its local communities have been using the fruits of the country's immense biodiversity for medicinal and farming purposes, through traditional knowledge. So it was quite natural that Brazil kept the matter under close scrutiny and that it saw it as in its interests that no new standard should be created in haste. In the end, despite extending considerably the frontiers of patentability, the TRIPS negotiators were not able to find appropriate answers to resolve the quandary of the compatibility with the criteria for patent protection and their application to living materials in a manner that could also take into account the genuine concerns of farmers and holders of traditional knowledge. Though deciding for the availability of protection, the Agreement left it to national legislations to establish the system of protection, whether by patents or by a UPOV-type[5] regime for plant varieties, or by a combination of both. It also determined to review the matter four years after the entry into force of the TRIPS Agreement.

Compulsory licensing

For Brazil, this was a key clause in the negotiations. The ability to apply compulsory licensing had long been a feature of Brazil's policies regarding the use of industrial property rules to induce industrial development. Since the early 1970s, Brazil had taken the leadership, alongside other developing countries, in the negotiations in

WIPO on the revision of the Paris Convention for the Protection of Industrial Property Rights, in particular, to secure further flexibilities in its Article 5A and 5*quater* that set the parameters within which governments can grant compulsory licences. In TRIPS negotiations, the developed countries were actually demanding the opposite, that is, less flexibility for governments on the matter. Granted, some developed countries also had reservations on proposals that could result in limiting their authorities' capacity to extract concessions from companies, by threatening to have recourse to compulsory licensing clauses.

The long exchanges on the matter in the Negotiating Group led to the conclusion that it would be practically impossible to negotiate on compulsory licences from the angle of reasons or grounds, as originally advocated by the US delegation, in that no one was ready to forsake the liberty to determine the circumstances to avail of such a tool. It was then convenient to opt for an approach based on conditions.

By setting clearer and firmer conditions, the *demandeurs* believed it was also possible to reduce the ability of governments to use compulsory licences for purposes of furthering industrial policies, their main concern *vis-à-vis* the developing countries. Actually, the arguments used to uphold national positions on the matter reflected, by and large, a North–South divide on the extent of governments' interference with the private sector's decisions in promoting development. On the one hand, most of the developed countries, but especially the United States, favoured a limited role for governments and laid a greater emphasis on the private sector and market forces; on the other, a great number of developing countries, such as Brazil, advocated a primary role for governments in generating, by means of rules and market intervention, better conditions for economic development. Admittedly, the matter was not so clear cut. Even some developed countries appreciated a role for governments in allowing use of a patent without the consent of its owner in projects in their national interest. They strongly opposed, though, the imposition of compulsory licences for purposes of import substitution, which had, in the past, been one of the main objectives of developing countries.

Indeed, a particular concern for Brazil was how to continue to have the ability to grant compulsory licences to acquire manufacturing capacity whenever the patent owner made use of its monopolistic rights to serve the market only by importation. In its view, this would be tantamount to depriving the market of competition and offering consumers goods at more reasonable prices. For Brazil, the possibility of using compulsory licences to allow for local manufacturing was equivalent to the meaning of "working the patent", as provided for in the relevant articles of the Paris Convention, the validity of which was reconfirmed in Article 2 of the TRIPS Agreement. As the TRIPS Agreement expressly does not contradict those articles (for it has not set out the reasons for compulsory licences), but makes them subject to a non-discrimination clause, I think it can be assumed that countries are able to apply compulsory licences to obtain the working of the patent in those terms. Furthermore, in the negotiations of conditions, the Brazilian delegation endeavoured to keep for the government the maximum flexibility to apply compulsory licences, should it be needed, to meet its requirements of public health, combat abusive practices and encourage local manufacturing. Such a position could be sustained by the fact that a compulsory licence is granted on non-exclusive terms, that is, even if the local manufacturer is given the licence to produce the goods that are the object of a compulsory licence, the patent's owner is not barred from continuing to offer those goods by means of importation. I believe that that assumption was key in order for Brazil to eventually accept the clauses on compulsory licences in the TRIPS Agreement.

Computer programs (software)

In the light of the imprecise definition of software – whether a creation similar to a work of art or to a technology (expressive vs utilitarian) – Brazil and the group of 14 developing countries indicated their preference to leave to national laws how to protect software. A great number of developed countries held that computer programs should be protected as a literary work, as provided for in the Berne Convention, with some adjustments as to the term of protection and the exclusion of moral rights.

Most of the negotiations occurred among the developed countries, for there existed important gaps between the positions of the United States and the EC. Whereas the former supported a protection by copyright with the exclusion of moral rights (for it considered such programs the result of a business endeavour with many collaborators, whose rights are determined by contracts; the United States also considered as equals natural and legal persons for the enjoyment of copyrights), the latter maintained that computer programs should enjoy full status as literary works under the purview of the Berne Convention, including moral rights. Actually, the United States only became a signatory of that Convention in 1989, well after the start of the Uruguay Round. This must certainly have helped pave the way to the final agreement on this issue, which was also facilitated because the developing countries had already adjusted their national laws to acknowledge protection of software by copyright.

But in the TRIPS negotiations, the US position came out as the winner. The duration of the protection – at least 50 years for computer programs – was not exactly as that for a literary work. It would count as of the date of its publication or of its making. In addition, signatories were not obliged to recognize the author's moral rights. For many developing countries, such as Brazil, which, at the inception of the negotiations, questioned the assimilation of computer programs as literary works under the Berne Convention as they considered that such programs had a strong technological content, the fact that the TRIPS Agreement recognized the specificity of software – as expressed in the term of protection and the exclusion of moral rights – represented a somewhat late vindication of their stance.

Related rights

Brazil wanted to preserve the regime of the Rome Convention, to which it is a signatory. It had some misgivings as to the intention, in particular of the United States, which was not bound by that treaty, to introduce into any TRIPS agreement changes to the effect of extending the rights of producers of phonograms and of broadcasting organizations. In this respect, it could follow broadly the position of the EC, which also defended the regime of the Rome Convention. The United States, by the TRIPS Agreement, became indirectly bound by that regime, but was able to expand the scope of the rights set forth therein, or preserve the restrictions provided in its national legislation, in order to enhance the protection afforded to producers of phonograms and to broadcasting organizations.

Apart from the ability to submit possible violations of related rights to the WTO dispute settlement mechanisms, the main novelties introduced by the TRIPS negotiations concerned the inclusion of rental rights, that is, the possibility of producers of phonograms or right holders in them (viz. performers) to prohibit rentals; and the extension of the duration of the protection to 50 years for producers of phonograms and performances. In the end, the outcome was considered satisfactory for Brazil as the new provisions were acceptable. It also pointed to the new developments in the market with the increasing use of rentals of computer programs, phonograms, films, electronic games and so on. In addition, it clearly strengthened the position of right holders against piracy, to which Brazil could subscribe without hesitation.

Objectives and principles

The insertion of Articles 7 and 8 in the agreed text originated from deep concerns hinted at in the proposal submitted by the group of 14 developing countries, which included Brazil.

The proposal was of a pre-emptive nature. Since, after the mid-term review, it was decided that negotiations should aim at raising the standards of IP protection, in the view of that group of countries, objectives and principles should be observed in the implementation of the new standards. As such, they should reflect the recognition in the TRIPS Agreement of the need for the social, economic and technological development of all countries; of proper balance between the rights of IPR holders and those needs; of the inter-relationships between rights and obligations; of ensuring diffusion of technological knowledge and stimulus to innovation in all countries; and of preventing abuses derived from the exercise of IPRs. The new standards should also result in social and economic welfare, as well as recognize the right of countries to take measures to protect public morality, national security, public health and nutrition, and promote the public interest in sectors of vital importance to their socioeconomic and technological development.

It was evident that these proposals, which eventually found their way in a more succinct form into the Agreement, were intended to allow for some flexibility in national laws, which was of particular interest to developing countries. The proposals came about in a stage of the negotiations where it had become clear that it would be impossible for developing countries to succeed with their "minimalist" approach for standards. At that point, basically, all developed countries (but especially the major trading partners, which carried a considerable weight in the GATT) had formed a front to fight for the adoption of ambitious standards of IPR protection, which ran in opposition to the stance taken by that small group of developing countries.

It should be noted as well that, in the GATT (and for that matter in the WTO today) there is no negotiating bloc, like the Group of 77, thus rendering quite difficult the process of bringing together all the developing countries to field common negotiating positions. But I believe that the texts on principles and objectives could count on unanimous support among the developing countries. In the end, the adoption of Articles 7 and 8 could be seen as a concession by the *demandeurs*, though the latter made sure that the eventual measures taken under national legislations, in the light of those objectives and principles, should be consistent with the provisions of the TRIPS Agreement.

The matter was of great interest for Brazil, as it eventually permitted national authorities to obtain an agreement from manufacturers and their countries of origin that they would not contest, by resorting to the WTO's dispute settlement mechanism, decisions to make available to the public at affordable prices, through the compulsory licensing of patents, medicines used, for example, in treatments for HIV/AIDS.

Enforcement

The issue was of high priority for the *demandeurs*. They aimed to have national judicial systems following high standards in combating counterfeit goods both in domestic markets and at the borders, and in ensuring the availability of legal procedures for IPR holders to defend their rights in member countries' national courts.

Brazil's main concerns with the topic lay in the possibility of imposition by the TRIPS Agreement of excessive obligations on its national jurisdiction for the purpose of enforcing the protection of IPRs *vis-à-vis* its judicial system of enforcement of laws in general. In addition, it was mindful that the enforcement provisions could give rise to possible conflicts in the application of judicial procedures between national systems based on civil law – followed by Brazil – or on customary law adopted by countries that followed the British system of common law.

As to the gist of the proposals, with one or two exceptions, Brazil did not have major problems with the disciplines proposed by the main negotiating parties, as they were already integrated into its judicial system. But it had a conceptual problem. If the TRIPS Agreement was to be part of the dispute settlement mechanism of the GATT/WTO, Brazil would be admitting that its national legal procedures, which are the same used in the enforcement of laws in general, could be questioned by another member in a case regarding IPRs. One particular concern was that some delegations of developed countries seemed to propose that the enforcement of IP laws could take precedence over other laws. The matter was more or less solved with the inclusion of a caveat in Article 41.5 in the subsection on General Obligations, by which no member is affected in its capacity to enforce its laws in general, nor has an obligation to distribute resources as between enforcement of IPR and of laws in general.

Dispute settlement

Initially, Brazil and many other developing countries took the stance that the question of dispute settlement should be dealt with separately in keeping with the double-track approach of their original proposals. Thus, the relevant articles of the GATT on dispute settlement would apply only to disputes arising from trade of counterfeit goods. As to disputes regarding standards of IP protection, the group of 14 developing countries, in their proposal, suggested a simple procedure of consultations between the parties concerned. Eventually, they would be referred to a dispute settlement mechanism that was to be negotiated at WIPO (whose dispute settlement mechanism never materialized).

In the negotiations, and as the idea of a single undertaking took deeper root, the developing countries became more amenable to the submission of disputes under the TRIPS Agreement to the dispute settlement mechanism to be agreed to at the Uruguay Round. That view gained traction as the major trading partners showed increasing acceptance of the commitment to avoid resorting to unilateral trade sanctions against developing countries on questions related to IPRs. The developing countries, eventually, agreed to have the TRIPS Agreement submitted to the WTO's new dispute settlement mechanism, because they considered that it would not only give them better protection against unilateral measures but also reinforce the multilateral trading system.

It was agreed, then, that Articles XXII and XXIII of the GATT would be applicable to disputes under the TRIPS Agreement. But the question of whether or not the subsections (b) and (c) on non-violation of Article XXIII would be included was left to be solved at a later stage (possibly through consultations in the TRIPS Council).

Transition period for pharmaceutical and agrochemical products

As the proposal of the 14 developing countries did not contemplate substantial changes in the IP standards, it did not provide for a transition period. The question came about late in the negotiations as part of a deal that would involve acceptance, mainly by the developing countries, of higher standards of IP protection as proposed by the *demandeurs*.

The transition period concerned not only the time normally needed by national legislative authorities to approve a new agreement but, more concretely, the time needed to draft new national laws and to adjust development, industrial and health policies, mainly in developing countries, in order to give effect to the new IP standards in particular areas or sectors, such as pharmaceuticals and agrochemicals, as well as to adapt their national enforcement systems. Developing countries that, prior to the TRIPS Agreement, did not provide product patent protection, would have up to 2005 (ten years after the entry into force of the Agreement, as per Article 65.4) to do so. This was accepted as part of the deal that would involve a similar transitional period (ten years) for the implementation of the Agreement on Agriculture and Agreement on Textiles and Clothing in the respective negotiating groups of the Round. It was a procedure meant to ensure some balance in the overall concessions exchanged by trading partners in the Round.

However, the pharmaceuticals and agrochemicals producers in the main trading partners (essentially, the United States, the EC, Japan and Switzerland) succeeded in having the delegations of their respective countries introduce clauses (Articles 70.8 and 70.9) to ensure both immediate IP protection and the possibility of monopolistic marketing rights of their products in those developing countries, such as Brazil, that, up until then, did not provide product patent protection to inventions in those sectors. Those clauses established that developing countries in that situation would agree to start accepting the filing of patent applications as of the date of the entry into force of the TRIPS Agreement (1995), and examine the criteria for patentability as of the date of application of the Agreement (five years later or from 1 January 2000) but as if they were established at the date of entry into force (i.e. retroactively to 1995).

Moreover, according to Article 70.9, the developing country authorities must accept to examine applications for exclusive marketing rights to a member, and eventually grant them, even prior to the granting of the patent it had applied following procedure in Article 70.8.

The developing country in question was then obliged to grant a patent for the remaining period of protection counting from the filing date (1995). This could be construed as an exception to the novelty requirement of patentability.

In practice, Articles 70.8 and 70.9 qualified the transition period of ten years afforded to developing countries that, prior to the TRIPS Agreement, did not provide product patents in the above-mentioned sectors. It could even result, as per the case in question, in a substantial reduction of the timespan agreed as the "transition period". Such drafting creativity was meant to give satisfaction to stakeholders whose patents might fall into the public domain before the expiry of the transition period.

But unlike trade in goods, where the transition period would mean a phase-out of the pre-existing restrictions at the end of ten years, in the TRIPS Agreement, the transition period in such highly valued sectors as pharmaceuticals and agrochemicals could be much shorter than ten years. This is because the national authority in the country (where no product patent was available prior to the TRIPS Agreement) could grant in much less than ten years exclusive marketing rights to the applicant member. As it is known, the owner of an invention for which patent protection is claimed, can start, soon after obtaining marketing approval, putting on the market and selling, on an exclusive basis, the corresponding product, even if the patent has not yet been granted.

Be that as it may, the transition period in any TRIPS agreement, considered critical by the *demandeurs* if they were to agree to a final text, was a "price" deemed acceptable by the developing countries in general, as it would unblock the road to agreements in other areas of their main export interest, and ensure a successful conclusion of the Uruguay Round.

Conclusions

Throughout more than seven years of negotiations, I think Brazil gradually moved from a position of staunch opposition to the negotiations on trade-related aspects of IPRs that would result in the adoption of higher international IP standards and the incorporation of the subject matter into the jurisdiction of the WTO, to a somewhat hesitant acceptance of such an outcome. Though not entirely convinced of the benefit to its economy of the acceptance of higher IP standards, nor that the WTO would be the best place to lodge TRIPS-related disputes for resolution, Brazil eventually agreed to these provisions as it considered them a price to pay in order to have a strengthened multilateral trading system and some satisfaction for its main export interests.

I believe also that a number of factors could have played a role in such a development, most notably:

- pressures from its then main trading partner, the United States – the main proponent of the negotiations on IP in the Round – including by means of trade sanctions (exclusion from the Generalized System of Preferences benefits)

- change in the Brazilian political scenario with the coming to power of a government that was more favourable to market-friendly policies and to an increased share of private sector and foreign investments in the economy

- a rather unified position taken by the major trading partners on issues where Brazil and other key developing countries were the main targets of the proposed new standards, such as in pharmaceuticals and agrochemicals patents or enforcement

- the perception of the strategic value of TRIPS in the overall negotiations as a bargaining chip to achieve Brazil's main goals in the market access and rule-making sectors of the Round (agriculture, textiles, safeguards and dispute settlement)

- given the strong interest of the big corporations in the *demandeurs'* economies, and their robust lobbying in the capitals of the main developing countries, the "inevitability" of Brazil's agreeing to higher or new IP standards to address technological developments in informatics, computer software, pharmaceuticals and agrochemicals, in particular

- the absence of a unified position among the developing countries, which had either little expertise in the subject matter or limited capacity to resist the pressures from the main stakeholders in introducing higher IP standards and restrictions in the action by governments to use IP to promote industrial development.

Notwithstanding the outcome of the TRIPS negotiations and the high degree of unpreparedness by developing countries to engage in such a complex and technically demanding exercise, Brazil and many developing countries, to my mind, succeeded in inserting in the final text a few clauses in order to safeguard their national interests and to give their governments some latitude of action or policy space in implementing their development policies and to defend the public interest. This is exemplified in the provisions on objectives and principles, as well as on use without authorization of the right holder. These negotiations surely ought to be a lesson, especially for developing countries when engaging in future negotiating exercises in the WTO.

Endnotes

1   In the negotiations, *demandeurs* were usually considered those that submitted proposals for higher IPR protection, such as, *inter alia*, the European Communities (EC), Japan, Switzerland and the United States.

2   GATT document MTN.GNG/NG11/W/71, Negotiating Group on Trade-Related Aspects of Intellectual Property Rights, including Trade in Counterfeit Goods – Communication from Argentina, Brazil, Chile, China, Colombia, Cuba, Egypt, India, Nigeria, Peru, Tanzania and Uruguay, 14 May 1990.

3   GATT document MTN/TNC/11, Uruguay Round – Trade Negotiations Committee – Mid-Term Meeting, 21 April 1989.

4   GATT document MTN.GNG/NG11/W/71.

5   International Union for the Protection of New Varieties of Plants.

13

Negotiating for Argentina

Antonio Gustavo Trombetta[1]

Introduction

To prepare a chapter that presents the experiences of a negotiator of the TRIPS Agreement as close as possible to reality is not an easy task. This is because the Agreement is complex as it covers many subjects related to IP and is made up of a set of rules with varied degrees of specificity and detail. Approaching this task 25 years after the negotiations has introduced complications and involuntary distortions that have made this task even more difficult.

After some days of reflection on how to face the challenge, I came to the conclusion that the best contribution within my reach would be an honest attempt to describe what had been the major elements of concern to my delegation, the global context in which the Uruguay Round of multilateral negotiations had taken place and the elements I had been able to count on in order to undertake the negotiations.

This chapter will cover, in its first part, a summary of the main decisions and dates that decisively shaped the development of the Uruguay Round and, in particular, of the TRIPS Agreement. In the second part, I will address the phenomenal changes that took place in the global, political and economic arena that unfolded in parallel with the negotiations, and the inevitable, although sometimes intangible, effects that these had on governments, people and delegates. Substantial changes, but not for the same reasons, also took place in Argentina and significantly affected the finalization of national positions. Third, I will attempt to present in binary opposition (even though it contradicts my way of judging reality) the expression of Argentina's interests under the simple formula "offensive" – that is, gains in agriculture negotiations – vs "defensive" – that is, losses under the TRIPS negotiations. After this, I propose to develop some of the fundamental reasons on which our objectives were based concerning crucial aspects of the TRIPS text, in order to incorporate "breathing space" or "policy space" for national legislations to implement the most sensitive issues from the "defensive" position. In the last part, I express with candour some of the problems and restrictions an individual negotiator from a developing country has to cope with as compared with delegations benefiting from the support of experts on every element of the proposed TRIPS text. In closing, I take the liberty to share a couple of additional thoughts, which I hope can give some colour and perspective to what is expressed in this work.

What follows is a modest and honest attempt, while revisiting memories left dormant for a long time, to share with the younger generation of negotiators my experiences in dealing with IP in those volatile times. What I call "my experience" is a complex mix of memories of a technical nature, reconstruction of thoughts and discussions of a speculative nature of some 25 years ago and the rediscovery that, under the embers of time and distance, some old and faithful convictions that accompanied me throughout the whole process still survive.

Key events in the TRIPS process

- Punta del Este, Uruguay, September 1986. The decision is made to launch multilateral trade negotiations (the Uruguay Round). For the ensuing years, the mandate of negotiation in the field of IP will be subject to controversial and opposite interpretations between those who emphasize "the need to promote effective and adequate protection of intellectual property rights" and those who consider that "the negotiations shall aim to clarify GATT provisions" in order to "develop a multilateral framework ... dealing with international trade in counterfeit goods ...".[2]

- Montreal, Canada, December 1988. Mid-term review at ministerial level. Deep disagreements on four chapters lead to an impasse in the negotiations until a solution is found to unblock those substantial elements: textiles, agriculture, safeguards and IP.

- Geneva, April 1989. An understanding is reached in the Trade Negotiations Committee, substantially reformulating the mandate on IP. From that point onwards, negotiations shall encompass "basic principles", "adequate standards" and "effective and appropriate means for the enforcement of trade-related intellectual property rights", as well as a "multilateral framework of principles, rules and disciplines dealing with international trade in counterfeit goods".[3]

- Brussels, 1990. A TRIPS text has been outlined, but with a number of substantial differences still remaining among the negotiators.

- Geneva, December 1991. Draft Final Act of Negotiations – the Dunkel Draft – is put forward by the GATT Director-General, Arthur Dunkel, following the recommendations of the Chair of the Negotiating Group, Ambassador Lars Anell. Dunkel proposes texts on a host of questions not agreed between the delegations. Regarding TRIPS, the proposed solutions are in general in line with the ambitions of the most active promoters of this area of the negotiations.

- Marrakesh, April 1994. Agreement Establishing the WTO. The TRIPS provisions, as an integral part of the new organization, create treaty obligations for its members.

- Bern, December 2014. A dear voice, but distant in time, brought me – totally unexpectedly – 25 years back to the exciting and fascinating moments of the TRIPS negotiations. Jayashree Watal, the clever, forceful and trusted Indian colleague in so many crucial instances during the negotiations – now a member of the WTO Secretariat – wanted me to remove the dust, stir the grey matter in my brains and write a paper, "an account of your personal experience, Tony", and not a "technical, formal one".

The broader context

The substantial changes in the mandate of the Uruguay Round

The year 1989 was one of dramatic changes. In April, as previously mentioned, the new mandate for the TRIPS Negotiating Group completely altered the direction and substance of the work. Thereafter, negotiations would, *inter alia*, extend to the principles that would be the basis of a future agreement; the standards of protection that would be adopted for each of the IPRs; measures of enforcement that would be designed, including provisions on border measures; and procedures for dispute settlement that would be agreed to. This was a really overwhelming agenda.

The starting point for this new stage brought about difficulties at different levels. Developing countries, especially those that had domestic pharmaceuticals industries of a certain size, were particularly concerned because we were fully aware that the aim of the major trading powers was to ensure, at a global level, patents for pharmaceutical products. Later, I will specifically address this issue, but it suffices to mention, at this point, that we were deeply concerned by the potential costly effects on national health systems. In the case of Argentina, given the public policies in place on this matter, this was of utmost importance.

At the same time, there was an underlying fear of granting too strong a patent protection in the biotechnological area. Biotechnology was a relatively new field and international experience was scarce; the greatest biological diversity – from which the base material for new developments is often obtained – was found precisely in the developing countries. Understandably, we were afraid that the exercise might head towards a reinforced technological supremacy by international companies based, paradoxically, on our vast biodiversity.

The economic situation in Latin America

In a somewhat broader perspective, but one necessary in order to understand the time and the framework within which the negotiations developed, reference should be made to the so-called "lost decade for development" in Latin America. With greater or lesser intensity, most countries of the region were confronting a drop in economic activity, high rates of unemployment, reduction in real wages, increase in the general level of prices and declining terms of trade.

The combined effect of higher international interest rates and its impact on debt service – an increase of almost six times – with the decline of the inflow of foreign capital and the fall in the terms of trade, was devastating. The transfer of capital towards creditors outside the region was of such magnitude that the ambition of economic development seemed unattainable.

This gloomy picture was exacerbated, if that were possible, by the fact that several countries were undergoing the process of democratic recovery after turbulent *coups d'état* and were forced to deal with legitimate social demands under clearly adverse economic conditions.

1989: The crisis hits harder in Argentina

The same year that saw the redefinition of the mandates within the Uruguay Round, 1989, challenged Argentina with one of its most difficult episodes since the successful restoration of democracy in 1983. International prices of grains and meats – essential components of the trade balance of the country – declined significantly during the 1980s, thus creating further external restrictions in addition to those imposed by the high interests on sovereign debt. This combination of critically negative factors led to high inflation, unsatisfied social demands and, finally, to the early fall of the government.

The newly elected government decisively changed direction: it put into motion a vast plan of economic deregulation, with privatizations within the utilities sector, dramatically simplified the requirements for foreign investments and made a pledge of reforming Argentina's patent law.

The altered global order: The fall of the Berlin Wall

To add complexity to the overall picture in which the negotiations took place, it should also be taken into consideration that the same year, 1989, saw the fall of the Berlin Wall. With this event, all the certainties that had been brought about by the bipolar order collapsed: the USSR was practically dissolved within months and, with that, the strong ideological references, the economic regimes, the organization of society resulting from the post-war order, disappeared from one day to the next.

It is unnecessary to accentuate the global magnitude of the "revolutionary transformation" that such an event had, but I believe it pertinent to recall it because the shock waves inevitably hit senior policy-makers and negotiators alike, generalizing the feeling of bewilderment and demanding great efforts to comprehend the consequences of the emerging order.

In that context, only the United States remained in the centre of the new global order and, as a consequence, a central reference in the commercial architecture that was being outlined in Geneva. In parallel with this course of events, Europe also went through a period of substantive changes that consolidated its role as major player in the negotiations and as a global trading partner. The fall of the Wall would entail – inevitably – the reunification of Germany, the demand for accession to the European Communities of the vast majority of the countries of Eastern Europe and, therefore, the expansion of the market economy into new territories, populations and industries.

In short, since the end of 1989, changes felt in the global political, economic and social order were of magnitudes unknown up until then and affected hundreds of millions of people in one way or another, by the alteration of a whole set of principles governing existing systems.

In addition to that, another factor that had considerable influence on national authorities and negotiators alike was the fact that the United States adopted and unilaterally applied legal provisions of a punitive nature against selected countries under Section 301 of its Trade and Tariff Act of 1984. At different times, Japan, the Republic of Korea, India, Brazil, Argentina, Mexico and Chile were, among other countries, placed under a regime of special supervision (i.e. watch list, priority watch list or priority foreign country) with the consequent threat of withdrawing Generalized System of Preferences benefits – which were important for many developing countries or by the application of sanctions in the form of higher tariffs on products sensitive for the exporting country.

The prospect of facing threats or trade sanctions in the US market produced a corrosive and divisive effect in many countries – among them, Argentina – pitting companies exporting to the US market against those identified as a "target" of the US action. This divisive effect in the business world did not take long to be felt in the public and political spheres, adding to the elements of controversy.

It is true, looking back at those events, that we all understood that the changes would decisively influence our dealings and that they would lead us to places that we could not foresee. Nor could we foresee what we would find in them.

Argentina: Crucial interests in the Uruguay Round

It goes without saying that, for a country such as Argentina, such complex and comprehensive negotiations as were undertaken in the Uruguay Round cannot come down to two central issues, in a sort of dichotomy represented by the "offensive interests" and "defensive interests".

Indeed, the multiple interests of the country, of differing intensity, interacted dynamically in a way not always foreseeable. For instance, from the very beginning of the Uruguay Round, it was clear that negotiating areas such as agriculture and textiles had systemic value for the whole exercise; not all the other areas had the same intrinsic value. But the developments that took place in the course of the Uruguay Round altered that equation; the introduction of the notion of "a single undertaking", for instance, prompted additional demands, due to the fact that we were now confronting an exercise out of which, at the end of the road, an international organization would emerge that would house the results achieved in all areas of negotiations and that would subject those results to a unique and reinforced dispute settlements mechanism.

In this evolution, it soon became apparent in the work of the internal coordination of the Argentine delegation that the different negotiating groups would have a growing relevance, not only for their intrinsic value, but also by the reinforced importance that inevitably would be brought about by the new multilateral trading architecture.

Having said this, and at the risk of contradicting myself about being uncomfortable when referring to binary dichotomies of the national positions, I will present the tension "agriculture vs TRIPS" in order to transmit, as a sketch with illustrative character, two of the more visible interests of Argentina within the framework of the Uruguay Round.

The "offensive" interests: Agriculture

The original GATT did not contemplate the major exporting interests of Argentina; in fact, it made official in its rules the discrimination that was contrary to our agricultural interests. It is necessary to point out that, for Argentina, agricultural and food production is central, not only for the recognized efficiency of the farmers and the exceptional conditions of the land but also because of its contribution to the gross domestic product (GDP) as a whole and to the trade balance.

Due to the unfair treatment of agriculture in the GATT, it was natural for Argentina to place a high level of ambition on this area of the negotiations. At the same time, given previous experience, the launching of a new round of negotiations in the GATT was received with scepticism and mistrust. For that reason, the whole negotiating exercise was initially received with cautious and measured political support.

Notwithstanding these difficulties, it was clear to the negotiators that the inclusion of agriculture in the Uruguay Round was a unique opportunity to leave behind such discrimination in the GATT. In those years, a coalition of agricultural exporting countries was formed, the Cairns Group, exceptionally overcoming the cleavage between North (developed countries) and South (developing countries) that characterized, to a large extent, these multilateral trade negotiations. This coordinated approach among several countries under the umbrella of the Cairns Group, however, did not lead to an increased convergence or coordination in other matters, such as the TRIPS negotiations.

In Argentina, predictably, perceptions of what the Uruguay Round could hold for us leaned towards either a "defensive" or an "offensive" view, depending on the interests at stake – namely, as a threat to certain industrial sectors, or as an opportunity for the agricultural sector.

This duality was certainly not confined to the private actors directly involved. In the public sector, at both the national and provincial levels, in professional associations, academia and the press, the subject was a matter of lively debate and of uncertainty about the magnitude of what was really at stake for the country. The state of anxiety and distrust remained throughout the negotiations of the Uruguay Round (strictly speaking, there are still many voices expressing deep dissatisfaction over the actual results of the Round for Argentina).

The positive internal reception of Argentina's decision not to conform to the proposals in the mid-term review at the ministerial meeting in Montreal in 1989, therefore, did not come as a surprise. On the side of the "offensive" interests, the positive reception of this outcome was unsurprising, because the process did not give hope for elements of negotiation considered indispensable; the "defensive" interests were positive because no decisions were made that would immediately jeopardize the most sensitive matters.

The "defensive" interests: The national pharmaceuticals industry

In Argentina, foreign and domestic pharmaceuticals industries had lived with manageable tensions between themselves for decades. The relative importance of the industry as a whole is apparent in its several hundreds of millions of dollars' value in terms of production and employment and its role in various health systems. The fact that laboratories of national origin were stronger in relation to their peers in other countries in the region led to a promising phase of expansion of activities in several countries in Latin America, and even in Asia, adding to the adversarial relationship between foreign and domestic pharmaceuticals industries.

The public interest in Argentina is explained not only by the growing economic contribution of this sector but also by the conditions of negotiation of prices/ quantities of medicines arising from the particularities of the Argentine health systems. Indeed, under the federal public health system, medicines were supplied free of charge to the network of public hospitals, which were distributed throughout the country. Furthermore, provincial entities were also partially involved in providing health care, and a multiplicity of labour associations granted high subsidies to their affiliates on purchases of medicines and had their own facilities, including hospitals and laboratories. It is thus easy to understand the social and political sensitivity aroused by the issue of drug patents and their impact – real or potential – on prices.

Another element of concern was the fact that Argentina – like so many other developing countries – did not have in place the necessary legislation or experienced institutions dealing with competition laws or consumer protection. I underline this point because, during the negotiations, the question on how to effectively fight potential abuses, including increases in prices, arose repeatedly. The developed countries favoured this type of approach, but for many of the developing countries, the argument was not convincing.

Perhaps it is interesting to point out the way in which the Argentine administration prepared to face the TRIPS negotiations. An Interdepartmental Commission was set up, encompassing all the agencies with responsibilities in matters of IP (Foreign Affairs, Trade, Science and Technology, Agriculture, Public Health, Directorate for Copyright Protection, Customs, etc.), although the diversity of interests at play did not always facilitate the adoption of an agreed position.

The Argentinian pharmaceuticals industry lobbied intensively on several fronts – public agencies, Parliament, consumers' associations, trade unions and mass media – and it kept close contact with partners in countries that faced similar challenges.

I recall an occasion on which an important business delegation travelled to Geneva to get a first-hand impression of the state of the negotiations. It met with the Chair of the Negotiating Group, Ambassador Lars Anell, officials of the GATT Secretariat and the delegations of the United States, the EC, Japan and Switzerland. The message received was blunt: the delegation returned to Argentina with the impression that the industry's room for manoeuvre would be greatly reduced.

The central issues of TRIPS

Once the negotiations moved to define the standards of IP protection, the quandary shifted from the defensive point of view to how to construct a system allowing for flexibilities in future national legislation concerning, in particular, the patent regime. The challenge was not a minor one, given the lack of international experience on a subject that was a typically internal one – in addition to the negotiating imperative of not giving away in advance our positions on crucial points in the negotiations. On top of that, negotiators had to cope with the growing scepticism of national actors on what, they anticipated, would represent an unmitigated defeat.

Thanks to the valuable support of a small number of outside experts and colleagues from other developing countries, particularly those who were the "preferred target" to change national patent regimes, a reasonably effective combined action, although not necessarily very well coordinated, could be deployed in order to include in the provisions of the TRIPS Agreement a certain "breathing space" for our national legislators.

What were these elements and how did they interact with each other?

The question of "exhaustion of rights"

It is important to state in advance that the TRIPS Agreement leaves the issue of exhaustion open because it was impossible to find a common ground among delegations. Article 6 is a tangible example of this; hence, there is no internationally accepted definition of the principle of "exhaustion of rights".

Therefore, what I express next must not be seen, in any way, as an attempt to interpret this provision in 2015; rather, it should be seen as my effort to share what moved me 25 years ago to defend this principle.

The joint submission of 14 developing countries[4] does not specifically include any provision on this issue. However, in the course of discussions, we came to better understand the relevance of the topic. The central idea of exhaustion relies upon the fact that the right holder has the crucial right to decide whether or not to place the product on the market. However, once the right holder places the product on the market, the IPR is exhausted; the product is already on the market, and from there this product "flies with his own wings" (an expression borrowed from a doctoral thesis I studied at the time).

One of the arguments in favour of the inclusion of a clause on exhaustion was that the negotiating mandate itself indicated that new provisions on IPRs should not become barriers to legitimate trade. Following the logic from a commercial point of view – we were in a trade round, after all – if there was no infringement of IP rights, then no artificial barriers to trade should be created.

In practical terms, the importance that my delegation attached to this provision arose from the possibility of "parallel imports" from the market where the price determined by the right owner was the lowest without the consent of the right holder. It is essential, and goes without saying, that the product should be "legitimate", that is to say, it should not infringe the rights of the right holder or an authorized licensee. In defending this position, I believed that the ability of the right holder to compartmentalize markets, with the consequent power of imposition of prices, would be moderated.

The solution enshrined in the TRIPS Agreement – a sort of "agreement to disagree" – leaves freedom to national legislators to determine their own regimes of "exhaustion". There are various, conflicting interpretations on the scope of Article 6 and its reading with the footnote to Article 28 (on rights conferred by the patent), for the insertion of which I am partly responsible. I will not give my interpretation here; I will simply limit myself to recalling, as a former negotiator, some of the issues considered central in those days.

Compulsory licences

As we approached a substantially reinforced patent system, fear was growing of the intensity of the legal monopoly to be granted. On the one hand, we were confronting the risk that national legislation would not be allowed to impose the obligation of "local working" – that is, local manufacturing – of the patented product. That, in and of itself, would have constituted a major concession from developing countries that they were reluctant to make. Their argument was that, if the patent owner was entitled to territorial legal monopoly, he or she had, in turn, to contribute to the development of the industry in that territory.

On the other hand, we watched with increasing concern the possibility that the new agreement would eventually grant to the holder the exclusive right to import the patented product. The conjunction of the non-requirement of local working and the exclusive right of importation was a hard blow against the idea, predominant among many developing countries about the contribution by national patent regimes to industrial development. Adding to this dark picture was the wide latitude that the right holder would have to compartmentalize markets and impose abusive practices, including high prices.

This explains why, as a defensive element, an effort was made to make the clause of the so-called non-voluntary licences as wide as possible; the ability to locally exploit the patent without authorization of the owner as a result of an administrative or judicial decision was of crucial importance.

During the negotiation of the provision on compulsory licences, a convergence of interests emerged on different elements of the provision, sometimes with the support of some developed countries and, on other occasions, with that of others. This gave us, as a result, increased room for manoeuvre in national legislation.

As it was extremely difficult, if not impossible, to agree on the grounds for granting compulsory licences, the exercise continued on a double track: on the one hand, identifying concepts of general order that could be specified in national legislation (e.g. cases of emergency, anti-competitive practices, public interest), and on the other hand, developing a detailed set of conditions that should be met, such as that decisions must be taken on a case-by-case-basis, compensation must be based on the economic value of the licence, the legal validity of the grant must be reviewed by a higher body and so on.

Conditions to observe to grant this type of authorization were, in general, acceptable and tempered the rigidity introduced by the binary choices of either prohibiting the requirement of local working or permitting the exclusive right of importation. Another significant element of relief was the inclusion, in the same Article 31, of the ample authority given to the national authorities when facing cases of anti-competitive practices by the right holder – a hypothetical situation in which there was no need to observe some of the conditions applicable in other situations.

Control of anti-competitive practices

Another issue of concern to developing countries was how to avoid abuses in licensing contracts that could restrict not only trade but also the transfer of technology – a concern that had been the subject of intense but unsuccessful discussions in the United Nations Conference on Trade and Development (UNCTAD) for almost a decade. The purpose was to establish a comprehensive approach to the harmful effects that such practices may have on the transfer of technology and, therefore, on development.

In accordance with the experience and defensive interests at stake, some developing countries, using the draft Code of Conduct on Transfer of Technology as their model, proposed in the TRIPS negotiations a list of 14 practices to be prohibited in licensing agreements. Developed countries resisted a positive listing of anti-competitive *"per se"* practices, and only admitted to penalize those practices, which, in individual cases, would adversely affect competition.

The final TRIPS Agreement text is very far from the initial aspirations of the developing countries proponents. It does not contain specific obligations for the members of the WTO nor does it contain internationally agreed rules on a list of anti-competitive practices – except in some cases that were admitted as examples.

Despite these weak provisions, the added value of the TRIPS Agreement consists in the freedom that countries have to control and sanction such practices and the admission, in a multilateral treaty, that certain licensing conditions can adversely affect trade and the transfer of technology.

Undisclosed information: Test data

In general, in order to register pharmaceutical products, national authorities require the submission of relevant data relating to a drug's quality, safety and efficacy ("test data"), as well as information on the composition and physical and chemical characteristics of the product.

During the TRIPS negotiations, the obligations that should be assumed with regard to the information submitted to the authorities, as well as the rights and benefits to grant to the companies producing these data, were highly controversial.

The international standard in place prior to the TRIPS Agreement was limited to protection against unfair competition – Article 10*bis* of the Paris Convention for the Protection of Industrial Property. The concept was generally considered to mean "acts contrary to honest business practices". National legislators had, therefore, ample discretion on the definition of "unfair competition" and the means of protection.

The questions raised were, ultimately, simple, but of enormous relevance: what would be the legal obligations of the authorities concerning undisclosed data? How could one protect such data under the concept of "unfair competition"? Do the data belong exclusively to the company that originates them? If so, for how long does the data exclusively belong to the company? What treatment should be given to a second or subsequent company that files a submission for regulatory approval of a product based, partly or wholly, upon the information provided by the first company?

The answers to these questions might have serious ramifications on the generic drug industries of countries that did not grant patents on pharmaceuticals and agrochemicals, such as Argentina and India, and also on those countries that granted them but relied heavily on local companies producing generic products, such as Canada. The crux, therefore, was the possibility of using existing data "not unfairly obtained" so as to avoid very expensive and time-consuming duplication of tests that would, if required, keep companies from placing equivalent products on the market once the patent had expired. A substantial part of information on tests relating to approved drugs becomes publicly available, for instance, once published in a scientific journal or made public by the authority.

Historically, some national authorities relied on the first application's data for the evaluation of a second or subsequent entrant's application for similar products. If producers, typically generic manufacturers, are obliged to unnecessarily repeat long and costly testing, the impact would be felt by small and medium-sized companies – particularly in developing countries – with insufficient resources to undertake such testing. This would reduce the affordability of medicines that are off patent and should, in principle, be broadly available at the lowest price. In those cases, health authorities would normally require that the second or subsequent entrant proves that the product is similar or bio-equivalent to the one already registered.

In response to the strong demand for patent protection and in order to avoid the creation – directly or indirectly – of new forms of exclusive rights not internationally recognized, it was of the utmost importance to elaborate provisions on test data that would not expand the exclusive rights granted by the patent.

In the end, some leeway was allowed; the obligations under the TRIPS Agreement would refer to "undisclosed" information submitted to the authorities for the approval of new pharmaceutical and agrochemical products, and the basic element of data protection would be the obligation not to disclose the data, that is, to keep them confidential and to protect against acts contrary to honest commercial practices.

Clearly then, what a competitor of a pharmaceutical or agrochemical product cannot do is use the originator's test data through unfair commercial practices. There are "exclusive" rights over this data, and there is indeed the right and obligation of governments to grant protection against unfair conduct. National authorities thus retain a significant margin of manoeuvre.

In a nutshell, this chapter was considered crucial by many delegations that wanted to preserve the interests of national producers of generic medicines and, at the same time, protect sensitive data of the companies against unfair commercial practices.

With the passing of time, Argentina and the United States met several times in order to clarify a number of legal provisions of the Argentinian patent law and administrative measures concerning data protection. In June 2002, a mutually accepted solution on most of the issues involved was notified to the Chair of the WTO's Dispute Settlement Body; on the question of protection of test data against unfair commercial use, no common ground was reached. Nevertheless, the parties agreed that, if the Dispute Settlement Body should adopt recommendations and rulings to clarify Article 39.3, our national legislation would follow those recommendations.

Negotiating teams: Imbalances

This book affords us an excellent opportunity to share with younger generations of negotiators some of the facts about the conditions and resources available to those with the responsibility for TRIPS negotiations.

First, concerning the experience of national institutions on IP, in Latin America, including national offices dealing with IP, with a few exceptions, notably Brazil, most had a stronger tradition on copyright issues than on industrial property. They generally lacked financial autonomy and had little exposure to international negotiations. Furthermore, the approach on industrial property was mainly of an administrative nature; the task of developing a comprehensive and up-to-date view of the opportunities offered by, and the requirements of, a modern patent system remained in the hands of a small group of experts.

Second, there were imbalances in the limited availability of national experts during the negotiating process. The dynamic, sometimes overwhelming, pace that characterized the negotiations on TRIPS since 1989 allowed us to benefit from the presence of national experts only occasionally, as it was not possible for them to travel frequently from our capitals. Argentina, fortunately, had the permanent support of a prestigious expert, Professor Carlos Correa.

It is only fair to mention in this context the priceless support and guidance the developing countries were given in Geneva. The expertise provided by UNCTAD – oddly enough, not by WIPO – clearly contributed to the strengthening of our technical understanding of several elements and facilitated the submission by developing countries of specific proposals,[5] which was essential to balance the proposals made by developed countries.

Third, I should mention the obvious imbalance resulting from large and small delegations. Most developing countries had very few officials to cover a wide range of issues in all areas of TRIPS. Developed countries, on the other hand, benefited from extended human, technical and financial resources, whether in Geneva or in their capitals.

Finally, the negotiating process itself threw up some additional imbalances. For differing reasons, not all the developing countries who tabled document MTN. GNG/NG11/W/71 could actively take part in the entire negotiating process. Only a handful of those signatories were able to participate in all of the informal consultations of the "10+10" group, a grouping open, essentially, to those delegations with concrete issues on the part or section to be negotiated. On the developed countries side, the "10" participating were almost invariably the same – inevitably, they were either the *demandeurs* or their close allies. From the developing countries' side, participation was certainly not so homogeneous, which did not facilitate for all a full understanding of the evolution of the discussions.

A closing reflection

The brief, and inevitably incomplete, preceding comments are a modest attempt to reflect the impressions, experiences and conditions within which a negotiator of the TRIPS Agreement from a developing country discharged his duties.

Certainly, this work does not intend to develop theoretical foundations or extended interpretations of the provisions of the TRIPS Agreement. If that were the case, I would have unintentionally distorted the real positions and ambitions expressed by so many during the negotiations.

On the other hand, it is redundant to mention that the effect of time on memory leads to the emphasis on some elements or nuances over others – especially for someone whose ensuing professional experiences rarely involved the TRIPS Agreement. The accompanying emotions felt during the negotiating process can be part of this distorted lens.

In any case, I have tried to reflect the influence of some of the forces operating at that historical time – and the resulting effect they produced – as well as the constant intention, while negotiating, of not losing sight of the global evolution of the Uruguay Round and of identifying and preserving space for national actions in crucial issues.

I emphasize the historical moment because, whether or not related to what happened in other latitudes around the globe, in Argentina, an essential change concerning economic policy and response to external demands was put in motion. With variable intensity, this influenced the task of the negotiators in Geneva.

Regarding the TRIPS Agreement, the amendment of the negotiating mandate, as well as the tight time frame fixed to conclude the negotiations – a little more than a year and a half – brought about a highly dynamic process in which great attention was required almost each step of the way, thus imposing a substantive weight on the shoulders of smaller delegations.

It is true that, by the very nature of the issues involved in negotiating the TRIPS Agreement, many developing countries did not in practice have substantive offensive interests to propose. In the case of Argentina, the defensive nature of the exercise was enhanced by its also being a "target" priority country for non-patenting pharmaceutical products.

This imposed a strong emphasis on some of the elements that govern the Agreement, either on the section on principles or on the provisions related to the extension of patent rights, limitations or safeguards that could result from a compulsory licensing regime, or the attempt, which partially failed, to enshrine effective and universally recognized anti-competitive practices. Finally, there was a need to preserve policy space and provide a chance for survival for our domestic industries that would see a dramatically altered environment in which to continue their activities.

I am not judging whether the end result was due to our modest ambition. We have to bear in mind that the TRIPS Agreement does not reflect a perfect agreement among the negotiators on any of its elements. It is part of a broader framework – subject to debate on whether it was realistic or essential – that was arbitrated by third parties (e.g. Chairs of the negotiating groups, Directors-General of GATT) and included the results of bilateral or plurilateral agreements among some delegations on several components of the Uruguay Round.

However, no matter what opinion it deserves, the TRIPS Agreement constitutes unprecedented regulation in the area of IP by virtue of the near-universal membership of the WTO and the harmonizing nature of minimum obligations that must be observed by its members.

Endnotes

1 This chapter is dedicated to Ambassador Néstor Stancanelli, who never lost sight of the essential and who knew how to translate into action the notion of "national interest".

2 GATT document MIN.DEC, Multilateral Trade Negotiations – The Uruguay Round – Ministerial Declaration on the Uruguay Round, 20 September 1986.

3 GATT document MTN.TNC/11, Uruguay Round – Trade Negotiations Committee – Mid-Term Meeting, 21 April 1989.

4 GATT document MTN.GNG/NG11/W/71, Negotiating Group on Trade-Related Aspects of Intellectual Property Rights, including Trade in Counterfeit Goods – Communication from Argentina, Brazil, Chile, China, Colombia, Cuba, Egypt, India, Nigeria, Peru, Tanzania and Uruguay, 14 May 1990.

5 For example, GATT document MTN.GNG/NG11/W/71.

14

Negotiating for Malaysia

Umi K.B.A. Majid

Introduction

I was the lead TRIPS negotiator for Malaysia for about two years (from 1990 to 1992). The views I express derive from my personal knowledge, though they are limited due to the passage of time from then until today. I was the Senior Federal Counsel in the Advisory and International Law Division of the Malaysian Attorney-General's Chambers, which position was later designated as the Senior Federal Counsel in charge of matters concerning the GATT.

My terms of reference for negotiating the TRIPS Agreement at that time were largely determined by myself, after consulting the then Ministry of International Trade and Industry on certain aspects. My main concern was to protect the interests of the Government of Malaysia and of Malaysia generally.

This chapter will begin with an overview of the TRIPS Agreement from the perspective of Malaysia, followed by some aspects of the negotiating history of the Agreement, and the legislation passed by Malaysia in fulfilling its international commitments under the TRIPS Agreement.

Overview

Malaysia is a small, developing, Muslim-majority country that is very reliant on foreign investment. It is a large importer of IPRs, but has also generated its own IPRs.

Being part of the common law legal system, Malaysia had in place several laws pertaining to IP protection, such as on industrial designs, patents, trademarks and copyright. Local interest groups were largely interested in copyright issues and, to the extent that there was any pressure on the government by these groups, it was on enforcement matters.

At the time of the TRIPS negotiations, Malaysia was blacklisted by the United States for failing to adequately protect US nationals' interests in Malaysia. Without "safety in numbers" in the form of multilateral agreements on IP, Malaysia was under pressure to enter into bilateral agreements for IP protection, especially from the United States. I had occasion to vet the draft bilateral agreement between Malaysia and the United States on IP protection. This draft was the same as the agreement that was entered into by Indonesia with the United States. After perusing the draft, I made salient observations to the Government of Malaysia on the impact and ramifications of its contents on Malaysia, especially on its sovereignty *vis-à-vis* the United States. Malaysia did not conclude that bilateral agreement. Instead, and due to the unequal strengths between the United States and Malaysia, it was felt that Malaysia was in a better position to justify its laws on IP if they were benchmarked against international conventions for the protection of IPRs. This led Malaysia to join the Paris Convention for the Protection of Industrial Property[1] and the Berne Convention for the Protection of Literary and Artistic Works.[2] By joining these Conventions, Malaysia believed it was also fulfilling its international commitments, which was what foreign investors were looking for. In this manner, Malaysia was able to attract foreign investments to uplift its economy.

Being a rapidly developing country, Malaysia also acknowledged that it was also obliged to take care of the IPRs of its citizens *vis-à-vis* other countries. At the same time, Malaysia had to acknowledge that it had limited resources to protect and enforce IPRs. Bearing these factors in mind, Malaysia went into the negotiations for the TRIPS Agreement. In doing so, Malaysia had unwittingly expressed its concerns, which were shared by the other developing countries, including China. To a lesser extent, it had also reflected the concerns of other Muslim countries. The final form of the TRIPS Agreement reflected the commitment of Malaysia to the multilateral process as well as to the international norms.

Aspects of the TRIPS negotiations

Drafts of the TRIPS Agreement

We started in mid-1990 with two main draft agreements – one prepared by the United Nations Conference on Trade and Development (UNCTAD) on behalf of 14 developing countries, and the other combining the texts submitted by the European Communities (EC), United States, Japan, and Switzerland. We went through arduous process of bridging the gaps between these two drafts until we could come up with one draft to further negotiate on.

To this end, I was very much involved in the negotiations, which were carried on late into the night, for weeks at a time. There was a tight schedule to follow and the Chair of the TRIPS Negotiating Group, Ambassador Lars Anell, made sure that we kept to it, even if it meant we had to hold meetings into the night and the wee hours of the morning. I was made to understand that it is one of the strategies in negotiations to wear down your opponents until they are exhausted and they will then readily agree to anything. Hence, I vowed that I would not succumb to such tactics. I remember having contracted the worst case of influenza when I was in Geneva, with my nose running like a tap (probably due to exhaustion), but I stoically stuck it out at the late night sessions. I did not miss any negotiating session that I know of.

When the ministerial meeting was held in Brussels in the winter of 1990 – it was supposed to have been the meeting to finalize all the agreements of the Uruguay Round of multilateral negotiations by the contracting parties to the GATT – I did not attend, as the then Malaysian Minister of International Trade and Industry was present to represent Malaysia. I bumped into one of the delegates in the corridor, who asked me concernedly why I was not at the meeting and that he saw another "girl" from Malaysia sitting there. I had to correct him and stated that the "girl" was actually the then Malaysian Minister of International Trade and Industry!

Another piece of useful information that I had picked up very early in the process was that there was a lot of horse-trading occurring outside the negotiating room, not seen by others who were not "invited" to participate in the horse-trading. I persuaded my colleague from the Ministry to provide us with funds in order for Malaysia to play host to the main players who had submitted the drafts, at dinners or lunches. Doing so also meant that I could not have a relaxed time at the negotiations, which required me to feverishly pore over each new draft provisions and to prepare my response to them.

Nothing legal about the TRIPS negotiations

On one of the many trips back home from Geneva, I met two previous colleagues who had been appointed as Senior Federal Counsel (GATT) before me. They told me not to work so hard or worry so much because Malaysia is just a small country and anything we say would not make a difference to the negotiations. One of them even told me that there were not many legal problems in the negotiations as almost everything was a policy matter to be taken care of by the Ministry, meaning that no legal input was required by me as the Senior Federal Counsel. I proved them wrong! Instead, I felt the great weight of responsibility placed upon me to ensure that the TRIPS Agreement did not overburden my country to the extent that it would promote foreign IPRs at the expense of the Malaysian economy or people.

Geographical indications

One of the first things I had to research, when assigned as the GATT officer, was what is meant by "geographical indication" (GI). I remember that neither I nor any of my colleagues knew anything about it, and referring to legal dictionaries – or any dictionary – did not yield the answer, until I read the draft TRIPS Agreement and participated in the debate.

This topic was especially significant to me, coming from a Muslim-majority country. This was because the initial drafts required contracting parties to specifically legislate for the protection of GIs, especially in respect of the products of the vine. Malaysia was adamant that it could not fulfil this obligation, as to legislate on it would be interpreted as protecting wines and spirits themselves, which would invite outright condemnation of the government, and the government would be questioned about it in Parliament. Each revision of the draft text on GIs would see me anxiously poring over it and decrying its contents until the next draft came around. It would seem as if Malaysia was a great infringer of this IPR, whereas the truth was to the contrary. The non-Muslims in Malaysia very much enjoy the products of the vine and Malaysia does import large quantities of such products, which explained my many interventions.

Finally, after much debate, Malaysia could agree to providing protection for products of the vine via other actions, such as administrative rules and regulations. Hence, we now see the provisions of Article 23(1) being worded as follows, with a footnote that carries legal binding obligations:

> 1. Each Member shall provide the legal means for interested parties to prevent use of a geographical indication identifying wines for wines not originating in the place indicated by the geographical indication in question or identifying spirits for spirits not originating in the place indicated by the geographical indication in question, even where the true origin of the goods is indicated or the geographical indication is used in translation or accompanied by expressions such as "kind", "type", "style", "imitation" or the like.[4]

Footnote 4 reads:

> Notwithstanding the first sentence of Article 42, Members may, with respect to these obligations, instead provide for enforcement by administrative action.

I was made to understand that the United States paid particular attention to Malaysia's interventions because it had similar concerns and was also keen to have other Muslim countries sign up with the TRIPS Agreement.

Long-arm statute

The United States had a provision in the draft agreement to compel nationals of countries other than the United States to produce documents located in their home country when ordered to do so by the courts for the purposes of any legal suit/prosecution of an IP case in the United States. Malaysia was very firm, as were the rest of the delegations, in stating that it reserved its rights to legislate "blocking statutes" to prevent such "enforcement" of such orders within Malaysian territory. After much debate in opposition, this provision was finally dropped from the text.

Enforcement of intellectual property rights

Being conscious that it has limited resources with which to enforce IPR actions, and having just emerged from an economic recession, Malaysia was concerned about not being able to fulfil its obligations under the TRIPS Agreement if no exceptions were provided for. To this end, Malaysia fought at every turn for exceptions to be made. One such "exception" can be seen in Part III, Article 41 paragraph 5, which reads as follows:

> It is understood that this Part does not create any obligation to put in place a judicial system for the enforcement of intellectual property rights distinct from that for the enforcement of law in general, nor does it affect the capacity of Members to enforce their law in general. Nothing in this Part creates any obligation with respect to the distribution of resources as between enforcement of intellectual property rights and the enforcement of law in general.

Malaysia's concerns on the enforcement aspect were not misplaced at all, as could be seen from our experience several years later, during the time of the financial crisis faced by the Association of Southeast Asian Nations (ASEAN) countries in

1997–8. I was then serving as the Senior Sessions Court Judge in the state of Kelantan. I had to preside over criminal and civil matters. One day, I was informed by the court police that the remand prisoners could not be brought to court because the Police Department had had its budget slashed and there was no money for petrol to transport the remand prisoners from the lock-up to the court. It would be recalled at that critical point in time that, on the dictates of the International Monetary Fund, Malaysia had to tighten its spending belt before financial assistance would be rendered by the fund. Fortunately, the slashing of the police budget was short lived, as the Malaysian Government had decided not to proceed with the fund's plan of action.

In the TRIPS negotiations, my recounting of the Kelantan episode also brought home the point on the conflicting interests of enforcing criminal law *per se* as against enforcing what is essentially a civil right in the criminal law arena.

Another exception in the TRIPS Agreement can be seen in Article 31(b) in respect of patent rights, as follows (emphasis added):

Article 31

Other Use Without Authorization of the Right Holder

Where the law of a Member allows for other use of the subject matter of a patent without the authorization of the right holder, including use by the government or third parties authorized by the government, the following provisions shall be respected:

...

(b) such use may only be permitted if, prior to such use, the proposed user has made efforts to obtain authorization from the right holder on reasonable commercial terms and conditions and that such efforts have not been successful within a reasonable period of time. *This requirement may be waived by a Member in the case of a national emergency or other circumstances of extreme urgency or in cases of public non-commercial use.* In situations of national emergency or other circumstances of extreme urgency, the right holder shall, nevertheless, be notified as soon as reasonably practicable. In the case of public non-commercial use, where the government or contractor, without making a patent search, knows or has demonstrable grounds to know that a valid patent is or will be used by or for the government, the right holder shall be informed promptly;

…

I recall that, at a cocktail get-together held by the session Chair, after a very heated intervention by me on the exceptions which I had wanted to be included (I forget which in particular), a nice Japanese delegate walked up to me to express his appreciation of the sentiments I had expressed. He then informed me that, in doing so, I was "scolding" the delegates around the negotiating table. I was dumbstruck at his observations as I did not realise that I had come on that strongly on the subject.

Assistance rendered

Due to my active participation in the TRIPS negotiations, I had unwittingly played the role of coordinating the ASEAN group of countries on the positions to be taken on any subject under discussion.

I had also received a request from the Brazilian head of delegation to spend my weekend with his team to assist them in drafting provisions which they wish to be included in the draft TRIPS Agreement.

At that time, China was not a GATT contracting party, but was following the Uruguay Round negotiations very closely in order to prepare itself for joining it. One day, I was approached by the Chinese representative following the TRIPS negotiations, who requested my presence at a meeting with several of his country's team. His brief to me was that his team would like me to explain to them what the TRIPS negotiations were all about. When I entered the room, I was taken aback to see about eight Chinese officials all sitting in one row facing me, waiting for me to "brief" them. I remember feeling overwhelmed at first, at being given the trust and honour to brief them. The gist of it is, my advice to them was that the TRIPS Agreement is here to stay and there is no avoiding it. China needed to come on board so as to benefit from it in the long run, seeing that it had millions of talented people who would one day be the owners of IPRs and whom it would want to protect. In the meantime, there was nothing to prohibit China from infringing IPRs.

Injunctions, provisional measures

It was during the short interval when I was back in the office in Kuala Lumpur that I became aware from one of my colleagues that there were efforts being made to amend the High Court Rules 1980 to extend time regarding injunctions. It was fortunate for me to come to know this, as I advised my colleague on the regime that was then posited in the draft TRIPS Agreement and argued for the High Court Rules 1980 not to be so amended.

Transitional arrangements

Transitional arrangements are provided for under Part VI of the TRIPS Agreement. As a developing country, Malaysia was entitled under paragraph 2 of Article 65 to claim the period of four years to delay the implementation of the Agreement. The same provisions also applied to former communist countries (see paragraph 3 of Article 65). The "least-developed country Members" were given a reprieve of ten years under Article 66.

Post-TRIPS Agreement legislation

While negotiating the draft TRIPS Agreement, I became aware of the great need for Malaysia to legislate on competition law and I had so advised the Ministry concerned. This was because the TRIPS Agreement (like other IP conventions) would give rise to monopolistic regimes that would be detrimental to Malaysia's interests if the country did not have anti-competition law like those enforced in the EC and the United States. I am glad to say that Malaysia has now legislated the Competition Act 2010 (Act 712), which was brought into force on 1 January 2012, and the Competition Commission Act 2010 (Act 713), which came into force on 1 January 2011.

The other legislation passed by Malaysia in order to implement the TRIPS Agreement is as follows:

- Layout-Designs of Integrated Circuits Act 2000 (Act 601), which came into force on 15 August 2000

- Geographical Indications Act 2000 (Act 602), which came into force on 15 August 2001

- Intellectual Property Corporation of Malaysia Act 2002 (Act 617), which came into force on 3 March 2003.

Conclusion

I have often told my family, friends and colleagues of how the TRIPS negotiations had shaped and changed my professional life. Before the TRIPS negotiations, I was afraid to speak publicly and hardly ever intervened in any international fora. But because I found that, if I did not raise issues on behalf of Malaysia, Malaysia's interests would be jeopardised, I had plucked up the courage to speak my piece at TRIPS negotiations, and the rest, as they say, is history. So I would like to thank all my colleagues and those from the GATT Secretariat present at the TRIPS negotiating table for giving me the opportunity to hone my public speaking skills, at the very least.

Endnotes

1   On June 23, 1988. See www.wipo.int/treaties/en/remarks.jsp?cnty_id=270C (last accessed 7 June 2015).

2   On June 28, 1990. See www.wipo.int/treaties/en/remarks.jsp?cnty_id=990C (last accessed 7 June 2015).

15

Negotiating for Hong Kong

David Fitzpatrick[1]

By way of introduction, I was part of the Hong Kong TRIPS negotiating team, from December 1987 to January 1992 inclusive. Throughout this period, I was employed as a Senior Crown Counsel by the Hong Kong Attorney General's Chambers, though I had been informally seconded to the Trade and Industry Branch, from which I received my instructions and to which I directed my reports for onward circulation within the Hong Kong Government. Though then a United Kingdom dependent territory, Hong Kong plotted its own course throughout the negotiations as a separate contracting party to the GATT. The United Kingdom was represented, as a part of the European Communities (EC) negotiating team. I attended the formal negotiations before the Chair of the TRIPS Negotiating Group, and most of the informal meetings that took place from time to time with the other participants. These negotiations took place in Geneva, where Hong Kong maintained an office, but I also travelled to Brussels to pursue my task.

Hong Kong's overall approach to the TRIPS negotiations was made clear to the other participants from an early stage: Hong Kong held itself out as the exemplar of free trade, with a mature, respected legal system, providing comprehensive protection across the range of IP to right holders. IP was variously protected, by a combination of civil remedies, criminal investigation and prosecution, and administrative means. Though there was no means of making a comprehensive comparison, the Hong Kong Government was of the view that its overall regime was among the soundest in the trading world. I believe that this remains the case, now that Hong Kong is part of the People's Republic of China. In its basic elements, Hong Kong's legal system shared, and continues to share, many features with other common law jurisdictions. The legal system in 1987, as it related to IP, closely resembled that of the United Kingdom, and any practitioner in a country that also derived its system from the British imperial past would have had no difficulty in understanding how it worked. This was to be of considerable assistance, whether it was dealing with the United States or members of the

Commonwealth. Of course, there were differences in detail in the exercise of border controls and criminal enforcement. Hong Kong had accomplished a great deal in the 1980s, through its Customs and Excise Department, to suppress any trade in counterfeit goods. That Department was, and remains, well-funded and highly professional. Hong Kong was, and remains, user friendly from the point of view of the right holder. With all this in mind, Hong Kong's main concerns were to ensure that any obligations created by a TRIPS treaty did not present any unreasonable limit on legitimate trade nor allow indirect barriers to be erected by other participants in the guise of IP control. Despite the excellence of the Customs and Excise Department, Hong Kong was at pains to emphasize civil justice and actions by the right holder as the centrepiece and first call for enforcement. Finally, Hong Kong was most concerned to ensure that freedom remained with its legislature to determine the extent of the control of parallel importation, that is, the free flow of goods and services which had been manufactured or provided by, or otherwise put on the market by or with the consent of, the ultimate right holder. It was the view of the Hong Kong Government that no provision in international law was breached by its then existing regime regarding the exhaustion of IPRs. It was apparent from lobbying that had taken place that right holders were inclined to swell the obligations they were granted by the Berne Convention for the Protection of Literary and Artistic Works or the Paris Convention for the Protection of Industrial Property.

At the time I joined the negotiations, no working draft had been tabled. As it seemed to me from the speeches made before the Chair of the TRIPS Negotiating Group, participants were sparring. Nonetheless, it was instructive. Participants described their regimes and their hopes and fears for the progress of the negotiations. It was apparent that a working draft would need to emerge before any detailed negotiations could proceed and that it was likely to be produced by one of the "Quad", that is, Canada, the EC, Japan and the United States, who were perceived as the prime movers in the negotiations. It was not too difficult to predict the form that it needed to take: obviously, it had to be consistent with existing WIPO provisions, probably using a similar drafting style to the Berne and Paris Conventions, together with some means of describing its relationship to those existing obligations, but adding enforcement procedures, border controls and administrative arrangements, together with housekeeping and the mechanisms that would allow the gradual adoption by the members, depending on their different stages of development and where domestic limitations needed to be accommodated.

My own perspective on the negotiating round was quite narrow. My assistance and thus my input to the broad negotiations that culminated in the establishment of the World Trade Organization was limited to the TRIPS negotiations, though I was briefed in general terms on the objectives and progress of the other negotiating groups from time to time. The detail of the interplay between the negotiating groups was not my concern, though I was aware that nothing was agreed until everything was agreed. Obviously, any capital that could be gained in the TRIPS negotiations might assist elsewhere. It appeared to me that Hong Kong had a not-too-difficult task, being an advanced economy, with a small agricultural sector and limited pharmaceuticals industry. That did not mean that compulsory licensing of pharmaceuticals, in certain circumstances, was not significant to Hong Kong, but it was a cause that was led in the negotiating group by the developing world. A similar view appeared to have been held by other negotiators at a similar level of development to Hong Kong. Whatever accommodation could be reached between the *demandeurs* and developing economies, provided it was of general application, might well accommodate Hong Kong's concerns. Thus, the patent complex, including patentability of process and the availability of compulsory licenses, was an area I kept under careful scrutiny, but it did not appear that Hong Kong had a dog in the fight.

Historically speaking, the TRIPS Agreement was negotiated in a favourable environment. While copyright lawyers were alive to the dawn of the digital era, and the convergence of television, computer and telephone technology, the Internet was not then upon us. The negotiators did not indulge in futurology. That stated, it appeared to be inevitable that computer programs would be protected as literary works and that, to some extent, algorithms could figure in patent claims. The negotiations looked backward to the means of distribution contemplated by the current drafts of the Berne and Paris Conventions. Looking to the future of the TRIPS Agreement, it is not easy to see how new technologies can be adequately accommodated, to meet the demands of right holders and consumers. Beyond the Internet, which has turned the distribution models of copyright material upside down, legal and ethical problems lie ahead with developments in synthetic biology and gene manipulation. Cyber hacking of confidential data is also a subject that might well figure, albeit indirectly, where IP has been misappropriated; goods thus incorporating or derived from such wrongdoing may face civil action or border controls, even prosecution, where manufacture or distribution is knowingly undertaken.

At the TRIPS Symposium held in Geneva on 26 February 2015, I learned that the TRIPS Agreement was regarded as an outstanding example in trade treaty negotiation. In a complex field, a detailed and ambitious text had emerged as a treaty that looked forward to the next 30 years. It consisted in large part of hard obligations. Unlike WIPO treaties, the TRIPS Agreement would allow any deficient regime to be called to account at the risk of appropriate trade penalties. Besides incorporating ambitious IPRs, minimum standards were demanded for administrative measures, border controls, and civil and criminal justice systems. It may be that I am insensitive, but I was unaware of taking part in a miraculous creation. Nonetheless, it is worth considering the factors that allowed negotiators to make such progress.

The TRIPS negotiations were fortunate in having such an able chair. Under the guidance of Ambassador Lars Anell, assisted by an efficient secretariat, the negotiations appeared to move forward in an autonomous fashion. The initial sparring allowed negotiators to meet, develop their understanding, form alliances and establish an atmosphere of goodwill. It was almost collegial, the formal debates being passionate but highly civilized. Hong Kong was one of the Friends of Intellectual Property group, but I believe that the atmosphere created made all the negotiators ambitious for progress. When sufficient time had been spent to allow all parties to state their concerns, the Secretariat prepared a convenient distillation of issues in a tabular form, from which it became possible for them to draft a working text under the Chair's sponsorship. The working draft incorporated in square brackets the principal positions thus far aired. That did not mean that the concerns of any one negotiator had been cast aside. Given sufficient support and following a full explanation, new ideas could be easily incorporated into a further set of square brackets in the appropriate place. In this form, I believe the Chair's text allowed the parties to proceed to Brussels where the real horse-trading could take place.

As far as this process touched upon my own main areas of concern – parallel imports and the enforcement of rights – I was not present in the Hong Kong negotiating team beyond the spring of 1992, when I returned to private practice. I was in the tent in Brussels when the dramatic intervention led by the Argentinian delegation brought negotiations to a temporary halt in 1990. It is my understanding that little changed beyond the negotiating draft that was on the table at the time I departed, at least as far as parallel imports and enforcement are concerned, before the treaty was concluded in 1994.

To the best of my recollection, parallel imports and exhaustion of rights was not on the radar of the other delegates when I first arrived in Geneva. After Hong Kong had made its position clear in formal negotiations before the Chair, and after a round of informal consultation, I was instructed to prepare a paper for circulation among the other negotiators aimed at consciousness-raising. At this stage, it did not appear that the negotiating teams included many lawyers, nor were they fully alive to the dangers associated with inappropriate protection of parallel imports. Beyond trade in the most basic materials, at least one, if not more, IPRs were involved. My colleagues quickly moved up the learning curve. Hong Kong had already encountered lobbying and it was apparent that lobbyists wanted to go beyond Hong Kong's existing regime as far as control over parallel imports was concerned. It was claimed by lobbyists, wrongly in my view, that the Paris and Berne Conventions compelled the creation of stronger controls over parallels than were embodied in domestic law. My research and consultation with individuals engaged in a number of industries suggested that the subject of parallel importation and the exhaustion of IPRs is not straightforward, neither legally nor on economic terms. Research also revealed that Hong Kong's laws were similar to those adopted in jurisdictions of the regimes whose laws also derived from their colonial history. There was safety in numbers. The exhaustion regime in place comprised elements of national and international exhaustion, together with concepts of waiver. Hong Kong was most concerned to ensure that freedom to legislate in respect of parallel imports and exhaustion was not limited – beyond the bounds of the WIPO conventions – as a result of the TRIPS negotiations. Unlike some jurisdictions which offered greater control over parallel imports, Hong Kong did not then have competition laws to attack any misuse of monopoly. It was my opinion that competition laws were no substitute. They are not really practical for smaller jurisdictions, required commitment of considerable resources and expertise, and introduced commercial uncertainty. Ultimately, such laws are steered as much by political considerations as by any other factor.

I was somewhat surprised at the strength of the opposition to the position that Hong Kong advocated. This is particularly so because Hong Kong gave such strong protection to right holders in regard to any trade in counterfeit goods. Article 6, as it appears in the TRIPS Agreement, represents what I would call an honourable draw. It is my view that, if the subject of parallel imports and exhaustion of rights is to be dealt with in an adequate fashion, detailed drafting will need to be applied and each IP needs to be treated separately. There would also be a need to recognize that the enforcement of competition laws is resource intensive and possibly ineffectual without financial muscle.

If I made any particular contribution to the TRIPS negotiations it was where negotiations were concerned with the terms now embodied in Part III, the enforcement of IPRs. As part of the team, I had the advantage of having experience as a former prosecutor and litigator, and our efforts were backed up by way of briefings from the Customs and Excise Department in Hong Kong. That Department probably maintained as comprehensive a regime of border controls and administrative intervention as was then found within the trading world. From a personal point of view, I had also benefited from working with US Government lawyers in matters of joint concern in the areas of organized crime and offences in the financial services industry. While I do not claim to have been an expert in all enforcement fields, I believe the description of being an experienced journeyman would have been fitting. This allowed me to analyse quickly and with some confidence any language that was under consideration. In this regard, Hong Kong was as well supplied as any of the negotiators, at least as regards the teams that they brought to Geneva or took to the showdown in Brussels.

I was flattered by the invitation at the Symposium to provide insight into or analysis of the provisions concerning enforcement, which represent the reconciliation between the basic features of the common law and corresponding components of the civil system. I felt I should decline. That accommodation, in its essentials, I believe was achieved by the team representing the EC. Furthermore, as it appeared to me, the fact that the *demandeurs* – Canada, the EC, Japan and the United States – were able to make common cause meant that they had ironed out any substantial differences that otherwise might have existed among common law and civil jurisdictions. What I believe Hong Kong might have done was to offer explanation of how provisions in the draft might work or otherwise, or offer examples by reference to jurisdictions the practice of which was well known. Hong Kong did not build the car, but at least it helped to tune it up or make sure that the wheels were put on properly.

Returning to the detailed provisions of Part III, I recall comparing the language of proposed provisions against Hong Kong's existing regime. I was assured by research that, at least as far as civil procedure and the criminal law was concerned, there was a high degree of commonality between Hong Kong and other Commonwealth countries. I also had a reasonable knowledge of US criminal and civil procedure and evidence. My acquaintance with the various civil codes was far more limited. It proved possible at the end of the day to keep all parties on board by flexible use of language – what is sometimes referred to as "constructive ambiguity". Whatever panels must rule on the meaning of the language of the TRIPS Agreement, they should take these origins into account. Each participant in the negotiations took back to his or her capital the assurance that their system corresponded to the language employed or could be adjusted by acceptable reform. If a great range of meaning has been brought under the umbrella of language, I fear this will stand in the way of the development of a "common law" of the TRIPS Agreement.

At the Symposium I highlighted a number of problems that I foresaw for the future that concern enforcement, variously attaching to border measures, the criminal jurisdiction, civil remedies or administrative measures. I hope I did not labour the point that Hong Kong was convinced that the first call of any right holder seeking a remedy was the civil justice system. The criminal justice system, in particular as it relates to resources employed to maintain law and order, must necessarily have priorities in which the protection of IP comes somewhere down the list. In the jurisdiction with which I am most familiar, that of the United Kingdom, resources that were once applied to investigating fraud have now largely been drawn away to the needs of supporting counter-terrorism. The net result is that only very serious frauds or the simplest of crimes are fully investigated and prosecuted. Based on my experiences of civil litigation involving fraud or IP infringement in Asia, it should be noted that it is often difficult to collect information in support of litigation where the information is somehow the subject of laws designed to protect official secrets. Similar restrictions occur in some jurisdictions where it is necessary to advise and work with the authorities if one is to collect evidence for an overseas civil suit. This rankles with the common lawyer, where he or she who alleges must prove. Wearing my hat as a part-time academic, I would also flag concerns that had arisen in the last decade that law enforcement agencies or those responsible for administrative action may well favour local enterprises over those perceived to be based overseas. There is a respectable body of opinion in Europe that holds that the treatment meted out to European banks and financial institutions by US regulators has been somewhat harsher than that meted out to local institutions. It may be that parties to the TRIPS Agreement will need to consider whether the discretions legitimately granted to investigators, prosecutors or administrators are being fairly applied in matters that concern infringement of IP.

Endnotes

1   My first draft was submitted to the Secretariat in mid-January 2015. After attending the
    Symposium on 26 and 27 February 2015, I realized how much I have forgotten. With the
    presentations of my fellow negotiators still fresh and with the materials and guidance provided
    by the Secretariat I made this second effort, hoping it will serve in some way to record the history
    of the negotiations and assist those who take the treaty forward into the future.

Part V

Negotiating substantive areas of TRIPS

16

Patents: An Indian perspective

Jayashree Watal[1]

Introduction

In this chapter, I share my recollections as a representative of India from 1989–90 in the TRIPS negotiations, focusing on India's defensive interests with respect to the patent provisions of the TRIPS Agreement. I also include some relevant background information, as well as some recollections of my interaction with other parties to the TRIPS negotiations.

My role in the TRIPS negotiations began in May 1989, when I was a mid-level official in the Ministry of Industry, Department of Industrial Development. My then supervisor in the government, A.V. Ganesan,[2] chose to have me specialize in IPRs in order to fill a gap in our knowledge, after India was placed on the United States' Special 301 watch list in April 1989 for the first time, and after the mid-term ministerial review decision in Geneva later that month. My active engagement in the negotiations began in mid-May 1990 when I was sent by the then Secretary of the Department of Industrial Development[3] to Geneva on the eve of the presentation of the draft legal text jointly submitted by 14 developing countries.[4] From then onwards, up until the Brussels ministerial meeting in December 1990, by which time most of the TRIPS text was drafted and only some key political issues remained (see Adrian Otten, chapter 3), it became my task, under the close supervision of my seniors in government[5] to safeguard India's interests as best I could, particularly with respect to the patent provisions. As it was for many other authors in this volume, participating in the TRIPS negotiations was a particular highlight of my professional life.

Background to India's negotiating position on patents

A.V. Ganesan provides the reader with much of the background to India's negotiating position on TRIPS (see chapter 11), and his account should ideally be read before this one.[6] He eloquently describes the process of the revision of the

Indian patent law in 1970, the domestic opposition to India even joining the Paris Convention for the Protection of Industrial Property due, in large part, to the interests of the generic drugs industry, and the general public opinion against the grant of product patents for pharmaceuticals for fear of sharply increased prices.

In retrospect, India suffered from several unique drawbacks in the Uruguay Round of multilateral trade negotiations. First, it had few or no offensive trade interests at the time. India's trade-to-GDP ratio – an indicator of integration into the global economy – was low, as it had followed the policy of "self-reliance" in the decades since its independence from colonial rule in 1947.[7] Even in the textiles sector, where there was hope of increased exports for many Asian countries post-Uruguay Round, India was not seen to be as competitive as others in the region. The joke at the time was that India's bureaucrats were more efficient than its textile exporters, since the large textile quotas they negotiated with major markets such as the European Communities (EC) and the United States were, more often than not, not fully utilized.

Second, India's patent law had undergone revision in 1970 after a long, arduous process through several high-level committees and parliamentary debates. There was a politically powerful group of both left-leaning and right-leaning politicians, academics and even legal luminaries, not to mention India's growing generic drugs industry, who believed that no change should be made to India's patent law and strongly opposed India even joining the Paris Convention. In this regard, the commercial interests of the Indian generic drugs sector coincided with the interests of Indian patients or, more generally, with what was perceived to be national or public interest. This is because in India medicines, including prescription medicines, were and are still paid for out-of-pocket by the patient, making consumers very price-conscious in their choices. While it is common to have as many as 50 to 60 Indian companies producing identical generic versions of a popular medicine, most of the market is held by the top three or four well-known companies, among whom there is intense price competition. Several economic studies have tried to predict price and welfare effects of the introduction of product patents for pharmaceuticals in India. While the numbers vary according to the models used, almost all studies predicted sharp increases in the average price of patented medicines.[8]

However, recent empirical work does not corroborate these fears, showing instead that there is competition even in products where patents have been granted.[9] While the authors do not explain this result, this may well be the result of Section 11A of the revised Patents Act. This provision allows those who had made significant investment and were already producing and selling medicines for which patent applications were filed from 1995 onwards in the so-called mailbox (also called the "black box", since these applications were kept secret) to continue to produce and sell the product at the same scale as before upon payment of reasonable remuneration to the patent owner.[10] In addition, there has been much patent validity litigation in India, with several companies being present even in patented drug markets, particularly in commercially valuable ones. Further, innovator companies have been careful to use differential pricing or voluntary licensing strategies in India, especially after India granted its first compulsory licence. India's first and only compulsory licence was granted in 2012 for a cancer drug on grounds that the price was unaffordable and the patent owner was not supplying the market through imports nor working the patent adequately in India.[11] The threat of compulsory licences could be another factor working in favour of lower prices than anticipated. It is hard to predict whether the combination of price sensitivity of demand and such patent strategies will continue to keep the Indian market competitive in future for new generations of medicines.

Be that as it may, during my time in the Uruguay Round negotiations - 1989-90 - no government was willing to risk supporting changes to the patent law, in particular to accept product patents. This was compounded by the fact that, unlike other developing countries, particularly those in Latin America, India had few economically significant demands to make in other areas of the Uruguay Round negotiations in exchange for concessions on TRIPS.

I recall that, given this background, the Indian delegation to the Brussels ministerial meeting in December 1990 was not entirely clear on how to proceed on patentable subject matter. When a breakdown in agriculture negotiations caused a disruption of the Brussels ministerial meeting itself, no delegation was as relieved as the Indian one, as no IP agreement needed to be defended on our return home. That joy was short-lived, as the United States initiated bilateral negotiations to pursue its IP objectives. The counterfactual to the failure of the TRIPS negotiations was always going to be bilateral negotiations, which are generally known to be much more difficult for the weaker of the two parties.

Broader international background to negotiations in the area of patents

It is important to recall the broader international context at the time of the launch of the Uruguay Round. Developing countries had just failed in their attempt to weaken the Paris Convention, particularly with respect to patents. The proverbial straw that broke the camel's back was the demand of developing countries that compulsory licences be exclusive, meaning thereby that the patent owner be excluded from exploiting the invention in markets where a compulsory licence has been issued.[12] As is well known, this was one of the factors that led to the shifting of forum from WIPO to GATT and to the now-famous prefix "trade-related aspects of" before "intellectual property rights". This proved to be an unexpectedly capacious formula: the only non-trade-related aspect of IPRs that I remember being mentioned during my time in the TRIPS negotiations was moral rights in the context of copyright.

The literature in economics supports the idea that patents are uniquely important for the pharmaceuticals and specialized chemicals sectors. This has been shown through multisectoral industry surveys conducted well before the TRIPS negotiations, focusing on innovation in the United Kingdom and the United States, and repeated over the years in the United States and in other countries.[13] It is clear that the pharmaceuticals sector disproportionately relies on patents to capture returns to research and development (R&D), unlike other sectors which rely more on lead time, complementary assets, trade secrets and other means to do so.[14]

It is therefore no surprise that the pharmaceuticals industry was the main non-state actor influencing the *demandeurs*' position on the patents section of the TRIPS Agreement.[15] The key *demandeurs* were the United States, EC, Japan and Switzerland. The "Quad" that led the Uruguay Round was comprised of Canada, the EC, Japan and the United States. As we will see below, Canada's presence in the Quad was important in moderating the demands of the other three, as in trying to protect its generic drugs industry's interests, it supported those in other countries as well.

Others have noted in this volume and elsewhere that external factors such as the broader global acceptance of market-based policies and the increasingly unipolar nature of world politics formed an important background to the TRIPS negotiations. As the negotiations proceeded and as the United States Trade Representative notched up more and more bilateral successes in persuading the US' trading partners to agree to "effective and adequate" standards on IPRs,[16] especially in the pharmaceuticals sector, the greater or more expansive became the demands of its industry.

It was thus that, from initially demanding the introduction of product patents in all fields of technology, the United States upped the ante in 1991 to demand "pipeline protection" from 1986 onwards, the date of the launch of the Uruguay Round.

This meant that all pharmaceutical inventions for which patent applications were filed and granted in the United States and other jurisdictions from 1986 onwards would be protected for the balance of the patent term in the jurisdictions of all parties to the negotiations. While the United States did ask for transitional protection in its spring 1990 submission,[17] this found no support in any other Quad draft legal text submission in early 1990.

The United States, EC and others argued that the economic impact of the introduction of pharmaceutical product patents was delayed by ten or so years – the average time from the date of patent application to the marketing of patented pharmaceuticals – due to the extensive regulatory requirements of clinical trials, and hence they demanded protection from about ten years earlier than the date of application of the TRIPS Agreement.[18] This pipeline protection demand remained an important one up to the end of the negotiations in 1993 (see Catherine Field, chapter 8). India and other textile-exporting countries were keen on parity between the TRIPS Agreement and the Agreement on Textiles and Clothing, and asked for a ten-year clean transition period without such pipeline protection. The United States and others argued that this would delay the economic impact of the TRIPS Agreement for the pharmaceuticals sector by 20 years, which was unacceptable. Even the Swiss compromise pipeline protection proposal – namely, to grant protection to all pharmaceutical and agricultural chemical products for which patents were filed from 1 January 1995 for the balance of the patent term after the expiry of the transition period, and the interim grant of exclusive marketing rights during the transition period – which was accepted by India and others in December 1991, did not satisfy the United States fully since it reiterated its original demand in 1993, although without success. The 1991 compromise that is reflected in what is now TRIPS Article 70, paragraphs 8 and 9, left India – and other countries that did not yet have product patents for pharmaceuticals – with not even a day of a transition period for the most sensitive sector in the TRIPS negotiations, since patent applications for pharmaceuticals and agricultural chemicals had to be permitted to be filed from 1 January1995 onwards (see A.V. Ganesan, chapter 11). A similar outcome would have occurred had India accepted pharmaceutical product patents in the TRIPS Agreement without either a transition period or pipeline protection.[19] However, this outcome may, in retrospect, be seen as a compromise, given India's initial demand for a ten-year clean transition period – with its economic effect only kicking in after 20 years – and the United States' demand for pipeline protection for approximately minus ten years – with economic effect kicking in from day one.

Differences among developing country delegations

I have elsewhere contrasted the TRIPS negotiations with the WTO negotiation of the Doha Declaration on the TRIPS Agreement and Public Health, and looked at the reasons for the relative failure of developing countries in TRIPS negotiations and their nearly full victory achieved in the Doha Declaration.[20] My main conclusion was that the united front presented by developing countries in the Doha negotiations, as well as external factors such as the moral imperative of providing a reasonable solution to tackle the HIV/AIDS pandemic then ravaging the poorest populations in the world, helped these countries succeed in obtaining their objectives. Clearly, developing countries had differing priorities in the Uruguay Round and did not share common defensive objectives in the TRIPS negotiations.

The text of the document submitted by 14 developing countries in May 1990, was largely prepared by the United Nations Conference on Trade and Development (UNCTAD) Secretariat, although it was cleared in the capitals of the 14 countries.[21] However, I recall that after its initial presentation by the delegate from Peru on 14 May 1990, it soon became an orphan: in other words, it became a text of which none of the 14 signatories really took ownership.

There were many reasons for this lack of ownership, the most important being that the text itself was not authored by anyone present in the negotiations. It was also, by its collective nature, a compromise text full of contradictions. I recall that on the very day of its presentation, other delegations, notably that of Hong Kong, expressed extreme dissatisfaction, claiming that it provided no guidance whatsoever on what its proponents wanted in the negotiations.

The text was presented in two parts: Part I was titled "Intellectual Property and International Trade", and only dealt with trade in counterfeit and pirated goods. This part consisted of nine articles and was meant to be the draft TRIPS agreement to be lodged in the GATT from the point of view of these 14 countries. However, Part II on standards of IPRs was also added for safe measure, in order to counter the draft legal texts already submitted by industrialized jurisdictions such as the EC, the United States, Switzerland and Japan. This part was full of further contradictions. For example, Article 4, titled "Patent Protection", proposed in its first paragraph that patent protection shall be available for inventions in all fields of technology, with five quite reasonable exclusions – most of which find place in the TRIPS Agreement – while adding in its second paragraph further open-ended optional exclusions on grounds of public interest, national security, public health or nutrition. Similarly, provisions on compulsory licences find mention in multiple provisions, namely Articles 5, 6 and 13, while remedies for anti-competitive practices find mention in Articles 5, 13, 15 and 16.

By about six months after its submission, at the time of the Brussels text,[22] the section on patents had evolved a lot from the text of the document submitted by the 14 developing countries and only largely political points remained for ministers to resolve, such as the scope of the subject matter of protection and the term of protection. By this time, India stood largely isolated in its opposition to product patents for pharmaceuticals. India's erstwhile comrade in arms, Brazil, had already, in early 1990, accepted that it would have to concede on this point in order to protect its larger trading interests in agriculture (see Piragibe dos Santos Tarragô, chapter 12). The Brazilian delegation openly conceded this point in the informal TRIPS negotiations in the autumn of 1990, well before the Brussels meeting, leaving no doubt that this issue was not a "make-or-break" one for Brazil. For Argentina, too, provisions in the TRIPS Agreement were mere bargaining chips to obtain its goals in the agriculture negotiations (see Antonio Gustavo Trombetta, chapter 13). However, both delegations continued to battle out the details of the provisions, and their participation proved invaluable to obtaining some concessions in wording in the patents section.

Differences among developed country delegations

Many subsequent commentators and analysts have maintained that the TRIPS negotiations were essentially a North–South negotiation, in which the South was largely ineffective in defending its position or traded off the entire IPRs sector wholesale in pursuit of gains elsewhere. The truth was that on a lot of issues, including in the politically sensitive areas such as patents, trade secrets and test data protection, there were North–North differences that persisted until the end. Developing countries such as India participated in negotiating each provision of the TRIPS Agreement, contrary to certain accounts. They seized opportunities that were offered on account of these intra-North differences, wherever they became aware of such discord. One such case is described in the next section. In many cases, however, the North presented a united front and their differences were either negotiated away bilaterally or aired in informal gatherings such as the Friends of Intellectual Property group to which, to the best of my recollection, perceived hard-core opponents such as Argentina, Brazil and India were never invited (see Thomas Cottier, chapter 4).

In those days, for developing countries with one- or two-person delegations dealing with such a new and complex subject as IPRs, it was not easy to research and comprehend all the nuances of the laws and practices of even the key developed countries. UNCTAD had hardly any IPR specialists on staff, although there were brilliant international law scholars who had helped prepare the submission of the 14 developing countries.[23] Local expertise in IP policy, as opposed to IP administration, was also rare in developing country capitals. Domestic interests typically wanted the government to resist all demands but offered no realistic compromise solutions. Such expertise was practically absent in the Geneva missions of developing countries, especially in the area of patents. Moreover, during the latter half of 1990, when the negotiations continued with only short breaks, many developing country governments, including that of India, chose, for financial reasons, to keep capital-based delegates in Geneva for months on end, making consultations with local experts difficult.[24]

Clearly, the core demand for stronger IPR protection worldwide came from private sector entities in certain sectors of the EC, Japan and the United States. The document, *Basic framework of GATT provisions on intellectual property*, jointly produced by the industry associations of these three jurisdictions,[25] largely formed the basis for the draft TRIPS legal texts submitted by these parties in early 1990, although earlier submissions to the TRIPS Negotiating Group made by these parties also echoed their essential demands.

A close reading of the different submissions made by the EC, Japan and the United States beginning in 1987 shows nuanced differences in emphasis and wording, particularly with respect to compulsory licensing. It also shows that these Quad members did not originally have such high ambitions. For example, initial submissions made by the United States on inadequacies in existing national IPR systems speak only of exclusive compulsory licences and non-respect of the Paris Convention standards.[26] It seems that, for all three, the level of ambition on the working requirements and compulsory licences in 1987-8 was only to get all countries to adhere to the Paris Convention 1967 standard of time limits before issuing a compulsory licence or direct non-revocation of patents on grounds of non-working. Even in later submissions, when the United States wanted to limit the grounds for compulsory licences to declared national emergency and adjudicated violation of antitrust laws, while not accepting such limitations for government use, the only prohibition the United States sought for non-working of patents was against revocation. By implication, the United States might, at this stage – given the views of the other members of the Quad – have reconciled itself to compulsory licences for non-working, provided Paris Convention 1967 rules were respected.[27] Later, in 1991, the United States pushed for language on non-discrimination on the enjoyment of patent rights through importation or local production, which is now in Article 27.1, although this language has been subject to different interpretations by commentators.[28]

Not surprisingly, Canada, though one of the Quad members, did not submit a draft legal text in the spring of 1990. In its submission of October 1989 on Standards for Trade-related IPRs, Canada argued for strengthening the patent compulsory licensing disciplines in the Paris Convention only insofar as to require transparency, non-exclusivity, adequate compensation and access to judicial review.[29] Canada's extensive use of compulsory licences on pharmaceutical patents in the 1980s, with a uniform royalty rate of 4 per cent, is now well-documented.[30] Canada was indeed the target of some of the demands of the EC, Japan and the United States in the patents area. Yet, quietly and, in my view, effectively, it played an important role in moderating the demands of other Quad members, particularly in the pharmaceuticals sector, with respect to both patents and test data protection.

Even while the United States was the strongest *demandeur* for higher IPR standards in the TRIPS Agreement, particularly in the patents area, it had laws and policies that could not be easily changed. This provided a useful basis for me to consider how to maintain the compulsory licence provisions in the Indian law.

India's role in the negotiations of compulsory licences

By autumn 1990, the overall dynamics of the negotiations made it inevitable that product patents for pharmaceuticals would have to be conceded at a political level in the forthcoming Brussels ministerial meeting. Given the inevitability of the acceptance of product patents for pharmaceuticals (since leaving the GATT was not really an option for India), my focus was to save India's compulsory licence/licence of right system to the extent possible.

India's 1970 Patents Act had four systems of non-voluntary licences in place:

- Use by or on behalf of government for purposes of government, including public interest

- Compulsory licences on grounds of non-working or that the reasonable requirements of the public have not been met, including making the patented invention available at reasonable terms

- Compulsory licences for dependent patents

- Automatic availability of "licences of right" on patents relating to food or drugs or medicines or chemicals on the expiration of three years from the date of grant of the patents.

Around October 1990, India, led by its Ambassador,[31] initiated an alliance with other Commonwealth countries that had very similar wording on compulsory licences and use of patents by governments. These laws were based on the United Kingdom patent law, hence the commonality of interest. The idea was to ensure that as much as possible of our respective national provisions be retained in the final agreement. This alliance worked well and, for the first time, "Friends of Intellectual Property", such as Australia and Hong Kong, spoke in one voice with India, espousing grounds for compulsory licences such as when the "reasonable requirements of the public are not met". On the government use provision we had less difficulty, as even the United States was on our side and did not want any restriction on grounds for such use. Suddenly India, which had been seen as sitting at one extreme end of the spectrum with little support even from other developing countries, was seen as having credible friends, even if on a limited issue. Alas, this alliance proved very short-lived – no more than a fortnight long – for reasons best known to our Commonwealth allies.

Almost overnight, India became isolated in its opposition to limiting the grounds for compulsory licences to remedy a declared national emergency or adjudicated cases of anti-competitive practices. The government use provision remained broad and had the support of the United States as before. As there was a real danger of the text getting set in this way, I began to contemplate alternatives. Not being the age of the Internet, it was not easy to research the reason why the United States supported the government use provision.

Scouring the draft legal texts, I found the EC approach in its 29 March 1990 submission to be most suitable, as it did not restrict the grounds for compulsory licences but only contained a chapeau stating,

> Where the law of a contracting party allows for the grant of compulsory licences, such licences shall not be granted in a manner which distorts trade, and the following provision shall be respected …[32]

I also looked at the United States' submission of 11 May 1990 and found some similar language.[33] For example, some of the conditions in Article 27 of that document, such as that each case shall be considered on its individual merits, were common with the EC submission.

Before drafting any proposal to the informal TRIPS negotiating group, I had informally checked the ideas I was contemplating with Mogens Peter Carl of the EC and John Gero of Canada.[34] Mogens Peter Carl, with whom I had spoken on the telephone from Geneva, said he could consider this approach in principle but would, of course, like to see the proposal in writing and could not commit. John Gero, whom I met in person, also supported the approach in principle. He was the one who drew my attention to the existence of 28 USC Section 1498(a), which, as I later discovered, states:

> Whenever an invention described in and covered by a patent of the United States is used or manufactured by or for the United States without license of the owner thereof or lawful right to use or manufacture the same, the owner's remedy shall be by action against the United States in the United States Court of Federal Claims for the recovery of his reasonable and entire compensation for such use and manufacture. (…) For the purposes of this section, the use or manufacture of an invention described in and covered by a patent of the United States by a contractor, a subcontractor, or any person, firm, or corporation for the Government and with the authorization or consent of the Government, shall be construed as use or manufacture for the United States.

This wording explained to me why the United States delegation was on the same page as India on government use and I sought to exploit this difference of position with that on compulsory licences. Late one night, with the permission of the head of my delegation, I drafted a provision combining the two separate provisions on compulsory licences and government use under one article titled "Use without authorization of the right holder". The term "right holder" was used in the initial proposal since India wanted this provision to apply to compulsory licences for other types of industrial property, such as industrial designs and lay-out designs for integrated circuits. In order to establish credibility, we conceded that the remuneration should be "reasonable" in all cases – in other words, while the use would be without the authorization of the right holder, he or she would be reasonably remunerated. Another upfront concession was giving up the demand for exclusive compulsory licences, seen as a major concession in the light of the Paris revision process referred to above.

India scored a major negotiating victory when the Indian non-paper or room document, submitted on an ad-referendum basis the next day, was accepted as a basis for further negotiations after it gained the support of the EC and Canada, as well as - unexpectedly - of Japan. It might have been that the US government use provisions were hurting Japanese industry. This led to the isolation of the US delegation within the Quad on this issue.

As anticipated, in the further course of the TRIPS negotiations, the US delegation could no longer insist on restriction of the grounds for compulsory licences. Instead it began to weaken this common text further to accommodate US laws. It proposed two types of exceptions to the listed conditions in what is now TRIPS Article 31: one, for public non-commercial use and two, for compulsory licences that are granted as a remedy in adjudicated cases of anti-competitive practices.

This explains why there are no restrictions on grounds for use without the authorization of the right holder in the TRIPS Agreement. Without a doubt, this could not have happened without the active support of the delegations of EC, Canada and Japan. The US delegation introduced the text of what is now in TRIPS Article 31(a), that each case of such use would be considered on its "individual merits". This was meant to tighten the provision for other countries, while allowing US government agents and contractors to use patents for public non-commercial purposes within the wording of what is now TRIPS Article 31(b).

Other delegations helped in making the conditions to be followed in what is now TRIPS Article 31 even less restrictive. My recollection is that Australia wanted review to reside with a distinct higher authority and not necessarily with a court of law, a provision that India has used to establish the Indian Intellectual Property Appellate Board. Argentina wanted only the legal validity of the authorization to be subject to higher, independent review.[35] Canada weakened the condition on exports by proposing the addition of the word "predominantly" in TRIPS Article 31(f). Without restrictions on the grounds for such use without the right holder's authorization, some of the conditions become far less strict than they seem.[36]

On the question of whether or not the Indian automatic licence of right system for food and pharmaceuticals could be saved with this proposal, my reasoning was that the provision contemplated only "use" without authorization of the right holder and not the "grant" of a licence. The Indian law did contemplate the Controller General of Patents Designs and Trademarks arbitrating the terms and conditions of the licence of right in the case of disagreement between the patent owner and the potential licensee. Such arbitration necessarily took place before "use" without authorization. However, the ceiling of 4 per cent royalty in the Indian law was unique and untenable – it was something that could be conceded as long as the remuneration was set by and renewed by national authorities, as was already the case.

There were some doubts about what "individual merits" of use could mean when there is no restriction on grounds for compulsory licences. At the time, I was reassured by GATT dispute settlement experts that, if India decided that certain sectors were of vital public interest, such as medical or food technologies, then the individual merits would require the authorities to determine whether the particular patent being considered for the grant of a compulsory licence belongs to these fields of technology or not. With this assurance, I believed at the time that the draft proposal I had submitted could save the broad contours of India's licence of right system.

Subsequently, in 1991, the text of what is now Article 27.1 introduced the clause of non-discrimination in the grant and enjoyment of patent rights with respect to the field of technology and whether the patented product is imported or locally produced. This was meant to block the automatic licence of right systems such as the Indian one, and the compulsory "working" requirement in patent laws. There may have been creative ways around this provision when drafting legislation in India and, indeed, Canada showed the way with its "early working" or Bolar-type provision under its regulatory review requirements, which was adjudicated at the WTO in 2000, by making its provision technology neutral.[37]

As for the working requirement, many countries' laws, including India's, continue to contain this provision without specifying, as some others have done, that importation would satisfy the working requirement. A WTO dispute case that the United States brought against Brazil in 2000 resulted in a mutually agreed settlement, and so there has been no express finding on whether such provisions are TRIPS-compliant or not.[38]

At the time of the TRIPS negotiations, I was convinced by the arguments put forward by economists that it was undesirable and inefficient to make technology transfer dependent on compulsory patent-working requirements, when there are more effective policy variables that can be used.[39] Indeed, it is difficult to find an example of any country in modern times where such patent-working requirements, with their broad carve-outs for justifiable reasons of technical or economic feasibility, were the main pathway to industrialization or technology transfer. Since Brazil was keen to defend this requirement in the negotiations, given the historical sensitivities on this issue in that country,[40] India did not strain itself too much on this issue.

All in all, the TRIPS Agreement provision on compulsory licences and use by governments – unlike, for example, that on the term of patent protection – has not only not led to harmonization of national patent laws but has not increased convergence nor improved coherence. In November 2001, WTO members adopted by consensus the Doha Declaration on the TRIPS Agreement and Public Health, which states in no uncertain terms in its paragraph 5(b) that "Each Member has the right to grant compulsory licences and the freedom to determine the grounds upon which such licences are granted." Importantly, this part of the Doha Declaration did not entail any amendment to the text of the TRIPS Agreement, because such freedom to determine the grounds for compulsory licences was already part of the original text (see Mogens Peter Carl, chapter 6). In this context, the Declaration simply served to state expressly what was inherent in the logic of the text.

Factors that came into play for India in negotiating other patent provisions

Subject matter and other exclusions

The subject matter of patents and, more importantly, permitted exclusions of patentable subject matter, was the most sensitive issue for both the *demandeurs* and for India. Even well before December 1990, it became clear to us that the Latin American countries that were supporting the position of the group of developing countries or "approach B" in document W/76[41] – that certain products or processes could be excluded on grounds of public interest, national security, public health or nutrition, including food, chemicals and pharmaceuticals – were ready to give up these exclusions in return for perceived gains in agriculture or other areas in the Uruguay Round.[42]

African countries were not active in the TRIPS negotiations, except, to some extent, Egypt, Nigeria, Tanzania and the Republic of Zaire[43] (at the early stages), where the latter two sought special provisions for least-developed countries (LDCs), almost all of which were conceded in Articles 66.1 and 66.2 of the TRIPS Agreement. Well before the TRIPS Negotiating Group began working on the legal text of the TRIPS Agreement, Bangladesh, on behalf of the group of LDCs, had made clear that LDCs wanted to be exempt from applying TRIPS obligations, and wanted technical assistance to eventually implement them, as well as provisions relating to transfer of technology, all of which they obtained, to a large extent, in the final Agreement.[44] It was thus that India found itself alone in its opposition to product patents in pharmaceuticals and chemicals – clearly, an unsustainable position in multilateral negotiations. That the term "invention" or the criteria of patentability were left undefined in what is now TRIPS Article 27.1 was not due to any major foresight in the negotiations, but because they were considered to be sufficiently clear for patent examination purposes. That India could use this "loophole" to insert Section 3(d) in its patent law to prevent incremental, trivial innovation that is allegedly used to extend the patent term of pharmaceutical products was thus not anticipated at the time of the negotiations.

On the optional exclusion of plant and animal inventions, there were considerable intra-North differences, with Canada in particular opposing the patenting of multi-cellular organisms. Canada submitted in October 1989 that it would not be reasonable to oblige all governments to extend patents to multi-cellular life forms, as this area required more technical study to determine the most appropriate form of protection.[45] At the time, the EC had not yet passed its Biotechnology Directive[46] and had difficulties in accepting an immediate obligation to provide patents for plant and animal inventions.[47] The Nordic countries also wanted such exclusions.

The Association of Southeast Asian Nations (ASEAN) countries, and even some Latin American countries, had no problem supporting the patentability of micro-organisms and microbiological and non-biological processes for the production of plants and animals, but could not support the patentability of plant and animal inventions. It was due to these positions that TRIPS Article 27.3(b) is drafted the way it is.

India had difficulties accepting even the patenting of micro-organisms, as its 1970 Patents Act limited patentable inventions to any new and useful:

- Art, process, method or manner of manufacture

- Machine, apparatus or other article

- Substance produced by manufacture and any new or useful improvement thereof.

Not only did India exclude product patents for food, medicine and chemicals, granting only process patents in these fields, it also excluded methods of agriculture and horticulture, so the patenting of microbiological and non-biological processes pertaining to these two sectors was also a problem. Accepting plant variety protection was also controversial in India even post-TRIPS despite assurances by the then GATT Director-General, Peter Sutherland, on permissible exceptions and limitations.[48]

India also wanted patent exclusion for nuclear fissionable material. While Brazil and Japan lent some support for such exclusion, in the end, the general security exception, now found in Article 73 of the TRIPS Agreement, was considered sufficient by all.

India also wanted the exclusion of methods of treatment for humans, animals and plants – it was the only country to seek such exclusion for plants. One view was that such methods, unlike products used for treatment, were not susceptible to industrial application. However, since the TRIPS text held "industrial applicability" to be synonymous with "usefulness", India and others thought it prudent to retain such an exclusion. Only the United States opposed the optional exclusion of methods of medical treatment, wanting these to be confined only to surgical methods. In the end, the United States' view did not prevail. In 1996, the US amended its patent law to exclude the availability of some enforcement remedies for patents on medical or surgical procedures used by medical practitioners for the treatment of humans.[49]

For India, conceding product patents for pharmaceuticals was clearly a call that was politically sensitive and had to be taken at the highest levels of government. Civil society groups, notably the National Working Group on Patent Laws which strongly opposed India agreeing to anything in the TRIPS Negotiating Group and even opposed India joining the Paris Convention, continued to campaign against these negotiations. When the so-called Dunkel Draft containing the results of the Uruguay Round became public at the end of 1991, the TRIPS text was pored over by many activists and academics in India and an active campaign was launched to reject the text. "Down with Dunkel" was a slogan painted on many walls around the capital and elsewhere in the country, and this is how Arthur Dunkel unexpectedly came to be a household name in India.

In June 1993, A.V. Ganesan gave an interview to the *Economic Times*, headlined "We don't have a choice",[50] in which he said that India would have to accept the Dunkel Draft and, with it, product patents for pharmaceuticals. This view began to gather public support. He said that the government could devise new mechanisms to minimize the impact of high drug prices, if required, such as price control mechanisms and compulsory licences. He emphasized that India would not accept patents for plants but would only institute a *sui generis* system for the protection of new plant varieties, which did not necessarily have to be based upon the International Convention for the Protection of New Varieties of Plants (1991), and that India would benefit from a ten-year transition period for the introduction of drug patents. It is my view that it was through the detailed explanations coming from a civil servant widely respected in India that Indians came to accept the inevitability of product patents for pharmaceuticals and plant variety protection as required by the TRIPS Agreement. By then, India had also had two years of successful implementation of economic reforms and was beginning to become rapidly integrated into the global economy.

Despite this, it took many more battles in India's parliament and India's loss of two WTO dispute settlement cases on transitional arrangements[51] before its laws were amended to introduce its TRIPS obligations in these contentious areas.

Rights of process patent owners and reversal of burden of proof

For India, extending the rights of process patent owners to the products directly obtained through the use of the process remained controversial so long as India did not accept product patents for pharmaceuticals and chemicals. India initially hoped that the extension of the rights of owners of process patents to the products directly obtained through the use of the patented processes would serve as a middle ground in lieu of product patents. But clearly this idea was a non-starter, and was not even proposed by India, since conceding product patents or not was clearly to be a binary decision left to the end-game: in my time, it was meant to be left to trade ministers at Brussels.

Indeed, given the sharp sensitivities on this point expressed by the Indian generic drugs industry and the more technical National Working Group on Patent Laws that served to espouse its interest, even such extension was not acceptable in India and remained in square brackets in the draft TRIPS text until well after Brussels.

To me, it was evident that, if product patents were going to be conceded at a political level, little purpose would be served by not extending the rights of process patent owners to the direct product. Indeed, I found the arguments on this particular point made by Michael Kirk, the US negotiator for patents, to be persuasive. How could a process patent owner take infringement action against someone who was simply using the patent elsewhere where the patentee held no process patent and was exporting the product to undercut the patentee's sales in key jurisdictions? Nevertheless, I had no authority to concede this point and so the square brackets remained at Brussels.

On reversal of the burden of proof in litigation involving process patent infringement, the EC and US legal texts of early 1990 contained this provision for the first time. As the text sent to Brussels[52] shows, the language of this article was largely negotiated with only one choice left to negotiators, namely, to decide whether the provision should be made optional or obligatory.

There was strong push-back in India to the leaked 1990 draft TRIPS text from the National Working Group on Patent Laws.[53] The main fear was that the alleged infringer would be forced to reveal his or her business secrets (despite the proviso to take such a scenario into account) and that the courts would presumptively favour the process patent owner. Even the second option, where the process patentee must first show a "substantial likelihood" that his or her patented process was used, was said to be weak, as hard facts need not be required to be presented. My own assessment was that, since the burden of proof shifts from the plaintiff to the defendant only when the plaintiff has established "substantial likelihood" that his or her patented process is being used, we could accept this provision with all the safeguards built into it with respect to business secrets of the defendant. Section 104A of the amended Indian patent law incorporates both options given in the TRIPS Agreement Article 34 instead of choosing one.

All in all, the criticism of the reversal of burden of proof turned out to be much ado about nothing, once product patents for pharmaceuticals and chemicals were accepted, since this would apply only to cases where process patents alone were taken out.

Limited exceptions

On exceptions to patent rights, the lack of agreement among the *demandeurs* on a positive list approach, which was based on different lists of exceptions proposed originally[54] and in the course of the negotiations, made the alternative language eventually proposed, in what is now TRIPS Article 30, acceptable to developing countries, including India. The positive list approach was followed in the draft WIPO Patent Law Harmonization Treaty,[55] which was being negotiated simultaneously with the TRIPS Agreement, but parties eventually failed to reach agreement and this treaty was dropped after a failed Diplomatic Conference in 1991.[56]

The limits of TRIPS Article 30 were tested under the WTO's dispute settlement mechanism (DS114, see endnote 37), where Canada's regulatory review exception was upheld, the result eventually being that the provision that the EC complained about is now part of European Union law. The TRIPS Agreement has ensured that the regulatory review exception has become an explicit part of patent laws around the world, where it was not so earlier because doubt had been cast on its legitimacy. This is the case in India's Patents Act, 1970, where Section 107A(a) now states:

> For the purposes of this Act,—
>
> (a) any act of making, constructing, using, selling or importing a patented invention solely for uses reasonably related to the development and submission of information required under any law for the time being in force, in India, or in a country other than India, that regulates the manufacture, construction, use, sale or import of any product; ...

Term of protection

It is clear that at the beginning, extremely short patent terms, such as five years, were not acceptable to the *demandeurs*. But the initial idea did not seem to be to oblige all governments to adhere to a 20-year patent term: it seemed to be accepted that the norm was anywhere between 15 and 20 years. While the United States, the EC, Japan, Switzerland, the Republic of Korea, Hong Kong and the Nordic countries supported an obligation of 20 years from the date of filing of the patent application, Australia and New Zealand, at least, preferred a term of 15 or 16 years only.

By taking the position that the term of patents should be left to countries to determine, developing countries might possibly have lost an opportunity to negotiate a shorter length of patent protection. On the other hand, while there may have been some flexibility for some sectors, it was clear that the patent term would have to be at least 20 years from the date of filing for pharmaceuticals. The United States wanted to have patent term extension in this sector to compensate for regulatory delays – a demand that it has successfully achieved in its bilateral and plurilateral agreements. Again, the patent term was a provision that was left to the end-game for a political decision.

Revocation

On revocation of patents, there was an attempt in the negotiations to list the grounds and conditions of revocation. The Paris Convention already allows revocation of the patent on grounds of patent abuse, such as failure to work, but lays down conditions that revocation is permitted only if, after two years of the grant of a compulsory licence to remedy the situation, the abuse continues. Australia, in its submissions, supported this provision. The EC and Japan, in their earlier submissions, supported the Paris Convention provisions. India, in Section 66 of its 1970 Patents Act, allowed revocation of patents in public interest, which it continues to maintain and use. Brazil, not being party to the 1967 version of the Paris Convention, supported direct revocation of patents on grounds of failure to work. The United States and Switzerland took the position that revocation should be allowed only on grounds of patent invalidity, that is, if the patent was wrongly granted in the first place. In the end, the *demandeurs* considered it prudent to only oblige judicial review in case of patent revocation.

There was an interesting discussion in the TRIPS Council in 1996 on what the single sentence in TRIPS Article 33 means. India took the position that it means that there are no restrictions on the grounds for revocation other than those contained in the Paris Convention, while the United States, and several other delegations that supported the United States, claimed that it meant that patents could only be revoked on grounds of patent invalidity.[57] Needless to add, no WTO dispute has been brought regarding the implementation of this provision.

Concluding remarks

While developing countries were undoubtedly disadvantaged in terms of their numbers of delegates dedicated to TRIPS negotiations or their level of expertise, I did not experience any bias against us on the part of the GATT Secretariat team, ably led by David Hartridge and Adrian Otten, nor on the part of our genial and effective Chair, Ambassador Lars Anell. Being a part of the WTO Secretariat now, I realize that actions of the Secretariat are motivated by its desire to see that members reach an agreement that all are willing to live with. It is up to members to carefully reflect on their "make-or-break" points and ensure that these are adequately reflected in the text. In general, in the GATT then and in the WTO now, while decision-making still follows the consensus rule, a proposal needs support of at least some of the major players. Today in the WTO arriving at a consensus is becoming more difficult in areas where there are widely divergent interests and no agreement can be reached without accommodating the interests of a number of developing countries, particularly those with growing economic clout owing to their increased integration into the global economy.

The narrative of the TRIPS negotiations illustrates that the package was much more balanced than some TRIPS commentators assume, since they make the mistake of taking the TRIPS text as representing only what its key *demandeurs* had wanted, rather than a genuine product of a multilateral negotiation, with concomitant checks and balances. For my part, I feel proud that, as a representative of India, I was able to contribute to the balance in the text of the Agreement in a way that improved the armoury of policy measures that WTO members can use to attenuate the adverse effects of patents, where needed. But this could not have happened without the crucial support of some key developed countries as well. Thus, cooperation, coalition-building and compromise are the key words in any successful trade negotiation.

Endnotes

1   I gratefully acknowledge helpful comments made on an earlier draft by A.V. Ganesan, John Gero, Catherine Field, Meagan McCann, Adrian Otten, Piragibe dos Santos Tarragô, Antony Taubman, Antonio Gustavo Trombetta, Hannu Wager and Thu-Lang Tran Wasescha.

2   A.V. Ganesan, who has a chapter (11) in this volume, was then Additional Secretary in the same department. He later became a member of the Appellate Body of the WTO, for two consecutive terms.

3   A.N. Verma, who later became Principal Secretary to the Indian Prime Minister, P.V. Narasimha Rao, spearheaded the economic reform process in India from 1991 onwards.

4   GATT document MTN.GNG/NG11.W/71, Negotiating Group on Trade-Related Aspects of Intellectual Property Rights, including Trade in Counterfeit Goods – Communication from Argentina, Brazil, Chile, China, Colombia, Cuba, Egypt, India, Nigeria, Peru, Tanzania and Uruguay, 14 May 1990.

5   Anwarul Hoda, as Additional Secretary and later Special Secretary, Ministry of Commerce, coordinated India's position in the Uruguay Round of multilateral trade negotiations overall. He later became Deputy Director General of the WTO in 1995.

6   I would also refer the interested reader to chapters I and IV of Jayashree Watal, *Intellectual property rights in the WTO and developing countries* (New Delhi: Oxford University Press and London/The Hague/Boston: Kluwer Law International, 2001). Chapter I describes in more detail the TRIPS negotiating process from Punta del Este to Marrakesh and chapter IV covers the negotiations on patents and exclusive marketing rights.

7   India's trade-to-GDP (gross domestic product) ratio was only 15 per cent in 1990 and is now over 54 per cent. See the World Bank note on India's foreign trade policy at http://web. worldbank.org/WBSITE/EXTERNAL/COUNTRIES/SOUTHASIAEXT/ EXTSARREGTOPINTECOTRA/0,,content MDK:20592520~menuPK:1465890~pagePK:34004173~piPK:34003707~theSitePK:57 9448,00.html and the WTO country profile of India at http://stat.wto.org/CountryProfile/ WSDBCountryPFView.aspx?Country=IN&Language=F (both last accessed 7 July 2015).

8   I, too, was curious about these price and welfare effects and was among the first to model them. See Jayashree Watal, "Pharmaceutical patents, prices and welfare losses: Policy options for India under the WTO TRIPS Agreement", *World Economy*, 23(5) (2000), 733-52.

9   See a recent paper that estimates that price rises may have been of the order of 3–6 per cent only, mostly on newer medicines: see Duggan, et al. "The market impacts of pharmaceutical product patents in developing countries: Evidence from India", NBER Working Paper 20548 (Cambridge, MA: National Bureau of Economic Research, 2014), www.nber.org/papers/ w20548.pdf (last accessed 7 July 2015).

10 The relevant provision reads: "Provided also that after a patent is granted in respect of applications made under sub-section (2) of section 5, *the patent-holder shall only be entitled to receive reasonable royalty* from such *enterprises which have made significant investment and were producing and marketing the concerned product prior to the 1st day of January, 2005* and which continue to manufacture the product covered by the patent on the date of grant of the patent and *no infringement proceedings shall be instituted against such enterprises*." (emphasis added).

11 See full text of the speaking order at: www.ipindia.nic.in/iponew/compulsory_license_12032012. pdf (last accessed 7 July 2015).

12 See Susan K. Sell, *Power and ideas: North–South politics of intellectual property and anti-trust* (New York: State University of New York Press), 107-140.

13 For a survey of the literature, see *The economics of intellectual property: Suggestions for further research in developing countries and countries with economies in transition* (Geneva: World Intellectual Property Organization, 2009), chapter 5.

14 Ibid. See chapters 1 and 5.

15 An interesting, if one-sided, account of the TRIPS negotiating process is that written by Jacques Gorlin, principal advisor to the R&D-based pharmaceuticals industry, titled *An analysis of the pharmaceutical-related provisions of the WTO TRIPS (intellectual property) Agreement* (London: Intellectual Property Institute, 1999). Ambassador Clayton Yeutter, United States Trade Representative from 1985–8, in a foreword to the book, commends the close industry involvement in TRIPS negotiations.

16 The words "effective and adequate protection of intellectual property rights" are part of the Punta del Este Ministerial Declaration, which set the mandate for TRIPS negotiations, and the words "adequate and effective protection of intellectual property rights" are part of the US statute governing Special 301 - see 19 U.S. Code § 2242 - Identification of countries that deny adequate protection, or market access, for intellectual property. rights, available at https://www.law.cornell.edu/uscode/text/19/2242 (last accessed 9 July 2015).

17 See GATT document MTN.GNG/NG11/W/70, Negotiating Group on Trade-Related Aspects of Intellectual Property Rights, including Trade in Counterfeit Goods – Draft Agreement on the Trade-Related Aspects of Intellectual Property Rights – Communication from the United States, 11 May 1990, in which the United States sought transitional protection for the balance of the patent term for subject matter that becomes patentable after the entry into force of the Agreement, if a patent has been obtained in another contracting party and the product has not been marketed in the jurisdiction providing the transitional protection.

18 This figure of "ten years" was considered to be authentic at the time and comes from a reputed study: *Pharmaceutical R&D: Costs, risks, and rewards* (US Congress, Office of Technology Assessment, OTA-H-522 (Washington, DC: US Government Printing Office, February 1993) http://ota.fas.org/reports/9336.pdf (last accessed 7 July 2015), but is increasingly being questioned by health activists who claim that this period is much shorter and could be as low as 4-5 years or less for priority pharmaceutical products.

19 See Jayashree Watal, *Intellectual property rights in the WTO and developing countries* (Oxford: Oxford University Press, 2001), pp. 36-39. See also A.V. Ganesan (chapter 11), on India's request for a clean transition period of five years.

20 See my article "From Punta del Este to Doha and beyond: Lessons from the TRIPS negotiating processes", in *WIPO Journal* (3)1 (2011): 24-35, www.wipo.int/edocs/pubdocs/en/intproperty/ wipo_journal/wipo_journal_3_1.pdf (last accessed 7 July 2015).

21 GATT document MTN.GNG11.W/71.

22 GATT document MTN.TNC/W/35/Rev.1, Uruguay Round – Trade Negotiations Committee – Draft Final Act Embodying the Results of the Uruguay Round of Multilateral Trade Negotiations – Revision, 3 December 1990.

23 One key expert, Abdulqawi Yusuf, moved on to other responsibilities in the UN and is now a judge in the International Court of Justice. I am truly grateful to Abdi for the long, illuminating discussions I had with him on IPRs in the period 1989-90.

24 I consulted widely on TRIPS enforcement provisions with Pravin Anand, a private IP lawyer in New Delhi who had a great deal of experience with litigation in the trademark and copyright areas. Consulting with Indian industry or academics was more to keep them informed of the negotiating process than to seek advice on negotiating strategy or positions.

25 See Intellectual Property Committee (US), Keidanren (Japan), Union of Industrial and Employers' Confederations of Europe (UNICE), (June 1988), *Basic framework of GATT provisions on intellectual property: Statement of views of the European, Japanese and United States business communities.*

26 See GATT document MTN.GNG/NG11/W/7, Negotiating Group on Trade-Related Aspects of Intellectual Property Rights, including Trade in Counterfeit Goods – Submissions from Participants on Trade Problems Encountered in Connection with Intellectual Property Rights, 29 May 1987.

27 See the section on patents in GATT document MTN.GNG/NG11/W/32, Negotiating Group on Trade-Related Aspects of Intellectual Property Rights, Including Trade in Counterfeit Goods – Synoptic Tables Setting Out Existing International Standards and Proposed Standards and Principles – Prepared by the Secretariat, 2 June 1989; this provides a comparison between existing international standards and the submissions of the following: the EC (GATT document MTN.GNG/NG11/W/26, Negotiating Group on Trade-Related Aspects of Intellectual Property Rights, including Trade in Counterfeit Goods – Guidelines and Objectives Proposed by the European Community for the Negotiations on Trade Related Aspects of Substantive Standards of Intellectual Property Rights, 7 July 1988); Japan (GATT document MTN.GNG/NG11/W/17, Negotiating Group on Trade-Related Aspects of Intellectual Property Rights, including Trade in Counterfeit Goods – Suggestion by Japan for Achieving the Negotiating Objective, 23 November 1987); and the United States (GATT document MTN.GNG/NG11/W/14, Negotiating Group on Trade-Related Aspects of Intellectual Property Rights, including Trade in Counterfeit Goods – Suggestion by the United States for Achieving the Negotiating Objective, 20 October 1987).

28 Carlos Correa, for example, argues that, since patent rights are negative rights, this language only obliges non-discrimination with respect to the right to protect against infringement, whether it takes place through importation or domestic production. Carlos M. Correa, "Can the TRIPS Agreement foster technology transfer to developing countries?", in Keith E. Maskus and Jerome H. Reichman, eds., *International public goods and transfer of technology under a globalized intellectual property regime* (Cambridge: Cambridge University Press, 2005), 243.

29 See GATT document MTN.GNG/NG11/W/47, Negotiating Group on Trade-Related Aspects of Intellectual Property Rights, including Trade in Counterfeit Goods – Standards for Trade-Related Intellectual Property Rights – Submission from Canada, 25 October 1989.

30 See, for example, F.M. Scherer and Jayashree Watal, "Post-TRIPS options for access to patented medicines in developing nations", *Journal of International Economic Law*, 1(4) (2002): 913-39.

31 Ambassador B.K. Zutshi also wrote an interesting account of TRIPS negotiations: "Bringing TRIPS into the multilateral trading system" in *The Uruguay Round and Beyond, Essays in Honour of Arthur Dunkel,* Jagdish Bhagwati and Mathias Hirsch, eds. (Berlin: Springer, 1998).

32 GATT document MTN.GNG/NG11/W/68, Negotiating Group on Trade-Related Aspects of Intellectual Property Rights, Including Trade in Counterfeit Goods – Draft Agreement on Trade-Related Aspects of Intellectual Property Rights, 29 March 1990.

33 GATT document MTN.GNG/NG11/W/70.

34 Mogens Peter Carl and John Gero, who have also contributed to this book, have permitted me to mention them.

35 Argentina was ably represented by Antonio Gustavo Trombetta, who also has a thoughtful chapter (13) in this book.

36 See chapter 10 of Jayashree Watal, *Intellectual property rights in the WTO and developing countries* (Oxford: Oxford University Press, 2001) for more on how none of the conditions in Article 31 are particularly restrictive, given the lack of restrictions on the grounds for the grant of such use.

37 See WTO document WT/DS114/R, Canada – Patent Protection of Pharmaceutical Products – Complaint by the European Communities and their Member States – Report of the Panel, 17 March 2000. See one-page summary at: www.wto.org/english/tratop_e/dispu_e/cases_e/ds114_e.htm (last accessed 7 July 2015).

38 See the one-page summary of this case at: www.wto.org/english/tratop_e/dispu_e/cases_e/ds199_e.htm (last accessed 7 July 2015).

39 Arvind Subramanian, "Compulsory licensing in patent legislation: superfluous and misleading", *Economic and Political Weekly*, 25 August 1990, 1880-1.

40 Brazil was ably represented by Piragibe dos Santos Tarragô who has written a brilliant and honest account of his country's position in the TRIPS negotiations in a chapter (12) in this volume.

41 MTN.GNG/NG11/W/76, Negotiating Group on Trade-Related Aspects of Intellectual Property Rights, Including Trade in Counterfeit Goods – Status of Work in the Negotiating Group – Chairman's Report to the GNG, 23 July 1990.

42 For Brazil, it was early 1990 when a new more market-oriented government took office. See Piragibe dos Santos Tarragô (chapter 12).

43 Now the Democratic Republic of the Congo.

44 See GATT document MTN.GNG/NG11/W/50, Negotiating Group on Trade-Related Aspects of Intellectual Property Rights, including Trade in Counterfeit Goods – Proposals on Behalf of the Least-Developed Countries – Communication from Bangladesh, 16 November 1989. LDCs continue to have a transition period up to July 2021 to implement TRIPS obligations other than national treatment and most-favoured-nation status.

45 See GATT document MTN.GNG/NG11/W/47.

46 This, Directive 98/44/EC of the European Parliament and of the Council of 6 July 1998 on the legal protection of biotechnological inventions, came much later. See http://eur-lex.europa.eu/LexUriServ/LexUriServ.do?uri=CELEX:31998L0044:EN:HTML.

47 See GATT document MTN.GNG/NG11/W/68 in which the EC asked for the exclusion of plant and animal varieties and, essentially, biological processes for their production.

48 Peter Sutherland, "Seeds of Doubt - Assurance on 'Farmers' Privilege", *Times of India*, 15 March 1994.

49 See 35 U.S. Code § 287(c) for details.

50 See "The Tuesday Interview", *Economic Times*, New Delhi, 8 June 1993. In 1994, A.V. Ganesan authored a "Layman's guide to the Dunkel Draft" that was widely circulated by the Rajiv Gandhi Foundation to parliamentarians in India.

51 See one-page summaries of DS50 (complainant: the US) and DS79 (complainant: the EC) at www.wto.org/english/tratop_e/dispu_e/cases_e/ds50_e.htm and www.wto.org/english/tratop_e/dispu_e/cases_e/ds79_e.htm (both last accessed 7 July 2015).

52 GATT document MTN.TNC/W/35/Rev.1.

53 See Rajeev Dhavan, "Making the world fit for prey: GATT and intellectual property rights" (New Delhi: National Working Group on Patent Laws, 1990). Dhavan's opinion piece in *The Hindu*, 10 December 2004, proposed that changes to the third amendment to the Patents Act should be resisted. This gives some idea of the continued opposition to the patent provisions in the TRIPS Agreement. See www.thehindu.com/2004/12/10/stories/2004121002361000.htm (last accessed 7 July 2015).

54 For example, the EC proposed in MTN.GNG/NG11/W/68: "Limited exceptions to the exclusive rights conferred by a patent may be made for certain acts, such as rights based on prior use, acts done privately and for non-commercial purposes and acts done for experimental purposes, provided that they take account of the legitimate interests of the proprietor of the patent and of third parties."

55 See the basic proposal text at www.wipo.int/edocs/mdocs/scp/en/scp_4/scp_4_3.pdf, Annex, page 35 (last accessed 7 July 2015).

56 See www.wipo.int/patent-law/en/patent_law_harmonization.htm (last accessed 7 July 2015).

57 See the discussion on the interpretation of TRIPS Article 32 in the TRIPS Council recorded in WTO documents IP/C/M/8, Council for Trade-Related Aspects of Intellectual Property Rights – Minutes of Meeting – Held in the Centre William Rappard from 22 to 25 July 1996, 14 August 1996, and IP/C/M/9, Council for Trade-Related Aspects of Intellectual Property Rights – Minutes of Meeting – Held in the Centre William Rappard on 18 September 1996, 30 October 1996.

17

Copyright: A Nordic perspective

Hannu Wager[1]

During the Uruguay Round of multilateral trade negotiations, I worked at the Finnish Ministry of Education and Culture, where my main responsibilities included copyright law and policy. I participated in coordination of the Nordic countries (Finland, Iceland, Norway and Sweden) in the capitals and represented the Nordic countries in the later stages of the TRIPS negotiations in Geneva. During the same period, I was also actively involved in WIPO's work on copyright and the protection of layout-designs of integrated circuits, and also contributed to the intergovernmental work under various other international and European fora, such as the International Convention for the Protection of Performers, Producers of Phonograms and Broadcasting Organizations (Rome Convention). Since January 1995, I have served at the WTO Secretariat, IP Division.

I have written this chapter partly as the recollections of a representative of the Nordic countries during the negotiations. But I have also tried to take some distance and share some personal reflections on how I saw these negotiations in the area of copyright in the broader context of the development of international copyright law, in particular, the ongoing convergence of the civil law authors' rights and common law copyright traditions.[2] I have, therefore, chosen to focus on certain selected issues that related to the philosophical differences between these two traditions, and which turned out to be difficult to resolve.

Finally, I have added some personal observations on how the international IP law had evolved, since the 1970s, in respect of two new areas of information technology, namely, computer software and layout-designs of integrated circuits, and how this evolution influenced the way these issues were addressed in the TRIPS negotiations.

Broader negotiation dynamics

During the Uruguay Round of negotiations under the GATT, the Nordic countries coordinated closely their positions and shared representation in various negotiating groups.[3] This enabled them to effectively pool together their expertise and other resources, and increase their bargaining power. As small countries dependent on foreign trade, they shared an interest in the maintenance and further development of a well-functioning, rules-based international trading system. This included adequate rules on IPRs and their enforcement, based on the recognition that distortions to international trade could result from an inappropriate level of protection, "be it inadequate or excessive".[4]

In the area of copyright, the Nordic countries, together with other industrialized countries, sought to reinforce the application of the pre-existing international standards as contained in the Berne Convention for the Protection of Literary and Artistic Works through their wider acceptance and rules concerning domestic enforcement. They shared the view that the latest act of the Berne Convention, the Paris Act of 1971, already adequately dealt with most of the key issues, such as the definition of protectable subject matter, minimum rights, permissible exceptions and the term of protection.

Beyond the readiness to build on this pre-existing level of protection, most of the substantive differences on copyright matters arose between the two copyright systems in the world, the civil law tradition of authors' rights and the US and British Commonwealth common law tradition of copyright. These differences were essentially perceived as North–North problems.

Although cross-cutting differences between industrialized and developing countries on issues such as the proper forum for substantive norms extended to the area of copyright, developing countries could agree to the Paris Act of 1971 as an appropriate standard for international copyright protection. Many of them had long traditions in copyright protection, including Argentina, Brazil, India and Mexico. In fact, of the 77 parties to the Berne Convention in 1986, some 42 could be classified by today's standards as developing countries. North–South divisions appeared mostly in regard to certain Berne-plus proposals, in particular whether computer programs should be protected as "literary works", which implied the full 50-year term of protection, or whether and to what extent exclusive rental rights were justified. But even in that regard, the picture was mixed: India had already provided protection to computer programs as literary works since 1983 and, with its flourishing film industry, was in favour of exclusive rental rights in respect of films, and opposed to the eventually successful US proposal to make that right subject to the so-called "impairment test".[5]

That the area of copyright was less contentious between the North and the South was further evidenced by the adoption of two important new treaties on copyright matters, under the auspices of WIPO, in December 1996, less than two years after the entry into force of the Marrakesh Agreement Establishing the WTO (WTO Agreement). The principal purpose of these "Internet treaties" – the WIPO Copyright Treaty (WCT) and the WIPO Performances and Phonograms Treaty (WPPT) – was to adapt international rules for the protection of copyright and the rights of performers and producers of sound recordings to the digital revolution, in particular, the distribution of copyright material over the Internet. They are self-standing treaties, which build on the TRIPS Agreement (which, in its turn, had built on the Berne Convention and, to a certain extent, the Rome Convention). The successful conclusion of the negotiations among some 130 countries on these two treaties showed that WIPO was able to build on the TRIPS Agreement in a way similar to that in which the TRIPS Agreement had built on the earlier WIPO Conventions. The majority of the 51 signatories of the WCT and the 50 signatories of the WPPT were either developing countries or economies in transition from a centrally planned to a market economy.[6]

In the negotiations leading up to the adoption of the Internet treaties, the tensions between the civil law and common law traditions that had been evident in the TRIPS negotiations had been eclipsed by the struggle between content providers (such as the film and music industries, keen to protect their rights) and service providers (i.e. those who transmit content over the Internet, worried about possible liability for their carriage of infringing material). This reflected the rapidly changing technological and commercial environment. Individual countries, both developed and developing, sought to align their positions in respect of these new realities.

Bridging the historical divide between civil law and common law traditions

Let me return to the philosophical differences that played an important role in defining the above-mentioned North–North issues during the TRIPS negotiations. Within the civil law system, the policy rationale for authors' rights has traditionally been rooted in the twin notions of justice – authors of literary and artistic works deserve to have their economic and moral interests protected as a matter of justice – and the broader benefit to the society at large. Copyright legislation was also seen as a tool for cultural policy. Therefore, among some European policy makers and scholars, there was a degree of discomfort with the common law system's predominant focus on the utilitarian rationale of providing incentives for copyright industries, and treating copyright as a general system of market regulation.

On the occasion of the centenary of the Berne Convention in 1986, the Assembly of the Berne Union reasserted these twin claims by "solemnly declar[ing] … that copyright is based on human rights and justice and that authors, as creators of beauty, entertainment and learning, deserve that their rights be recognised and effectively protected both in their own country and in all other countries of the world", and "that the law of copyright has enriched and will continue to enrich mankind by encouraging intellectual creativity and by serving as an incentive for the dissemination throughout the world of expressions of the arts, learning and information for the benefit of all people".[7]

Against this background, some European policy makers felt that the emphasis of the utilitarian objectives in the draft TRIPS Agreement, as eventually expressed in its Article 7, was difficult to reconcile with the Berne Convention's author-centric approach, built on the notion of natural justice or equity.

A major step in bridging this divide was the United States' accession to the Berne Convention in 1988, effective on 1 March 1989. Until then, US international copyright relations had primarily been governed under the 1952 Universal Copyright Convention. The move was strongly supported by US software, film and other copyright industries, which underlined their increasing share of US exports. This also strengthened the United States' efforts to include copyright and other IPRs in the ongoing Uruguay Round negotiations, and made it possible for it to reach agreement with other GATT parties to take the Paris Act of 1971 of the Berne Convention as the point of departure for copyright negotiations.

From a philosophical perspective, the United States had thus moved half-way across the ocean towards the European position. In the meantime, the Europeans had been moving closer to the US thinking with their new emphasis on the economic importance of copyright-related industries as a proper justification for protection. As regards the Nordic countries, a Swedish study published in 1982 had found that the economic contribution of copyright-related industries amounted to 6.6 per cent of Sweden's gross domestic product (GDP).[8] A study published in Finland in 1988 had indicated that the contribution amounted to 3.5 per cent of Finnish GDP in 1981 and 3.98 per cent in 1985.[9] In introducing that study, Jukka Liedes of the Finnish Ministry of Education and Culture noted that there was an ongoing shift from the production of and trade in tangible goods to the production of and trade in services and immaterial commodities, which emphasized the importance of know-how *per se*, and its importance for competitiveness.[10]

During this period, similar studies were also published in Canada (1977), the United States (1984), the United Kingdom (1985), the Netherlands (1986), Germany (1988) and Austria (1988). These studies concluded that the contribution of copyright-related industries was from 2 to 3 per cent of the GDP. Although the methodologies used in the studies varied and, at best, only gave indications of the order of magnitude, they created a new awareness among policy makers about the importance of copyright law and helped to put it front and centre on the international trade agenda.[11]

Practical challenges

Although the TRIPS negotiators across this divide approached their shared interest in strengthening the international protection of copyright in a pragmatic manner, these underlying differences in philosophy and tradition resulted in a number of intractable problems that were eventually left to the Chair of the TRIPS Negotiating Group, Ambassador Lars Anell, to resolve. These differences included two interrelated sets of questions: the first was the treatment of moral rights, and the second concerned initial ownership of copyright, transfer of rights and related elements of the distribution of collective remunerations.

From the European perspective, the authors' rights system stood on two pillars, the authors' economic and moral rights, the latter being the right to claim authorship and to object to any derogatory action in relation to a work prejudicial to the author's honour or reputation, as recognized in Article 6*bis* of the Berne Convention. The Nordic countries and the European Communities (EC), therefore, wished to include moral rights along with economic rights in the future TRIPS Agreement. In the meantime, in adhering to the Berne Convention in 1988, the United States had taken the view that the protection available under its statutory and common law already provided an adequate equivalent to the Berne Article 6*bis* rights, without a need for a further amendment of the US Copyright Act. The United States objected to the inclusion of moral rights in the TRIPS Agreement on the grounds that they were not "trade-related".

Under the civil law tradition, the original owner of copyright is normally the natural person who creates the work; an employer can only acquire the rights by means of contractual arrangements. Some laws, furthermore, contained extensive regulations on copyright contracts, including on the inalienability of moral rights and, in some cases, certain economic rights. Under the common law tradition, including the US "work for hire" doctrine, the rights in a work created in the course of employment may initially be vested in the employer, and there are few regulations on transfer of rights. It should be noted, though, that, in this respect, the gap between the two traditions was already narrowing as a number of civil law jurisdictions had amended their copyright laws, or were contemplating doing so, to the effect that the rights in respect of computer programs created in the course of employment could be considered or presumed to have been transferred to the employer.

These differences raised difficult questions concerning the law applicable to the determination of authorship and the validity of contractual arrangements that did not comply with the requirements of the country where protection was claimed. The United States, therefore, sought specific rules that, in general, would have leaned towards applying the law of the country of origin to the initial ownership of and contractual relations in respect of works, while the Nordic countries and the EC preferred to maintain the pre-existing provisions of the Berne Convention and the generally applicable rules of private international law.

The Nordic countries and a number of others had introduced blank tape levies, at that time mostly applied on audiocassette tapes (c-cassettes) and videotapes, to compensate widespread private copying of music and films. The legal characterization of these levies varied from proper copyright fees to taxes or the mixture thereof, and such characterizations were sometimes challenged in domestic courts. In some countries, a part of the collected revenue was distributed to right holders while another part was reserved for common cultural purposes. The use of c-cassettes and videotapes had already started to decline as a support for media content in the late 1980s, with the introduction of compact discs (CDs) and, a few years later, of DVDs. A number of European countries had also introduced, or were introducing, collective remunerations for holders of copyright and certain neighbouring rights for uses such as commercial rental of films, another form of exploitation that has since declined as a result of changes in technology and markets. The United States sought provisions that would have clarified how the international law should apply to these schemes, including the treatment of contractual arrangements, neighbouring rights and revenue reserved for common cultural purposes. Again, the Europeans preferred to apply the cross-cutting provisions of the TRIPS Agreement, including the provisions of the Berne Convention, to be incorporated into the Agreement.

Resolution and subsequent developments

While almost all of the copyright provisions in the so-called Dunkel Draft (the Draft Final Act Embodying the Results of the Uruguay Round of Multilateral Trade Negotiations) were agreed in the negotiations, negotiators failed to reach agreement on these two sets of issues concerning moral rights and contractual arrangements, thus leaving their resolution to the Chair of the Negotiating Group. In his attempt to read the delegations' offensive and defensive red lines, Ambassador Anell chose not to include either the protection of moral rights or the proposed texts relating to the second set of issues in the consolidated text of the agreement that was published as part of the Draft Final Act on 20 December 1991.[12]

As it turned out, the TRIPS negotiations were largely over with the publication of the Dunkel Draft. Some further attempts to reopen the second set of issues were made after the circulation of that draft. Eventually, only two changes were made to the TRIPS provisions between the 1991 Draft Final Act and the 1993 Final Act: first, to introduce a text on the moratorium on so-called non-violation complaints in dispute settlement cases (Articles 64.2 and 64.3); and, second, to limit the scope of compulsory licensing of semi-conductor technology (Article 31(c)).

The practical consequence of the exclusion of moral rights from the scope of the Agreement meant that such rights could not be enforced under the WTO dispute settlement system. In my view, the fact that the Agreement did not broaden or strengthen the application of moral rights obligations was, however, not intended to affect moral rights obligations that countries already had under the Berne Convention. This was made clear in Article 2.2 of the Agreement, which contains a safeguard clause. It provides that the provisions of the TRIPS Agreement cannot be understood to derogate from the existing obligations that countries may have to each other under the Berne Convention.

In fact, the international protection of moral rights was reaffirmed soon after the conclusion of the TRIPS Agreement by their inclusion by reference in Article 1.4 of the WCT, in December 1996. The preparatory works of the WCT indicate that this was "because the [proposed] Treaty is not limited to trade-related aspects of copyright".[13] At the same time, the protection of moral rights was extended to cover performers in respect of their musical performances or, more precisely, "live aural performances or performances fixed in phonograms" in Article 5 of the WPPT. In June 2012, Article 5 of the Beijing Treaty on Audiovisual Performances further extended moral rights to actors or, more precisely, to performers "as regards [their] live performances or performances fixed in audiovisual fixations".

The differences concerning original ownership, contractual arrangements and applicable law resurfaced soon after the conclusion of the TRIPS Agreement in WIPO's work aimed at improving the protection of actors' rights in respect of their performances on audiovisual fixations. As I will discuss later, a solution was not found until 2011, which allowed the conclusion of the Beijing Treaty in June 2012.

More broadly, as mentioned above, the TRIPS negotiators approached their shared interest in strengthening the international protection of copyright in a pragmatic manner. Certain issues that, to a large extent, arose from the differences between the authors' rights and copyright traditions were, in the end, not specifically addressed in the text of the Agreement but left to the pre-existing public and private international law.

As a result, the final text of the TRIPS Agreement can be considered as being strictly neutral as between the two main legal traditions. In that sense, the negotiators succeeded in reinforcing the protection under both these traditions, and the conceptual starting points under the two traditions remain complementary rather than mutually exclusive. Reflecting this broad approach, a WTO panel in *US – Copyright Act* noted in 2000 that "the Berne Convention and the TRIPS Agreement form the overall framework for multilateral protection", and that "it is a general principle of interpretation to adopt the meaning that reconciles the texts of different treaties and avoids a conflict between them".[14]

As mentioned above, within the civil law tradition, copyright legislation was often seen, *inter alia*, as a tool for cultural policy. Arguably, cultural objectives have always been an element underlying the multilateral copyright law under the Berne Convention. Although the only pre-existing explicit reference to such objectives in the text of the Berne Convention can be found in its Appendix,[15] the preparatory works of the Convention discuss the impact of copyright on cultural activities. It is worth noting that, apart from the Berne Appendix, cultural objectives found their first explicit recognition in the form of treaty text in the 1996 WCT, which recognizes in its Preamble "the need to introduce new international rules and clarify the interpretation of certain existing rules in order to provide adequate solutions to the questions raised by new economic, social, *cultural* and technological developments" (emphasis added). Similar provisions were included in the preambles of the 1996 WPPT and the 2012 Beijing Treaty.

Related rights

One of the major differences between the civil law and common law systems is their approach to the protection of rights neighbouring copyright, in particular the protection of performers, producers of phonograms (or sound recordings) and broadcasting organizations. Finding common ground on how to treat their protection was bound to be a challenging task for the negotiators.

From early on, the United States sought strong protection for sound recordings, including exclusive reproduction and rental rights. Under the US Copyright Act, sound recordings are considered as subject matter of copyright, that is, a category of works of authorship. Under the civil law tradition, producers of phonograms enjoy a separate "neighbouring right", which is on par with similar neighbouring rights of performers and broadcasting organizations. The Nordic countries and the EC, therefore, wished to see all of the three categories of right holders covered by the new agreement.

These three categories of neighbouring rights benefited from international protection under the Rome Convention. The membership of that Convention was, however, mostly limited to countries from the civil law tradition, and amounted, at the time of the negotiations, to only 34 parties (by the end of 1990). Therefore, there was no general agreement at the global level on the merits of protecting these categories through special rights.

This explains why the negotiators chose an approach to the Rome Convention that differs from that to the Berne Convention, as well as to the Paris Convention and the Treaty on Intellectual Property in Respect of Integrated Circuits (IPIC or Washington Treaty). The TRIPS Agreement does not contain any general obligation to comply with the provisions of the Rome Convention, although there are direct references to certain provisions of the Convention that determine, for example, the criteria for eligibility for protection and permissible conditions, limitations and exceptions. The level of protection is, in certain respects, higher but, in some other respects, lower than that under the Rome Convention. The safeguard clause of Article 2.2, however, applies also to related rights. Thus, nothing in the TRIPS Agreement may be interpreted as derogating from the existing obligations that WTO members also parties to the Rome Convention may have to each other under the Rome Convention. Furthermore, the negotiators chose to use a neutral term, "related rights", rather than the term "neighbouring rights" associated with the civil law tradition to refer to these categories.

The United States was successful in securing strong protection for sound recordings, in particular, exclusive reproduction and rental rights for phonogram producers. At Japan's suggestion,[16] the latter, however, became subject to a grandfather clause, allowing its substitution with a system of equitable remuneration under certain circumstances.[17]

As mentioned above, in my view, the TRIPS Agreement can be considered as being strictly neutral as between the two main legal traditions. This is also reflected in the way it addresses the protection of producers of phonograms. It simply defines the kind of protection that has to be available for producers. The obligations can be complied with by granting either copyright or neighbouring rights to them. Even here, the Agreement bridges the two approaches.

The EC, in turn, secured the inclusion of the protection of performers and broadcasting organizations in the Agreement. The final text provides that performers must have the possibility of preventing the unauthorized fixation of their performance on a phonogram and certain other acts. The wording used in the relevant provision, "possibility of preventing the following acts when taken without their authorization", follows that of the Rome Convention. In the latter context, it has been understood to leave freedom of choice to members as to the means used to implement the obligation. These include granting of an exclusive right or law of employment, of unfair competition or criminal law.[18] Although, from the European perspective, the level of protection achieved under these provisions was modest, the provisions established, for the first time, a truly multilateral recognition that performers should benefit from international IP protection.

In respect of broadcasting organizations, the Agreement provides that they shall have the right to prohibit the unauthorized fixation, the reproduction of fixations, and the rebroadcasting by wireless means of broadcasts, as well as the communication to the public of their television broadcasts. To accommodate common law jurisdictions that do not provide special related rights to broadcasting organizations, it was agreed that it is not necessary to grant such rights to broadcasting organizations, if owners of copyright in the subject matter of broadcasts are provided with the possibility of preventing these acts, subject to the provisions of the Berne Convention. While these provisions are also flexible, and take into account the differences between the two main legal traditions, they bridge the two approaches.

Unlike in other areas of IPRs covered by the Agreement, the minimum level of protection provided to related rights was set at a relatively modest level. This was due to the lack of broader agreement about the need for special related rights. The provisions, therefore, left substantial differences in the level of protection granted under the laws of different countries. The Nordic countries were concerned that major differences in the level of protection, coupled with full national and most-favoured-nation (MFN) treatment, would make it politically difficult to further develop the protection of neighbouring rights; the resulting imbalances might even risk the maintenance of the current levels of protection in those countries where such rights were very advanced. The EC shared this concern.

It was noted that Article 2.2 of the Rome Convention already had a narrower formulation of the national treatment of neighbouring rights. Together with the other conditions of the Rome Convention, this would also be applicable under the draft TRIPS provisions. The Nordic countries and the EC, however, wished to clarify the legal situation. This was not objected to by other delegations, although some questioned whether it was necessary. Eventually, agreement was reached to clarify the national and MFN treatment clauses of the TRIPS Agreement by excluding from their coverage those rights of performers, producers of phonograms and broadcasters that were not provided under the TRIPS Agreement.

After the circulation of the Dunkel Draft, there were some attempts to reopen the scope of non-discrimination rules concerning related rights and, to some extent, copyright. But, as mentioned above, in the end, no further changes were made to the copyright section between the 1991 Draft Final Act and the 1993 Final Act. In subsequent treaties on related rights, the national treatment obligations were formulated in a similar manner, namely, in Article 4(1) of the 1996 WPPT and Article 4(1) of the 2012 Beijing Treaty.

As it turned out, the inclusion of the related rights in the TRIPS Agreement provided impetus for the further development of international protection of related rights, leading to the adoption of the WPPT in December 1996. Building on the provisions of the TRIPS Agreement, the WPPT provides enhanced protection for the rights of performers and producers of sound recordings. Among important improvements was that, under the WPPT, performers were provided an "exclusive right of authorizing" certain acts in regard to their performances, rather than the mere "possibility of preventing" those acts.

The WPPT did not cover the rights of performers in audiovisual fixations of their performances. While many delegations were in favour of extending the application of its provisions to actors' rights in relation to films and other audiovisual productions, some others were not yet willing to go that far. The WIPO Diplomatic Conference of December 1996 adopted a resolution calling for further work. Questions relating to initial ownership, contractual arrangements and applicable law resurfaced in this work. This led to the Diplomatic Conference of December 2000 that reached a provisional agreement on 19 of 20 substantive articles. The two leading film producers from common law jurisdictions, India and the United States, favoured strong copyright protection for their film industries but wished to ensure that the contractual relationships between their producers and actors would be internationally recognized. While in favour of improving actors' protection, European governments and performers resented the prospect of the new rights provided under the Treaty to actors being in practice enjoyed by producers.

The remaining provision on the transfer of rights was finally settled by the WIPO Standing Committee on Copyright and Related Rights at its June 2011 meeting. It, *inter alia*, allows a contracting party to provide in its national law that, once a performer has consented to fixation of his or her performance in an audiovisual fixation, the exclusive rights are owned or exercised by or transferred to the producer; independent of such transfer of exclusive rights, national laws or individual, collective or other agreements may provide the performer with the right to receive royalties or equitable remuneration for any use of the performance.[19] This compromise took into account the different rules and practices that countries applied at that time. It enabled the adoption of the Beijing Treaty in June 2012.

Contrary to the TRIPS Agreement and the Rome Convention, the WPPT does not cover the protection of broadcasting organizations. In response to a request by the Philippines, which had been concerned about the earlier exclusion of the rights of broadcasting organizations from the mandate for the preparatory work of the WPPT, an international forum was held in April 1997 in the Philippines, where these rights were discussed. The issue was put on the agenda of the newly formed WIPO Standing Committee on Copyright and Related Rights in November 1999; it is continuing its discussions on a potential treaty that would update the international norms relating to the rights of broadcasting organizations in the light of technological developments.

Computer programs and layout-designs of integrated circuits

In the 1970s, the international community was faced with two new types of information technology products that seemed to need IP protection: computer software and layout-designs of integrated circuits. There are many similarities between the two: both are functional products that involve incremental technological innovation and direct the operation of a machine. They are constructed by using either text or three-dimensional designs, which could be conceived as protectable works falling under the notion of a "production in the literary, scientific and artistic domain".[20]

In both cases, discussions at WIPO and in other international fora initially focused on new *sui generis* forms of protection, although copyright and patent protection were also explored. The approaches, however, gradually diverged as copyright became the preferred form of protection for computer software while *sui generis* laws were applied to layout-designs. This had important implications on certain aspects of the substantive protection of these two categories, in particular, the term of protection. Developments at the domestic level, particularly in the United States, influenced the direction of the multilateral work.

This evolution of international IP law, including the previous and, to some extent, parallel work done at WIPO, became the point of departure for how these issues were addressed and eventually resolved in the TRIPS negotiations.

During that period, the protection of computer programs and layout-designs of integrated circuits also came up in the Nordic cooperation to revise Nordic copyright laws. Following the broader international developments, both issues were initially taken up in the context of this cooperation in the area of copyright, but the *sui generis* approach was soon selected for layout-designs.

Computer programs

Work at WIPO on computer software initially started under the auspices of the Paris Union for the Protection of Industrial Property. This work resulted in 1978 Model Provisions on the Protection of Computer Software,[21] prepared by the International Bureau of WIPO with the assistance of experts. The Model Provisions followed a *sui generis* approach, although they built on copyright concepts. They provided for a term of protection of 20 years from the first use or sale, but not more than 25 years from the creation.

In the further work, the focus gradually shifted towards the copyright approach in the protection of computer software. The then Assistant Director-General of WIPO, Mihály Ficsor, identifies the critical shift in thinking as occurring in the mid-1980s, explaining that the 1985 meeting of the Group of Experts on the Copyright Aspects of the Protection of Computer Software, jointly convened by WIPO and the United Nations Educational, Scientific and Cultural Organization (UNESCO), "produced a breakthrough towards the general recognition of computer programs as works to be protected under the Berne Convention (and the UCC)".[22]

In the meantime, there was an ongoing trend towards the copyright approach at the domestic level. A working document prepared for the aforementioned meeting showed that five countries had already explicitly covered computer programs under their domestic copyright laws (in chronological order, the Philippines, the United States, Hungary, Australia and India) and, in some other countries, this had resulted from court decisions.[23] A number of other countries soon followed suit.

The prime motivation of the proponents of this approach appeared to be that, if computer programs were to be considered as works, they would automatically benefit from the international protection already available under the pre-existing conventions. Or, as two leading scholars of international copyright law, Sam Ricketson and Jane Ginsburg, have put it, "copyright protection provided a ready pigeon-hole into which software could be slotted with a minimum of trouble".[24]

By the late 1980s, the most contentious remaining issue at WIPO was less whether computer programs should be protected under copyright than whether they should be considered as literary works. The main implication was that their recognition specifically as "literary" works would mean that the general term of 50 years *post mortem auctoris* (after an author's death) would become applicable, excluding the 25-year term from the making applicable to works of applied art.[25] For example, the summary record of a 1989 meeting of a WIPO Committee of Experts indicates that some delegations argued that "the 50-year term of protection after the authors' [sic] death is unrealistic". The proponents responded that "[t]he alleged problem of the long term of protection is of an academic nature; there are a number of other categories of literary and artistic works which may become obsolete within a much shorter period than 50 years after the authors'[sic] death which should be considered nothing else but an upper limit".[26]

In the TRIPS negotiations, the United States sought from the outset the protection of computer programs as literary works.[27] The EC initially took the view that "the term of protection of computer programs shall in no event be shorter than the minimum term provided for in the Berne Convention for certain categories of works, i.e. 25 years from the date of creation".[28] Later on, its position shifted to support the view that computer programs should be protected as literary works.[29] This was also the approach favoured by the Nordic countries. Many developing countries advocated for a shorter term of protection, such as 25 years from the creation. The text submitted by 14 developing countries suggested leaving "the nature, scope and term of protection to be granted to such works" to domestic law.[30]

Eventually, agreement was reached on the present Article 10.1, which provides that computer programs, whether in source or object code, shall be protected as literary works under the Berne Convention (1971). This agreement was subsequently reconfirmed in Article 4 of the 1996 WCT.

During the negotiations, Japan proposed to clarify the scope of protection by specifically excluding programming languages and algorithms used for making such works.[31] It was, however, recognized that this already would follow from the idea/expression dichotomy that was understood to apply to all categories of works under the Berne Convention.[32] It was, therefore, agreed to include this as a general principle in Article 9.2, which confirms that copyright protection shall extend to expressions and not to ideas, procedures, methods of operation or mathematical concepts as such. A similar wording was subsequently included in Article 2 of the 1996 WCT.

Layout-designs of integrated circuits

As mentioned earlier, the international work on the protection of layout-designs of integrated circuits steadily moved towards a *sui generis* solution. This was influenced by the domestic developments in the United States and Japan, the two leading producers at that time.

After initially considering protecting layout-designs (or "mask works") by incorporating them into copyright law,[33] in 1984, the US Congress passed a Semiconductor Chip Protection Act opting for a *sui generis* approach. Protection was made available to foreign right holders on the basis of reciprocity. Japan passed an Act Concerning the Circuit Layout of a Semiconductor Integrated Circuit in 1985, which also adopted a *sui generis* approach. In 1986, the EC adopted a Directive on the Legal Protection of Topographies of Semiconductor Products based on a similar approach.

These domestic developments gave impetus to the development of multilateral norms at WIPO. It set up an expert committee to consider a possible treaty in respect of integrated circuits. In response to a question raised at its first meeting in 1985 concerning the relationship between the draft treaty and the pre-existing copyright conventions, the then WIPO Director-General Árpád Bogsch observed that "[i]t is believed that neither the Berne Convention nor the Universal Copyright Convention requires a State party to it to consider layout-designs of integrated circuits as works, in the sense that that word is used in copyright law, and to protect them as works under their copyright legislation or under the Berne Convention or the Universal Copyright Convention".[34] Later on, he elaborated his view on both the Berne Convention and the Paris Convention by stating that "if the [domestic] regulation is made in a *sui generis* law, such law needs to be compatible *only* with the proposed Treaty", but if such regulation treated layout-designs as works or subject matter of industrial property, they also needed to comply with the Berne and/or Paris Conventions, including the 50 years term of protection after the death of the author.[35]

This work eventually led to the convening of a Diplomatic Conference for the adoption of the IPIC Treaty in Washington in May 1989. After three weeks of negotiations, it failed to reach agreement on a number of remaining differences, among which were the term of protection, lack of compensation in case of innocent infringement, and compulsory licensing. It adopted the IPIC Treaty only after a vote, with 48 votes in favour and five abstentions. The two biggest producers of integrated circuits, Japan and the United States, voted against. Together, they represented around 85 per cent of the global production. Some of the other industrialized countries had voted in favour to show their support for multilateralism, but remained uncomfortable with the contents of the treaty. As a result, they refrained from signing it. In the end, only eight countries signed it.[36] Since only three countries have ratified it, the Treaty has not entered into force.

The extensive work on this highly technical matter that had gone into the negotiations of the IPIC Treaty was not wasted, however. The substantive content of the Treaty was revived as part of the TRIPS negotiations. Developing countries that had actively participated at the Washington Diplomatic Conference and in its preparations did not have difficulties in taking that Treaty as the basis for TRIPS negotiations. Japan and the United States, in turn, sought to address the issues they saw as deficiencies in the level of protection it provided. They were eventually successful in reaching agreement on texts that addressed their concerns. As a result, the TRIPS Agreement is based on an IPIC-plus approach, incorporating most of the substantive provisions of that Treaty, while including some additional obligations on the aforementioned matters.

Endnotes

1 Helpful comments received from Jukka Liedes, Adrian Otten and Jayashree Watal are gratefully acknowledged.

2 For a description of this broader context, see Sam Ricketson and Jane C. Ginsburg, *International copyright and neighbouring rights: The Berne Convention and beyond*, second edition (Oxford: Oxford University Press, 2006).

3 Denmark, as a member of the European Communities (EC), did not participate in this coordination. During the same period, it actively participated in the Nordic cooperation aimed at updating the Nordic countries' copyright laws.

4 Communication by the Nordic countries circulated as GATT document MTN.GNG/NG11/W/29, Negotiating Group on Trade-Related Aspects of Intellectual Property Rights, including Trade in Counterfeit Goods – Communication by the Nordic Countries, 20 October 1988, para. 4.

5 See Article 11 of the TRIPS Agreement, second sentence.

6 The WCT and WPPT were adopted on 20 December 1996, and entered into force on 6 March 2002 and 20 May 2002, respectively.

7 The "solemn declaration" adopted by the Assembly of the Berne Union on 9 September 1986, as reproduced in *Copyright* 11 (1986): 373.

8 A. Henry Olsson, "Copyright in the national economy", *Copyright* 4 (1982): 130-133.

9 Finnish Copyright Society, *A study of the economic importance of copyright-related industries in Finland*, October 1988.

10 Jukka Liedes, "A study of the economic importance of copyright-related industries in Finland" in Association Littéraire et Artistique Internationale, "The economic importance of copyright: Issues involving the distribution of exemplars of copyright-protected works", *Journées d'Étude* (Munich, 6-7 October 1988): 44.

11 During this period, the EC had started its work of harmonizing the copyright laws of its member states, which also involved reconciling the continental authors' rights system with the British common law system. Familiarity with the two systems enabled the EC to take the lead in suggesting solutions concerning enforcement of IPRs that would be compatible with both systems.

12 GATT document MTN/TNC/W/FA, Uruguay Round – Trade Negotiations Committee – Draft Final Act Embodying the Results of the Uruguay Round of Multilateral Trade Negotiations, 20 December 1991.

13 WIPO documents CRNR/DC/3-5, Basic Proposals for the Administrative etc. Clauses (drafted by the International Bureau), and for the Substantive Provisions of Treaty I and II (drafted by the Chairman), note 1.05.

14 *US – Copyright Act, WT/DS160/R*, para. 6.66.

15 Article I(1) of the Appendix to the Berne Convention refers to the "economic situation and [...] social and *cultural* needs" (emphasis added) of a developing country wishing to avail itself of the flexibilities under the Appendix.

16 GATT document MTN.GNG/NG11/W/74, Negotiating Group on Trade-Related Aspects of Intellectual Property Rights, including Trade in Counterfeit Goods – Main Elements of a Legal Text for Trips – Communication from Japan, 15 May 1990, Section I, para. 2(2).

17 Article 14.4 of the TRIPS Agreement, second sentence.

18 *Guide to the Rome Convention and to the Phonograms Convention* (Geneva: World Intellectual Property Organization, 1981), 34-35.

19 It was subsequently included as Article 12 in the Beijing Treaty.

20 Article 2(1) of the Berne Convention.

21 *Copyright* 1 (1978): 6-19.

22 Mihály Ficsor, *The law of copyright and the Internet: The 1996 WIPO treaties, their interpretation and implementation* (Oxford: Oxford University Press, 2002), 7. "UCC" refers to the Universal Copyright Convention of 1952.

23 Document UNESCO/WIPO/GE/CCS/2, Legal protection for Computer Programs: A Survey and Analysis of National Legislation and Case Law; A study by Michael S. Keplinger.

24 Ricketson and Ginsburg, supra note 2, p. 493.

25 Article 7(4) of the Berne Convention.

26 Summary record of the discussion, see WIPO document CE/MPC/I/3, Committee of Experts on Model Provisions for Legislation in the Field of Copyright, First Session, Geneva, February 20 to March 3 1989 – Report adopted by the Committee, 3 March 1989, paras. 83 and 85, respectively.

27 GATT document MTN.GNG/NG11/W/14/Rev.1, Negotiating Group on Trade-Related Aspects of Intellectual Property Rights, including Trade in Counterfeit Goods – Suggestion by the United States for Achieving the Negotiating Objective – Revision, 17 October 1988, Section III, para. C.2.

28 GATT document MTN.GNG/NG11/W/26, Negotiating Group on Trade-Related Aspects of Intellectual Property Rights, including Trade in Counterfeit Goods – Guidelines and Objectives Proposed by the European Community for the Negotiations on Trade Related Aspects of Substantive Standards of Intellectual Property Rights, 7 July 1988, Section 3, para .c.3.

29 GATT document MTN.GNG/NG11/W/68, Negotiating Group on Trade-Related Aspects of Intellectual Property Rights, Including Trade in Counterfeit Goods – Draft Agreement on Trade-Related Aspects of Intellectual Property Rights, 29 March 1990, Part II, Article 2.

30 GATT document MTN.GNG/NG11/W/71, Negotiating Group on Trade-Related Aspects of Intellectual Property Rights, including Trade in Counterfeit Goods - Communication from Argentina, Brazil, Chile, China, Colombia, Cuba, Egypt, India, Nigeria, Peru, Tanzania and Uruguay. 14 May 1990, Chapter IV, Article 11.

31 GATT document MTN.GNG/NG11/W/74, Section I, para. 1(3)(ii).

32 See, for example, *Guide to the Berne Convention for the Protection of Literary and Artistic Works (Paris Act, 1971)* (Geneva: World Intellectual Property Organization, 1978), 12.

33 See Robert W. Kastenmeier and Michael J. Remington, "The Semiconductor Chip Protection Act of 1984: A swamp or firm ground?", *Minnesota Law Review*, 1985, 70: 417.

34 WIPO document IPIC/CE/II/3, Committee of Experts on Intellectual Property in respect of Integrated Circuits, Second Session, 23-27 June 1986 – The Draft Treaty and the Copyright Conventions; Memorandum of the Director General, 27 March 1986, para. 4.

35 WIPO document IPIC//CE/IV/2, Committee of Experts on Intellectual Property in respect of Integrated Circuits, Fourth Session, 7-22 November 1988 – Draft Treaty with Explanatory Notes – Document presented by the Director General, 1 September 1988, para. 30.

36 Ghana, Liberia, Yugoslavia, Zambia, Guatemala, Egypt, China and India.

18

Copyright: An Indian perspective

Jagdish Sagar

My unexpected participation in the TRIPS negotiations, as my country's sole negotiator on copyright, remains one of the unforgettable experiences of a 38-year civil service career. I shall try to put this across to the reader as I remember it, which means no specific dates; I shall also avoid names since I remember fewer of them than I do faces.

In India, the upper echelons of the civil service are notoriously "generalist". Thus, in the late 1980s and early 1990s, after extremely varied experience in other fields, and in vastly different parts of India, I found myself in the Ministry of Human Resources Development, Department of Education, in charge of the Book Promotion Division.

The Book Promotion Division was responsible for copyright – an arrangement that already reflected an antiquated notion of what copyright is about. And I was the only senior person anywhere in the Government of India who was expected to know the law of copyright; the Registrar and Deputy Registrars of Copyright – middle-ranking officers – were, like me, birds of passage. WIPO exposed me to some training and I learned much from interactions with the leading copyright industry associations in publishing, music and software. It was fascinating, but I did not expect that what I was learning would be of any great practical importance, to me or anyone else, in the foreseeable future. The Book Promotion Division was a backwater – but would not be so for long.

Now, before I proceed with my own experience of the TRIPS negotiations, some background is necessary. The Uruguay Round of multilateral trade negotiations had been much in the news. The media, and public opinion as expressed by some very vocal persons, supported the Indian Government's position that IP had no place in multilateral trade agreements. That was, of course, a battle already lost. Nevertheless, most of the people one met seemed firmly of the view that IP was an imposition of the developed countries to keep us down: we needed free access to information to catch up with them.[1] One sometimes heard such concerns voiced quite emotively in terms of national sovereignty.

India had always been subject to the Berne Convention for the Protection of Literary and Artistic Works under the "colonial clause" and the (British) Government of India had acceded to the 1928 Rome Act of the Convention as a contracting party. This had continued without remark, and a body of judicial interpretation had been built up over the years[2] when the Joint Parliamentary Committee, convened to study the Copyright Bill, 1956, recommended that the term of copyright be reduced from 50 (the Berne minimum) to 25 years. Fortunately, the government overruled this idea and pushed through a Berne-compliant version of the Bill, which became the Copyright Act, 1957.

But the mindset that the parliamentary committee gave expression to has never gone away. India was in the forefront of those countries which, refusing to accede to the 1967 Stockholm Act of the Berne Convention, compelled the adoption of the 1971 Paris Act adding an Appendix to the Convention to allow developing countries to issue compulsory licences in certain cases. This was supposed to be necessary for our educational system, but India did not bother to amend its own law to provide for such compulsory licences until 1984; thereafter, it never even issued a single compulsory licence to avail itself of this hard-won right and, in the late 1990s, actually allowed this special right that we enjoyed to lapse by failing to renew its ten-year declaration under Article I of the Appendix. Few noticed, nobody complained. Here again was a very clear case of our ideological position having no relationship at all with any actual national interest; not for the last time.

In my area of copyright law, there was (and is) a real issue about our place in the world. With our productivity in film, music, software (already coming up in those days) and even print media, we have a strong interest, vocally expressed by the stakeholders involved, in strong copyright protection. We had (and still have) the world's largest film industry, which is closely tied to a very large music industry; our software industry held out great promise at the time, which has since been realized. Whatever the politics of our relationship with other developing countries in regard to other and broader issues, we did not then, and certainly do not now, have common interests with many of them in the sphere of copyright. At the same time, there is an influential section of opinion in India which, on the strength of ideological prejudices (though these are widely prevalent and have very little to do with any overtly political considerations), favours a much more relaxed copyright regime.

To return to the story, one day I received a telephone call from someone in the Commerce Ministry telling me I was required for the TRIPS negotiations in Geneva. Eventually, I would make over a dozen trips to Geneva, honing my very limited skills in the French language, getting very familiar with the geography of that town and (on a couple of days when copyright was not on the agenda) sneaking out of Geneva for a few excursions. Normally, for a civil servant to be deputed abroad, there is a certain amount of processing and approval-taking, but now the Commerce Ministry handled all that, bought my tickets, booked my hotel room and paid me my per diem. I retained the diplomatic passport that was issued on a short-term basis for such purposes and I would quite often find myself at the airport at a day's notice.

Looking back, the sequence of events is impossible to recover but the memories are vivid. This was unlike most international conferences that I had attended: it was more businesslike, with not much in the way of carefully worded speeches read from prepared texts; rather, it was much more face-to-face, in both seating and style. We were a proud Indian team of two: I handled copyright and neighbouring rights and Jayashree Watal (who consequently did much more of the talking and spent more time in Geneva) handled almost everything else. We both knew enough of our areas to be sufficiently confident, and were not really daunted by the size of some of the delegations, but it was no advantage to face much larger teams, particularly from the developed countries – there were never fewer than half a dozen Americans in the room at any given time.

The first time round, true to our general brief on the TRIPS negotiations at the time, I was non-committal about the main innovations that were on the table, which would require us to amend our copyright law. These were the introduction of rental rights for films, software and sound recordings, and performers' rights. By the next session, and from then on, I felt confident enough to take an independent line in consultation with the Indian stakeholders concerned. Of course, I did not do so without in-house approval where amendments to our law might be necessitated, but I found such approval to be readily forthcoming.

I cannot, at this remove in time, recount the negotiations sequentially, but will do so by topic, and will carry the story forward to subsequent outcomes.

Computer programs

By the time of the TRIPS negotiations, we had a burgeoning software industry. We had no issues about protecting computer programs as literary works, which had already been done by amendment of our Act in 1984, though the definition of a computer program was (if adequate) not really satisfactory; nor do I remember much controversy about this internationally, though, at the time, a few countries did contemplate having *sui generis* protection for computer programs. To comply with the treaty as it was taking shape, we would also have to further expand the definition of literary works to include electronic databases, but that posed no problem for our government. It does, however, bear mention that this protection in India remains strictly limited to copyright protection as specified in Article 10(2) of the TRIPS Agreement, that is, to the extent that the database constitutes an intellectual creation by virtue of the selection or arrangement of its contents. Nor does copyright subsist in data *per se*, which Article 10(2) seems to envisage as a possibility. To this date, there is no database right, as in the European Union, even distantly on the horizon. (It is another matter that the courts have sometimes applied copyright in databases quite liberally.)

Rental rights

The whole concept of rental rights was novel in India and, for want of understanding, I was conservative and non-committal about it the first time the topic was discussed. However, on my coming home and interacting with our film, music and software industries, its importance became obvious. Those were the days of videocassettes for audiovisual works and, besides, in India, audiocassettes were the most common form of recorded music on the market – in the early 1990s, compact discs (CDs) were more expensive and the repertoire available on them was limited, and vinyl was disappearing. Videocassettes and audiocassettes were much easier to reproduce than anything known hitherto, and seemed very liberating to those (and there were many) who did not set much store by the law of copyright.

There were many rental shops for videocassettes and small "video parlours" were not rare: these were mini-theatres, sometimes, but not always, clandestine, where the contents of videocassettes were projected onto screens, giving a small audience an actual (and infringing) theatrical experience. The film industry, which still depended mainly on theatrical exhibition, was getting hurt. Video parlours were, of course, obviously infringing, but public opinion was not particularly friendly to copyright and the police had other priorities. However, it was the much larger business of hiring out videocassettes that posed the most serious problem: it was changing the way of consuming film, keeping audiences away from the cinema theatres, and the film industry was getting nothing out of this new mode of distribution. The film industry was helpless, not only because of the scale of the problem but, more fundamentally, because of lacunae in copyright laws that had been enacted for a different era. In India, the hiring out of a copy of a videocassette was not *per se* an infringing act: to establish infringement it was necessary to establish both that the copy being rented out was an infringing copy, and that the person who produced the copy had no authorization to do so. The industry itself could be faulted for not anticipating this situation by making video available at reasonable prices before the problem had assumed such serious proportions, but now, clearly, something had to be done.

The idea of rental rights, when put to representatives of the film industry – who, in those days, unlike now, were not very IP-savvy – was welcomed. It was as novel to them as it had been to me. The music industry in India, then, as now, was rather sophisticated about how it went about protecting its rights: it had the advantage of much greater international exposure, since the larger Indian record labels had traditionally been subsidiaries of multinationals. They knew about rental rights and, of course, supported them. The same was true of the software business which, though homegrown, served international markets and understood IP.

For us, the only real sticking point in the negotiations on rental rights was the United States' insistence on exempting itself from the obligation to introduce rental rights in its own law, on the grounds that it needed rental rights abroad (where infringement was rife) but not at home (where the American delegation said it was not). This was called the "impairment test". The American delegation explained to us that, if they were to introduce rental rights at home, it would upset the comfortable relationship that already existed in their country between the video rental business and the film industry; hence, they felt they could impose on the rest of the world what they felt they did not need themselves. This was a grossly unequal provision but, after discussion with the Commerce Ministry, we accepted that we needed rental rights in our own country anyway. Therefore, and because the Government of India had to choose its battles, we decided, reluctantly, to go along with it. Now, over two decades later, we do hear complaints of Indian films being widely pirated in the United States: that, certainly, is "impairment".

Following the TRIPS Agreement, in India we enacted provisions on rental rights that were actually TRIPS-plus. Because of the difficulty of defining "commercial" (which can mean different things in different contexts in our judicial precedents), we improved on the requirements of the TRIPS Agreement by dropping that qualifier and conferring exclusive rental rights. Further, we included sale or offer for sale of a copy in the exclusive rights of the copyright owner – in effect, abolishing the exhaustion rule for these classes of work.

This has since been modified; the word "commercial" has been inserted, and "commercial rental" does not include rental, lease or lending for non-profit purposes by non-profit libraries or non-profit educational institutions.

Performers' rights

Performers' rights serendipitously offered a solution to a peculiarly Indian problem. South Asia is possibly the only civilization with a classical music that is as sophisticated as that of the West – indeed, unlike in South-East Asian countries, for example, there are few takers for Western classical music in India. But our classical music does not fit the traditional copyright paradigm, in which the work is distinct from the performance. In India, the classical musician is both a composer and a performer: he or she improvises, within a strict and difficult discipline that it takes a lifetime to acquire, on any one of a range of traditional, well-identified themes. Every performance is a composition, a once-and-for-all creation that gives a distinct identity to every recorded performance by the same maestro. However, our law at the time defined a musical work in terms of notation, in blind adherence to the language of the earlier law enacted during the British Raj. This was actually an irrelevant, alien concept for our music. In 1977, the Supreme Court, in passing, suggested that the government should consider giving performers a right, but the government did not respond, I believe for want of understanding. India never acceded to the 1961 International Convention for the Protection of Performers, Producers of Phonograms and Broadcasting Organizations (Rome Convention), but now the new compulsion to amend our Act to introduce performers' rights was put to good use. We not only introduced performers' rights into our Act, but simultaneously amended the definition of a "musical work" to drop the requirement of notation. As a result, the Indian classical musician now has, so to speak, two strings to his or her bow: a performance, once fixed, is now protected both as a performance and as a musical work.

The neighbouring rights of phonogram producers posed no problem: like other common law countries, we already protected phonograms as copyrighted works, and our protection of phonograms was already TRIPS-plus. The rights of broadcasting organizations, again, were no problem. Nor did any of the other innovations, including the extension of the three-step test to all rights, pose any problem for us.

The first thing to do, once the TRIPS Agreement was signed, was to push through the necessary amendments to the Copyright Act. This proved surprisingly easy – our Minister, the late Arjun Singh, was a literate and cultivated person who had no difficulty understanding the questions involved and, once he had been briefed, actively pushed the process. This turned into an exercise to review the whole Act, and we ended up modifying about a quarter of the text, not only to meet the requirements of the TRIPS Agreement but to address numerous other issues. We updated the provisions on collective administration, strengthened criminal remedies for infringement, updated a number of definitions, completely revamped the section spelling out exclusive rights and updated the provisions on limitations and exceptions.

But the most important thing that we did in the amendments was to introduce a right of making available the copyrighted work, as a form of communication to the public – in this, we were way ahead of much of the world. It seems odd, looking back, that the Internet never figured in the TRIPS negotiations: at least, I do not remember any mention of it and the treaty itself took no account of it. But, soon after the TRIPS Agreement, 1995 was being called the "year of the Internet". India has yet to accede to the WIPO Copyright Treaty (WCT) and WIPO Performances and Phonogram Treaty (WPPT) but, with just this one TRIPS-plus amendment in place, our courts have been able to enforce copyright on the Internet. In recent years, courts have: ordered Internet service providers to block infringing websites; ordered them to block any uploading of the plaintiff's copyrighted works, and, for the purpose, required them to block infringing web addresses – in effect, a "John Doe" order; and restrained social networking sites from allowing the plaintiff's content to be uploaded.

I was able to see our Bill to amend the Copyright Act introduced in Parliament and into the committee stage. Then, as my term in the Ministry of Human Resources Development ended, I moved on to other, very different work. But, until I retired in February 2004, the Ministry kept me on one committee after another and I found myself returning to its conference rooms from wherever I was and whatever I was doing. I was involved in developing our position during the negotiations leading up to the 1996 Diplomatic Conference on Certain Copyright and Neighboring Rights Questions, which accepted the WCT and WPPT, and in the formulation of draft legislation to comply with the requirements of these two treaties.

It is a matter of regret, I feel, that legislation to make our law compliant with the WCT and WPPT was not introduced until 2010 and not enacted until 2012, and that India has still to accede to either of these treaties. Nor do I believe our amended legislation is wholly compliant, particularly in regard to technological measures. The main focus of the amendments was not on the WCT and WPPT but, rather, more on provisions intended to help authors in the entertainment business – itself a laudable object – which, unfortunately, were so drafted as to create confusion and ambiguity: professionally, I am currently involved in constitutional challenges to some of these amendments. The old populism has come back and there seems currently to be much more enthusiasm for the treaties on limitations and exceptions. The 2013 Marrakesh Treaty to Facilitate Access to Published Works for Persons Who Are Blind, Visually Impaired, or Otherwise Print Disabled was, of course, laudable, but the Indian position on educational and library exceptions seems weighted too far against the rights of copyright owners, to the point, arguably, of not appearing to be TRIPS compliant in regard particularly to the three-step test: at times, I have felt that there is insufficient appreciation of the fact that the TRIPS Agreement imposes inescapable obligations which cannot be derogated from in any possible WIPO treaty. One longs for the more pragmatic and businesslike approach that I believe India managed to retain during the general negotiations that culminated in the establishment of the WTO, not least those leading to the TRIPS Agreement.

There is, for me personally, a happy epilogue. I acquired the reputation of a person who knew a thing or two about copyright, with the result that I am able, over a decade after I retired, to be rewardingly and gainfully employed as a practising copyright lawyer. The TRIPS negotiations did that for me.

Endnotes

1 Trademarks did not particularly figure in this kind of discussion. My own remarks here apply mainly to copyright; the issues regarding patents were different and are dealt with by Jayashree Watal (chapter 16).

2 India is, of course, a common law jurisdiction, and its statutory law on copyright has much in common with that of other Commonwealth countries.

19

Dispute settlement in TRIPS: A two-edged sword

Adrian Macey

In the Uruguay Round of multilateral trade negotiations under the GATT, the negotiations on the TRIPS Agreement were not alone in making a slow start. IPRs were a radically new subject matter for the GATT. There was both uncertainty as to just what could be considered trade-related aspects of IPRs, and disagreement over the appropriateness of trying to incorporate them into a negotiation about goods. The constructive ambiguity of the mandate – necessary to achieve consensus at Punta del Este – led to strong disagreement over what did or did not fall within it. This disagreement continued throughout most of the negotiations, and was only attenuated towards the end.

It was the first indent of the mandate, the clarification of GATT provisions and the elaboration "as appropriate" of new rules and disciplines, that was problematic. There was no major challenge to the relevance of the GATT to the second indent covering international trade in counterfeit goods. This was, after all, clearly about goods crossing borders, and could be seen as building on work already conducted within the organization.

The major concerns held by developing countries – clearly not the *demandeurs* in this negotiation – were twofold: first, that it was inappropriate to use the GATT to set IP standards, since they were the prerogative of other bodies, notably WIPO;[1] second (and related to the first), the fear that trade sanctions under the GATT dispute settlement mechanism could be used, in effect, to enforce IP standards. The latter was not a hypothetical fear. The US Section 301 action against Brazil took place early in the TRIPS negotiations, and only served to heighten the concerns:

> Brazil informed the Group that on 20 October 1988 unilateral restrictions had been applied by the United States to Brazilian

exports as a retaliatory action in connection with an intellectual property issue. This type of action seriously inhibited Brazilian participation in the work of the Group, since no country could be expected to participate in negotiations while experiencing pressures on the substance of its position. The action of the United States Government was a blatant infringement of GATT rules and was thus contrary to the standstill commitment of the Declaration of Punta del Este. The United States action was an attempt to coerce Brazil to change its intellectual property legislation. However, Brazil's legislation was fully consistent with the relevant intellectual property conventions. Furthermore, it represented an attempt by the United States to improve its negotiating position in the Uruguay Round, specifically in this Group.[2]

Not long afterwards, others finding themselves on the watch lists of the US Special Section 301 also expressed their concern in the TRIPS Negotiating Group:

A number of participants stated their deep concern about certain decisions taken by the United States under Section 301 of its Tariff Act, in particular the listing under "special" Section 301 relating to IPRs of countries on a "priority watch list". These decisions were jeopardising the work of the Negotiating Group and threatened to wreck the Uruguay Round as a whole.[3]

The possibility of institutionalizing such action, through what became known as "cross-retaliation" or, alternatively, "cross-compensation",[4] under a TRIPS agreement, was simply unacceptable to many countries.[5] The United States had drawn attention to this possibility in an early submission to the TRIPS Negotiating Group.[6] A typical reaction was as follows:

Concerning the provision in the dispute settlement part of the US paper for retaliation to include the possibility of withdrawal of equivalent GATT concessions, some participants said that such a linkage would be unacceptable. It was also asked what would be the incentive to a country to join such an agreement if it thereby put at risk its GATT benefits in a way that would not occur if it stayed out.[7]

The rationale given by the United States was:

> (…) the possibility of retaliation taking the form of withdrawal of
> GATT benefits had been included because experience of trade
> disputes had shown that limiting the ways of restoring the
> appropriate balance of concessions in cases of non-compliance
> made more difficult the satisfactory resolution of disputes.[8]

In other words, the United States wanted to ensure that there was full scope for
the type of measures already provided for under Section 301.

Cross-retaliation became equally important to the other major proponent of the
TRIPS negotiations, the European Communities (EC). Coming several years after
the US proposal, the following rationale given by the EC for its proposal[9] shows
the extent of the common ground on this point:

> [T]he achievement of this objective would be dependant[sic] on the
> establishment of an effective dispute settlement mechanism (…) It
> was therefore necessary to provide for the possibility of meaningful
> sanctions in cases where other measures had proved insufficient
> to solve a dispute. The Community proposal therefore suggested
> that, in conformity with Article XXIII of the General Agreement,
> such sanctions could include the possible suspension by a
> contracting party of the application of any concession or other
> obligation under the GATT, as determined to be appropriate by the
> Contracting Parties.[10]

So, from the developing countries' point of view, the two parties most likely to
pursue dispute settlement action against them were both advocating the ability to
use trade sanctions for IPR breaches.

There was no reference to dispute settlement in the Punta del Este Ministerial
Declaration that established the TRIPS mandate. But, as a result of the April 1989
mid-term review, the importance of dispute settlement to a TRIPS outcome was
acknowledged by a new agenda item in the Negotiating Group's work, namely,
"the provision of effective and expeditious procedures for the multilateral
prevention and settlement of disputes between governments, including the
applicability of GATT procedures".[11] This enabled greater momentum on the topic,
and a more in-depth exploration of the issues. At the same time, there was some
important reassurance given in response to the concerns about unilateral
measures:

Ministers emphasise the importance of reducing tensions in this area by reaching strengthened commitments to resolve disputes on trade-related intellectual property issues through multilateral procedures.[12]

The New Zealand/Colombia/Uruguay proposal

Since the mid-term review then determined that IPRs would be the subject of substantive negotiations within the GATT, it became even more important to resolve the differences over dispute settlement. An informal initiative was taken by New Zealand and Colombia, later supported by Uruguay, to try to deal with some of the issues at a conceptual level. It was hoped that this might make dispute settlement less of an impediment to advancement of the negotiations. The rejection out of hand of cross-retaliation, an idea that was of key importance to the principal proponents of a TRIPS agreement, would have created a distraction from the rest of the increasingly complex subject matter of the negotiations. So it was felt worth floating some ideas that could bridge the differences and perhaps take some heat out of the discussion. At the time, I was New Zealand's negotiator for dispute settlement, and we wanted to see whether it was possible, while still allowing for cross-retaliation, to make it a less threatening prospect, and hence a less divisive topic at this point in the negotiations. I could also make use of my knowledge of this negotiation to try to advance the subject within TRIPS negotiations more generally.

There were difficulties in that it was not known what shape the GATT dispute settlement provisions would take, or what institutional structure would apply under the TRIPS Agreement. The idea of a TRIPS council (rather than the default assumption of a committee) came much later. Any ideas in the proposal could thus not be over prescriptive and had to be flexible enough to cover a range of dispute settlement and institutional outcomes.

To this end, rather than come up with yet another detailed proposal, we decided to produce a flow chart of how a dispute settlement process might work, with a minimum of textual description. We wanted something that was relatively simple and, in any case, easily understandable. So it did not attempt to reflect the full dispute settlement procedure. Further, it was not presented as a formal proposal since its aim was more to facilitate progress and compromise in the negotiations than to be a complete template (see figure 2).

Figure 2: New Zealand/Columbia/Uruguay proposal for TRIPS dispute settlement

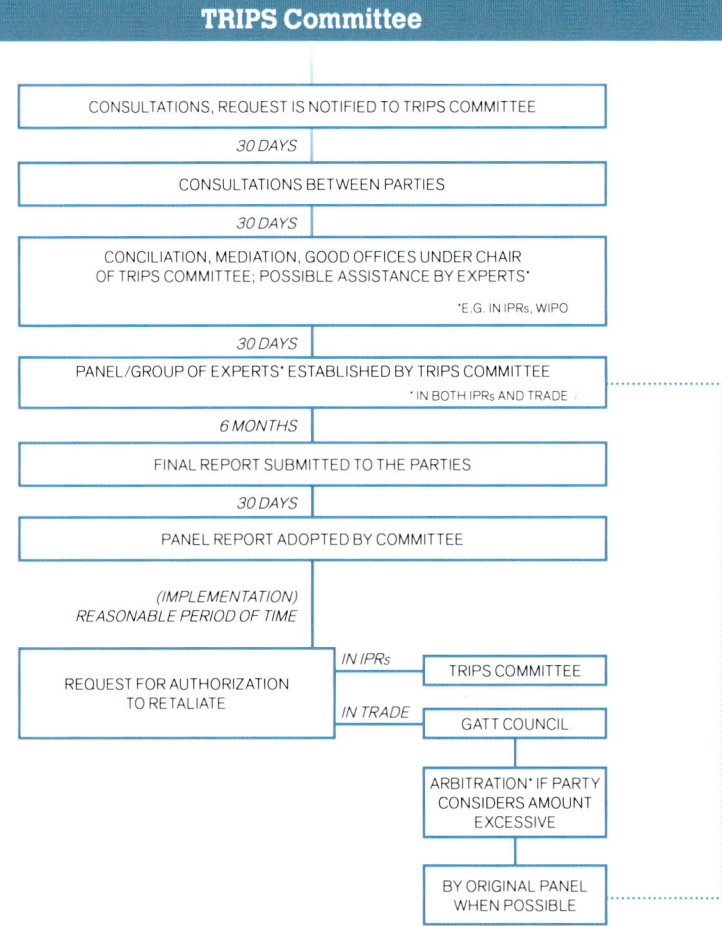

TRIPS Committee

CONSULTATIONS, REQUEST IS NOTIFIED TO TRIPS COMMITTEE

30 DAYS

CONSULTATIONS BETWEEN PARTIES

30 DAYS

CONCILIATION, MEDIATION, GOOD OFFICES UNDER CHAIR OF TRIPS COMMITTEE; POSSIBLE ASSISTANCE BY EXPERTS*

*E.G. IN IPRs, WIPO

30 DAYS

PANEL/GROUP OF EXPERTS* ESTABLISHED BY TRIPS COMMITTEE

* IN BOTH IPRs AND TRADE

6 MONTHS

FINAL REPORT SUBMITTED TO THE PARTIES

30 DAYS

PANEL REPORT ADOPTED BY COMMITTEE

(IMPLEMENTATION)
REASONABLE PERIOD OF TIME

REQUEST FOR AUTHORIZATION TO RETALIATE

IN IPRs — TRIPS COMMITTEE

IN TRADE — GATT COUNCIL

ARBITRATION* IF PARTY CONSIDERS AMOUNT EXCESSIVE

BY ORIGINAL PANEL WHEN POSSIBLE

Notes

1. The only assumption made about the final form of a TRIPS Agreement is the establishment of a TRIPS Committee.

2. The suggested procedures are intended to be compatible with the procedures being negotiated in the Dispute Settlement Negotiating Group.

3. The time limits are approximate, and for illustrative purposes only.

4. The diagram is a simplified representation of dispute settlement procedures. Not all intermediate steps are shown, nor are such new suggestions as a review stage for panel reports or an appellate review mechanism.

5. Final decisions on dispute settlement for TRIPS will be dependent on:
   - the final legal form of the TRIPS Agreement.
   - decisions on dispute settlement taken at TNC [Trade Negotiations Committee] level.

It was not easy to disseminate this chart. In the pre-information technology age of the late 1980s, we were restricted to what now seem primitive means. We could not simply reach for a software program and construct the chart electronically. So it was done rather laboriously on large sheets of paper with hand-drawn boxes and lines. The sheets had to be taped together end on end to show the full chart. After the chart's first airing, the Secretariat helped us out by tidying up our initial efforts in order to make it more presentable.

The key principles of a possible TRIPS dispute settlement mechanism put forward in the proposal were:

- A consultation and panel process that would follow, as far as possible, standard GATT procedures and timetables

- Use of both IPR and trade experts on panels

- A possibility of recourse to retaliation in IPRs

- A higher bar to retaliation in goods, with a requirement to seek authorization from a higher body – the General Council

- A safeguard against potential excessive cross-retaliation via an arbitration process.

We suggested that these ideas could be adapted to work under a range of possible Uruguay Round dispute settlement outcomes. The only institutional assumption we made was the establishment of a TRIPS committee.

The most important signal was that there would be no direct route to cross-retaliation. Not only would it have a higher threshold by needing to go the General Council rather than the TRIPS committee, but there would also be a built-in safeguard through recourse to arbitration.

The initiative did succeed in sparking off a constructive discussion in the Negotiating Group. Some other participants suggested amendments. Later in the negotiation, more ideas emerged. These became quite complicated – for example, a Chilean proposal described as a two- or possibly three-stage process, involving WIPO at the first stage.[13]

On the most sensitive point of cross-retaliation, the possibility of retaliation in the other direction, from goods to IP, was hardly touched on in the early stages of the negotiations. The discussions were dominated by the fear of developing countries of coming under pressure from developed countries. After the mid-term review, there was some further discussion on the basis of the texts annexed to the draft TRIPS agreement. A view was expressed that, if cross-retaliation from TRIPS to trade were to be allowed, logically, the reverse should also apply, allowing TRIPS benefits to be withdrawn if there were a failure to implement market access obligations under the GATT.[14] There was some discussion among developing countries, in the margins of the negotiations, about their potential use of cross-retaliation.[15] But this never made it to the floor of the Negotiating Group. The extent that retaliation in IPRs could be an effective weapon for developing countries was not fully or widely realized at the time, either by the proponents of cross-retaliation or by the developing countries themselves.

Influence of the New Zealand/Colombia/Uruguay ideas

The ideas embodied in the chart found their way into the text forwarded to the 1990 Brussels ministerial meeting, and were the basis for most of the discussion. This finally put some of the ideas in the chart into a textual form, as option 1, which provided for application *mutatis mutandis* of GATT dispute settlement procedures. On the question of retaliation, the distinction between retaliation "in kind" and cross-retaliation, with a higher threshold for the latter, was maintained. The safeguard of arbitration was also included:

> If a PARTY fails to implement the recommendations and rulings of the Committee within the reasonable period of time, the complaining PARTY may:
>
> – request the Committee for authorisation to suspend obligations under this Agreement; or
>
> – request the GATT Council for authorisation to suspend concessions or other obligations under the General Agreement on Tariffs and Trade. If the PARTY that would be subject to such measures objects to the level of suspension proposed, the matter shall be referred to arbitration. Such arbitration shall where possible be carried out by the original panel. The arbitration body shall determine whether the amount of trade covered is appropriate in the circumstances.[16]

The Chair recognized that the extent to which it was possible to carry forward these discussions and settle differences had been limited by the linkage with institutional arrangements, whose outcome could only be known at the end of the negotiations, and the lack of clarity on the future dispute settlement mechanism.

In the final period of the negotiations, the institutional arrangements, notably, the three councils (on goods, services and IP) and the dispute settlement system, became clearer. This evolution made some of the discussion in the TRIPS negotiations redundant. Some of the concerns could be accommodated through these discussions. Some of the more complex proposals involving other organizations were able to be put aside, and the result is the integrated arrangements under the Dispute Settlement Understanding (DSU).

Key ideas in the proposal can be seen in the current dispute settlement procedures, which allow for retaliation across the three domains of goods, services and IP. The requirement of Article 22.3 that retaliation should first be sought in the area of the complaint retains the concept of the higher threshold. The recourse to arbitration is also retained in Article 22.6, and has been used. Compared with its initial discussion in TRIPS, cross-retaliation has thus been both broadened and simplified.

While not specifically related to cross-retaliation, another level of safeguard or reassurance about dispute settlement action under the TRIPS Agreement was given by the moratorium on non-violation and situational disputes.[17] This is a troublesome enough area when applied to goods concessions and is likely to be even more uncertain in its application to IP. Indeed, 20 years later, the parties had still not managed to agree on the scope and modalities for these types of disputes under the TRIPS Agreement.[18]

Cross-retaliation and intellectual property under the WTO in practice

Cross-retaliation now has a sound legal footing in the DSU, and actual experience with it is building up. Indeed, it has come to be primarily a weapon for developing countries for whom withdrawal of goods concessions risks not only being ineffective but also causing harm at home, for example, through increased prices.

The first three cases featuring authorization of cross-retaliation between IP and other domains have involved as complainants one large and two small developing countries. Antigua and Barbuda, Brazil and Ecuador have been authorized to suspend concessions under the TRIPS Agreement on cases as diverse as online gambling, cotton and bananas, respectively.[19] In the Brazilian case, it is notable that the concept of a threshold was applied. As a large developing economy, Brazil had some capacity for leverage in goods; retaliation under the TRIPS Agreement was thus only authorized after a threshold value of retaliation in goods had been reached. The DSU thus maintains the concept of the New Zealand/Colombia/ Uruguay proposal that retaliation should first be sought in the area of the violation. The arbitrators' report on the Ecuador case[20] has deepened the understanding of the role of cross-retaliation; it contains the fullest and most coherent exposition yet of the rationale for cross-retaliation under the TRIPS Agreement.

Conclusion

Cross-retaliation has thus proved to be a two-edged sword. There is no evidence from the negotiations that the original proponents of cross-retaliation saw the extent that it could become a weapon that could be used by the weak against the strong. As Brazil commented on the arbitration decision on its case:

> The present award contributes to strengthen the WTO dispute settlement mechanism, demonstrating that the system is capable of recognising the evident asymmetries between developed and developing countries.[21]

The DSU provisions not only compensate for such asymmetries but also allow more effective targeting of countermeasures through the greater choice available to the complaining party. This allows more scope for measures to be applied where pressure will be most effective in the jurisdiction of the WTO member that has failed to implement rulings of a panel or the Appellate Body.

From a more theoretical point of view, this history of cross-retaliation in the WTO is an illustration of the role that some informal creative thinking can play in negotiations. Such initiatives were frequent in the Uruguay Round, and often depended on the relationships and trust formed among Geneva-resident negotiators. It is questionable whether individual negotiators in subsequent years have had as much freedom to act as did those in the Uruguay Round, given both the greater dominance of capital-based officials and the emergence of various groupings of countries as WTO membership has expanded.

Endnotes

1   The following comment is typical: "It was not the task of the Group or of the GATT to create an international system for the production [sic – presumably 'protection'] of intellectual property parallel to that existing in WIPO and elsewhere. If countries considered the international protection under that system inadequate, they had full opportunities to raise the matter in the appropriate fora." GATT document MTN.GNG/NG11/8, Negotiating Group on Trade-Related Aspects of Intellectual Property Rights, including Trade in Counterfeit Goods – Meeting of 5-8 July 1988 - Note by the Secretariat, 29 August 1988, para. 30.

2   GATT document MTN.GNG/NG11/10, Negotiating Group on Trade-Related Aspects of Intellectual Property Rights, Including Trade in Counterfeit Goods – Meeting of 17-21 October 1988 – Note by the Secretariat, 30 November 1988, para. 27.

3   GATT document MTN.GNG/NG11/13, Negotiating Group on Trade-Related Aspects of Intellectual Property Rights, Including Trade in Counterfeit Goods – Meeting of 3-4 July 1989 – Note by the Secretariat, 16 August 1989, para. 4.

4   The Chair considered the latter term more accurate, but it did not supplant the first one. GATT document MTN.GNG/TRIPS/2, Uruguay Round – Group of Negotiations on Goods (GATT) – Negotiating Group on Trade-related Aspects of Intellectual Property Rights Including Trade in Counterfeit Goods – Meeting of Negotiating Group of 16 and 20 September 1991 – Note by the Secretariat, 7 October 1991, para. 8.

5   See, for example, GATT document MTN.GNG/NG11/4, Negotiating Group on Trade-Related Aspects of Intellectual Property Rights, Including Trade in Counterfeit Goods – Meeting of 28 October 1987 – Note by the Secretariat, 17 November 1987, para. 20.

6   GATT document MTN.GNG/NG11/W/14, Negotiating Group on Trade-Related Aspects of Intellectual Property Rights, including Trade in Counterfeit Goods – Suggestion by the United States for Achieving the Negotiating Objective, 20 October 1987.

7   GATT document MTN.GNG/NG11/4, Negotiating Group on Trade-Related Aspects of Intellectual Property Rights, Including Trade in Counterfeit Goods - Meeting of 28 October 1987 – Note by the Secretariat, para. 20.

8   Ibid.

9   GATT document MTN.GNG/NG11/W/49, Negotiating Group on Trade-Related Aspects of Intellectual Property Rights, including Trade in Counterfeit Goods – Trade-Related Aspects of Intellectual Property Rights – Submission from the European Communities, 14 November 1989, section B.d.

10 GATT document MTN.GNG/NG11/17, Negotiating Group on Trade-Related Aspects of Intellectual Property Rights, Including Trade in Counterfeit Goods – Meeting of 11, 12 and 14 December 1989 – Note by the Secretariat, 23 January 1990.

11 GATT document MTN.TNC/11, Uruguay Round – Trade Negotiations Committee – Mid-Term Meeting – [Held in Montreal on 5-9 December 1988 and in Geneva on 5-8 April 1989], 21 April 1989.

12 Ibid.

13 GATT document MTN.GNG/NG11/W/61, Negotiating Group on Trade-Related Aspects of Intellectual Property Rights, including Trade in Counterfeit Goods – Communication from Chile, 22 January 1990.

14 GATT document MTN.GNG/NG11/17, para. 11.

15 Personal communication, Adrian Otten.

16 GATT document MTN.TNC/W/35/Rev.1, Uruguay Round – Trade Negotiations Committee – Draft Final Act Embodying the Results of the Uruguay Round of Multilateral Trade Negotiations – Revision, 3 December 1990, page 230.

17 Article 64 para. 2 of the TRIPS Agreement.

18 See Article 64 para. 3 of the TRIPS Agreement.

19 DS27– European Communities – Regime for the Importation, Sale and Distribution of Bananas; DS267 – United States – Subsidies on Upland Cotton; DS285 – United States – Measures Affecting the Cross-Border Supply of Gambling and Betting Services.

20 WTO document WT/DS27/ARB/ECU, European Communities – Regime for the Importation, Sale and Distribution of Bananas – Recourse to Arbitration by the European Communities under Article 22.6 of the DSU – Decision by the Arbitrators, 24 March 2000.

21 Catherine Saez, "WTO ruling on Brazil-US cotton opens door to cross-retaliation against IP rights", Intellectual Property Watch, www.ip-watch.org/2009/09/07/wto-ruling-on-brazil-cotton-opens-door-to-cross-retaliation-against-ip-rights/ (last accessed 11 April 2015).

Appendices

Keynote speech at the TRIPS Symposium, 26 February 2015

Lars Anell

I would like to thank you very much for inviting me to this Symposium. It is really great to be back in Geneva. I have, indeed, very fond memories of my long stay here and coming back gives me the great pleasure to meet dear, old friends.

It is a bit intimidating to appear as a keynote speaker. According to the dictionary, one is supposed to "set the underlying tone, summarize the core message, and arouse unity and enthusiasm" among you – well, we will see about that. What I will do is to share with you some recollections about what happened here some 25 years ago – because it was 25 years ago that we actually negotiated the TRIPS Agreement – and some reflections on where we are today, and that will be from my vantage point as Chair of the Swedish Research Council.

I think I was drafted as Chair of the Negotiating Group by default. I was asked whether I would be ready to chair one of the many negotiating groups and I thought that was part of the job description of a Permanent Representative in Geneva, so I said "Yes". And, when asked about my particular preferences, I gave the same answer as Marlon Brando did in a classic movie, *The Wild One*, when a nice young woman asked him what he was rebelling against: "What have you got?" Not much, it turned out. Well, it was not much at the beginning, but it turned out to be quite a lot at the end of the [Uruguay] Round.

It had to be a slow start and a steep learning curve. It was a new subject, very few experts on intellectual property (IP), if any, were posted in Geneva, and many delegations could not rely on high-level expertise in their capitals. Negotiations revealed, quite brutally, the extent to which GATT, as it was then, was run by the members, called contracting parties. That all draft proposals for the Agreement came from participating countries was as it had to be, but there was also a tremendous reluctance to allow the Secretariat, and me as Chair, to produce factual information, and to ask WIPO to provide fact sheets was completely out of the question. The most important task in the beginning was to establish a basis for our negotiations. Several contracting parties submitted more or less complete text for a TRIPS agreement and these documents did not have even the ordering of subjects in common. Real negotiations were all but impossible. The obvious solution was, of course, to ask the Secretariat to put together a composite text as a basis. It was very difficult to convince everybody, and, as you know, in those days all decisions had to be unanimous. It took a long time and it was agreed only when I promised that nothing would be discarded. Literally everything that had been put on the table would be part of that composite text.

This composite text, called the Chair's Draft, appeared in June 1990, and the most important effect of that was that it put the negotiations on a solid track. It was, of course, a rather thick document with a lot of redundancy, but all negotiators in the room now referred to the same paragraph on the same page in the same document. Another unforeseen consequence was that we made rapid progress. Quite often, it was easy to see that the alternative texts said almost the same thing. In other words, we had an abundant crop of low-hanging fruits. We did not resolve the key issues, but we began to see what an agreement could and would look like. Why did we succeed? Certainly, David Hartridge and Adrian Otten and the other Secretariat staff did an excellent job, but we were, of course, part of the overall dynamics of the Round. The simple fact is that, without a comprehensive TRIPS Agreement, there would not have been a Uruguay Round as we know it today.

It is no secret that the United States was the main proponent in favour of putting TRIPS on the agenda, supported by countries such as Japan, the Nordic countries, Switzerland, Canada, Australia, New Zealand, Singapore, Malaysia, Uruguay, and Colombia, all keen to start a round for several other reasons. The European Communities (EC) was less enthusiastic and I think that Brussels could have lived without [a TRIPS agreement] when the Round started, but not when it ended. Several EC member states needed TRIPS to compensate for what were regarded as important concessions in other areas. Many other countries were less enthusiastic about TRIPS but realized that they needed to swallow that pill in order to get the rest of the package. The Nordic countries are free-traders, even if some of my friends were and are very keen on agriculture protection. I do not think any of our governments thought twice about the opportunity to launch a new round. However, as an afterthought, the Norwegian Government initiated an investigation of its balance sheet – What is actually in it for us? Where are the net gains for Norway? I was invited to Oslo for a discussion with members of the

Norwegian Government. It turned out that, among the gains that could be identified, design protection took pride of place.

After five or six years of pretty hard work, I allowed myself to feel some satisfaction with what we had accomplished, and in that "we" I include the Secretariat and all members of what was the biggest negotiating group of them all. But my enthusiasm was somewhat moderated by an experience I had in Hamburg. I was invited as a keynote speaker, together with the head of the London Port Authority. I spoke about the possible outcome of the negotiations (the text was more or less finished by then), and my colleague from the London Port Authority talked about activities to fight trade in counterfeit goods, and he showed a list of political priorities based on a survey of opinion in England. Among the 40 topics people had been asked to place in order of precedence, action against trade in counterfeit goods ended up next to last, beating a pay rise for MPs by a slim margin.

Ending this trip down memory lane, let me just say what I have already placed on record, that the Secretariat that I worked with was possibly the most talented and devoted group that I have ever worked with. I enjoyed the whole experience thoroughly, even if it may be too much to say that I enjoyed every minute of it. In particular, I remember one occasion when I had to leave the meeting with the informal group to attend to some other duty in Geneva. As Permanent Representative, I had a number of other obligations. I had agreed with David or Adrian that they should call my place and inform my family if, and when, the informal meeting would continue the day after. My then-11-year-old daughter took the call and placed a note on my desk saying "the infernal meeting will continue". I am certain that David or Adrian did not say that, but it was a rare exception to what was, on the whole, a stimulating experience, perhaps for all of us. I think I remember that Jayashree Watal once told me it was indeed hard work, but also a lot of fun. Since I see Thomas Cottier here, I cannot help mentioning something I noted down very late one night. We were all very tired, and Thomas maybe a little bit more than the rest of us. When he was reminded by someone sitting next to him that he had the floor, he woke up and said "Oh, it's me speaking, then I'd better say something" – but I do not remember whether he said much more than that.

Before turning my attention to the future, let us remind ourselves about how particular the situation was when we negotiated the TRIPS Agreement in 1991 and 1992. Some few years before that, Tim Berners-Lee had presented his idea for the World Wide Web at CERN [the European Organization for Nuclear Research], some 10 kilometres from here. All the components were at hand, but he was the genius who put it together and, towards the end of 1989, he implemented the first successful communication between a hypertext transfer protocol client and a server – the beginning of it all. Was anyone aware of the revolutionary implications? I was also Sweden's representative to CERN and, for personal reasons, I kept in touch with the Swedish researchers coming to CERN to conduct experiments, and also with a few Swedes who were employed by CERN. I remember very well that the aim of one of the most important projects conducted at CERN was, and I quote, "to recreate the situation that prevailed one millisecond after the Big Bang" – the idea was to create the situation existing *before* all the basic laws of physics were established. This I remember very vividly, but I cannot remember that I ever heard them talk about the web or the Internet. Another development, also with huge implications for IP, was that patent law in the United States had recently been extended to cover software. The US Supreme Court had ruled in 1972 that abstract software algorithms could not be protected, but, 10 years later, a special Court of Appeal was created to hear all appeals in patent cases. I do not know to what extent we were aware of these developments and their implications for IP protection.

The basic proposition is still valid – in order to encourage private investors to spend money to develop new products and processes, the state is willing to protect them from competition for a certain period of time. The key challenge is still to strike a balance. How much protection is too much protection? Another key issue is what we shall require in order for something to be an innovation – how big must a step be in order to be an innovative step?

The TRIPS Agreement was a massive increase in IP protection globally, and it was primarily driven by corporate interest. The business community will continue to push but there will be, and should be, countervailing forces. There are good reasons to believe that too generous protection will stifle research, unduly restrict competition and increase transaction costs. There is an emerging consensus in the international research community that research financed with public money should be made available without costs to all other scientists – to the general public, in fact. The objective is that research results should be made available immediately, which is called Open Access Gold. Today, many institutions accept a delay of six to 12 months. This approach has been adopted by many of the major research councils in Europe and North America – the National Institutes of Health (NIH), British research councils, Max-Planck-Gesellschaft, European Union, my own organization and Wellcome Trust – we are among many others in the driver's seat. It has the support of a large part of the research community. The reason for open access is simple – it will promote the advancement of science. All scientific endeavour builds upon what others have done in the past: "I see further because I stand on the shoulders of giants" is a saying that has been attributed to Bernard of Chartres as well as to Isaac Newton and a couple of others. Scientific journals are today so expensive that they are difficult to obtain, even for researchers at European universities; thus, open access will not only speed up the transmission of new knowledge but make it available to a much larger community. The issue is far from uncontested in the academic community. A number of decisions regarding allocation of funding are at present based on citations in peer-reviewed high-impact journals that do not allow articles to be made available on the Internet.

Many scientists see a risk if this system is replaced too quickly. An even thornier issue is the demand that, also, databases should be made available to the whole research community. It is easy to see the advantage, but one has to ask oneself about what happens to the incentives to invest time and effort to put together a new database. Even if there is no open conflict with the protection of copyright, I think it is important to note the general philosophy behind this approach – what is paid with public money should stay in the public domain. I might add that publishers of prestigious scientific journals seem to be far more lucrative than "Big Pharma".

By the way – is the pharmaceutical industry profitable? Yes and no – many pharmaceutical companies are highly profitable and what is sometimes called Big Pharma is doing well. At the same time, according to the CEO of Genentech, Arthur Levinson, biotech is – and I quote him – "one of the biggest money-losing industries in the history of mankind, having lost since 1976 and until 2008 a staggering amount of US$ 3,100 billion". We could discuss at length the cost of new drugs – I will mention a few pertinent points only. It is, of course, not a new issue – we have had the discussion about the cost of treating AIDS victims in Africa and what could have been the consequences of the anthrax scare in the United States. Today, we already have drugs on the market that cost more than US$ 100,000 per course of treatment. Even in not-so-poor countries, some drugs are not prescribed because of the cost – the reason given is often that the effect is not good enough, or even dubious. But it is more than probable that we will soon have a number of drugs that are more effective, and a lot more expensive. The pharmaceuticals industry is already in the era of biologics and produces drugs that consist of giant molecules, hundreds of times the size of a conventional drug molecule. True or not, I cannot tell, but representatives of the industry claim that those new drugs have one great advantage: they do only what we want them to do and nothing else – there are no or few side-effects. Some biologic drugs will use viruses to deliver gene therapy, the replacement of a faulty gene. We are coming close to designer drugs. The total cost effect is difficult to predict, and I will refrain from guessing.

The most important point I wish to make concerns patents on human genes. If this were to happen, in a way that actually restricts research and the possibility to make new discoveries, it would be very serious indeed. I think the best way to illustrate my point is to relate a story that many of you may be familiar with. It concerns the two human genes, BRCA1 and BRCA2, which significantly increase women's risk of developing breast and ovarian cancer. It started in 1990 when a geneticist at Berkeley announced that her laboratory had located BRCA1 on chromosome no.17. After that, it was just simply a matter of time – who would be the first to isolate the gene? Supported by venture capital, funds and collaborators from the NIH, the race was won by a respected scientist and entrepreneur at the University of Utah. His team was also able to locate and isolate BRCA2. They formed a company and applied for patents in 1994 and 1995. The US Patent and Trademark Office awarded a total of seven patents on the two genes, various fragments of them and the diagnostic tests to find them. Some 10 years later, some organizations filed a lawsuit in an effort to overturn the decision of the patent office. The plaintiffs argued that it was wrong to award a patent on a product made by nature and claimed that the patents granted prevented others from using the genes in cancer research, diagnostics and treatment. I will not review all the arguments made in different courtrooms by several judges. However, I must note that I found it alarming that a judge considered that patents should be granted in order to satisfy the "settled expectations" of the pharmaceuticals industry. It ended up in the Supreme Court which, in a unanimous decision, struck down the patent on the two genes held by the Utah-based biotech company. In its decision, the Supreme Court stressed the need for an inventive step and argued that patent law should not inhibit further discovery or impede innovation more than it would tend to promote it.

Diffuse and vague-sounding patents are a main reason for the emergence of so-called "patent trolls", which are companies that exist only to buy and litigate patents. They thrive particularly in software territory. In 2011, some 5,000 firms in the United States paid US$ 30 billion to the trolls and their lawyers. It is a major issue for some start-ups that cannot afford to defend themselves. One infamous case is a patent for "an information-manufacturing machine" at "a point of sale location". To me, that sounds like anything happening anywhere, and that was also the interpretation of the troll that bought the patent to sue more than 100 companies.

Finally, let me very briefly mention William Baumol's theory of competition – since it is based on the existence of patent consortia. It is presented in his book *The Free Market Innovation Machine*, one of the few – maybe the only – academic texts on economic theory that can be read and recognized by a CEO of a major company. If you think about the textbook treatment of what is called perfect competition, you realize that it is characterized by an absence of competition and of profits. None of the companies producing a homogenous product in a perfect market can by definition earn more than what is needed to survive. Baumol's point of departure is that, for competition to be productive, it must be between companies that have the resources to invest in new processes and products, in research and product development. His ideal is the oligopolistic market – a few, big, high-tech companies in relentless pursuit of new ideas, products and cost-saving processes. But this is a dangerous game for the companies. If someone made a truly game-changing innovation and patented it, survival itself would be at stake for all the others. In order to eliminate this risk, and, I suppose, reduce the cost of litigation, companies pool their patented knowledge and these consortia, according to Baumol, tend to be stable because it is very risky to strike out on your own. There is not an abundance of empirical evidence in the book but it is an intriguing theory.

Revisiting the text we agreed upon, reflecting on what has happened since and thinking about the future – which, as an American Congressman observed, has no lobbyists – I must admit that I have some concerns. First and foremost, I am convinced that it would be very serious if protection of IP were to stifle and prevent research. In a sense it would be self-defeating. There would be less genuine progress to protect. My other concern is more general. I think both politicians and the business community should consider the obvious need to demand a clear, visible, inventive step in order to award 20 years' protection from competition.

Thank you very much for your attention. I look forward to the Symposium. I will pick up where I left off in 1994 and expect to learn a lot.

Negotiating Group on Trade-Related Aspects of Intellectual Property Rights, including Trade in Counterfeit Goods: Status of Work in the Negotiating Group, Chairman's Report to the GNG

MTN.GNG/NG11/W/76
23 July 1990

Annexed to this note is a draft text which is intended to provide a profile of the current state of work in the Negotiating Group and of the options for the possible results of the negotiations. The text is produced on the Chairman's responsibility in the hope that it will assist the further work of the Group and does not commit any participant. It is essentially a compilation of the options for legal commitments as they have emerged from a process of informal consultations. In this sense it is intended as a basis for further negotiation.

The two basic approaches to the negotiations on TRIPS are identified in the text by the letters A and B. These approaches differ not only in substance but also in structure. In broad terms approach A envisages a single TRIPS agreement, encompassing all the areas of negotiation and dealing with all seven categories of intellectual property on which proposals have been made; this agreement would be implemented as an integral part of the General Agreement. Approach B provides for two parts, one on trade in counterfeit and pirated goods (reflected in Part IX of the attached text) and the other on standards and principles concerning the availability, scope and use of intellectual property rights (reflected in Parts I-VIII). Under this approach, the latter part would cover the same categories of intellectual property as approach A, with the exception of the protection of trade secrets, which its proponents do not accept as a category of intellectual property; this part would be implemented in the "relevant international organisation, account being taken of the multidisciplinary and overall aspects of the issues involved".

Options within an approach, A or B, are indicated by the use of square brackets or little "a"s, "b"s etc.

However, it must be emphasised that no point in this text is presented as having been agreed by all participants, even where it appears without an alternative. During the consultations participants said on many occasions that in their view particular provisions should be omitted as being undesirable or unnecessary, and I considered whether these provisions should be identified in the composite text as being subject to objection. I decided against doing so, however, on the ground that this would have carried the false implication that provisions not so identified had been agreed, and the stage has not yet been reached in the work where it would be appropriate to imply agreement. Furthermore, it may well be that in the effort to simplify the text points have been omitted to which participants attach importance. I would therefore emphasise that in no way should this text be construed as limiting the scope for participants to raise such points in the further negotiations.

I should like, in communicating this text, to express my appreciation for the very constructive approach of participants to the informal consultations I held. It is inevitable that in a document like this, which aims to be a rendering of the options for legal commitments and not a descriptive record of discussions, it is impossible to reflect adequately the full richness of the contributions made by participants, especially where those contributions took the form of explaining the difficulties in accepting some of the proposals made. I have no doubt that these points will continue to prove valuable in informing the further discussions and negotiations.

One of the issues which will have to be given further consideration in the autumn is the appropriateness of the technique of incorporating commitments by making reference to the provisions of existing international intellectual property conventions.

The Annex to this document reproduces those Parts of a composite draft text that I informally made available earlier to the Negotiating Group that concern preambular provisions and objectives, dispute prevention and settlement, transitional arrangements, institutional arrangements and final provisions. These Parts have not been the subject of detailed consultations, which have focused mainly on the proposals for substantive commitments. I have therefore decided to reproduce these sections of the earlier draft composite text tel quel in order to ensure that this document provides a complete picture of the state of work of the

Negotiating Group. It should be noted that the notation used in the Annex is not identical to that in the body of this paper.

TABLE OF CONTENTS

Part II: General Provisions; Basic Principles

Part III: Standards

1. Copyright and related rights

2. Trademarks

3. Geographical indications, including appellations of origin

4. Industrial designs

5. Patents

6. Lay-out designs of integrated circuits

7. Protection of undisclosed information

8. Remedies for non-fulfilment of obligations

9. Control of abusive or anti-competitive practices in contractual licences

Part IV: Enforcement

Part V: Acquisition of Intellectual Property Rights and Related Inter-Partes Procedures

*

Part IX: Trade in Counterfeit and Pirated Goods.

ANNEX Parts I, VI, VII and VIII of the draft composite text of 12 June 1990

Part I: Preambular Provisions; Objectives

Part VI: Dispute Prevention and Settlement

Part VII: Transitional Arrangements

Part VIII: Institutional Arrangements; Final Provisions

NOTES ON THE COMPOSITE TEXT

1.   The numbering and lettering in the left column have been included to facilitate reference. Related points have been grouped with a common number. Alternative proposals on the same issue have been indicated in the left column by letters: A and B where these alternatives relate to the two broad approaches before the Group, and lower case letters where they relate to alternatives within an approach. Where a number appears without an A or a B, this either indicates a point of common approach or a point where the basic differences in the Group are not those between the A approach and the B approach (this is, for example, the situation for geographical indications, including appellations of origin). As emphasised in the covering note, the absence of an A or a B should not be taken to imply that no participants have difficulty with that point. The same applies with respect to the absence of alternatives signalled by lower case letters or square brackets within an A or a B approach.

2.   "Paris Convention" refers to the Paris Convention for the Protection of Industrial Property. "Paris Convention (1967)" refers to the Stockholm Act of this Convention of 14 July 1967. "Berne Convention" refers to the Berne Convention for the Protection of Literary and Artistic Works. "Berne Convention (1971)" refers to the Paris Act of this Convention of 24 July 1971. "Rome Convention" refers to the International Convention for the Protection of Performers, Producers of Phonograms and Broadcasting Organisations, adopted at Rome, 26 October 1961.

PART II: GENERAL PROVISIONS AND BASIC PRINCIPLES

1.   <u>Scope and Coverage</u>

For the purposes of this agreement, the term "intellectual property" refers to all categories of intellectual property that are the subject of Sections ... to ... of Part III. This definition is without prejudice to whether the protection given to that subject matter takes the form of an intellectual property right.

2.   <u>Beneficiaries Eligible for Treatment Provided for in the Agreement</u>

2.1   Parties shall accord the treatment provided for in this agreement to the nationals of other PARTIES. [In respect of the relevant intellectual property right, the term "nationals" shall be understood as those natural or legal persons meeting the criteria for eligibility for protection under the Paris Convention (1967), the Berne Convention (1971), [the Rome Convention] and the Treaty on Intellectual Property in Respect of Integrated Circuits[1].] [Any PARTY not a party to the Rome Convention and availing itself of the possibilities as provided for in Articles 5.3 or 6.2 of that Convention shall make the notification foreseen in that provision to (the committee administering this agreement).]

2.2A   The term "right holder" means the right holder himself, any other natural or legal persons authorized by him [who are exclusive licensees of the right-holder], or [other authorized] persons, including federations and associations, having legal standing under domestic law to assert such rights.

3.   <u>Freedom to Grant More Extensive Protection</u>

3A   Unless expressly stated otherwise, nothing in Parts III-V of this agreement shall prevent PARTIES from granting more extensive protection to intellectual property rights than that provided in this agreement.

---

1   The relevant provisions would appear to be Articles 2 and 3 of the Paris Convention, Articles 3 and 4 of the Berne Convention, Articles 4, 5 and 6 of the Rome Convention and Article 5(1) of the Treaty on Intellectual Property in Respect of Integrated Circuits.

4. Relation to Obligations under the GATT

4A   Nothing in this agreement shall derogate from existing obligations of PARTIES to each other under the GATT.

5. Intellectual Property Conventions

5A   PARTIES shall comply with the [substantive] provisions [on economic rights] of the Paris Convention (1967), of the Berne Convention (1971) [and of the Rome Convention].

6. National Treatment

6.1   Each PARTY shall accord to the nationals of other PARTIES [treatment no less favourable than] [the same treatment as] that accorded to the PARTY's nationals with regard to the protection of intellectual property, [subject to the exceptions already provided in, respectively,] [without prejudice to the rights and obligations specifically provided in] the Paris Convention [(1967)], the Berne Convention [(1971)], [the Rome Convention] and the Treaty on Intellectual Property in Respect of Integrated Circuits[2]. [Any PARTY not a party to the Rome Convention and availing itself of the possibilities as provided in Article 16(1)(a)(iii) or (iv) or Article 16(1)(b) of that Convention shall make the notification foreseen in that provision to (the committee administering this agreement).]

6.2A   Any exceptions invoked in respect of procedural requirements imposed on beneficiaries of national treatment, including the designation of an address for service or the appointment of an agent within the jurisdiction of a PARTY, shall not have the effect of impairing access to, and equality of opportunity on, the market of such PARTY and shall be limited to what is necessary to secure reasonably efficient administration and security of the law.

6.3A   Where the acquisition of an intellectual property right covered by this agreement is subject to the intellectual property right being granted or registered, PARTIES shall provide granting or registration procedures

2   For the first two and the last of these conventions, the exceptions have been listed by WIPO in document NG11/W/66. For the Rome Convention, the relevant provisions would appear to be Articles 15, 16(1)(a)(iii) and (iv) and (b), and 17.

not constituting any <u>de jure</u> or <u>de facto</u> discrimination in respect of laws, regulations and requirements between nationals of the PARTIES.

6.4A   With respect to the protection of intellectual property, PARTIES shall comply with the provisions of Article III of the General Agreement on Tariffs and Trade, subject to the exceptions provided in that Agreement.[3]

7.   <u>Most-Favoured-Nation Treatment/Non-Discrimination</u>

7.1aA   PARTIES shall ensure that the protection of intellectual property is not carried out in a manner [which would constitute an arbitrary or unjustifiable discrimination between nationals of a PARTY and those of any other country or which would constitute a disguised restriction on international trade] [that has the effect of impairing access to and equality of opportunity on their markets].

7.1b.1 With regard to the protection of intellectual property, any advantage, favour, privilege or immunity granted by a PARTY to the nationals of any other [country] [PARTY] shall be accorded [immediately and unconditionally] to the nationals of all other PARTIES.

7.1b.2 Exempted from this obligation are any advantage, favour, privilege or immunity accorded by a PARTY:

- Deriving from international agreements on judicial assistance and law enforcement of a general nature and not particularly confined to the protection of intellectual property rights.

- Concerning procedures provided under international agreements relating to the acquisition and maintenance of protection for intellectual property in several countries, provided that accession to such agreements is open to all PARTIES.

- Granted in accordance with the provisions of the Berne Convention (1971) [and the Rome Convention] authorising that the treatment accorded be a function not of national treatment but of the treatment accorded in another country.[4]

---

3   This provision would not be necessary if, as proposed by some participants, the results of the negotiations were to be an integral part of the General Agreement on Tariffs and Trade.

4   The relevant provisions would appear to be Articles 2(7), 6(1), 7(8), 14<u>ter</u>(1) and (2), 18 and 30(2)(b) of the Berne Convention and Articles 15 and 16(1)(a)(iv) and (b) of the Rome Convention.

- Deriving from international agreements related to intellectual property law which entered into force prior to the entry into force of this agreement, provided that such agreements do not constitute an arbitrary and unjustifiable discrimination against nationals of other PARTIES and provided that any such exception in respect of another PARTY does not remain in force for longer than [X] years after the coming into force of this agreement between the two PARTIES in question.

- Exceeding the requirements of this agreement and which is provided in an international agreement to which the PARTY belongs, provided that [such agreement is open for accession by all PARTIES to this agreement] [any such PARTY shall be ready to extend such advantage, favour, privilege or immunity, on terms equivalent to those under the agreement, to any other PARTY so requesting and to enter into good faith negotiations to this end.]

7.2A   With respect to the protection of intellectual property, PARTIES shall comply with the provisions of Article I of the General Agreement on Tariffs and Trade, subject to the exceptions provided in that Agreement.[5]

8.   Principles

8B.1   PARTIES recognize that intellectual property rights are granted not only in acknowledgement of the contributions of inventors and creators, but also to assist in the diffusion of technological knowledge and its dissemination to those who could benefit from it in a manner conducive to social and economic welfare and agree that this balance of rights and obligations inherent in all systems of intellectual property rights should be observed.

8B.2   In formulating or amending their national laws and regulations on IPRs, PARTIES have the right to adopt appropriate measures to protect public morality, national security, public health and nutrition, or to promote public interest in sectors of vital importance to their socio-economic and technological development.

---

5   This provision would not be necessary if, as proposed by some participants, the results of the negotiations were to be an integral part of the General Agreement on Tariffs and Trade.

8B.3   PARTIES agree that the protection and enforcement of intellectual property rights should contribute to the promotion of technological innovation and enhance the international transfer of technology to the mutual advantage of producers and users of technological knowledge.

8B.4   Each PARTY will take the measures it deems appropriate with a view to preventing the abuse of intellectual property rights or the resort to practices which unreasonably restrain trade or adversely affect the international transfer of technology. PARTIES undertake to consult each other and to co-operate in this regard.

PART III: STANDARDS CONCERNING THE AVAILABILITY, SCOPE AND USE OF INTELLECTUAL PROPERTY RIGHTS

SECTION 1: COPYRIGHT AND RELATED RIGHTS

1.   Relation to Berne Convention

1A   PARTIES shall grant to authors and their successors in title the [economic] rights provided in the Berne Convention (1971), subject to the provisions set forth below.

1B   PARTIES shall provide to the nationals of other PARTIES the rights which their respective laws do now or may hereafter grant, consistently with the rights specially granted by the Berne Convention.

2.   Protectable Subject Matter

2.1   PARTIES shall provide protection to computer programs [,as literary works for the purposes of point 1 above,] [and to databases]. Such protection shall not extend to ideas, procedures, methods [, algorithms] or systems.

2.2B.1   For the purpose of protecting computer programs, PARTIES shall determine in their national legislation the nature, scope and term of protection to be granted to such works.

2.2B.2   In view of the complex legal and technical issues raised by the protection of computer programs, PARTIES undertake to cooperate with each other to identify a suitable method of protection and to evolve international rules governing such protection.

3.   Rights Conferred

(Right of Importation and Distribution)

3A.1   Economic rights shall include:

3A.1.1   the right to import or authorize the importation into the territory of the PARTY of lawfully made copies of the work as well as the right to prevent the importation into the territory of the PARTY of copies of the work made without the authorization of the right-holder;

3A.1.2   the right to make the first public distribution of the original or each authorized copy of a work by sale, rental, or otherwise except that the first sale of the original or such copy of, at a minimum, acomputer program shall not exhaust the rental or importation right therein.[1]

(Rental Rights)

3A.2.1   [At least in the case of computer programs [,cinematographic works] [and musical works,]] PARTIES shall provide authors and their successors in title the [right to authorise or prohibit the rental of the originals or copies of their copyright works] [or, alternatively,] [the right to obtain an equitable remuneration] [corresponding to the economic value of such a use] [whenever originals or copies are rented or otherwise made available against payment]. [It is understood that granting to authors the right to authorise or prohibit the rental of their works for a certain period of time and to claim an equitable remuneration for the remaining period is sufficient to fulfil this provision.]

3A.2.2   For the purposes of the previous point, rental shall mean the disposal [for a limited period of time] of the possession of the original or copies for [direct profit-making purposes][direct or indirect commercial advantage].

---

1   It is understood that, unless expressly provided to the contrary in this agreement, nothing in this agreement shall limit the freedom of PARTIES to provide that any intellectual property rights conferred in respect of the use, sale, importation and other distribution of goods are exhausted once those goods have been put on the market by or with the consent of the right holder.

3A.2.3 There shall be no obligation to provide for a rental right in respect of works of applied art or architecture.

4.   Protection in Respect of Private Copying

4A   Protected works shall enjoy the same protection in respect of private or personal copying accorded under the domestic law of a PARTY to works of national origin.

5.   Definition of "Public Communication"

5A   With respect to the right to make a public communication of a work (e.g. to perform, display, project, exhibit, broadcast, transmit, or retransmit a work), public communication shall include:

5A.1   communicating a work in a place open to the public or at any place where a substantial number of persons outside of a normal circle of a family and its social acquaintances is gathered; or

5A.2   communicating or transmitting a work, a performance, or a display of a work, in any form, or by means of any device or process to a place specified in point 5A.1 or to the public, regardless of whether the members of the public capable of receiving such communications can receive them in the same place or separate places and at the same time or at different times.

6.   Transfers of Rights

6A   Protected rights shall be freely and separately exploitable and transferable. [Assignees and exclusive licensees shall enjoy all rights of their assignors and licensors acquired through voluntary agreements, and shall be entitled to enjoy, exercise and enforce their acquired exclusive rights [in their own names.]]

7.   Term of Protection

7A.1   The term of protection of a work whose author is a legal entity shall be no less than 50 years from the end of the year of authorised publication, or, failing such authorised publication within 50 years from the making of the work, 50 years from the end of the year of making.

7A.2   The term of protection of computer programs shall be no less than 50 years after the end of the year of creation.

8. Limitations, Exemptions and Compulsory Licensing

8A.1 In respect of the rights provided for at point 3, the limitations and exemptions, including compulsory licensing, recognised under the Berne Convention (1971) shall also apply mutatis mutandis. [Limitations made to the rights in favour of private use shall not apply to computer software.] [PARTIES may also provide for other limited exceptions to rights in respect of computer programs, consistent with the special nature of these works.]

8A.2 PARTIES shall confine any limitations or exemptions to exclusive rights (including any limitations or exceptions that restrict such rights to "public" activity) to clearly and carefully defined special cases which do not impair an actual or potential market for or the value of a protected work.

8A.3 Translation and reproduction licensing systems permitted in the Appendix to the Berne Convention (1971):

8A.3.1 shall not be established where legitimate local needs are being met by voluntary actions of copyright owners or could be met by such action but for intervening factors outside the copyright owner's control; and

8A.3.2 shall provide an effective opportunity for the copyright owner to be heard prior to the grant of any such licences.

8A.4 Any compulsory licence (or any restriction of exclusive rights to a right of remuneration) shall provide mechanisms to ensure prompt payment and remittance of royalties at a level consistent with what would be negotiated on a voluntary basis.

8B (See Sections 8 and 9 below.)

9. Protection of Works Existing at Time of Entry into Force

9A A PARTY shall provide protection, consistent with this agreement, for all works not yet in the public domain in its territory at the time of entry into force of this agreement. In addition, a PARTY that has afforded no effective copyright protection to works or any class of works of other PARTIES prior to its entry into force in its territory shall provide protection, consistent with this agreement, for all works of other PARTIES that are not in the public domain in their country of origin at the time of entry into force of this agreement in its territory.

10.   Relation to Rome Convention

10A   PARTIES shall, as minimum substantive standards for the protection of performers, broadcasting organisations and producers of phonograms, provide protection consistent with the substantive provisions of the Rome Convention. [Articles 1 to 20 of the Rome Convention could be considered to constitute the substantive provisions.]

11.   Rights of Producers of Phonograms (Sound Recordings)

11A.1   PARTIES shall extend to producers of phonograms the right to authorise or prohibit the direct or indirect reproduction of their phonograms [by any means or process, in whole or in part].

11A.2a   [In regard to the rental of phonograms,] the provisions of point 3 in respect of computer programs shall apply _mutatis mutandis_ in respect of producers of phonograms [or performers or both].

11A.2b   The protection provided to producers of phonograms shall include the right to prevent all third parties not having their consent from putting on the market, from selling, or from otherwise distributing copies of such phonograms.

11A.3   The provisions of point 4A shall apply _mutatis mutandis_ to the producers of phonograms.

12.   Rights of Performers

12A   The protection provided for performers shall include the possibility of preventing:

12A.1   the broadcasting [by any technical means or process such as by radio wave, by cable or by other devices] [by wireless means and the communication to the public of their live performance];

12A.2   the fixation of their unfixed performance [on phonograms or data carriers and from reproducing such fixations];

12A.3   the reproduction of a fixation of their performance;

12A.4   the production of their performance in any place other than that of the performance;

12A.5 the offering to the public, selling, or otherwise distributing copies of the fixation containing the performance.

13. Rights of Broadcasting Organisations

13.1 Broadcasting organisations shall have the possibility of preventing:

13A.1 the fixation of their broadcasts [on phonograms or data carriers, and from reproducing such fixations];

13A.2 the reproduction of fixations;

13A.3 the communication to the public of their [television] broadcasts;

13A.4 the rebroadcasting by wireless means of their broadcasts;

13A.5 the retransmitting of their broadcast;

13A.6 the putting on the market, sale, or other distribution of copies of the broadcast.

14. Public Communication of Phonograms

14A If a phonogram published for commercial purposes, or a reproduction of such a phonogram, is used directly for broadcasting or for any communication to the public, a single equitable remuneration shall be paid by the user to the performers, or to the producers of the phonogram, or to both.

15. Term of Protection

15A.1a The term of protection granted to producers of phonograms, performers and broadcasting organisations shall last at least until the end of a period of [20][50] years computed from the end of the year in which the fixation was made or the performance or broadcast took place.

15A.2a PARTIES may, however, provide for a period of protection of less than 50 years provided that the period of protection lasts at least for 25 years and that they otherwise assume a substantially equivalent protection against piracy for an equivalent period.

15Ab Point 7 shall apply mutatis mutandis to the producers of phonograms.

16.   Exceptions

16Aa   PARTIES may, in relation to the rights conferred by points 11, 12, 13 and 14, provide for limitations, exceptions and reservations to the extent permitted by the Rome Convention.

16Ab   Points 8A.2-4 of this Part shall apply mutatis mutandis to phonograms.

16B   (See Section 8 of this Part.)

17.   Acquisition of Rights

17A.1   The provisions of points 6 and 9 of this Part shall apply mutatis mutandis to the producers of phonograms.

17A.2   PARTIES shall protect phonograms first fixed or published in the territory of another PARTY, including phonograms published in the territory of a PARTY within thirty days of their publication elsewhere; and phonograms the producer of which is a national of a PARTY, or is a company headquartered in the territory of a PARTY.

17A.3   The acquisition and validity of intellectual property rights in phonograms shall not be subject to any formalities, and protection shall arise automatically upon their creation.

SECTION 2: TRADEMARKS

1.   Protectable Subject Matter

1A.1   A trademark is a sign capable of distinguishing goods or services of one undertaking from those of other undertakings. It may in particular consist of words and personal names, letters, numerals, the shape of goods and of their packaging, combinations of colours, other graphical representations, or any combination of such signs.

1A.2   Trademarks which are:

(i)   devoid of any distinctive character;

(ii)   of such a nature as to deceive the public, for instance as to the nature, quality or geographical origin of the goods or services; or

(iii)   in conflict with earlier rights,

[shall not be protected] [cannot be validly registered]. Protection may also be denied in particular to trademarks contrary to morality or public order.

1A.3   The term "trademark" shall include service marks, as well as collective [and] [or] certification marks.

1B   PARTIES shall provide protection for trademarks and service marks registered in their territories in compliance with the formalities and requirements laid down in their respective national legislation.

2.   Acquisition of the Right and Procedures

2A.1   PARTIES shall enable the right to a trademark to be acquired by registration or by use. For the acquisition of the right to a trademark by use, a PARTY may require that the trademark is well-known among consumers or traders of the PARTY.

2A.2   A system for the registration of trademarks shall be provided. The nature of the goods [or services] to which a trademark is to be applied shall in no case form an obstacle to registration of the trademark.

2A.3   [[Actual] use of a trademark prior to [the application for] registration shall not be a condition for registration.] [Use of a trademark may be required as a prerequisite for registration.]

2A.4   PARTIES are encouraged to participate in a system for the international registration of trademarks.

2A.5   PARTIES shall publish each trademark either before it is registered or promptly after it is registered and shall afford other parties a reasonable opportunity to petition to cancel the registration. In addition, PARTIES may afford an opportunity for other parties to oppose the registration of a trademark.

2B   Parties shall provide protection for trademarks and service marks registered in their territories in compliance with the formalities and requirements incorporated or laid down in their respective national law.

3.   Rights Conferred

3.1   [The owner of a registered trademark shall have exclusive rights therein.] The owner of a registered trademark [or service mark] shall be entitled to prevent all third parties not having his consent from using in the course of trade identical or similar signs for goods or services which are identical or similar to those in respect of which the trademark registration has been granted [where such use would result in a likelihood of confusion.] [However, in case of the use of an identical sign for identical goods or services, a likelihood of confusion shall be presumed.]

3.2A   Protection for registered or unregistered trademarks shall extend under trademark law or other law to the use in the course of trade of any sign which is identical with, or similar to, the trademark in relation to goods or services which are not similar to those in respect of which the right to the trademark has been acquired, where the latter has a reputation and where use of that sign without due cause takes unfair advantage of, or is detrimental to, the distinctive character or the repute of the trademark.

3.3A   PARTIES shall refuse to register or shall cancel the registration and prohibit use of a trademark likely to cause confusion with a trademark of another which is considered to be well-known [in that country]. [This protection shall be extended inter alia against the use of such marks for goods or services which are dissimilar to original goods or services.] [In determining whether a trademark is well-known, the extent of the trademark's use and promotion in international trade must be taken into consideration. A PARTY may not require that the reputation extend beyond the sector of the public which normally deals with the relevant products or services.]

3.4A   The owner of a trademark shall be entitled to take action against any unauthorised use which constitutes an act of unfair competition.

4.   Exceptions

4A   Limited exceptions to the exclusive rights conferred by a trademark, such as fair use of descriptive terms, may be made, provided that they take account of the legitimate interests of the proprietor of the trademark and of third parties.

4B   Rights shall be subject to exhaustion if the trademarked goods or services are marketed by or with the consent of the owner in the territories of the PARTIES.

5.   Term of Protection

5A   Initial registration of a trademark shall be for a term of no less than ten years. The registration of a trademark shall be renewable indefinitely.

5B   It shall be a matter for national legislation to determine the duration of the protection granted.

6.   Requirement of Use

6.1   If use of a registered trademark is required to maintain the right to a trademark, the registration may be cancelled only after [an uninterrupted period of at least [five years] [three years]] [a reasonable period] of non-use, unless valid reasons based on the existence of obstacles to such use are shown by the trademark owner.

6.2A   Use of the trademark by another person with the consent of the owner shall be recognized as use of the trademark for the purpose of maintaining the registration.

6.3A   Valid reasons for non-use shall include non-use due to circumstances arising independently of the will of the proprietor of a trademark which constitute an obstacle to the use of the trademark, such as import restrictions on or other governmental requirements for products protected by the trademark.

7.   Other Requirements

7A   The use of a trademark in commerce shall not be [unjustifiably] encumbered by special requirements, such as use with another trademark, a use requirement which reduces the function of the trademark as an indication of source, [or use in a special form].

7B   It shall be a matter for national legislation to determine the conditions for the use of a mark.

8.   Licensing and Compulsory Licensing

8A   Compulsory licensing of trademarks shall not be permitted.

8B   It will be a matter for national legislation to determine the conditions for the use of a mark. (See also Section 8 below)

9.   Assignment

9A   The right to a [registered] trademark may be assigned with or without the transfer of the undertaking to which the trademark belongs. [PARTIES may require that the goodwill to which the trademark belongs be transferred with the right to the trademark.] [PARTIES may prohibit the assignment of a registered trademark which is identical with, or similar to, a famous mark indicating a state or a local public entity or an agency thereof or a non-profit organisation or enterprise working in the public interest.]

9B   It will be a matter for national legislation to determine the conditions for the use or assignment of a mark. (See also Section 8 below)

SECTION 3: GEOGRAPHICAL INDICATIONS

1.   Definition

1.1   Geographical indications are any designation, expression or sign which [aims at indicating] [directly or indirectly indicates] that a product [or service] originates from a country, region or locality.

1.2   [Geographical indications] [Appellations of origin] are for the purpose of this agreement [geographical] indications which designate a product as originating from the territory of a PARTY, a region or locality in that territory where a given quality, reputation or other characteristic of the products is attributable [exclusively or essentially] to its geographical origin, including natural [and] [or] human factors. [A denomination which has acquired a geographical character in relation to a product which has such qualities, reputation or characteristics is also deemed to be an appellation of origin.]

1.3   PARTIES agree that the provisions at point 2b.1 and 2b.2 below shall also apply to a geographical indication which, although literally true as to the territory, region or locality in which the goods originate, falsely represents to the public that the goods originate in the territory of another PARTY.

2. Protection

2a PARTIES shall provide protection for geographical indications by complying with the provisions under the Madrid Agreement for the Repression of False or Deceptive Indications of Source on Goods of 1891, as last revised in 1967.

2b.1 PARTIES shall protect [, at the request of an interested party,] geographical [or other] indications [denominating or suggesting the territory of a PARTY, a region or a locality in that territory] against use with respect to products not originating in that territory if that use [constitutes an act of unfair competition in the sense of Article 10bis of the Paris Convention (1967), including use which] [might mislead] [misleads] the public as to the true origin of the product.

[Such protection shall notably be afforded against:

- any direct or indirect use in trade in respect of products not originating from the place indicated or evoked by the geographical indication in question;

- any usurpation, imitation or evocation, even where the true origin of the product is indicated or the appellation or designation is used in translation or accompanied by expressions such as "kind", "type", "style", "imitation" or the like;

- the use of any means in the designation or presentation of products likely to suggest a link between those products and any geographical area other than the true place of origin.]

2b.2 PARTIES shall [, at the request of an interested party,] refuse or invalidate the registration of a trademark which contains or consists of:

[an indication denominating or suggesting a geographical indication,]

[a geographical or other indication denominating or suggesting the territory of a PARTY, or a region or locality in that territory,]

with respect to products not originating in the territory indicated [, if use of such indication [for such products] is of such a nature as to mislead or confuse the public [as to the true place of origin]]. [National laws shall provide the possibility for interested parties to oppose the use of such a trademark.]

2b.3   Appropriate measures shall be provided by PARTIES to enable interested parties to impede a geographical indication [, generally known in the territory of the PARTY to consumers of given products or of similar products as designating the origin of such products manufactured or produced in the territory of another PARTY,] from developing, as a result of its use in trade for [identical or similar] products of a different origin, into a designation of generic character [for these products or for similar products] [, it being understood that appellations of origin for products of the vine shall not be susceptible to develop into generic designations].

2c.1   PARTIES shall protect geographical indications that certify regional origin by providing for their registration as certification or collective marks.

2c.2   PARTIES shall provide protection for non-generic appellations of origin for wine by prohibiting their use when such use would mislead the public as to the true geographic origin of the wine. To aid in providing this protection, PARTIES are encouraged to submit to other PARTIES evidence to show that each such appellation of origin is a country, state, province, territory, or similar political subdivision of a country equivalent to a state or country; or a viticultural area.

2d   PARTIES undertake to provide protection for geographical indications including appellations of origin against any use which is likely to confuse or mislead the public as to the true origin of the product.

3.   International Register

PARTIES agree to cooperate with a view to establishing an international register for protected geographical indications, in order to facilitate the protection of geographical indications including appellations of origin. In appropriate cases the use of documents certifying the right to use the relevant geographical indication should be provided for.

4.   Exceptions

4.1   No PARTY shall be required to apply the provisions for the protection of geographical indications:

(a)   to the prejudice of holders of rights relating to an indication identical with or similar to a geographical indication or name and used or filed in good faith before the date of the entry into force of this agreement in the PARTY;

(b) with regard to goods for which the geographical indication or name is in the common language the common name of goods in the territory of that PARTY, or is identical with a term customary in common language

4.2a PARTIES agree that the preceding paragraphs shall not prevent the conclusion pursuant to Article 19 of the Paris Convention (1967) of bilateral or multilateral agreements concerning the rights under those paragraphs, with a view to increasing the protection for specific geographical or other indications, and further agree that any advantage, favour, privilege or immunity deriving from such agreements are exempted from the obligations under point 7 of Part II of this agreement.

4.2b Given the country specific nature of [geographical indications] [appellations of origin], it is understood that in connection with any advantage, favour, privilege or immunity stemming from bilateral agreements on such [indications] [appellations] and exceeding the requirements of this agreement, the most-favoured nation treatment obligations under point 7 of Part II of this agreement shall be understood to require each PARTY belonging to such an agreement to be ready to extend such advantage, favour, privilege or immunity, on terms equivalent to those under the agreement, to any other PARTY so requesting and to enter into good faith negotiations to this end.

SECTION 4: INDUSTRIAL DESIGNS

1.   Requirements for Protection

1.1 PARTIES shall provide for protection for industrial designs which are new [and] [or] original [, ornamental and non-obvious].

1.2 PARTIES [may] [shall] condition such protection on registration [or other formality].

1.3 PARTIES may provide that protection shall not extend to features required by technical reasons.

1.4 Such protection shall be provided without affecting any protection under copyright law [or other law].

2.   Textiles Designs

2A   The acquisition of industrial design rights in textiles or clothing shall not be encumbered by any special requirements such as <u>ex officio</u> examination of novelty before registration, compulsory publication of the design itself or disproportionate fees for multiple users of the registration.

3.   Industrial Design Rights

3.   The owner of a [protected] [registered] industrial design shall have the right to prevent third parties not having his consent from:
>   manufacturing;
>   [selling] [offering, putting on the market];
>   using;
>   or importing for commercial purposes;

[an object which is the subject matter of the industrial design right] [their industrial designs] [articles the appearance of which does not differ substantially from that of the protected design] [articles bearing a design which is a copy or substantially a copy of the protected design].

4.   Obligations of Industrial Design Owners

4B   With respect to the obligations of an industrial design owner, the requirements for patent inventions under point 3 of Section 5 below shall apply.

5.   Term of Protection and Renewal

5A.1   The term of protection available shall be at least ten years.

5A.2   PARTIES shall provide for an initial term of protection of registered industrial designs of at least five years [from the date of application], with a possibility of renewal for [at least another period] [two consecutive periods] of five years.

5B   The term of protection shall be provided under national legislation.

6.   Remedial Measures under National Legislations; Compulsory Licensing of Industrial Designs

6A.1   [PARTIES shall not issue compulsory licences for industrial designs except to remedy adjudicated violations of competition law to which the conditions set out at point 3 of Section 5 below shall apply <u>mutatis</u>

mutandis.] [The compulsory licensing of an industrial design shall not be permitted.]

6A.2   The protection of industrial designs shall not be subject to any forfeiture by reason of failure to exploit.

6B   (See Section 8 below)

SECTION 5: PATENTS

1.   Patentable Subject Matter

1.1   Patents shall be [available] [granted] for [any inventions, whether products or processes, in all fields of technology,] [all products and processes] which are new, which are unobvious or involve an inventive step and which are useful or industrially applicable.

1.2   Patents shall be available according to the first-to-file principle.

1.3   Requirements such as filing of an adequate disclosure in a patent application and payment of reasonable fees shall not be considered inconsistent with the obligation to provide patent protection.
         (See also point 3.1 below)

1.4   The following [shall] [may] be excluded from patentability:

1.4.1   Inventions, [the publication or use of which would be], contrary to public order, [law,] [generally accepted standards of] morality, [public health,] [or the basic principle of human dignity] [or human values].

1.4.2   Scientific theories, mathematical methods, discoveries and materials or substances [already existing] [in the same form found] in nature.

1.4.3   Methods of [medical] treatment for humans [or animals].

1.4.4   [Any] plant or animal [including micro-organisms] [varieties] or [essentially biological] processes for the production of plants or animals; [this does not apply to microbiological processes or the products thereof]. [As regards biotechnological inventions, further limitations should be allowed under national law].

1.4.5   [Production, application and use of] nuclear and fissionable material, [and substances manufactured through nuclear transformation].

1.5B   PARTIES may exclude from patentability certain kinds of products, or processes for the manufacture of those products on grounds of public interest, national security, public health or nutrition.

1.6A   PARTIES shall provide for the protection of plant varieties by patents and/or by an effective _sui generis_ system.

2.   Rights Conferred

2.1A   A patent shall confer on its owner at least the following exclusive rights:

(a)   to prevent third parties not having his consent from the acts of: making, using, [putting on the market, offering] [or selling] [or importing] [or importing or stocking for these purposes] the product which is the subject matter of the patent.

(b)   where the subject matter of a patent is a process, to prevent third parties not having his consent from the act of using the process, and from the acts of: using, [putting on the market, offering] [selling,] [or importing,] [or importing or stocking for these purposes,] at least the product obtained directly by that process.

2.1B   Once a patent has been granted, the owner of the patent shall have the following rights:

(a)   The right to prevent others from making, using or selling the patented product or using the patented process for commercial or industrial purposes.

(b)   The right to assign, or transfer by succession, the patent and to conclude licence contracts.

(c)   The right to a reasonable remuneration when the competent authorities of a PARTY to the present agreement use a patent for government purpose or provide for the granting of a licence of right or a compulsory licence. Such reasonable remuneration will be determined having regard to the economic situation of the PARTY, the nature of the invention, the cost involved in developing the patent and other relevant factors.

(See also point 5A.3.9 below)

2.2 Exceptions to Rights Conferred

2.2 [Provided that legitimate interests of the proprietor of the patent and of third parties are taken into account,] limited exceptions to the exclusive rights conferred by a patent may be made for certain acts, such as:

2.2.1 Rights based on prior use.

2.2.2 Acts done privately and for non-commercial purposes.

2.2.3 Acts done for experimental purposes.

2.2.4 Preparation in a pharmacy in individual cases of a medicine in accordance with a prescription, or acts carried out with a medicine so prepared.

2.2.5A Acts done in reliance upon them not being prohibited by a valid claim present in a patent as initially granted, but subsequently becoming prohibited by a valid claim of that patent changed in accordance with procedures for effecting changes to patents after grant.

2.2.6B Acts done by government for purposes merely of its own use.

2.3 Reversal of Burden of Proof

2.3A.1 If the subject matter of a patent is a process for obtaining a product, the same product when produced by any other party shall, in the absence of proof to the contrary, be deemed to have been obtained by the patented process in [at least one of] the following situation[s]:

(a) if the product is new, [or,

(b) where the product is not new, if there is a substantial likelihood that the product was made by the process [and the owner of the patent has been unable through reasonable efforts to determine the process actually used].

2.3A.2 In the adduction of proof to the contrary, the legitimate interests of the defendant in protecting his manufacturing and business secrets shall be taken into account.

2.3B   Where the subject matter of a patent is a process for obtaining a product, whether new or old, the burden of establishing that an alleged infringing product was made by the patented process shall always be on the person alleging such infringement.

3.   Obligations of Patent Owners

The owner of the patent shall have the following obligations:

3.1   to disclose prior to grant the invention in a clear and complete manner to permit a person versed in the technical field to put the invention into practice [and in particular to indicate the best mode for carrying out the invention];
(See also point 1.3 above)

3.2   to give information concerning corresponding foreign applications and grants;

3.3B   to work the patented invention in the territory of the Party granting it within the time limits fixed by national legislation;

3.4B   in respect of licence contracts and contracts assigning patents, to refrain from engaging in abusive or anticompetitive practices adversely affecting the transfer of technology, subject to the sanctions provided for in Sections 8 and 9 below.

4.   Term of Protection

4A.1   The term of protection shall be [at least] [15 years from the date of filing of the application, except for inventions in the field of pharmaceuticals for which the term shall be 20 years] [20 years from the date of filing of the application] [or where other applications are invoked in the said application, 20 years from the filing date of the earliest filed of the invoked applications which is not the priority date of the said application].

4A.2   PARTIES are encouraged to extend the term of patent protection in appropriate cases, to compensate for delays regarding the exploitation of the patented invention caused by regulatory approval processes.

4B   It shall be a matter for national legislation to determine the duration of protection.

5. Compulsory Licences/Licences of Right/ Use for Government Purposes

5A.1 The term "compulsory licence" shall be understood to cover licences of right [and government use without the authorisation of the patent owner]. PARTIES shall minimise the grant of compulsory licences in order not to impede adequate protection of patent rights.

5A.2 A compulsory licence may [only] be granted for the following purposes:

5A.2.1 To remedy an adjudicated violation of competition laws.

5A.2.2a To address, only during its existence, a [declared] national emergency.

5A.2.2b On the grounds of the public interest concerning national security, or critical peril to life of the general public or body thereof.

5A.2.2c Where the exploitation of the patented invention is required by reason of an overriding public interest, the possibility of exploitation of the patented invention by the government, or by third persons authorized by it.

5A.2.3 Where the invention claimed in a later patent cannot be exploited without infringing an earlier patent, a compulsory licence may be given to the extent necessary to avoid infringement of the patent, provided that the invention claimed in the later patent involves an important technical advance in relation to the invention claimed in the earlier patent or serves an entirely different purpose.

5A.2.4 In the event [of failure to exploit the patented invention or that its exploitation] [that the acts of manufacturing, selling or importing of the patented product or using of the patented process and the performance of any of these acts regarding the product obtained by the process] does not satisfy the [basic] needs of the local market before the expiration of a period of four years from the date of the patent application, or three years from the date of the grant of the patent, whichever period expires last, [unless legitimate reasons as viewed from Government's regulation or normal commercial practices exist].

5A.3   Where the law of a PARTY allows for the grant of compulsory licences, [such licences shall be granted in a manner which minimises distortions of trade[.To this end] [and]] the following provisions shall be respected:

5A.3.1   A compulsory licence may only be granted after unsuccessful efforts have been made by the applicant to negotiate a voluntary licence in line with normal commercial practices with the right holder, [except in the case of a manifest national emergency].

5A.3.2   Compulsory licences for non-working or insufficiency of working on the territory of the granting authority shall not be granted if the right holder can show that the lack or insufficiency of local working is justified by the existence of legal, technical or commercial reasons.

5A.3.3   The scope of a compulsory licence shall be limited to the precise extent necessary for the purpose for which it was granted.

5A.3.4   Compulsory licences shall be non-exclusive [and non-assignable except with that part of the enterprise or goodwill which exploits such licence].

5A.3.5   Compulsory licences shall be granted to permit manufacture for the local market only.

5A.3.6   Each case involving the possible grant of a compulsory licence shall be considered on its individual merits.

5A.3.7   Compulsory licences shall not require the transfer of know-how related to the exploitation of the invention.

5A.3.8   Any compulsory licence shall be revoked when the circumstances which led to its granting cease to exist and are unlikely to recur, subject to adequate protection of the legitimate interests of the right holder and of the licensee. The continued existence of these circumstances shall be reviewed upon request of the right holder.

5A.3.9   The payment of [an equitable remuneration to the right holder corresponding to the economic value of the licence] [remuneration to the right holder adequate to compensate the right holder fully for the licence] [reasonable compensation to the patentee] shall be

required [, except for compulsory licences to remedy adjudicated violations of competition law].
(See also point 2.1B(c))

5A.3.10   Any decision relating to the grant and continuation of compulsory licences and the compensation provided therefor shall be subject to [judicial review] [review by a distinct higher authority].

5B   Nothing in this Agreement shall be construed to prevent any PARTY from taking any action necessary: (i) for the working or use of a patent for governmental purposes; or (ii) where a patent has been granted for an invention capable of being used for the preparation or production of food or medicine, for granting to any person applying for the same a licence limited to the use of the invention for the purposes of the preparation or production and distribution of food and medicines.
(See also point 2.1B(c) above and Section 8 below)

6.   Revocation/Forfeiture

6A.1   A patent [[may not be revoked or forfeited [merely] on grounds [of non-working] stipulated in 5A.2 above]] [may only be revoked on grounds that it fails to meet the requirements of 1.1 and 1.3 above].

6A.2   Judicial review shall be available in the case of forfeiture of a patent where applicable.

6B   A patent may be revoked on grounds of public interest and where the conditions for the grant of compulsory licences are not fulfilled.

7.   Transitional Protection

7A.1   PARTIES shall provide transitional protection for products embodying subject matter deemed to be unpatentable under its patent law prior to its acceptance of this Agreement, where the following conditions are satisfied:

(a)   the subject matter to which the product relates will become patentable after acceptance of this Agreement;

(b)   a patent has been issued for the product by another PARTY prior to the entry into force of this Agreement; and

(c)   the product has not been marketed in the territory of the PARTY providing such transitional protection.

7A.2   The owner of a patent for a product satisfying the conditions set forth above shall have the right to submit a copy of the patent to the PARTY providing transitional protection. Such PARTY shall limit the right to make, use, or sell the product in its territory to such owner for a term to expire with that of the patent submitted.

8.   Formalities

8B   It shall be a matter for national legislation to determine the formalities required for the granting of patents.

SECTION 6: LAYOUT-DESIGNS (TOPOGRAPHIES) OF INTEGRATED CIRCUITS

1.   Relation to Washington Treaty

1.   PARTIES agree to provide protection to the layout-designs (topographies) of integrated circuits in accordance with the [substantive] provisions of the Treaty on Intellectual Property in Respect of Integrated Circuits as open for signature on 26 May 1989 [, subject to the following provisions].

2.   Legal Form of Protection

2A   The protection accorded under this agreement shall not prevent protection under other laws.

3.   Scope of the Protection

3A   Any PARTY shall consider unlawful the following acts if performed without the authorisation of the holder of the right:

3A.1   incorporating the layout-design (topography) in an integrated circuit;

3A.2   importing, selling, or otherwise distributing for commercial purposes a protected layout-design (topography), an integrated circuit in which a protected layout-design (topography) is incorporated or a product incorporating such an integrated circuit.

4. Acts not Requiring the Authorization of the Holder of the Right

4A.1 PARTIES may exempt from liability under their law the reproduction of a layout-design (topography) for purposes of teaching, analysis, or evaluation in the course of preparation of a layout-design (topography) that is itself original. This provision shall replace Articles (2)(a) and (b) of the Washington Treaty.

4A.2 The act of importing, selling, or otherwise distributing for commercial purposes [an unlawfully reproduced layout-design (topography),] [an integrated circuit incorporating an unlawfully reproduced layout-design (topography) or] a product incorporating an unlawfully reproduced layout-design (topography) [shall] [may] not itself be considered an infringement if, at the time of performance of the act in question, the person performing the act [establishes that he] did not know and had [no reasonable grounds to believe] that the layout-design (topography) was unlawfully reproduced. However, PARTIES [shall] [may] provide that, after the time [of receipt of notice] [that the person comes to know or has reasonable grounds to believe] that the layout-design (topography) was unlawfully reproduced, he may perform any of the acts with respect to the stock on hand or ordered before such time, but shall be liable to pay [a reasonable royalty] [an equitable remuneration] to the right holder.

4A.3a Non-voluntary licences shall not be granted for purposes or on terms which could result in a distortion of international trade.

4A.3b The conditions set out at point 5 of Section 5 above shall apply _mutatis mutandis_ to the grant of any non-voluntary licences for layout-designs (topographies).

4A.3c Non-voluntary licences shall not be granted for layout-designs (topographies).

5. Term of Protection

5A (i) In PARTIES requiring registration as a condition of protection, layout-designs (topographies) shall be protected for a term of no less than 10 years from the date of [filing an application for registration] [registration] or of the first commercial exploitation wherever in the world it occurs, whichever is the earlier [, except that if neither of the above events occurs within 15 years of the first fixation or encoding there shall no longer be any obligation to provide protection].

(ii)   In PARTIES not requiring registration as a condition for protection, layout-designs (topographies) shall be protected for a term of no less than 10 years from the date of the first commercial exploitation wherever in the world it occurs [, except that if a layout-design (topography) is not so exploited within a period of 15 years of the first fixation or encoding, there shall no longer be any obligation to provide protection].

[(iii)   If registration is required by law, and no application is filed, the protection of the layout-design (topography) shall lapse after two years from the date of the first commercial exploitation wherever in the world it occurs.

(iv)   Notwithstanding (i),(ii) and (iii) above, protection shall lapse 15 years after the creation of the layout-design (topography).]

SECTION 7: ACTS CONTRARY TO HONEST COMMERCIAL PRACTICES INCLUDING PROTECTION OF UNDISCLOSED INFORMATION

1.   Protection of Undisclosed Information

1A.1   In the course of ensuring effective protection against unfair competition as provided for in Article 10bis of the Paris Convention (1967), PARTIES shall provide in their domestic law the legal means for natural and legal persons to prevent information within their control from being disclosed to, acquired by, or used by others without their consent in a manner contrary to honest commercial practices insofar as such information:

1A.1.1   is secret in the sense that it is not, as a body or in the precise configuration and assembly of its components, generally known or readily accessible; and

1A.1.2   has actual [or potential] commercial value because it is secret; and

1A.1.3   has been subject to reasonable steps, under the circumstances, by the person in possession of the information, to keep it secret.

1A.2   "A manner contrary to honest commercial practice" is understood to encompass, practices such as theft, bribery, breach of contract, breach of confidence, inducement to breach, electronic and other forms of commercial espionage, and includes the acquisition of trade secrets by third parties who knew [, or had reasonable grounds to know] that such practices were involved in the acquisition.

1A.3   PARTIES shall not limit the duration of protection under this section so long as the conditions stipulated at point 1A.1 exist.

2.   Licensing

2Aa   PARTIES shall not discourage or impede voluntary licensing of undisclosed information by imposing excessive or discriminatory conditions on such licences or conditions which dilute the value of such information.

2Ab   There shall be no compulsory licensing of proprietary information.

3.   Government Use

3Aa   PARTIES, when requiring the publication or submission of undisclosed information consisting of test [or other] data, the origination of which involves a considerable effort, shall protect such data against unfair exploitation by competitors. The protection shall last for a reasonable time commensurate with the efforts involved in the origination of the data, the nature of the data, and the expenditure involved in their preparation, and shall take account of the availability of other forms of protection.

3Ab.1   PARTIES which require that trade secrets be submitted to carry out governmental functions, shall not use the trade secrets for the commercial or competitive benefit of the government or of any person other than the right holder except with the right holder's consent, on payment of the reasonable value of the use, or if a reasonable period of exclusive use is given the right holder.

3Ab.2   PARTIES may disclose trade secrets to third parties, only with the right holder's consent or to the degree required to carry out necessary government functions. Wherever practicable, right holders shall be given an opportunity to enter into confidentiality agreements with any non-government entity to which the PARTY is disclosing trade secrets to carry out necessary government functions.

3Ab.3   PARTIES may require right holders to disclose their trade secrets to third parties to protect human health or safety or to protect the environment only when the right holder is given an opportunity to enter into confidentiality agreements with any non-government entity receiving the trade secrets to prevent further disclosure or use of the trade secret.

3Ac.1   Proprietary information submitted to a government agency for purposes of regulatory approval procedures such as clinical or safety tests, shall not be disclosed without the consent of the proprietor, except to other governmental agencies if necessary to protect human, plant or animal life, health or the environment. Governmental agencies may disclose it only with the consent of the proprietor or to the extent indispensable to inform the general public about the actual or potential danger of a product. They shall not be entitled to use the information for commercial purposes.

3Ac.2   Disclosure of any proprietary information to a third party, or other governmental agencies, in the context of an application for obtaining intellectual property protection, shall be subject to an obligation to hear the applicant and to judicial review. Third parties and governmental agencies having obtained such information shall be prevented from further disclosure and commercial use of it without the consent of the proprietor.

SECTION 8: REMEDIES FOR NON-FULFILMENT OF OBLIGATIONS

1.   Remedial Measures under National Legislation

1B   PARTIES may adopt appropriate measures to remedy the non-fulfilment of obligations arising from the protection provided for intellectual property rights under the provisions of this agreement or in accordance with national legislation. Such measures may include:

(i)   in respect of non-working or insufficient working of patents, the granting of a compulsory licence;
         (See also point 3 of Section 5 above)

(ii) compulsory licence may also be granted wherever necessary in public interest and to secure free competition and to prevent abuses by the holder of the right;
         (See also point 8 of Section 2, point 6 of Section 4, point 5 of Section 5, point 4.3 of Section 6 and point 2 of Section 7 above)

(iii) where the use of a trademark is required by national legislation to maintain trademark rights, the cancellation of the registration of such a trademark after a reasonable period, unless valid reasons based on the existence of obstacles to such use are shown by the trademark owner;
         (See also point 6 of Section 2 above)

(iv) in respect of abusive or anti-competitive practices in licensing contracts, the annulment of the contract or of those clauses of the contract deemed contrary to the laws and regulations governing competition and/or transfer of technology.

2.   <u>Co-operation to Ensure Fulfilment of Obligations</u>

2B   PARTIES undertake to ensure that intellectual property right holders who are nationals or domiciliaries of their territories comply with the obligations prescribed by this agreement or by the national legislation of any other PARTY in accordance with the provisions of this agreement.

SECTION 9: CONTROL OF ABUSIVE OR ANTI-COMPETITIVE PRACTICES IN CONTRACTUAL LICENCES

1.   <u>National Legislation</u>

1B   PARTIES may specify in their national legislation practices in licensing contracts deemed to constitute an abuse of intellectual property rights or to have an adverse effect on competition in the relevant market, and adopt appropriate measures to prevent or control such practices.

(See also point 6B of Part IX and point 6 of Section 4, points 5 and 6 of Section 5 and point 4.3 of Section 6 above)

2.   Consultation and Co-operation

2B   PARTIES agree that practices which restrain competition, limit access to the technology or to markets or foster monopolistic control, and which are engaged in by licensors, may have harmful effects on trade and transfer of technology among their countries. Accordingly, each PARTY agrees upon the request of any other PARTY to consult with respect to any such practices and to co-operate with other PARTIES with a view to ensuring that IPR owners, who are nationals or domiciliaries of its country, comply with the obligations prescribed in this respect by the national legislation of the PARTY granting them such rights.

PART IV: ENFORCEMENT OF INTELLECTUAL PROPERTY RIGHTS

SECTION 1: GENERAL OBLIGATIONS

1.   PARTIES shall ensure that effective [and appropriate] enforcement procedures are available under their national laws so as to enable action against any act of infringement of intellectual property rights covered by the agreement, including effective and expeditious remedies to stop [or prevent] infringements and remedies which constitute an effective deterrent to further infringements. In conformity with the provisions below, they shall provide such procedures [,internally and at the border,] by means of civil law, administrative law, or, where appropriate, criminal law, or a combination thereof. [Such procedures shall be provided consistently with each PARTY's legal and judicial systems and traditions and within the limits of its administrative resources and capabilities.] These procedures shall be applied in such a manner as to avoid the creation of barriers to legitimate trade and provide for safeguards against their abuse.

2. Procedures concerning the enforcement of intellectual property rights shall be fair and equitable. They shall be [simple and expeditious] [not unnecessarily complicated, costly or time consuming, nor shall they be subject to unreasonable time-limits or unwarranted delays].

3A Decisions on the merits of a case shall [, as a general rule,] [preferably] be in writing and reasoned. They shall be made known at least to the parties to the dispute without undue delay. Decisions on the merits of a case shall only be based on such evidence in respect of which parties were offered the opportunity to be heard.

4A Parties to a dispute shall have an opportunity to appeal to a court of law against final administrative decisions [and [subject to jurisdictional provisions in national laws concerning the importance of a case, against the legal aspects of] all initial judicial decisions] on the merits of a case concerning the enforcement of an intellectual property right. However, there shall be no obligation to provide an opportunity to appeal against acquittals in criminal cases.

4B Provision shall be made for appeal against initial judicial orders and for judicial review of administrative orders.

SECTION 2: CIVIL AND ADMINISTRATIVE PROCEDURES AND REMEDIES

5. Fair and Equitable Procedures

5A.1 PARTIES shall make available to right holders civil judicial procedures concerning the enforcement of any intellectual property right covered by this agreement.

5A.2 Defendants shall have the right to written notice which is timely and contains sufficient detail, including the basis of the claims.

5A.3 Parties shall be allowed to be represented by independent legal counsel, and procedures shall not impose overly burdensome requirements concerning personal appearances.

5A.4   All parties to such procedures shall be duly entitled to substantiate their claims and to present evidence.

5A.5   The procedure shall provide a means to identify and protect confidential information [without prejudice to the legitimate interests of any party to substantiate its claims].

5B   There shall be prior notice given to parties to a legal proceeding and adequate opportunities for defence.

6.   <u>Evidence of Proof</u>

6A.1   PARTIES shall provide courts with the authority, where a party has presented a [justifiable] [coherent] case and has identified evidence relevant to substantiation of its claim and which lies in the control of the opposing party, to order that this evidence be produced by the opposing party, subject to conditions which ensure the protection of confidential information. [For the purposes of this agreement, a justifiable case is one in which a party has presented to the court reasonably available evidence sufficient to [indicate that its claims are not without foundation] [support its claims]].

6A.2   In addition to the preceding procedure, PARTIES may also provide access to relevant evidence through, for example, measures to preserve evidence, use of search and seizure authority, by rule or by exercise of other judicial or administrative authority.

6A.3   In cases in which another PARTY refuses access to or impedes a party's compliance with a request to provide necessary information or a party to the proceeding refuses access to, or otherwise does not provide necessary information within a reasonable period, or significantly impedes a procedure relating to an enforcement action, [a PARTY may provide that] preliminary and final determinations, affirmative or negative, may be made on the basis of the complaint or the allegation presented by the party adversely affected by the denial of access to information and/or on other facts and evidence before the court, subject to providing the parties an opportunity to be heard on the allegations or evidence.

7. <u>**Injunctions**</u>

7A   The judicial authorities shall have the authority to issue upon request an order that an infringement be refrained from or discontinued, irrespective of whether the defendant has acted with intent or negligence.

7B   Injunctions must be available.

8. <u>**Damages**</u>

8A   The right holder shall be entitled to [obtain] [claim] from the infringer [adequate] [full] compensation for the injury he has suffered because of a [deliberate or negligent] infringement of his intellectual property right. The right holder shall also be entitled to claim remuneration for costs, including attorney fees, reasonably incurred in the proceedings. In appropriate cases, PARTIES may provide for recovery of profits and/or pre-established damages to be granted even where the infringer has not acted intentionally or negligently.

8B   Courts shall have the authority to award damages.

9. <u>**Remedies against Governments**</u>

9A   Notwithstanding the other provisions of this Part, when a government is sued for infringement of an intellectual property right as a result of the use of that right by or for the government, PARTIES may limit remedies against the government to payment of [full] [adequate] compensation to the right holder.

10. <u>**Other Remedies**</u>

10A   Where an intellectual property right has been found to be infringed, the court shall have the authority to order, upon request of the right holder, that the infringing goods, as well as materials and implements the predominant use of which has been in the creation of the infringing goods, be, without compensation of any sort, destroyed or disposed of outside the channels of commerce in such a manner as to minimise any harm caused to the right holder. In considering such a request, the need for proportionality between the seriousness of the infringement and the remedies ordered as well as the interests of third parties shall be taken into account. [In regard to counterfeit goods] [Other than in exceptional cases], the simple removal of the trade mark [or geographical indication] unlawfully affixed shall not be ordered.

11.   Right of Information

11A   [PARTIES may provide that,] unless this would be out of proportion to the seriousness of the infringement, the infringer may be ordered by a court to inform the right holder of the identity of third persons involved in the production and distribution of the infringing goods or services and of their channels of distribution.

12.   Indemnification of the Defendant

12A.1   Parties wrongfully enjoined or restrained by any measures taken for the purpose of enforcing intellectual property rights shall be entitled to claim from the party at whose request the measures were taken adequate compensation for the injury suffered because of an abuse of enforcement procedures and to claim reimbursement for the costs, including attorney fees, reasonably incurred in the proceedings.

12A.2   PARTIES may provide for the possibility that such parties [may] [shall] be entitled to claim compensation from [authorities] [public officials] in appropriate cases, such as negligent or deliberate improper conduct. [They shall provide for such possibility in the case of administrative ex officio action.]

13.   Administrative Procedures

13A   Administrative procedures concerning the enforcement of intellectual property rights shall [conform to principles equivalent] [correspond in substance] to those set forth in this Section for application to judicial proceedings.

SECTION 3: PROVISIONAL MEASURES

14A.1.1   The judicial authorities shall have the authority to order, upon request, prompt and effective provisional measures:

> (i)   to prevent an infringement of any intellectual property right from occurring or being continued, and in particular to prevent the goods from entering commercial channels;

(ii) to preserve relevant evidence in regard to the alleged infringement.

14A.1.2   Where appropriate, provisional measures may be adopted <u>inaudita altera parte</u>, [in particular] where any delay is likely to cause irreparable harm to the right holder, or where there is a demonstrable risk of evidence being destroyed.

14A.2   The applicant shall be required to provide any reasonably available evidence so as to permit the court to establish with a sufficient degree of certainty that he is the right holder and that his right is being infringed or that such infringement is imminent [, and to provide a security or equivalent assurance sufficient [to protect the defendant and] to prevent abuse].

14A.3   Where provisional measures have been adopted <u>inaudita altera parte</u>, the parties affected shall be given notice, at the latest immediately after the execution of the measures. A review, including a right to be heard, shall take place upon request of the defendant with a view to deciding, within a reasonable period after the notification of the measures, whether these measures shall be modified, revoked or confirmed.

14A.4   Where provisional measures according to point 14A.1.1(i) are to be carried out by customs authorities, the applicant may be required to supply any other information necessary for the identification of the goods concerned.

14A.5   Without prejudice to point 14A.3, provisional measures taken on the basis of point 14.1 shall, upon request by the defendant, be revoked or otherwise cease to have effect, if proceedings leading to a decision on the merits of the case are not initiated within a reasonable period not exceeding [one month] [two weeks] after the notification of the provisional measures, unless determined otherwise by the court.

14A.6   Where the provisional measures are revoked or where they lapse due to any act or omission by the applicant, or where it is subsequently found that there has been no infringement or threat of infringement of an intellectual property right, the defendant shall be entitled to claim from the applicant adequate compensation for any injury caused [intentionally or negligently] by these measures, unless the parties reach an out-of-court settlement of the case.

14.7   Point 13 of this Part shall apply [accordingly] [mutatis mutandis] to provisional administrative procedures.

SECTION 4: SPECIAL REQUIREMENTS RELATED TO BORDER MEASURES[1]

15.   Suspension of Release by Customs Authorities

15A   Without prejudice to point 21 of this Part, PARTIES shall, in conformity with the provisions set out below, establish procedures according to which a right holder, who has valid grounds for suspecting that the importation of [goods which infringe his intellectual property right]

[counterfeit trademark or pirated copyright goods] may take place, may lodge an application in writing with the competent authorities, administrative or judicial, for the suspension by the customs authorities of the release into free circulation of such goods. [This provision does not create an obligation to apply such procedures to parallel imports].

15B   See point 8B of Part IX below.

15A.2   PARTIES may provide for corresponding procedures concerning the suspension by the customs authorities of the release of such goods destined for exportation from their territory.

16.   Application

16A   The application under point 15 must contain prima facie evidence of the alleged infringement and [evidence] that the applicant is the right holder. It must contain all pertinent information known or reasonably available to the applicant to enable the competent authority to act in knowledge of the facts at hand, and a sufficiently detailed description of the goods to make them readily recognisable by the customs authorities. [It must specify the length of period for which the customs authorities are

---

1   It will be made clear at an appropriate place in any agreement that, for the European Communities and for the purposes of this Section, the term "border" is understood to mean the external border of the European Communities with third countries.

requested to take action.] The applicant may also be required to supply any other information necessary for the identification of the goods concerned. The competent authorities shall inform the applicant within a reasonable period whether they have accepted the application and the period for which it will remain in force.

16B   See point 9B(i) of Part IX.

17.   Security or Equivalent Assurance

17A   PARTIES shall seek to avoid border enforcement procedures being abused by means of unjustified or frivolous applications. For this purpose, they [may] [shall] require a right holder, who has lodged an application according to point 16 to provide a security or equivalent assurance. Such security or equivalent assurance shall not unreasonably deter recourse to these procedures.

17B   See point 9B(ii) of Part IX.

18.   Duration of Suspension

18A   The importer and the applicant shall be promptly notified of the suspension of the release of goods according to point 15 above. If, within ten working days after the applicant has [been served with a notice of the] [received] notification of the suspension, the customs authorities have not been informed that the matter has been referred to the authority competent to take a decision on the merits of the case, or that the duly empowered authority has taken provisional measures, the goods shall be released, provided that all other conditions for importation or exportation have been complied with [and unless this would be contrary to provision of domestic law]. In exceptional cases, the above time-limit may be extended by another ten working days.

18B   See points 8B (last sentence) and 9B(iii) of Part IX.

19.   Indemnification of the Importer and of the Owner of the Goods

19A   The importer and the owner of the goods shall be entitled to claim from the applicant adequate compensation for any injury caused [intentionally or negligently] to them through the wrongful detention of goods or through the detention of goods released pursuant to point 18 above.

20.   Right of Information and Inspection

20A   Without prejudice to the protection of confidential information, the competent authority shall be empowered to give the right holder sufficient opportunity to inspect any product detained by the customs authorities in order to substantiate his claims. [Unless this would be contrary to provisions of domestic law, the customs authorities shall inform the right-holder, upon request, of the names and addresses of the consignor, importer, consignee and of the quantity of the goods in question.]

21.   Ex Officio Action

21A.1.1   PARTIES may provide that the customs authorities have the right, but not an obligation, to inform the right-holder or his representative, wherever they have reasons to suspect an imminent importation of products the release of which into free circulation would contravene intellectual property rights of that right-holder.

21A.1.2   The exercise of this right of information shall not imply any liability for the customs authorities.

21A.1.3   This right of information is without prejudice to the provisions at points 15 to 20, 22 and 23.

21A.2.1   PARTIES may require the competent authorities to act upon their own initiative and to suspend the release of goods in respect of which they have acquired [a sufficient degree of certainty] [prima facie evidence] that an intellectual property right is being infringed.

21A.2.2   In this case, the competent authorities may at any time seek from the right holder any information that may assist them to exercise these powers.

21A.2.3   The importer and the right holder shall be promptly notified of the suspension. Where the importer has lodged an appeal against the suspension with the competent authorities, the suspension shall be subject to the conditions, mutatis mutandis, set out at point 18 above.

21A.2.4   With regard to the importer's rights to claim compensation, the provisions at point 19 shall apply, mutatis mutandis.

22. Remedies

22A   Without prejudice to the other rights of action open to the right holder, and subject to the right of the defendant to lodge an appeal to the judicial authorities, the competent authorities shall provide for the destruction or disposal of the infringing goods in accordance with the principles set out at point 10 above. [Other than in exceptional circumstances] [With respect to counterfeit goods], the authorities shall not allow the re-exportation of the infringing goods in an unaltered state or subject them to a different customs procedure.

22B   See point 10B of Part IX below.

23.   De Minimis Imports

23A   PARTIES may exclude from the application of the above provisions small quantities of goods of a non-commercial nature contained in travellers' personal luggage or sent in small consignments.

SECTION 5: CRIMINAL PROCEDURES

24.   PARTIES shall provide for criminal procedures and penalties to be applied in cases of wilful [trademark counterfeiting and copyright piracy on a commercial scale] [infringements of trademarks and copyright on a commercial scale] [infringements on a commercial scale of intellectual property rights concerned by this agreement]. Remedies available shall include imprisonment and monetary fines sufficient to provide an effective deterrent and in appropriate cases the seizure, forfeiture and destruction of the infringing goods and of any device [the predominant use of which has been] [used] in the commission of the offence. PARTIES may provide for criminal procedures and penalties to be applied in cases of infringement of any other intellectual property right, in particular where it is committed wilfully and on a commercial scale.

PART V: ACQUISITION OF INTELLECTUAL PROPERTY RIGHTS AND RELATED INTER-PARTES PROCEDURES

1A   Where the acquisition of an intellectual property right covered by this Annex is subject to the intellectual property right being granted or registered, PARTIES shall provide for procedures which permit, subject to the substantive conditions for acquiring the intellectual property right being fulfilled, the granting or registration of the right [within a reasonable period of time so as to avoid that the period of protection is unduly curtailed] [and] [at reasonable cost] [at a cost commensurate with the service rendered].

2A   Procedures concerning the acquisition or renewal of such intellectual property rights shall be governed by the general principles set out in Part IV at points 3 and 5.

3A   Where the national law provides for opposition, revocation, cancellation or similar inter-partes procedures, they shall be [at reasonable cost] expeditious, effective, fair and equitable. [Such procedures shall give all parties concerned an opportunity to present their views and provide for rulings to be made on the basis of equitable and clear criteria.]

4A   Final administrative decisions concerning the acquisition of an intellectual property right or any other matter subject to an inter-partes procedure referred to at point 3 above [other than pre-grant opposition procedures], shall be subject to the right of appeal in a court of law or quasi-judicial body.

PART IX: TRADE IN COUNTERFEIT AND PIRATED GOODS

1.   Preamble

1B.1   Desirous of providing for adequate procedures and remedies to discourage international trade in counterfeit and pirated goods while ensuring an unimpeded flow of trade in legitimate goods;

1B.2 <u>Deeming</u> it highly desirable to ensure competition in international trade and to prevent arrangements which may restrain such competition;

1B.3 <u>Recognizing</u> the need to take into consideration the public policy objectives underlying national systems for the protection of intellectual property, including developmental and technological objectives;

1B.4 <u>Recognizing</u> also the special needs of the least developed countries in respect of maximum flexibility in the application of this Agreement in order to enable them to create a sound and viable technological base.

2.   Objectives

2B   With respect to intellectual property and international trade, PARTIES agree on the following objectives:

(i)   To clarify GATT provisions related to the effects of the enforcement of intellectual property rights on international trade, in particular articles IX and XX(d), and to provide for adequate procedures and remedies to discourage international trade in counterfeit and pirated goods.

(ii)   To ensure that such procedures and remedies do not themselves become barriers to legitimate trade and are not applied in a discriminatory manner to imported goods.

(iii) To ensure free flow of goods and prevent arrangements, effected by private or public commercial enterprises, which may result in the division of markets or otherwise restrain competition, thus having harmful effects on international trade.

SECTION 2: GUIDING PRINCIPLES AND NORMS

3.   Trade in Counterfeit and Pirated Goods

3B.1   PARTIES undertake to discourage trade in counterfeit and pirated goods and to combat such trade without inhibiting the free flow of legitimate trade. For this purpose, PARTIES shall exchange information and promote cooperation between customs authorities with respect to trade in counterfeit and pirated goods. They shall also adopt in their respective national legislation the necessary measures, procedures and remedies in this respect.

3B.2   For the purposes of this Agreement, trade in counterfeit goods means trade in goods which infringe a trademark validly registered in respect of such goods in the importing country, while trade in pirated goods means trade in goods which constitute a slavish copy of a work protected by copyright under the legislation of the country of importation.

4. Safeguard against Creation of Trade Impediments in the Application of Measures and Procedures to Enforce Intellectual Property Rights

4B   In the application of national measures and procedures to enforce intellectual property rights, PARTIES undertake to avoid the creation of impediments or distortions to international trade, and to refrain from applying their national legislation in a discriminatory manner to imports from the territories of other PARTIES. For this purpose, they shall observe the principles of national treatment and MFN enshrined in the GATT.

5. Non-recourse to Unilateral Measures

5B   PARTIES shall refrain, in relation to each other, from threatening or having recourse to unilaterally decided economic measures of any kind aimed at ensuring the enforcement of intellectual property rights.

6. Control of Anti-competitive and Trade-distorting Practices

6B   PARTIES shall co-operate with each other to ensure the free flow of goods and prevent that intellectual property rights are used, through arrangements among enterprises, to create restrictions or distortions to international trade or to engage in anti-competitive practices having adverse effects on their trade. For this purpose, they undertake to exchange information and to agree upon the request of any other PARTY to consult with respect to any such practices and to take such measures in their territory as may be deemed appropriate with a view to eliminating the adverse effects of such practices.

7.   Transparency

7B   Laws, regulations, judicial decisions and administrative rulings pertaining to the application of the principles and norms prescribed in points 2 to 5 shall be made publicly available in the official language of the Party adopting such texts and, shall be provided, upon request, to any other Party.

SECTION 3: BORDER MEASURES RELATED TO COUNTERFEIT OR PIRATED GOODS

8.   Suspension of Customs Clearance

8B   PARTIES shall adopt the necessary measures and procedures, whether judicial or administrative, to enable intellectual property right holders, who may have valid grounds for suspecting that imported goods infringe their trademark or constitute a slavish copy of a work protected by copyright in accordance with the national legislation of the importing country, to obtain the suspension by the customs authorities of clearance from customs of such goods. Such suspension shall be for a limited period of time pending a determination by the competent authorities whether the goods are infringing.

8A   (See point 15A of Part IV above).

9.   Safeguards against Obstacles to Legitimate Trade

9B   (i) Persons initiating the procedure for the suspension of clearance from customs shall be required to provide adequate documentary evidence to satisfy the competent authorities that prima facie there is an infringement of their right to protection in accordance with the relevant laws of the country of importation.

(ii) Such persons shall also be required to provide security by bond or deposit of money in an amount sufficient to indemnify the authorities or to hold the importer harmless from loss or damage resulting from the action undertaken.

(iii) The importers of such goods or other persons affected by the procedure shall be informed promptly of actions taken and shall be entitled to a judicial review of any final decision taken by an administrative authority.

9A   (See points 16A, 17A and 18A of Part IV above).

10.   Disposal of Infringing Goods

10B   Where it is finally determined that the goods are infringing in accordance with the relevant laws of the importing country, the competent authorities shall provide for the forfeiture, destruction or disposal of the goods in a manner not prejudicial to the interests of the right holder.

10A   (See point 22 of Part IV above).

ANNEX

PARTS I, VI, VII AND VIII OF THE COMPOSITE DRAFT TEXT OF 12 JUNE 1990

This Annex reproduces tel quel Parts I, VI, VII and VIII of the composite draft text which was circulated informally by the Chairman of the Negotiating Group on 12 June 1990. The text was prepared on the basis of the draft legal texts submitted by the European Communities (NG11/W/68), the United States (NG11/W/70), Argentina, Brazil, Chile, China, Colombia, Cuba, Egypt, India, Nigeria, Peru, Tanzania and Uruguay, and subsequently also sponsored by Pakistan and Zimbabwe (NG11/W/71), Switzerland (NG11/W/73), Japan (NG11/W/74) and Australia (NG11/W/75).

The notes that follow reproduce the explanatory notes of the composite draft text. It should be noted that the system of notation is somewhat different from that of the profile contained in the body of this document, particularly that the letters A and B refer not to different general approaches but simply to different suggested formulations in regard to a specific point. The cross-references contained in this Annex refer to the draft composite text.

Notes on the composite text

1.   In most of the text the language of the various proposals has been reproduced tel quel. In a few cases, slight modifications of a non-substantive nature have been made to the wording or structure of a sentence in order to simplify the common presentation of the various proposals. For this reason, the signatories of the proposed agreements have been referred to uniformly as "PARTIES", except in relation to those questions where it is important for the meaning to retain the original formulations, notably in the area of dispute settlement and institutional arrangements.

2.   The numbers in bold type at the end of a paragraph or sub-paragraph indicate the NG11/W numbers of the proposals reproduced in that paragraph or sub-paragraph. Variations between those proposals are indicated by the use of square brackets within the paragraph or sub-paragraph.

3.　　The numbering and lettering in the left column has been included to facilitate reference. Related points have been grouped with a common number. Alternative proposals on the same issue have been indicated in the left column by capital letters. Where possible, the headings put forward in the proposals have been used; they are reproduced in bold type. To make the presentation as clear as possible, some additional headings have been employed; they are in ordinary type and placed in parentheses.

4.　　"Paris Convention" refers to the Paris Convention for the Protection of Industrial Property. "Paris Convention (1967)" refers to the Stockholm Act of this Convention of 14 July 1967. "Berne Convention" refers to the Berne Convention for the Protection of Literary and Artistic Works. "Berne Convention (1971)" refers to the Paris Act of this Convention of 24 July 1971. "Rome Convention" refers to the International Convention for the Protection of Performers, Producers of Phonograms and Broadcasting Organisations, adopted at Rome, 26 October 1961.

PART I: PREAMBULAR PROVISIONS; OBJECTIVES

1.　　<u>Preamble</u> (71); <u>Objectives</u> (73)

1.1　　<u>Recalling</u> the Ministerial Declaration of Punta del Este of 20 September 1986; **(73)**

1.2　　<u>Desiring</u> to strengthen the role of GATT and its basic principles and to bring about a wider coverage of world trade under agreed, effective and enforceable multilateral disciplines; **(73)**

1.3　　<u>Recognizing</u> that the lack of protection, or insufficient or excessive protection, of intellectual property rights causes nullification and impairment of advantages and benefits of the General Agreement on Tariffs and Trade and distortions detrimental to international trade, and that such nullification and impairment may be caused both by substantive and procedural deficiencies, including ineffective enforcement of existing laws, as well as by unjustifiable discrimination of foreign persons, legal entities, goods and services; **(73)**

1.4   <u>Recognizing</u> that adequate protection of intellectual property rights is an essential condition to foster international investment and transfer of technology; **(73)**

1.5   <u>Recognizing</u> the importance of protection of intellectual property rights for promoting innovation and creativity; **(71)**

1.6   <u>Recognizing</u> that adequate protection of intellectual property rights both internally and at the border is necessary to deter and persecute piracy and counterfeiting; **(73)**

1.7   <u>Taking into account</u> development, technological and public interest objectives of developing countries; **(71)**

1.8   <u>Recognizing</u> also the special needs of the least developed countries in respect of maximum flexibility in the application of this Agreement in order to enable them to create a sound and viable technological base; **(71)**

1.9   <u>Recognizing</u> the need for appropriate transitional arrangements for developing countries and least developed countries with a view to achieve successfully strengthened protection and enforcement of intellectual property rights; **(73)**

1.10   <u>Recognizing</u> the need to prevent disputes by providing adequate means of transparency of national laws, regulations and requirements regarding protection and enforcement of intellectual property rights; **(73)**

1.11   <u>Recognizing</u> the need to settle disputes on matters related to the protection of intellectual property rights on the basis of effective multilateral mechanisms and procedures, and to refrain from applying unilateral measures inconsistent with such procedures to PARTIES to this PART of the General Agreement; **(73)**

1.12   <u>Recognizing</u> the efforts to harmonize and promote intellectual property laws by international organizations specialized in the field of intellectual property law and that this PART of the General Agreement aims at further encouragement of such efforts; **(73)**

2.   <u>Objective of the Agreement</u> (74)

2A   The PARTIES agree to provide effective and adequate protection of intellectual property rights in order to ensure the reduction of distortions and impediments to [international (68)] [legitimate (70)] trade. The protection of intellectual property rights shall not itself create barriers to legitimate trade. **(68, 70)**

2B   The objective of the present Agreement is to establish adequate standards for the protection of, and effective and appropriate means for the enforcement of intellectual property rights; thereby eliminating distortions and impediments to international trade related to intellectual property rights and foster its sound development. **(74)**

2C   With respect to standards and principles concerning the availability, scope and use of intellectual property rights, PARTIES agree on the following objectives:

(i)   To give full recognition to the needs for economic, social and technological development of all countries and the sovereign right of all States, when enacting national legislation, to ensure a proper balance between these needs and the rights granted to IPR holders and thus to determine the scope and level of protection of such rights, particularly in sectors of special public concern, such as health, nutrition, agriculture and national security. **(71)**

(ii)   To set forth the principal rights and obligations of IP owners, taking into account the important inter-relationships between the scope of such rights and obligations and the promotion of social welfare and economic development. **(71)**

(iii)   To facilitate the diffusion of technological knowledge and to enhance international transfer of technology, and thus contribute to a more active participation of all countries in world production and trade. **(71)**

(iv)   To encourage technological innovation and promote inventiveness in all countries. **(71)**

(v)   To enable participants to take all appropriate measures to prevent the abuses which might result from the exercise of IPRs and to ensure intergovernmental co-operation in this regard. **(71)**

PART VI. DISPUTE PREVENTION AND SETTLEMENT

1.   **<u>Transparency</u> (68, 70, 71, 73, 74)**

1.1.1   [National (73)] (<u>Publication</u>) laws, regulations, judicial decisions and administrative rulings [of general application (68, 70, 74)] [of a precedential value (73)], [and all international agreements and decisions of international bodies (73)] [made effective by any PARTY, (70, 74)] pertaining to [the availability, scope, acquisition and enforcement of (68)] [the protection of (74)] intellectual   property [rights (68, 74)] [laws (73)] (68, 70, 73, 74)] [the application of the principles and norms prescribed at points 9 and 11 of Part I and point 2A.1 of Part IV above (71)] shall be:

- published promptly by PARTIES. **(73)**

- [published, or where such publication is not practicable, (74)] made [publicly (74)] available [promptly (74)] in such a manner as to enable governments [of the PARTIES (74)] and [traders (68)] [other interested parties (74)] to become acquainted with them. **(68, 74)**

- shall be subject to the provisions of Article X of the General Agreement. **(70)**

- made publicly available in the official language of the PARTY adopting such texts and, shall be provided, upon request, to any other PARTY. **(71)**

1.1.2   Agreements concerning the protection of intellectual property rights which are in force between the government or governmental agency of any PARTY and the government or a governmental agency of any other PARTY to the Agreement shall also be published or made publicly available. The provision of this paragraph shall not require PARTIES to disclose confidential information which would impede law enforcement or otherwise be contrary to the public interest or would prejudice the legitimate commercial interests of particular enterprises, public or private. **(74)**

(<u>Notification</u>)

1.2A   PARTIES shall notify the laws and regulations referred to above to the Committee on Trade Related Intellectual Property Rights in order to assist the Committee in its review of the operation of this Annex. The Committee shall enter into consultations with the World Intellectual

Property Organisation in order to agree, if possible, on the establishment of a common register containing these laws and regulations. If these consultations are successful, the Committee may decide to waive the obligation to notify such laws and regulations directly to the Committee. **(68)**

1.2B.1   The Committee established under point 1B of Part VIII below shall ensure, in co-operation with the World Intellectual Property Organization and other international organizations, as appropriate, access to all international agreements, decisions of international bodies, national laws, regulations, judicial decisions and administrative rulings of a precedential value, related to the intellectual property laws of the PARTIES. **(73)**

1.2B.2   PARTIES shall promptly notify all international agreements, national laws and regulations, judicial decisions and administrative rulings of a precedential value relying upon an exception of the principles of National Treatment and Most-Favoured Nation Treatment through the Committee to the other PARTIES. **(73)**

1.2C   PARTIES shall inform the TRIPS Committee, established under point 1C of Part VIII below, of any changes in their national laws and regulations concerning the protection of intellectual property rights (and any changes in their administration). PARTIES engaged in a special arrangement as stipulated in point 8B.2C.2 of Part II above shall inform the TRIPS Committee of the conclusion of such a special arrangement together with an outline of its contents. **(74)**

          (Information on Request)

1.3A   A PARTY, having reason to believe that a specific judicial decision, administrative ruling or bilateral agreement in the area of intellectual property rights affects its rights under this Annex, may request in writing to be given access to or be informed in sufficient detail of such specific judicial decisions and administrative rulings or bilateral agreement. **(68)**

1.3B   PARTIES shall, upon request from other PARTIES, provide information as promptly and as comprehensively as possible concerning application and administration of their national laws and regulations related to the protection of intellectual property rights. PARTIES shall notify the TRIPS Committee of the request and the provision of such information and shall provide the same information, when requested by other PARTIES, to the TRIPS Committee. **(74)**

1.3C   PARTIES shall ensure that an enquiry point exists which is able to answer all reasonable enquiries from other PARTIES and persons and legal entities thereof regarding the PARTY's laws, regulations, and requirements for protection and enforcement of intellectual property rights. **(73)**

2.   Prior Consultation (68), Dispute Prevention (73)

2A   PARTIES shall make reasonable efforts within the framework of their constitutional systems to inform and, upon request, to consult with the other PARTIES on possible changes in their intellectual property right laws and regulations, and in the administration of such laws and regulations relevant to the operation of this Annex. **(68)**

2B.1   Whenever laws, regulations and practices relevant to, and affecting, the protection and enforcement of intellectual property rights are under review or intended to be introduced by a PARTY to this Agreement, such PARTY shall

- publish, in an official GATT language, a notice in a publication at an early appropriate stage that it proposes to introduce, amend or abolish legislation or regulation; **(73)**

- promptly provide, upon request, draft legislation and draft regulations, including explanatory materials, to such PARTIES; **(73)**

- allow, without discrimination, reasonable time of no less than [X] months for other PARTIES to submit comments in writing on the basis of the General Agreement; **(73)**

- consult with interested PARTIES, upon request, on the basis of comments submitted. **(73)**

2B.2   None of these obligations is meant to limit the sovereignty of PARTIES to legislate, regulate and adjudicate in conformity with international obligations. **(73)**

3.   Dispute Settlement (68, 71, 73); Consultation, Dispute Settlement (74)

3A   Contracting parties agree that in the area of trade related intellectual property rights covered by this Annex they shall, in relation to each other, abide by the dispute settlement rules and procedures of the General Agreement, and the recommendations, rulings and decisions of the

CONTRACTING PARTIES, and not have recourse in relation to other contracting parties to unilaterally decided economic measures of any kind. Furthermore, they undertake to modify and administer their domestic legislation and related procedures in a manner ensuring the conformity of all measures taken thereunder with the above commitment. **(68)**

3B   (i)   Disputes arising under this PART shall be settled on the basis of Article XXII and Article XXIII and in accordance with the consolidated instrument [name]. **(73)**

        (ii)   Non-compliance with obligations under this PART shall be deemed to cause nullification and impairment of advantages and benefits accruing under the General Agreement on Tariffs and Trade. **(73)**

        (iii)   PARTIES shall refrain from taking any measure against another PARTY other than those provided for under the rules on dispute settlement within the General Agreement on Tariffs and Trade. **(73)**

3C   A PARTY shall not suspend, or threaten to suspend, its obligations under the Agreement without abiding by the procedures for settlement of disputes set out in this section. **(74)**

3D.1   Consultations (71)

(a) Where a dispute arises concerning the interpretation or implementation of any provisions of this Agreement, a PARTY may bring the matter to the attention of another PARTY and request the latter to enter into consultations with it. **(71)**

(b) The PARTY so requested shall provide promptly an adequate opportunity for the requested consultations. **(71)**

(c) PARTIES engaged in consultations shall attempt to reach, within a reasonable period of time, a mutually satisfactory solution to the dispute. **(71)**

3D.2   Other Means of Settlement (71)

If a mutually satisfactory solution is not reached within a reasonable period of time through the consultations referred to at point 3D.1, PARTIES to the dispute may agree to resort to other means designed to lead to an amicable settlement of their dispute, such as good offices, conciliation, mediation and arbitration. **(71)**

3D.3   <u>Non-Recourse to Unilateral Measures</u> (71)

PARTIES shall refrain, in relation to each other, from threatening or having recourse to unilaterally decided measures of any kind aimed at ensuring the enforcement of intellectual property rights. **(71)**

(See also point 11 of Part II above)

PART VII: TRANSITIONAL ARRANGEMENTS

1.   <u>Transitional Period</u> (68); <u>Transitional Arrangements for Developing Countries and Technical Cooperation</u> (73); <u>Transitional Arrangements</u> (74)

1A   PARTIES shall take all necessary steps to ensure the conformity of their laws, regulations and practice with the provisions of this Annex within a period of not more than [-] years following its entry into force. The Committee on Trade Related Intellectual Property Rights may decide, upon duly motivated request, that developing countries which face special problems in the preparation and implementation of intellectual property laws, dispose of an additional period not exceeding [-] years, with the exception of points 6, 7 and 8 of PART II, in respect of which this additional period shall not apply. Furthermore, the Committee may, upon duly motivated request, extend this additional period by a further period not exceeding [-] years in respect of least developed countries. **(68)**

1B.1   <u>Developing Countries</u> (73)

(i)   With a view to achieve full and successful adjustment and compliance with levels of protection and enforcement set forth in Parts III and IV above, and provided that existing levels of protection and enforcement are not reduced, developing PARTIES may not apply such standards for a period of a total of [X] years beginning with the date of acceptance or accession of such PARTY, but not later than the year [Z]. **(73)**

(ii)   Delay in implementation of obligations under Parts III and IV above may be extended upon duly motivated request for a further period not exceeding [X] years by the Committee established under point 1B of Part VIII below. Such decision shall take into account the level of technological and commercial development of the requesting PARTY. **(73)**

(iii)   Non-application of levels of protection set forth in Parts III and IV above after final expiration of the transitional period agreed shall entitle other PARTIES, without prejudice to other rights under the General Agreement, to suspend the application points 7 and 8 of Part II above and grant protection of intellectual property rights on the basis of reciprocity. **(73)**

1B.2   Least-Developed Countries (73)

(i) With a view to achieve full and successful adjustment and compliance with levels of protection and enforcement set forth in Parts III and IV above, least developed PARTIES are not expected to apply such standards for a period of a total of [X+Y] years. **(73)**

(ii) Delay of implementation of obligations may be further extended upon request by the Committee established under point 1B of Part VIII below. **(73)**

2.   Technical Assistance (68); Technical Cooperation (73); International Cooperation, Technical Assistance (74)

2A   Developed PARTIES shall, if requested, advise developing PARTIES on the preparation and implementation of domestic legislation on the protection and enforcement of intellectual property rights covered by this Annex as well as the prevention of their abuse, and shall grant them technical assistance on mutually agreed terms and conditions, regarding the establishment of domestic offices and agencies relevant to the implementation of their intellectual property legislation, including the training of officials employed in their respective governments. **(68)**

2B   PARTIES to this Agreement shall provide for technical co-operation to developing and least developed PARTIES upon coordination by the Committee established under point 1B of Part VIII below in collaboration with the World Intellectual Property Organization, and other international organizations, as appropriate. Upon request, such co-operation includes support and advice as to training of personnel, the introduction, amendment and implementation of national laws, regulations and practices, and assistance by the Committee for settlement of disputes. **(73)**

PART VIII: INSTITUTIONAL ARRANGEMENTS; FINAL PROVISIONS

Committee on Trade-Related Intellectual Property Rights (68); The Committee on Trade-Related Aspects of Intellectual Property Law (73); The TRIPS Committee (74)

1A   PARTIES shall establish a Committee on Trade Related Intellectual Property Rights composed of representatives from each PARTY. The Committee shall elect its own chairman, establish its own rules of procedures and shall meet not less than once a year and otherwise upon request of any PARTY. The Committee shall monitor the operation of this Annex and, in particular, PARTIES' compliance with their obligations hereunder, and shall afford PARTIES the opportunity of consulting on matters relating to trade related intellectual property rights. It shall carry out such other responsibilities as assigned to it by the CONTRACTING PARTIES, and it shall, in particular, provide any assistance requested by them in the context of procedures under Articles XXII and XXIII of the General Agreement. In carrying out its functions, the Committee may consult with and seek information from any source they deem appropriate. **(68)**

1B   (i) All PARTIES shall be represented in the Committee on Trade-Related Aspects of Intellectual Property Rights (hereinafter the Committee). It shall elect its Chairman annually and meet as necessary, but not less than once a year. It shall carry out its responsibilities as assigned to it under this PART or by the PARTIES. It may establish working groups. **(73)**

(ii) The Committee shall monitor the implementation and operation of this PART, taking into account the objectives thereof. It shall examine periodical country reports prepared by the GATT Secretariat on laws, regulations, practices and international agreements related to, and affecting, the protection of intellectual property rights. It shall make recommendations, as appropriate, to the PARTIES concerned. **(73)**

(iii) The Committee shall periodically agree upon a schedule of country reports. It shall adopt a work programme and coordinate activities of PARTIES in the field of technical cooperation. **(73)**

(iv) The Committee shall annually report to the CONTRACTING PARTIES. It may submit recommendations.**(73)**

(v) The Committee is entitled to elaborate and adopt guidelines for the interpretation, in particular of PARTS III and IV above. It shall take into account relevant findings of adopted panel reports. **(73)**

1C   The TRIPS Committee composed of representatives of the PARTIES shall be established. The TRIPS Committee shall carry out functions under this Agreement or otherwise assigned to it by the PARTIES. **(74)**

Joint Expert Group (68), Joint Group of Experts (73)

2A   In order to promote cooperation between the Committee on Trade Related Intellectual Property Rights and bodies under the World Intellectual Property Organisation, the latter shall be invited by the Committee to serve together with the GATT Secretariat as Secretariat for a joint Expert Group which shall consist of representatives of the CONTRACTING PARTIES and of the Member States of the Paris and Berne Unions. The Expert Group shall, when requested to do so by the Committee, advise the Committee on technical matters under consideration. **(68)**

2B   In order to promote co-operation between the Committee and bodies under the World Intellectual Property Organization, the Committee may establish, as appropriate, Joint Groups of Experts consisting of representatives of the PARTIES and of the Member States of the Unions created by the Paris Convention (1967) and the Berne Convention (1971) respectively. Upon request of the Committee, the Joint Groups of Experts shall give advice on technical matters under consideration. **(73)**

3.   Other Conventions (68)

PARTIES shall, within a period of [-] years, adhere to the Paris Convention (1967), and the Berne Convention (1971). They shall also give careful consideration to adhering to other international conventions on intellectual property with a view to strengthening the international framework for the protection of intellectual property rights and furthering the development of legitimate trade. **(68)**

4.   **International Cooperation** (68)

PARTIES agree to co-operate with each other with a view to eliminating international trade in goods infringing intellectual property rights. For this purpose they shall establish and notify contact points in their national administrations, and shall be ready to exchange information on trade in infringing goods. They shall, in particular, promote the exchange of information and co-operation between customs authorities with regard to trade in counterfeit goods. **(68)**

(See also point 1.1 of Part IX below)

5.   **Relationship to Other Parts of the General Agreement on Tariffs and Trade** (73)

Other provisions of the General Agreement shall apply to the extent that this PART does not provide for more specific rights, obligations and exceptions thereof. **(73)**

(See also point 5 of PART II)

6.   **Provisional Application** (73)

Pending the entry into force in accordance with Article XXX:1, this PART shall be applied provisionally. It shall become effective between PARTIES upon acceptance at [date]. For each other contracting party, it shall apply provisionally with the thirtieth day following the date of accession. **(73)**

7.   **Review and Amendment** (68); **Amendments** (73)

7A   PARTIES shall review the implementation of this Annex after the expiration of the transitional period referred to at point 1 of Part VII above. They shall, having regard to the experience gained in its implementation, review it [-] years after that date, and at identical intervals thereafter. The PARTIES shall also undertake reviews in the light of any relevant new developments which might warrant modification or amendment of this annex. **(68)**

7B   (i) Amendments to this PART shall take effect in accordance with the provisions on entry into force and on provisional application. **(73)**

(ii) Amendments merely serving the purpose to adjust to higher levels of protection of intellectual property rights achieved, and in force, in other multilateral agreements and accepted by all PARTIES may be adopted by the Committee.**(73)**

8.   <u>Withdrawal</u> **(73)**

Pending the entry into force, withdrawal from this PART shall be effected in accordance with the Protocol of Provisional Application of the General Agreement on Tariffs and Trade or the respective Protocol of Accession of contracting parties to the General Agreement on Tariffs and Trade. **(73)**

APPENDIX 3

Draft Final Act Embodying the Results of the Uruguay Round of Multilateral Trade Negotiations (Dunkel Draft), excerpts pertaining to TRIPS

MTN.TNC/W/FA
20 December 1991

This document is being tabled by the Chairman of the Trade Negotiations Committee at Official Level with the following understanding:

(a) It offers a concrete and comprehensive representation of the final global package of the results of the Uruguay Round;

(b) No single element of the Draft Final Act can be considered as agreed till the total package is agreed;

(c) Final agreement on the attached Draft Final Act will depend on substantial and meaningful results for all parties being achieved in the ongoing market access negotiations, including those related to tariffs and non-tariff measures: this applies to areas such as natural resource-based products, tropical products, agriculture and textiles and clothing.

(d) Final agreement similarly applies to the ongoing negotiations pertaining to initial liberalization commitments in the area of services.

AGREEMENT ON TRADE-RELATED ASPECTS OF INTELLECTUAL PROPERTY RIGHTS, INCLUDING TRADE IN COUNTERFEIT GOODS (Annex III)

TABLE OF CONTENTS

AGREEMENT ON TRADE-RELATED ASPECTS OF INTELLECTUAL PROPERTY RIGHTS, INCLUDING TRADE IN COUNTERFEIT GOODS

The PARTIES to this Agreement (hereinafter referred to as "PARTIES"),

Desiring to reduce distortions and impediments to international trade, and taking into account the need to promote effective and adequate protection of intellectual property rights, and to ensure that measures and procedures to enforce intellectual property rights do not themselves become barriers to legitimate trade;

Recognising, to this end, the need for new rules and disciplines concerning:

(a)   the applicability of the basic principles of the GATT and of relevant international intellectual property agreements or conventions;

(b)   the provision of adequate standards and principles concerning the availability, scope and use of trade-related intellectual property rights;

(c)   the provision of effective and appropriate means for the enforcement of trade-related intellectual property rights, taking into account differences in national legal systems;

(d)   the provision of effective and expeditious procedures for the multilateral prevention and settlement of disputes between governments; and

(e)   transitional arrangements aiming at the fullest participation in the results of the negotiations;

Recognising the need for a multilateral framework of principles, rules and disciplines dealing with international trade in counterfeit goods;

Recognising that intellectual property rights are private rights;

Recognising the underlying public policy objectives of national systems for the protection of intellectual property, including developmental and technological objectives;

Recognising also the special needs of the least-developed countries in respect of maximum flexibility in the domestic implementation of laws and regulations in order to enable them to create a sound and viable technological base;

Emphasising the importance of reducing tensions by reaching strengthened commitments to resolve disputes on trade-related intellectual property issues through multilateral procedures;

Desiring to establish a mutually supportive relationship between GATT and WIPO as well as other relevant international organisations;

Hereby agree as follows:

PART I: GENERAL PROVISIONS AND BASIC PRINCIPLES

Article 1: Nature and Scope of Obligations

1.   PARTIES shall give effect to the provisions of this Agreement. PARTIES may, but shall not be obliged to, implement in their domestic law more extensive protection than is required by this Agreement, provided that such protection does not contravene the provisions of this Agreement. PARTIES shall be free to determine the appropriate method of implementing the provisions of this Agreement within their own legal system and practice.

2.   For the purposes of this Agreement, the term "intellectual property" refers to all categories of intellectual property that are the subject of Sections 1 to 7 of Part II.

3.   PARTIES shall accord the treatment provided for in this Agreement to the nationals of other PARTIES.[1] In respect of the relevant intellectual property right, the nationals of other PARTIES shall be understood as those natural or legal persons that would meet the criteria for eligibility for protection provided for in the Paris Convention (1967), the Berne Convention (1971), the Rome Convention and the Treaty on Intellectual Property in Respect of Integrated Circuits, were all PARTIES members of those conventions. Any PARTY availing itself of the possibilities provided in Articles 5.3 or 6.2 of the Rome Convention shall make a notification as foreseen in those provisions to the Council on Trade-Related Aspects of Intellectual Property Rights.

Article 2: Intellectual Property Conventions

1.   In respect of Parts II, III and IV of this Agreement, PARTIES shall comply with Articles 1-12 and 19 of the Paris Convention (1967).

2.   Nothing in Parts I to IV of this Agreement shall derogate from existing obligations that PARTIES may have to each other under the Paris Convention, the Berne Convention, the Rome Convention and the Treaty on Intellectual Property in Respect of Integrated Circuits.

---

1   When "nationals" are referred to in this Agreement, they shall be deemed, in the case of Hong Kong, to mean persons, natural or legal, who are domiciled or who have a real and effective industrial or commercial establishment in Hong Kong.

Article 3: National Treatment

1.   Each PARTY shall accord to the nationals of other PARTIES treatment no less favourable than that it accords to its own nationals with regard to the protection[1] of intellectual property, subject to the exceptions already provided in, respectively, the Paris Convention (1967), the Berne Convention (1971), the Rome Convention and the Treaty on Intellectual Property in Respect of Integrated Circuits. In respect of performers, producers of phonograms and broadcasters, this obligation only applies in respect of the rights provided under this Agreement. Any PARTY availing itself of the possibilities provided in Article 6 of the Berne Convention and Article 16.1(b) of the Rome Convention shall make a notification as foreseen in those provisions to the Council on Trade-Related Aspects of Intellectual Property Rights.

2.   PARTIES may avail themselves of the exceptions permitted under paragraph 1 above in relation to judicial and administrative procedures, including the designation of an address for service or the appointment of an agent within the jurisdiction of a PARTY, only where such exceptions are necessary to secure compliance with laws and regulations which are not inconsistent with the provisions of this Agreement and where such practices are not applied in a manner which would constitute a disguised restriction on trade.

Article 4: Most-Favoured-Nation Treatment

With regard to the protection of intellectual property, any advantage, favour, privilege or immunity granted by a PARTY to the nationals of any other country shall be accorded immediately and unconditionally to the nationals of all other PARTIES. Exempted from this obligation are any advantage, favour, privilege or immunity accorded by a PARTY:

(a)   deriving from international agreements on judicial assistance and law enforcement of a general nature and not particularly confined to the protection of intellectual property rights;

(b)   granted in accordance with the provisions of the Berne Convention (1971) or the Rome Convention authorising that the treatment

---

1   For the purposes of Articles 3 and 4 of this Agreement, protection shall include matters affecting the availability, acquisition, scope, maintenance and enforcement of intellectual property rights as well as those matters affecting the use of intellectual property rights specifically addressed in the Agreement.

accorded be a function not of national treatment but of the treatment accorded in another country;

(c)   in respect of the rights of performers, producers of phonograms and broadcasters not provided under this Agreement;

(d)   deriving from international agreements related to the protection of intellectual property which entered into force prior to the entry into force of this Agreement, provided that such agreements are notified to the Council on Trade-Related Aspects of Intellectual Property Rights and do not constitute an arbitrary or unjustifiable discrimination against nationals of other PARTIES.

Article 5: Multilateral Agreements on Acquisition or Maintenance of Protection

The obligations under Articles 3 and 4 above do not apply to procedures provided in multilateral agreements concluded under the auspices of the World Intellectual Property Organization relating to the acquisition or maintenance of intellectual property rights.

Article 6: Exhaustion

For the purposes of dispute settlement under this Agreement, subject to the provisions of Articles 3 and 4 above nothing in this Agreement shall be used to address the issue of the exhaustion of intellectual property rights.

Article 7: Objectives

The protection and enforcement of intellectual property rights should contribute to the promotion of technological innovation and to the transfer and dissemination of technology, to the mutual advantage of producers and users of technological knowledge and in a manner conducive to social and economic welfare, and to a balance of rights and obligations.

Article 8: Principles

1.   PARTIES may, in formulating or amending their national laws and regulations, adopt measures necessary to protect public health and nutrition, and to promote the public interest in sectors of vital importance to their socio-economic and technological development, provided that such measures are consistent with the provisions of this Agreement.

2.   Appropriate measures, provided that they are consistent with the provisions of this Agreement, may be needed to prevent the abuse of intellectual property rights by right holders or the resort to practices which unreasonably restrain trade or adversely affect the international transfer of technology.

SECTION 1: COPYRIGHT AND RELATED RIGHTS

Article 9: Relation to Berne Convention

1.   PARTIES shall comply with Articles 1-21 and the Appendix of the Berne Convention (1971). However, PARTIES shall not have rights or obligations under this Agreement in respect of the rights conferred under Article 6bis of that Convention or of the rights derived therefrom.

2.   Copyright protection shall extend to expressions and not to ideas, procedures, methods of operation or mathematical concepts as such.

Article 10: Computer Programs and Compilations of Data

1.   Computer programs, whether in source or object code, shall be protected as literary works under the Berne Convention (1971).

2.   Compilations of data or other material, whether in machine readable or other form, which by reason of the selection or arrangement of their contents constitute intellectual creations shall be protected as such. Such protection, which shall not extend to the data or material itself, shall be without prejudice to any copyright subsisting in the data or material itself.

Article 11: Rental Rights

In respect of at least computer programs and cinematographic works, a PARTY shall provide authors and their successors in title the right to authorise or to prohibit the commercial rental to the public of originals or copies of their copyright works. A PARTY shall be excepted from this obligation in respect of cinematographic works unless such rental has led to widespread copying of such works which is materially impairing the exclusive right of reproduction conferred in that PARTY on authors and their successors in title. In respect of computer programs, this obligation does not apply to rentals where the program itself is not the essential object of the rental.

Article 12: Term of Protection

Whenever the term of protection of a work, other than a photographic work or a work of applied art, is calculated on a basis other than the life of a natural person, such term shall be no less than fifty years from the end of the calendar year of authorised publication, or, failing such authorised publication within fifty years from the making of the work, fifty years from the end of the calendar year of making.

Article 13: Limitations and Exceptions

PARTIES shall confine limitations or exceptions to exclusive rights to certain special cases which do not conflict with a normal exploitation of the work and do not unreasonably prejudice the legitimate interests of the right holder.

Article 14: Protection of Performers, Producers of Phonograms (Sound Recordings) and Broadcasts

1.   In respect of a fixation of their performance on a phonogram, performers shall have the possibility of preventing the following acts when undertaken without their authorisation: the fixation of their unfixed performance and the reproduction of such fixation. Performers shall also have the possibility of preventing the following acts when undertaken without their authorisation: the broadcasting by wireless means and the communication to the public of their live performance.

2.   Producers of phonograms shall enjoy the right to authorise or prohibit the direct or indirect reproduction of their phonograms.

3.   Broadcasting organisations shall have the right to prohibit the following acts when undertaken without their authorisation: the fixation, the reproduction of fixations, and the rebroadcasting by wireless means of broadcasts, as well as the communication to the public of television broadcasts of the same. Where PARTIES do not grant such rights to broadcasting organisations, they shall provide owners of copyright in the subject matter of broadcasts with the possibility of preventing the above acts, subject to the provisions of the Berne Convention (1971).

4.   The provisions of Article 11 in respect of computer programs shall apply mutatis mutandis to producers of phonograms and any other right holders in phonograms as determined in domestic law. If, on the date of signature of this Agreement, a PARTY has in force a system of equitable remuneration of right holders, it may maintain such system provided that the commercial rental of

phonograms is not giving rise to the material impairment of the exclusive rights of reproduction of right holders.

5.   The term of the protection available under this Agreement to performers and producers of phonograms shall last at least until the end of a period of fifty years computed from the end of the calendar year in which the fixation was made or the performance or broadcast took place. The term of protection granted pursuant to paragraph 3 above shall last for at least twenty years from the end of the calendar year in which the broadcast took place.

6.   Any PARTY to this Agreement may, in relation to the rights conferred under paragraphs 1-3 above, provide for conditions, limitations, exceptions and reservations to the extent permitted by the Rome Convention. However, the provisions of Article 18 of the Berne Convention (1971) shall also apply, _mutatis mutandis_, to the rights of performers and producers of phonograms in phonograms.

SECTION 2: TRADEMARKS

Article 15: Protectable Subject Matter

1.   Any sign, or any combination of signs, capable of distinguishing the goods or services of one undertaking from those of other undertakings, shall be capable of constituting a trademark. Such signs, in particular words including personal names, letters, numerals, figurative elements and combinations of colours as well as any combination of such signs, shall be eligible for registration as trademarks. Where signs are not inherently capable of distinguishing the relevant goods or services, PARTIES may make registrability depend on distinctiveness acquired through use. PARTIES may require, as a condition of registration, that signs be visually perceptible.

2.   Paragraph 1 above shall not be understood to prevent a PARTY from denying registration of a trademark on other grounds, provided that they do not derogate from the provisions of the Paris Convention (1967).

3.   PARTIES may make registrability depend on use. However, actual use of a trademark shall not be a condition for filing an application for registration. An application shall not be refused solely on the ground that intended use has not

taken place before the expiry of a period of three years from the date of application.

4.   The nature of the goods or services to which a trademark is to be applied shall in no case form an obstacle to registration of the trademark.

5.   PARTIES shall publish each trademark either before it is registered or promptly after it is registered and shall afford a reasonable opportunity for petitions to cancel the registration. In addition, PARTIES may afford an opportunity for the registration of a trademark to be opposed.

Article 16: Rights Conferred

1.   The owner of a registered trademark shall have the exclusive right to prevent all third parties not having his consent from using in the course of trade identical or similar signs for goods or services which are identical or similar to those in respect of which the trademark is registered where such use would result in a likelihood of confusion. In case of the use of an identical sign for identical goods or services, a likelihood of confusion shall be presumed. The rights described above shall not prejudice any existing prior rights, nor shall they affect the possibility of PARTIES making rights available on the basis of use.

2.   Article 6*bis* of the Paris Convention shall apply, *mutatis mutandis*, to services. In determining whether a trademark is well-known, account shall be taken of the knowledge of the trademark in the relevant sector of the public, including knowledge in that PARTY obtained as a result of the promotion of the trademark.

3.   Article 6*bis* of the Paris Convention shall apply, *mutatis mutandis*, to goods or services which are not similar to those in respect of which a trademark is registered, provided that use of that trademark in relation to those goods or services would indicate a connection between those goods or services and the owner of the registered trademark and provided that the interests of the owner of the registered trademark are likely to be damaged by such use.

Article 17: Exceptions

PARTIES may provide limited exceptions to the rights conferred by a trademark, such as fair use of descriptive terms, provided that such exceptions take account of the legitimate interests of the owner of the trademark and of third parties.

Article 18: Term of Protection

Initial registration, and each renewal of registration, of a trademark shall be for a term of no less than seven years. The registration of a trademark shall be renewable indefinitely.

Article 19: Requirement of Use

1.   If use is required to maintain a registration, the registration may be cancelled only after an uninterrupted period of at least three years of non-use, unless valid reasons based on the existence of obstacles to such use are shown by the trademark owner. Circumstances arising independently of the will of the owner of the trademark which constitute an obstacle to the use of the trademark, such as import restrictions on or other government requirements for goods or services protected by the trademark, shall be recognised as valid reasons for non-use.

2.   When subject to the control of its owner, use of a trademark by another person shall be recognised as use of the trademark for the purpose of maintaining the registration.

Article 20: Other Requirements

The use of a trademark in commerce shall not be unjustifiably encumbered by special requirements, such as use with another trademark, use in a special form or use in a manner detrimental to its capability to distinguish the goods or services of one undertaking from those of other undertakings. This will not preclude a requirement prescribing the use of the trademark identifying the undertaking producing the goods or services along with, but without linking it to, the trademark distinguishing the specific goods or services in question of that undertaking.

Article 21: Licensing and Assignment

PARTIES may determine conditions on the licensing and assignment of trademarks, it being understood that the compulsory licensing of trademarks shall not be permitted and that the owner of a registered trademark shall have the right to assign his trademark with or without the transfer of the business to which the trademark belongs.

SECTION 3: GEOGRAPHICAL INDICATIONS

Article 22: Protection of Geographical Indications

1.   Geographical indications are, for the purposes of this Agreement, indications which identify a good as originating in the territory of a PARTY, or a region or locality in that territory, where a given quality, reputation or other characteristic of the good is essentially attributable to its geographical origin.

2.   In respect of geographical indications, PARTIES shall provide the legal means for interested parties to prevent:

    (a)   the use of any means in the designation or presentation of a good that indicates or suggests that the good in question originates in a geographical area other than the true place of origin in a manner which misleads the public as to the geographical origin of the good;

    (b)   any use which constitutes an act of unfair competition within the meaning of Article lObis of the Paris Convention (1967).

3.   A PARTY shall, ex officio if its legislation so permits or at the request of an interested party, refuse or invalidate the registration of a trademark which contains or consists of a geographical indication with respect to goods not originating in the territory indicated, if use of the indication in the trademark for such goods in that PARTY is of such a nature as to mislead the public as to the true place of origin.

4.   The provisions of the preceding paragraphs of this Article shall apply to a geographical indication which, although literally true as to the territory, region or locality in which the goods originate, falsely represents to the public that the goods originate in another territory.

Article 23: Additional Protection for Geographical Indications for Wines and Spirits

1.   Each PARTY shall provide the legal means for interested parties to prevent use of a geographical indication identifying wines for wines not originating in the place indicated by the geographical indication in question or identifying spirits for spirits not originating in the place indicated by the geographical indication in question, even where the true origin of the goods is indicated or the geographical

indication is used in translation or accompanied by expressions such as "kind", "type", "style", "imitation" or the like.[1]

2.   The registration of a trademark for wines which contains or consists of a geographical indication identifying wines or for spirits which contains or consists of a geographical indication identifying spirits shall be refused or invalidated, ex officio if domestic legislation so permits or at the request of an interested party, with respect to such wines or spirits not having this origin.

3.   In the case of homonymous geographical indications for wines, protection shall be accorded to each indication, subject to the provisions of paragraph 4 of Article 22 above. Each PARTY shall determine the practical conditions under which the homonymous indications in question will be differentiated from each other, taking into account the need to ensure equitable treatment of the producers concerned and that consumers are not misled.

4.   In order to facilitate the protection of geographical indications for wines, negotiations shall be undertaken in the Council on Trade-Related Aspects of Intellectual Property Rights concerning the establishment of a multilateral system of notification and registration of geographical indications eligible for protection in those PARTIES participating in the system.

Article 24: International Negotiations; Exceptions

1.   PARTIES agree to enter into negotiations aimed at increasing the protection of individual geographical indications under Article 23. The provisions of paragraphs 4-8 below shall not be used by a PARTY to refuse to conduct negotiations or to conclude bilateral or multilateral agreements. In the context of such negotiations, PARTIES shall be willing to consider the continued applicability of these provisions to individual geographical indications whose use was the subject of such negotiations.

2.   The Council on Trade-Related Aspects of Intellectual Property Rights shall keep under review the application of the provisions of this Section; the first such review shall take place within two years of the entry into force of this Agreement. Any matter affecting the compliance with the obligations under these provisions may be drawn to the attention of the Council, which, at the request of a PARTY, shall consult with any PARTY or PARTIES in respect of such matter in

---

1   Notwithstanding the first sentence of Article 42, PARTIES may, with respect to these obligations, instead provide for enforcement by administrative action.

respect of which it has not been possible to find a satisfactory solution through bilateral or plurilateral consultations between the PARTIES concerned. The Council shall take such action as may be agreed to facilitate the operation and further the objectives of this Section.

3.　　　In implementing this Section, a PARTY shall not diminish the protection of geographical indications that existed in that PARTY immediately prior to the date of entry into force of this Agreement.

4.　　　Nothing in this Section shall require a PARTY to prevent continued and similar use of a particular geographical indication of another PARTY identifying wines in connection with goods or services by any of its nationals or domiciliaries who have used that geographical indication in a continuous manner with regard to the same or related goods or services in the territory of that PARTY either (a) for at least ten years preceding its signature of this Agreement or (b) in good faith preceding its signature of this Agreement.

5.　　　Where a trademark has been applied for or registered in good faith, or where rights to a trademark have been acquired through use in good faith either:

(a)　before the date of application of these provisions in that PARTY as defined in Part VI below; or

(b)　before the geographical indication is protected in its country of origin;

measures adopted to implement this Section shall not prejudice eligibility for or the validity of the registration of a trademark, or the right to use a trademark, on the basis that such a trademark is identical with, or similar to, a geographical indication.

6.　　　Nothing in this Section shall require a PARTY to apply its provisions in respect of a geographical indication of any other PARTY with respect to goods or services for which the relevant indication is identical with the term customary in common language as the common name for such goods or services in the territory of that PARTY. Nothing in this Section shall require a PARTY to apply its provisions in respect of a geographical indication of any other PARTY with respect to products of the vine for which the relevant indication is identical with the customary name of a grape variety existing in the territory of that PARTY as of the date of entry into force of this Agreement.

7.　　　A PARTY may provide that any request made under this Section in connection with the use or registration of a trademark must be presented within five years after the adverse use of the protected indication has become generally known in that PARTY or after the date of registration of the trademark in that PARTY provided that the trademark has been published by that date, if such date is earlier than the date on which the adverse use became generally known in that PARTY, provided that the geographical indication is not used or registered in bad faith.

8.   The provisions of this Section shall in no way prejudice the right of any person to use, in the course of trade, his name or the name of his predecessor in business, except where such name is used in such a manner as to mislead the public.

9.   There shall be no obligation under this Agreement to protect geographical indications which are not or cease to be protected in their country of origin, or which have fallen into disuse in that country.

SECTION 4: INDUSTRIAL DESIGNS

Article 25: Requirements for Protection

1.   PARTIES shall provide for the protection of independently created industrial designs that are new or original. PARTIES may provide that designs are not new or original if they do not significantly differ from known designs or combinations of known design features. PARTIES may provide that such protection shall not extend to designs dictated essentially by technical or functional considerations.

2.   Each PARTY shall ensure that requirements for securing protection for textile designs, in particular in regard to any cost, examination or publication, do not unreasonably impair the opportunity to seek and obtain such protection. PARTIES shall be free to meet this obligation through industrial design law or through copyright.

Article 26: Protection

1.   The owner of a protected industrial design shall have the right to prevent third parties not having his consent from making, selling or importing articles bearing or embodying a design which is a copy, or substantially a copy, of the protected design, when such acts are undertaken for commercial purposes.

2.   PARTIES may provide limited exceptions to the protection of industrial designs, provided that such exceptions do not unreasonably conflict with the normal exploitation of protected industrial designs and do not unreasonably prejudice the legitimate interests of the owner of the protected design, taking account of the legitimate interests of third parties.

3.   The duration of protection available shall amount to at least ten years.

SECTION 5: PATENTS

Article 27: Patentable Subject Matter

1.   Subject to the provisions of paragraphs 2 and 3 below, patents shall be available for any inventions, whether products or processes, in all fields of technology, provided that they are new, involve an inventive step and are capable of industrial application.[1] Subject to paragraph 4 of Article 65 and paragraph 3 of this Article, patents shall be available and patent rights enjoyable without discrimination as to the place of invention, the field of technology and whether products are imported or locally produced.

2.   PARTIES may exclude from patentability inventions, the prevention within their territory of the commercial exploitation of which is necessary to protect ordre public or morality, including to protect human, animal or plant life or health or to avoid serious prejudice to the environment, provided that such exclusion is not made merely because the exploitation is prohibited by domestic law.

3.   PARTIES may also exclude from patentability:

   (a)   diagnostic, therapeutic and surgical methods for the treatment of humans or animals;

   (b)   plants and animals other than microorganisms, and essentially biological processes for the production of plants or animals other than non-biological and microbiological processes. However, PARTIES shall provide for the protection of plant varieties either by

---

1   For the purposes of this Article, the terms "inventive step" and "capable of industrial application" may be deemed by a PARTY to be synonymous with the terms "non-obvious" and "useful" respectively.

patents or by an effective <u>sui generis</u> system or by any combination thereof. This provision shall be reviewed four years after the entry into force of this Agreement.

Article 28: Rights Conferred

1.   A patent shall confer on its owner the following exclusive rights:

    (a)   where the subject matter of a patent is a product, to prevent third parties not having his consent from the acts of: making, using, offering for sale, selling, or importing[1] for these purposes that product;

    (b)   where the subject matter of a patent is a process, to prevent third parties not having his consent from the act of using the process, and from the acts of: using, offering for sale, selling, or importing for these purposes at least the product obtained directly by that process.

2.   Patent owners shall also have the right to assign, or transfer by succession, the patent and to conclude licensing contracts.

Article 29: Conditions on Patent Applicants

1.   PARTIES shall require that an applicant for a patent shall disclose the invention in a manner sufficiently clear and complete for the invention to be carried out by a person skilled in the art and may require the applicant to indicate the best mode for carrying out the invention known to the inventor at the filing date or, where priority is claimed, at the priority date of the application.

2.   PARTIES may require an applicant for a patent to provide information concerning his corresponding foreign applications and grants.

Article 30: Exceptions to Rights Conferred

PARTIES may provide limited exceptions to the exclusive rights conferred by a patent, provided that such exceptions do not unreasonably conflict with a normal exploitation of the patent and do not unreasonably prejudice the legitimate interests of the patent owner, taking account of the legitimate interests of third parties.

---

1   This right, like all other rights conferred under this Agreement in respect of the use, sale, importation or other distribution of goods, is subject to the provisions of Article 6 above.

Article 31: Other Use Without Authorisation of the Right Holder

Where the law of a PARTY allows for other use[1] of the subject matter of a patent without the authorisation of the right holder, including use by the government or third parties authorised by the government, the following provisions shall be respected:

(a)   authorisation of such use shall be considered on its individual merits;

(b)   such use may only be permitted if, prior to such use, the proposed user has made efforts to obtain authorisation from the right holder on reasonable commercial terms and conditions and that such efforts have not been successful within a reasonable period of time. This requirement may be waived by a PARTY in the case of a national emergency or other circumstances of extreme urgency or in cases of public non-commercial use. In situations of national emergency or other circumstances of extreme urgency, the right holder shall, nevertheless, be notified as soon as

(c)   the scope and duration of such use shall be limited to the purpose for which it was authorised;

(d)   such use shall be non-exclusive;

(e)   such use shall be non-assignable, except with that part of the enterprise or goodwill which enjoys such use;

(f)   any such use shall be authorised predominantly for the supply of the domestic market of the PARTY authorising such use;

(g)   authorisation for such use shall be liable, subject to adequate protection of the legitimate interests of the persons so authorised, to be terminated if and when the circumstances which led to it cease to exist and are unlikely to recur. The competent authority shall have the authority to review, upon motivated request, the continued existence of these circumstances;

(h)   the right holder shall be paid adequate remuneration in the circumstances of each case, taking into account the economic value of the authorisation;
reasonably practicable. In the case of public non-commercial use, where the government or contractor, without making a patent search, knows or has demonstrable grounds to know that a valid

---

1   "Other use" refers to use other than that allowed under Article 30.

patent is or will be used by or for the government, the right holder shall be informed promptly;

(i) the legal validity of any decision relating to the authorisation of such use shall be subject to judicial review or other independent review by a distinct higher authority in that PARTY;

(j) any decision relating to the remuneration provided in respect of such use shall be subject to judicial review or other independent review by a distinct higher authority in that PARTY;

(k) PARTIES are not obliged to apply the conditions set forth in sub-paragraphs (b) and (f) above where such use is permitted to remedy a practice determined after judicial or administrative process to be anti-competitive. The need to correct anti-competitive practices may be taken into account in determining the amount of remuneration in such cases. Competent authorities shall have the authority to refuse termination of authorisation if and when the conditions which led to such authorisation are likely to recur;

(l) where such use is authorised to permit the exploitation of a patent ("the second patent") which cannot be exploited without infringing another patent ("the first patent"), the following additional conditions shall apply:

   (i) the invention claimed in the second patent shall involve an important technical advance of considerable economic significance ,in relation to the invention claimed in the first patent;

   (ii) the owner of the first patent shall be entitled to a cross-licence on reasonable terms to use the invention claimed in the second patent; and

   (iii) the use authorised in respect of the first patent shall be non-assignable except with the assignment of the second patent.

Article 32: Revocation/Forfeiture

An opportunity for judicial review of any decision to revoke or forfeit a patent shall be available.

Article 33: Term of Protection

The term of protection available shall not end before the expiration of a period of twenty years counted from the filing date.[1]

Article 34: Process Patents: Burden of Proof

1.   For the purposes of civil proceedings in respect of the infringement of the rights of the owner referred to in Article 28.1(b), if the subject matter of a patent is a process for obtaining a product, the judicial authorities shall have the authority to order the defendant to prove that the process to obtain an identical product is different from the patented process. Therefore, PARTIES shall provide, in at least one of the following circumstances, that any identical product when produced without the consent of the patent owner shall, in the absence of proof to the contrary, be deemed to have been obtained by the patented process:

   (a)   if the product obtained by the patented process is new;

   (b)   if there is a substantial likelihood that the identical product was made by the process and the owner of the patent has been unable through reasonable efforts to determine the process actually used.

2.   Any PARTY shall be free to provide that the burden of proof indicated in paragraph 1 shall be on the alleged infringer only if the condition referred to in sub-paragraph (a) is fulfilled or only if the condition referred to in sub-paragraph (b) is fulfilled.

3.   In the adduction of proof to the contrary, the legitimate interests of the defendant in protecting his manufacturing and business secrets shall be taken into account.

---

1   It is understood that those PARTIES which do not have a system of original grant may provide that the term of protection shall be computed from the filing date in the system of original grant.

SECTION 6: LAYOUT-DESIGNS (TOPOGRAPHIES) OF INTEGRATED CIRCUITS

Article 35: Relation to IPIC Treaty

PARTIES agree to provide protection to the layout-designs (topographies) of integrated circuits (hereinafter referred to as "layout-designs') in accordance with Articles 2-7 (other than Article 6.3), 12 and 16.3 of the Treaty on Intellectual Property in Respect of Integrated Circuits as opened for signature on 26 May 1989 and, in addition, to comply with the following provisions.

Article 36: Scope of the Protection

Subject to the provisions of Article 37.1 below, PARTIES shall consider unlawful the following acts if performed without the authorisation of the holder of the right: importing, selling, or otherwise distributing for commercial purposes a protected layout-design, an integrated circuit in which a protected layout-design is incorporated, or an article incorporating such an integrated circuit only insofar as it continues to contain an unlawfully reproduced layout-design.

Article 37: Acts not Requiring the Authorisation of the Holder of the Right

1.   Notwithstanding Article 36 above, no PARTY shall consider unlawful the performance of any of the acts referred to in that Article in respect of an integrated circuit incorporating an unlawfully reproduced layout-design or any article incorporating such an integrated circuit where the person performing or ordering such acts did not know and had no reasonable ground to know, when acquiring the integrated circuit or article incorporating such an integrated circuit, that it incorporated an unlawfully reproduced layout-design. PARTIES shall provide that, after the time that such person has received sufficient notice that the layout-design was unlawfully reproduced, he may perform any of the acts with respect to the stock on hand or ordered before such time, but shall be liable to pay to the holder of the right a sum equivalent to a reasonable royalty such as would be payable under a freely negotiated licence in respect of such a layout-design.

2.   The conditions set out in sub-paragraphs (a)-(k) of Article 31 above shall apply mutatis mutandis in the event of any non-voluntary licensing of a layout-design or of its use by or for the government without the authorisation of the right holder.

Article 38: Term of Protection

1.   In PARTIES requiring registration as a condition of protection, the term of protection of layout-designs shall not end before the expiration of a period of ten years counted from the date of filing an application for registration or from the first commercial exploitation wherever in the world it occurs.

2.   In PARTIES not requiring registration as a condition for protection, layout-designs shall be protected for a term of no less than ten years from the date of the first commercial exploitation wherever in the world it occurs.

3.   Notwithstanding paragraphs 1 and 2 above, a PARTY may provide that protection shall lapse fifteen years after the creation of the layout-design.

SECTION 7: PROTECTION OF UNDISCLOSED INFORMATION

Article 39

1.   In the course of ensuring effective protection against unfair competition as provided in Article 10bis of the Paris Convention (1967), PARTIES shall protect undisclosed information in accordance with paragraph 2 below and data submitted to governments or governmental agencies in accordance with paragraph 3 below.

2.   Natural and legal persons shall have the possibility of preventing information lawfully within their control from being disclosed to, acquired by, or used by others without their consent in a manner contrary to honest commercial practices[1] so long as such information:

-        is secret in the sense that it is not, as a body or in the precise configuration and assembly of its components, generally known among or readily accessible to persons within the circles that normally deal with the kind of information in question;

-        has commercial value because it is secret; and

---

1   For the purpose of this provision, "a manner contrary to honest commercial practices" shall mean at least practices such as breach of contract, breach of confidence and inducement to breach, and includes the acquisition of undisclosed information by third parties who knew, or were grossly negligent in failing to know, that such practices were involved in the acquisition.

-        has been subject to reasonable steps under the circumstances, by the person lawfully in control of the information, to keep it secret.

3.   PARTIES, when requiring, as a condition of approving the marketing of pharmaceutical or of agricultural chemical products which utilise new chemical entities, the submission of undisclosed test or other data, the origination of which involves a considerable effort, shall protect such data against unfair commercial use. In addition, PARTIES shall protect such data against disclosure, except where necessary to protect the public, or unless steps are taken to ensure that the data are protected against unfair commercial use.

SECTION 8: CONTROL OF ANTI-COMPETITIVE PRACTICES IN CONTRACTUAL LICENCES

Article 40

1.   PARTIES agree that some licensing practices or conditions pertaining to intellectual property rights which restrain competition may have adverse effects on trade and may impede the transfer and dissemination of technology.

2.   Nothing in this Agreement shall prevent PARTIES from specifying in their national legislation licensing practices or conditions that may in particular cases constitute an abuse of intellectual property rights having an adverse effect on competition in the relevant market. As provided above, a PARTY may adopt, consistently with the other provisions of this Agreement, appropriate measures to prevent or control such practices, which may include for example exclusive grantback conditions, conditions preventing challenges to validity and coercive package licensing, in the light of the relevant laws and regulations of that PARTY.

3.   Each PARTY shall enter, upon request, into consultations with any other PARTY which has cause to believe that an intellectual property right owner that is a national or domiciliary of the PARTY to which the request for consultations has been addressed is undertaking practices in violation of the requesting PARTY's laws and regulations on the subject matter of this Section, and which wishes to secure compliance with such legislation, without prejudice to any action under the law and to the full freedom of an ultimate decision of either PARTY. The PARTY addressed shall accord full and sympathetic consideration to, and shall

afford adequate opportunity for, consultations with the requesting PARTY, and shall cooperate through supply of publicly available non-confidential information of relevance to the matter in question and of other information available to the PARTY, subject to domestic law and to the conclusion of mutually satisfactory agreements concerning the safeguarding of its confidentiality by the requesting PARTY.

4.   A PARTY whose nationals or domiciliaries are subject to proceedings in another PARTY concerning alleged violation of that other PARTY's laws and regulations on the subject matter of this Section shall, upon request, be granted an opportunity for consultations by the other PARTY under the same conditions as those foreseen in paragraph 3 above.

PART III: ENFORCEMENT OF INTELLECTUAL PROPERTY RIGHTS

SECTION 1: GENERAL OBLIGATIONS

Article 41

1.   PARTIES shall ensure that enforcement procedures as specified in this Part are available under their national laws so as to permit effective action against any act of infringement of intellectual property rights covered by this Agreement, including expeditious remedies to prevent infringements and remedies which constitute a deterrent to further infringements. These procedures shall be applied in such a manner as to avoid the creation of barriers to legitimate trade and to provide for safeguards against their abuse.

2.   Procedures concerning the enforcement of intellectual property rights shall be fair and equitable. They shall not be unnecessarily complicated or costly, or entail unreasonable time-limits or unwarranted delays.

3.   Decisions on the merits of a case shall preferably be in writing and reasoned. They shall be made available at least to the parties to the dispute without undue delay. Decisions on the merits of a case shall be based only on evidence in respect of which parties were offered the opportunity to be heard.

4.   Parties to a dispute shall have an opportunity for review by a judicial authority of final administrative decisions and, subject to jurisdictional provisions in national laws concerning the importance of a case, of at least the legal aspects of initial judicial decisions on the merits of a case. However, there shall be no obligation to provide an opportunity for review of acquittals in criminal cases.

5.   It is understood that this Part does not create any obligation to put in place a judicial system for the enforcement of intellectual property rights distinct from that for the enforcement of laws in general, nor does it affect the capacity of PARTIES to enforce their laws in general. Nothing in this Part creates any obligation with respect to the distribution of resources as between enforcement of intellectual property rights and the enforcement of laws in general.

SECTION 2: CIVIL AND ADMINISTRATIVE PROCEDURES AND REMEDIES

Article 42: Fair and Equitable Procedures

PARTIES shall make available to right holders[1] civil judicial procedures concerning the enforcement of any intellectual property right covered by this Agreement. Defendants shall have the right to written notice which is timely and contains sufficient detail, including the basis of the claims. Parties shall be allowed to be represented by independent legal counsel, and procedures shall not impose overly burdensome requirements concerning mandatory personal appearances. All parties to such procedures shall be duly entitled to substantiate their claims and to present all relevant evidence. The procedure shall provide a means to identify and protect confidential information, unless this would be contrary to existing constitutional requirements.

Article 43: Evidence of Proof

1.   The judicial authorities shall have the authority, where a party has presented reasonably available evidence sufficient to support its claims and has specified evidence relevant to substantiation of its claims which lies in the control of the opposing party, to order that this evidence be produced by the opposing

---

1   For the purpose of this Part, the term "right holder" includes federations and associations having legal standing to assert such rights.

party, subject in appropriate cases to conditions which ensure the protection of confidential information.

2.   In cases in which a party to a proceeding voluntarily and without good reason refuses access to, or otherwise does not provide necessary information within a reasonable period, or significantly impedes a procedure relating to an enforcement action, a PARTY may accord judicial authorities the authority to make preliminary and final determinations, affirmative or negative, on the basis of the information presented to them, including the complaint or the allegation presented by the party adversely affected by the denial of access to information, subject to providing the parties an opportunity to be heard on the allegations or evidence.

Article 44: Injunctions

1.   The judicial authorities shall have the authority to order a party to desist from an infringement, <u>inter alia</u> to prevent the entry into the channels of commerce in their jurisdiction of imported goods that involve the infringement of an intellectual property right, immediately after customs clearance of such goods. PARTIES are not obliged to accord such authority in respect of protected subject matter acquired or ordered by a person prior to knowing or having reasonable grounds to know that dealing in such subject matter would entail the infringement of an intellectual property right.

2.   Notwithstanding the other provisions of this Part and provided that the provisions of Part II specifically addressing use by governments, or by third parties authorised by a government, without the authorisation of the right holder are complied with, PARTIES may limit the remedies available against such use to payment of remuneration in accordance with sub-paragraph (h) of Article 31 above. In other cases, the remedies under this Part shall apply or, where these remedies are inconsistent with national law, declaratory judgments and adequate compensation shall be available.

Article 45: Damages

1.   The judicial authorities shall have the authority to order the infringer to pay the right holder damages adequate to compensate for the injury the right holder has suffered because of an infringement of his intellectual property right by an infringer who knew or had reasonable grounds to know that he was engaged in infringing activity.

2.   The judicial authorities shall also have the authority to order the infringer to pay the right holder expenses, which may include appropriate attorney's fees.

In appropriate cases, PARTIES may authorise the judicial authorities to order recovery of profits and/or payment of pre-established damages even where the infringer did not know or had no reasonable grounds to know that he was engaged in infringing activity.

Article 46: Other Remedies

In order to create an effective deterrent to infringement, the judicial authorities shall have the authority to order that goods that they have found to be infringing be, without compensation of any sort, disposed of outside the channels of commerce in such a manner as to avoid any harm caused to the right holder, or, unless this would be contrary to existing constitutional requirements, destroyed. The judicial authorities shall also have the authority to order that materials and implements the predominant use of which has been in the creation of the infringing goods be, without compensation of any sort, disposed of outside the channels of commerce in such a manner as to minimise the risks of further infringements. In considering such requests, the need for proportionality between the seriousness of the infringement and the remedies ordered as well as the interests of third parties shall be taken into account. In regard to counterfeit goods, the simple removal of the trademark unlawfully affixed shall not be sufficient, other than in exceptional cases, to permit release of the goods into the channels of commerce.

Article 47: Right of Information

PARTIES may provide that the judicial authorities shall have the authority, unless this would be out of proportion to the seriousness of the infringement, to order the infringer to inform the right holder of the identity of third persons involved in the production and distribution of the infringing goods or services and of their channels of distribution.

Article 48: Indemnification of the Defendant

1.   The judicial authorities shall have the authority to order a party at whose request measures were taken and who has abused enforcement procedures to provide to a party wrongfully enjoined or restrained adequate compensation for the injury suffered because of such abuse. The judicial authorities shall also have the authority to order the applicant to pay the defendant expenses, which may include appropriate attorney's fees.

2.   In respect of the administration of any law pertaining to the protection or enforcement of intellectual property rights, PARTIES shall only exempt both public

authorities and officials from liability to appropriate remedial measures where actions are taken or intended in good faith in the course of the administration of such laws.

Article 49: Administrative Procedures

To the extent that any civil remedy can be ordered as a result of administrative procedures on the merits of a case, such procedures shall conform to principles equivalent in substance to those set forth in this Section.

SECTION 3: PROVISIONAL MEASURES

Article 50

1.   The judicial authorities shall have the authority to order prompt and effective provisional measures:

     (a)   to prevent an infringement of any intellectual property right from occurring, and in particular to prevent the entry into the channels of commerce in their jurisdiction of goods, including imported goods immediately after customs clearance;

     (b)   to preserve relevant evidence in regard to the alleged infringement.

2.   The judicial authorities shall have the authority to adopt provisional measures _inaudita altera parte_ where appropriate, in particular where any delay is likely to cause irreparable harm to the right holder, or where there is a demonstrable risk of evidence being destroyed.

3.   The judicial authorities shall have the authority to require the applicant to provide any reasonably available evidence in order to satisfy themselves with a sufficient degree of certainty that the applicant is the right holder and that his right is being infringed or that such infringement is imminent, and to order the applicant to provide a security or equivalent assurance sufficient to protect the defendant and to prevent abuse.

4.   Where provisional measures have been adopted _inaudita altera parte_, the parties affected shall be given notice, without delay after the execution of the measures at the latest. A review, including a right to be heard, shall take place

upon request of the defendant with a view to deciding, within a reasonable period after the notification of the measures, whether these measures shall be modified, revoked or confirmed.

5.   The applicant may be required to supply other information necessary for the identification of the goods concerned by the authority that will execute the provisional measures.

6.   Without prejudice to paragraph 4 above, provisional measures taken on the basis of paragraphs 1 and 2 above shall, upon request by the defendant, be revoked or otherwise cease to have effect, if proceedings leading to a decision on the merits of the case are not initiated within a reasonable period, to be determined by the judicial authority ordering the measures where national law so permits or, in the absence of such a determination, not to exceed twenty working days or thirty-one calendar days, whichever is the longer.

7.   Where the provisional measures are revoked or where they lapse due to any act or omission by the applicant, or where it is subsequently found that there has been no infringement or threat of infringement of an intellectual property right, the judicial authorities shall have the authority to order the applicant, upon request of the defendant, to provide the defendant appropriate compensation for any injury caused by these measures.

8.   To the extent that any provisional measure can be ordered as a result of administrative procedures, such procedures shall conform to principles equivalent in substance to those set forth in this Section

SECTION 4: SPECIAL REQUIREMENTS RELATED TO BORDER MEASURES[1]

Article 51: Suspension of Release by Customs Authorities

PARTIES shall, in conformity with the provisions set out below, adopt procedures[2] to enable a right holder, who has valid grounds for suspecting that the importation of counterfeit trademark or pirated copyright goods[3] may take place, to lodge an application in writing with competent authorities, administrative or judicial, for the suspension by the customs authorities of the release into free circulation of such goods. PARTIES may enable such an application to be made in respect of goods which involve other infringements of intellectual property rights, provided that the requirements of this Section are met. PARTIES may also provide for corresponding procedures concerning the suspension by the customs authorities of the release of infringing goods destined for exportation from their territories.

Article 52: Application

Any right holder initiating the procedures under Article 51 above shall be required to provide adequate evidence to satisfy the competent authorities that, under the laws of the country of importation, there is prima facie an infringement of his intellectual property right and to supply a sufficiently detailed description of

---

1   It is understood that there shall be no obligation to apply such procedures to imports of goods put on the market in another country by or with the consent of the right holder, or to goods in transit.

2   Where a PARTY has dismantled substantially all controls over movement of goods across its border with another PARTY with which it forms part of a customs union, it shall not be required to apply the provisions of this Section at that border.

3   For the purposes of this Agreement:
    - counterfeit trademark goods shall mean any goods, including packaging, bearing without authorisation a trademark which is identical to the trademark validly registered in respect of such goods, or which cannot be distinguished in its essential aspects from such a trademark, and which thereby infringes the rights of the owner of the trademark in question under the law of the country of importation;
    - pirated copyright goods shall mean any goods which are copies made without the consent of the right holder or person duly authorised by him in the country of production and which are made directly or indirectly from an article where the making of that copy would have constituted an infringement of a copyright or a related right under the law of the country of importation.

the goods to make them readily recognisable by the customs authorities. The competent authorities shall inform the applicant within a reasonable period whether they have accepted the application and, where determined by the competent authorities, the period for which the customs authorities will take action.

Article 53: Security or Equivalent Assurance

1.   The competent authorities shall have the authority to require an applicant to provide a security or equivalent assurance sufficient to protect the defendant and the competent authorities and to prevent abuse. Such security or equivalent assurance shall not unreasonably deter recourse to these procedures.

2.   Where pursuant to an application under this Section the release of goods involving industrial designs, patents, integrated circuits or undisclosed information into free circulation has been suspended by customs authorities on the basis of a decision other than by a judicial or other independent authority, and the period provided for in Article 55 has expired without the granting of provisional relief by the duly empowered authority, and provided that all other conditions for importation have been complied with, the owner, importer, or consignee of such goods shall be entitled to their release on the posting of a security in an amount sufficient to protect the right holder for any infringement. Payment of such security shall not prejudice any other remedy available to the right holder, it being understood that the security shall be released if the right holder fails to pursue his right of action within a reasonable period of time.

Article 54: Notice of Suspension

The importer and the applicant shall be promptly notified of the suspension of the release of goods according to Article 51 above.

Article 55: Duration of Suspension

If, within a period not exceeding ten working days after the applicant has been served notice of the suspension, the customs authorities have not been informed that proceedings leading to a decision on the merits of the case have been initiated by a party other than the defendant, or that the duly empowered authority has taken provisional measures prolonging the suspension of the release of the goods, the goods shall be released, provided that all other conditions for importation or exportation have been complied with; in appropriate cases, this time-limit may be extended by another ten working days. If proceedings leading to a decision on the merits of the case have been initiated, a review, including a right to be heard, shall take place upon request of the defendant with a view to deciding, within a reasonable period, whether these measures shall be modified, revoked or confirmed. Notwithstanding the above, where the suspension of the release of goods is carried out or continued in accordance with a provisional judicial measure, the provisions of Article 50, paragraph 6 above shall apply.

Article 56: Indemnification of the Importer and of the Owner of the Goods

Relevant authorities shall have the authority to order the applicant to pay the importer, the consignee and the owner of the goods appropriate compensation for any injury caused to them through the wrongful detention of goods or through the detention of goods released pursuant to Article 55 above.

Article 57: Right of Inspection and Information

Without prejudice to the protection of confidential information, PARTIES shall provide the competent authorities the authority to give the right holder sufficient opportunity to have any product detained by the customs authorities inspected in order to substantiate his claims. The competent authorities shall also have authority to give the importer an equivalent opportunity to have any such product inspected. Where a positive determination has been made on the merits of a case, PARTIES may provide the competent authorities the authority to inform the right holder of the names and addresses of the consignor, the importer and the consignee and of the quantity of the goods in question.

Article 58: Ex Officio Action

Where PARTIES require competent authorities to act upon their own initiative and to suspend the release of goods in respect of which they have acquired prima facie evidence that an intellectual property right is being infringed:

(a)   the competent authorities may at any time seek from the right holder any information that may assist them to exercise these powers;

(b)   the importer and the right holder shall be promptly notified of the suspension. Where the importer has lodged an appeal against the suspension with the competent authorities, the suspension shall be subject to the conditions, mutatis mutandis, set out at Article 55 above;

(c)   PARTIES shall only exempt both public authorities and officials from liability to appropriate remedial measures where actions are taken or intended in good faith.

Article 59: Remedies

Without prejudice to other rights of action open to the right holder and subject to the right of the defendant to seek review by a judicial authority, competent authorities shall have the authority to order the destruction or disposal of infringing goods in accordance with the principles set out in Article 46 above. In regard to counterfeit goods, the authorities shall not allow the re-exportation of the infringing goods in an unaltered state or subject them to a different customs procedure, other than in exceptional circumstances.

Article 60: De Minimis Imports

PARTIES may exclude from the application of the above provisions small quantities of goods of a non-commercial nature contained in travellers' personal luggage or sent in small consignments.

SECTION 5: CRIMINAL PROCEDURES

Article 61

PARTIES shall provide for criminal procedures and penalties to be applied at least in cases of wilful trademark counterfeiting or copyright piracy on a commercial scale. Remedies available shall include imprisonment and/or monetary fines sufficient to provide a deterrent, consistently with the level of penalties applied for crimes of a corresponding gravity. In appropriate cases, remedies available shall also include the seizure, forfeiture and destruction of the infringing goods and of any materials and implements the predominant use of which has been in the commission of the offence. PARTIES may provide for criminal procedures and penalties to be applied in other cases of infringement of intellectual property rights, in particular where they are committed wilfully and on a commercial scale.

PART IV: ACQUISITION AND MAINTENANCE OF INTELLECTUAL PROPERTY RIGHTS AND RELATED INTER-PARTES PROCEDURES

Article 62

1.　　　PARTIES may require, as a condition of the acquisition or maintenance of the intellectual property rights provided for under Sections 2-6 of Part II of this Agreement, compliance with reasonable procedures and formalities. Such procedures and formalities shall be consistent with the provisions of this Agreement.

2.　　　Where the acquisition of an intellectual property right is subject to the right being granted or registered, PARTIES shall ensure that the procedures for grant or registration, subject to compliance with the substantive conditions for acquisition of the right, permit the granting or registration of the right within a reasonable period of time so as to avoid unwarranted curtailment of the period of protection.

3.　　　Article 4 of the Paris Convention (1967) shall apply mutatis mutandis to service marks.

4.　　　Procedures concerning the acquisition or maintenance of intellectual property rights and, where the national law provides for such procedures, administrative revocation and inter partes procedures such as opposition, revocation and cancellation, shall be governed by the general principles set out in paragraphs 2 and 3 of Article 41.

5.　　　Final administrative decisions in any of the procedures referred to under paragraph 4 above shall be subject to review by a judicial or quasi-judicial authority. However, there shall be no obligation to provide an opportunity for such review of decisions in cases of unsuccessful opposition or administrative revocation, provided that the grounds for such procedures can be the subject of invalidation procedures.

PART V: DISPUTE PREVENTION AND SETTLEMENT

Article 63: Transparency

1.   Laws and regulations, and final judicial decisions and administrative rulings of general application, made effective by any PARTY pertaining to the subject matter of this Agreement (the availability, scope, acquisition, enforcement and prevention of the abuse of intellectual property rights) shall be published, or where such publication is not practicable made publicly available, in a national language, in such a manner as to enable governments and right holders to become acquainted with them. Agreements concerning the subject matter of this Agreement which are in force between the government or a governmental agency of any PARTY and the government or a governmental agency of any other PARTY shall also be published.

2.   PARTIES shall notify the laws and regulations referred to in paragraph 1 above to the Council on Trade-Related Aspects of Intellectual Property Rights in order to assist that Council in its review of the operation of this Agreement. The Council shall attempt to minimise the burden on PARTIES in carrying out this obligation and may decide to waive the obligation to notify such laws and regulations directly to the Council if consultations with the World Intellectual Property Organisation on the establishment of a common register containing these laws and regulations are successful. The Council shall also consider in this connection any action required regarding notifications pursuant to the obligations under this Agreement stemming from the provisions of Article 6ter of the Paris Convention (1967).

3.   Each PARTY shall be prepared to supply, in response to a written request from another PARTY, information of the sort referred to in paragraph 1 above. A PARTY, having reason to believe that a specific judicial decision or administrative ruling or bilateral agreement in the area of intellectual property rights affects its rights under this Agreement, may also request in writing to be given access to or be informed in sufficient detail of such specific judicial decisions or administrative rulings or bilateral agreements.

4.   Nothing in paragraphs 1 to 3 above shall require PARTIES to disclose confidential information which would impede law enforcement or otherwise be contrary to the public interest or would prejudice the legitimate commercial interests of particular enterprises, public or private.

Article 64: Dispute Settlement

The provisions of Articles XXII and XXIII of the General Agreement on Tariffs and Trade and the Understanding on Rules and Procedures Governing the Settlement of Disputes under Articles XXII and XXIII of the General Agreement on Tariffs and Trade as adopted by the CONTRACTING PARTIES shall apply to consultations and the settlement of disputes under this Agreement except as otherwise specifically provided herein.[1]

PART VI: TRANSITIONAL ARRANGEMENTS

Article 65: Transitional Arrangements

1.   Subject to the provisions of paragraphs 2, 3 and 4 below, no PARTY shall be obliged to apply the provisions of this Agreement before the expiry of a general period of one year following the date of entry into force of this Agreement.

2.   Any developing country PARTY is entitled to delay for a further period of four years the date of application, as defined in paragraph 1 above, of the provisions of this Agreement other than Articles 3, 4 and 5 of Part I.

3.   Any other PARTY which is in the process of transformation from a centrally-planned into a market, free-enterprise economy and which is undertaking structural reform of its intellectual property system and facing special problems in the preparation and implementation of intellectual property laws, may also benefit from a period of delay as foreseen in paragraph 2 above.

4.   To the extent that a developing country PARTY is obliged by this Agreement to extend product patent protection to areas of technology not protectable in its territory on the general date of application of this Agreement for that PARTY, as defined in paragraph 2 above, it may delay the application of Section 5 of Part II of this Agreement to such areas of technology for an additional period of five years.

---

1   This provision may need to be revised in the light of the outcome of work on the establishment of an Integrated Dispute Settlement Understanding under the Agreement Establishing the Multilateral Trade Organisation.

5.   Any PARTY availing itself of a transitional period under paragraphs 1, 2, 3 or 4 shall ensure that any changes in its domestic laws, regulations and practice made during that period do not result in a lesser degree of consistency with the provisions of this Agreement.

Article 66: Least-Developed Countries

1.   In view of their special needs and requirements, their economic, financial and administrative constraints, and their need for flexibility to create a viable technological base, least-developed country PARTIES shall not be required to apply the provisions of this Agreement, other than Articles 3, 4 and 5, for a period of 10 years from the date of application as defined under paragraph 1 of Article 65 above. The Council shall, upon duly motivated request by a least-developed country PARTY, accord extensions of this period.

2.   Developed country PARTIES shall provide incentives to enterprises and institutions in their territories for the purpose of promoting and encouraging technology transfer to least-developed country PARTIES in order to enable them to create a sound and viable technological base.

Article 67: Technical Cooperation

In order to facilitate the implementation of this Agreement, developed country PARTIES shall provide, on request and on mutually agreed terms and conditions, technical and financial cooperation in favour of developing and least-developed country PARTIES. Such cooperation shall include assistance in the preparation of domestic legislation on the protection and enforcement of intellectual property rights as well as on the prevention of their abuse, and shall include support regarding the establishment or reinforcement of domestic offices and agencies relevant to these matters, including the training of personnel.

PART VII: INSTITUTIONAL ARRANGEMENTS; FINAL PROVISIONS

Article 68: Council on Trade-Related Aspects of Intellectual Property Rights

The Council on Trade-Related Aspects of Intellectual Property Rights shall monitor the operation of this Agreement and, in particular, PARTIES' compliance with their obligations hereunder, and shall afford PARTIES the opportunity of consulting on matters relating to the trade-related aspects of intellectual property rights. It shall carry out such other responsibilities as assigned to it by the PARTIES, and it shall, in particular, provide any assistance requested by them in the context of dispute settlement procedures. In carrying out its functions, the Council may consult with and seek information from any source it deems appropriate. In consultation with the World Intellectual Property Organization, the Council shall seek to establish, within one year of its first meeting, appropriate arrangements for cooperation with bodies of that Organization.

Article 69: International Cooperation

PARTIES agree to cooperate with each other with a view to eliminating international trade in goods infringing intellectual property rights. For this purpose, they shall establish and notify contact points in their national administrations and be ready to exchange information on trade in infringing goods. They shall, in particular, promote the exchange of information and cooperation between customs authorities with regard to trade in counterfeit and pirated goods.

Article 70: Protection of Existing Subject Matter

1.   This Agreement does not give rise to obligations in respect of acts which occurred before the date of application of the Agreement for the PARTY in question.

2.   Except as otherwise provided for in this Agreement, this Agreement gives rise to obligations in respect of all subject matter existing at the date of application of this Agreement for the PARTY in question, and which is protected in that PARTY on the said date, or which meets or comes subsequently to meet the criteria for protection under the terms of this Agreement. In respect of this paragraph and paragraphs 3 and 4 below, obligations with respect to existing

copyrighted works shall be solely determined under Article 18 of the Berne Convention (1971), and with respect to the rights of producers of phonograms and performers in existing phonograms shall be determined solely under Article 18 of the Berne Convention (1971) as made applicable under Article 14.6 of this Agreement.

3.   There shall be no obligation to restore protection to subject matter which on the date of application of this Agreement for the PARTY in question has fallen into the public domain.

4.   In respect of any acts in respect of specific objects embodying protected subject matter which become infringing under the terms of legislation in conformity with this Agreement, and which were commenced, or in respect of which a significant investment was made, before the date of ratification of this Agreement by that PARTY, any PARTY may provide for a limitation of the remedies available to the right holder as to the continued performance of such acts after the date of application of the Agreement for that PARTY. In such cases the PARTY shall, however, at least provide for the payment of equitable remuneration.

5.   A PARTY is not obliged to apply the provisions of Article 11 and of paragraph 4 of Article 14 with respect to originals or copies purchased prior to the date of application of this Agreement for that PARTY.

6.   PARTIES shall not be required to apply Article 31, or the requirement in Article 27.1 that patent rights shall be enjoyable without discrimination as to the field of technology, to use without the authorisation of the right holder where authorisation for such use was granted by the government before the date this Agreement became known.

7.   In the case of intellectual property rights for which protection is conditional upon registration, applications for protection which are pending on the date of application of this Agreement for the PARTY in question shall be permitted to be amended to claim any enhanced protection provided under the provisions of this Agreement. Such amendments shall not include new matter.

8.   Where a PARTY does not make available as of the date of entry into force of this Agreement patent protection for pharmaceutical and agricultural chemical products commensurate with its obligations under Article 27, that PARTY shall:

    (i)   provide as from the date of entry into force of the Agreement a means by which applications for patents for such inventions can be filed;

(ii)   apply to these applications, as of the date of application of this Agreement, the criteria for patentability as laid down in this Agreement as if those criteria were being applied on the date of filing in that PARTY or, where priority is available and claimed, the priority date of the application;

(iii)   provide patent protection in accordance with this Agreement as from the grant of the patent and for the remainder of the patent term, counted from the filing date in accordance with Article 33 of this Agreement, for those of these applications that meet the criteria for protection referred to in sub-paragraph (ii) above.

9.   Where a product is the subject of a patent application in a PARTY in accordance with paragraph 8(i) above, exclusive marketing rights shall be granted for a period of five years after obtaining market approval in that PARTY or until a product patent is granted or rejected in that PARTY, whichever period is shorter, provided that, subsequent to the entry into force of this Agreement, a patent application has been filed and a patent granted for that product in another PARTY and marketing approval obtained in such other PARTY.

Article 71: Review and Amendment

1.   PARTIES shall review the implementation of this Agreement after the expiration of the transitional period referred to in paragraph 2 of Article 65 above. They shall, having regard to the experience gained in its implementation, review it two years after that date, and at identical intervals thereafter. The PARTIES may also undertake reviews in the light of any relevant new developments which might warrant modification or amendment of this Agreement.

2.   Amendments merely serving the purpose of adjusting to higher levels of protection of intellectual property rights achieved, and in force, in other multilateral agreements and accepted by all PARTIES may be adopted by the Council.

Article 72: Reservations

Reservations may not be entered in respect of any of the provisions of this Agreement without the consent of the other PARTIES.

Article 73: Security Exceptions

Nothing in this Agreement shall be construed:

(a)   to require any PARTY to furnish any information the disclosure of which it considers contrary to its essential security interests; or

(b)   to prevent any PARTY from taking any action which it considers necessary for the protection of its essential security interests;

    (i)   relating to fissionable materials or the materials from which they are derived;

    (ii)   relating to the traffic in arms, ammunition and implements of ward and to such traffic in other goods and materials as is carried on directly or indirectly for the purpose of supplying a military establishment;

    (iii)   taken in time of war or other emergency in international relations; or

(c)   to prevent any PARTY from taking any action in pursuance of its obligations under the United Nations Charter for the maintenance of international peace and security.